KENNEWICK MAN

PERSPECTIVES ON THE ANCIENT ONE

ARCHAEOLOGY AND INDIGENOUS PEOPLES SERIES

Sponsored by the World Archaeological Congress

Series Editorial Board:
Martin Wobst, University of Massachusetts, Amherst
Sonya Atalay, Indiana University, Bloomington
T.J. Ferguson, University of Arizona, Tucson
Dorothy Lippert, Smithsonian Institution, Washington, DC
Claire Smith, Institute of the Advanced Study for Humanity, The University of Newcastle, Australia
Joe Watkins, University of Oklahoma, Norman
Larry Zimmerman, Indiana University, Indianapolis

Books in this series:
Kennewick Man: Perspectives on the Ancient One, Heather Burke, Claire Smith, Dorothy Lippert, Joe Watkins, Larry Zimmerman, editors

KENNEWICK MAN

PERSPECTIVES ON THE ANCIENT ONE

HEATHER BURKE
CLAIRE SMITH
DOROTHY LIPPERT
JOE WATKINS
LARRY ZIMMERMAN

EDITORS

5

H2 Contributors

Left Coast
Press Inc.

WALNUT CREEK, CALIFORNIA

Left Coast Press Inc.

LEFT COAST PRESS, INC.
1630 North Main Street, #400
Walnut Creek, CA 94596
http://www.LCoastPress.com

ISBN 978-1-59874-347-0 hardcover
ISBN 978-1-59874-348-7 paperback

Library of Congress Cataloguing-in-Publication Data:
Kennewick Man : perspectives on the ancient one / Heather Burke ... [et
al.], editors.
p. cm. -- (Archaeology and indigenous peoples series)
ISBN 978-1-59874-347-0 (hardback : alk. paper) -- ISBN 978-1-59874-348-7
(pbk. : alk. paper) 1. Kennewick Man. 2. Human remains
(Archaeology)--Washington (State) 3. Indians of North
America--Anthropometry--Washington (State) 4. Indians of North
America--Washington (State)--Antiquities. 5. Washington
(State)--Antiquities. I. Burke, Heather, 1966-
E78.W3.K46 2008
979.7'01--dc22
2008014740

Printed in the United States of America

 The paper used in this publication meets the minimum requirements of American
National Standard for Information Sciences—Permanence of Paper for Printed Library
Materials, ANSI/NISO Z39.48–1992.

08 09 10 11 12 5 4 3 2 1

CONTENTS

IN MEMORY OF
ANDREW ALLEN-FARR,
WHO SPENT A SIGNIFICANT PART OF A SHORT LIFE
WORKING FOR ARCHAEOLOGY AND
INDIGENOUS PEOPLE.

THE DEAD HAVE NO RIGHTS?

David Hurst Thomas

The editors of this volume have assembled an extraordinarily diverse group of stakeholders to reflect on the broader implications and impacts of the Kennewick Man/Ancient One controversy.

I'm honored to offer a couple of personal thoughts to the dialog. My first point is largely historical and the second concerns the role of science in contemporary society.

* * * * *

The taproot of the Kennewick Man/Ancient One conflict runs deep, stretching far back in time.

The fundamental problems underlying the Kennewick Man/Ancient One dispute can be traced to the initial encounter between Christopher Columbus and the native Caribbean people living on an island they called Guanahani.[1] In October 1492, Columbus unfurled a white banner with a green-crowned cross and took possession of this "new" land for his God and the Spanish Crown. By his decree, this New World and all its riches now belonged to Spain and the people living on Guanahani would henceforth be Spanish subjects: Finders Keepers.

Setting up a rough wooden cross, the Admiral of the Ocean Sea then renamed the island, calling it "San Salvador" to honor the Holy Savior who had protected him during the perilous voyage. Columbus also renamed the indigenous people of Guanihani, calling them *los indios* (broadening the geographical subcontinent of India to denote all of Asia east of the Indus River). Even after Europeans discovered Columbus's navigational error (something about a pair of intervening continents), they retained his term *Indios* and translated it into the other languages of conquest— the French *Indien* and the English *Indian*. This invented word "Indian," rooted in a geographic confusion, still carries enormous colonial connotations, collapsing the massive complexities and variability among Native American people into a vastly oversimplified pan-tribal construct: The Name Game.

These two formalized rituals established the protocols to ensure that the conquest would be played out by European rules. From this point forward, when a conqueror discovered a patch of "unclaimed" land, he would proclaim the newly discovered lands to be his patron's domain, laying claim to the new-found riches, the natural resources, and all things living and inanimate: Finders Keepers. The conqueror then played the Name Game, renaming the spoils of the new "discovery" in a new tongue—because the power to name manifestly reflects an underlying control of lands, indigenous peoples, and histories.

Some centuries later, Thomas Jefferson reaffirmed these same basic protocols. Having convinced Congress to authorize a secret expedition westward, President

Jefferson dispatched his hand-picked representatives, Meriwether Lewis and William Clark, to map an all-water route to Cathay, directly across the American continent. This was, of course, precisely the same task assigned to young Columbus by Ferdinand and Isabella.

Cleverly situating his Corps of Discovery as a jointly scientific and commercial enterprise, Jefferson constructed perfect cover for expanding his trans-Mississippian empire. The polymath president personally instructed Captain Lewis in the basics of surveying, map reading, and scientific description (in the process, renaming the flora, the fauna, the rivers, the mountains—and the people). In so doing, the Lewis and Clark expedition precisely reprised the strategies employed by Christopher Columbus some three centuries earlier.

When Columbus renamed the land and people of the Caribbean, he reenacted a well-known biblical scenario—renaming was the very first act by Adam, the very first human.[2] As military naturalists, Lewis and Clark used Linnaean classification and binomial Latin terminology to take symbolic possession of Jefferson's new American West. Whether marching beneath the banner of God or Science, the basic rules of the Name Game still applied, imposing a European and/or American order on "new" territory, collecting, and curating the territorial resources—botanical, mineralogical, and human.[3]

When Lewis and Clark returned home with the material proof of conquest, they affirmed proprietorship over the distinctive natural resources of the American West—including those Native American people still living there. Many of these specimens ended up in the imposing entrance hall at Monticello, Virginia, where Thomas Jefferson proudly displayed the booty of the Corps of Discovery. Mastodon bones and other fossils lined one wall; a mix of prized Indian relics adorned another. Monticello became the nation's first natural history museum, and, in the view of Jefferson, American Indian people were redefined as scientific specimens, not terribly unlike mastodons and glaciers.[4]

So it was that intellectual study of natural history arose as an instrument of the state, and 19th-century natural historians followed Jefferson's lead, amassing the relics and bones of *Los Indios* for science. At one point, the U.S. surgeon general ordered his medics to collect the battlefield dead and ship the Indian remains back to the natural history museums of the eastern seaboard—all in the name of state-sanctioned science. Although contemporary attitudes in anthropology differ greatly from the biological determinism that Jefferson helped foster, it is hardly surprising that many native people still associate archaeology with robbing the graves of their ancestors.

This familiar scenario played out again in July 1996. When a nearly complete skeleton washed out of a riverbank near Kennewick, Washington, an archaeologist claimed the bones for science (Finders Keepers) and, following long-established scientific protocols, he named his find "Kennewick Man."

But the rules had changed, and Americanist archaeology found itself in an evolving ethical and legal landscape. With the 1990 passage of the Native American Graves Protection and Repatriation Act, archaeologists had lost their monopoly on the deep American past. For the first time, Native American people were bona fide stakeholders in the national narrative, and they demanded to be heard.

It is hardly surprising that members of the Umatilla tribe took exception to the scientific claim on "Kennewick Man." They pronounced the skeleton as one of their own and rejected the scientist's name, preferring their own term, "*Oyt.pa.ma.na.tit.tite*," or "The Ancient One."

The power to name and possess reflects the disparities among divergent histories. These twin processes created the Great American Skull Wars and its modern legacy in the dispute over Kennewick Man/Ancient One.

*   *   *   *   *

As a dirt archaeologist, I am struck by the monumental changes in the practice of Americanist archaeology during the last couple of decades. But as a practicing anthropologist, I am puzzled why it took so long.

I was schooled in the "explicitly scientific" archaeology of the 1960s. The processual paradigm (the self-proclaimed "New Archaeology") constructed itself as an objective way to generate rigorous (and sometimes even elegant) ways to explain and predict the past.[5] Processual archaeology became a generalizing social science—not unlike economics, political science, and sociology—with the stated goal of seeking universally valid generalizations about the human condition.

This search for timeless and spaceless understandings transcends, by definition, the specifics of individual cultures. In practice, this meant that specific historical events in specific places are blown off as mere "local history"—irrelevant to a nomothetic understanding of the human condition. With an unrelenting focus on ecology, subsistence, and generalization, the New Archaeology effectively ignored (and sometimes belittled) the significance of cultural and religious traditions of greatest interest to many Indian people.

The science-based New Archaeology sent a clear message to Indian Country: The 1906 Antiquities Act gave us absolute control over the archaeological record of Native America, and we intend to mine this past for objectives that have no particular relevance to living Indian people. Today, many archaeologists (me included) feel that the heavy-handed pursuit of law-like generalizations unintentionally alienated the very Native American communities that archaeologists wanted most to study.

Ironically, this same culture of New Archaeology simultaneously privileged pro-Indian sentiments—many of us really did care, if naively, about the plight of American Indian people—yet discouraged professional involvement with actual Indians. When I was a graduate student studying North American archaeology, my professors typically characterized modern Indian people as "troublemakers who'd lost their own culture," outsiders who championed radical causes and obstructed the pursuit of real science. I was assured that we [archaeologists] are "the ones who understand what the Indian past was all about," and if, someday, Indian people decided to discover their own history, they should read our scientific monographs.

This is why, for a quarter-century, I practiced an archaeology of Native America that avoided living, breathing Native American people.[6]

*   *   *   *   *

I've been a museum curator for a long time. For years, on the way to my office, I walked by hundreds of museum trays storing numbered human bones. Right outside my office were bones that once belonged to Qisuk and three other Eskimos from Smith Sound (Greenland); but now the bones belonged to my museum. These four people had arrived in Brooklyn in 1897 aboard Robert Peary's tall ship, the *Hope*. Franz Boas arranged for them to live at my museum, but when they died of tuberculosis, he faked a funeral and secretly rendered their bones, which he numbered and accessioned into the museum's skeletal collection. In 1902, Aleš Hrdlička published a picture of Qisuk's brain in the *American Anthropologist*. When Qisuk's son, Minik, had asked for the return of his father's bones, Boas refused to give them up, explaining to the press that the bones were critically important to science. Neither Franz Boas nor anybody else ever published a word about these bones; in the 1990s, my museum decided that the skeletons of these four Smith Sound people were "out of scope," and the bones were flown back to northern Greenland.[7]

Over the years, I have worked on archaeological collections stored in other natural history museums. Sometimes, I'd see museum trays containing the numbered bones of Indian people killed on 19th-century battlefields of the American West. Several of these skeletons have returned home as well.

Many have mused about the recent changes in Americanist archaeology—from an exclusionary, elitist academic enterprise to a more inclusive exercise that explicitly recognizes the importance of collaborating with descendant, stake-holding communities.

But on a personal level, I'm still wondering why I wasn't bothered by the bones of Qisuk and his friends right outside my office. I knew the story of Robert Peary and "his" Eskimos. I knew they'd died less than seventy-five years before I joined the museum staff. I knew that Minik had asked for the return of his father's bones. I knew that Boas had refused.

The New Archaeologists (me included) thought that museums should keep curating people's bones, even when close relatives wanted them back. I don't believe this anymore. Americanist archaeology has changed, and so have I.

But why did I think it was OK before?

*   *   *   *   *

Having thought about this a lot, I keep coming back to the story of Thomas Stolz Harvey, the man who owned Einstein's brain.

On April 18, 1955, Dr. Harvey, then chief pathologist at Princeton Hospital, looked down at the lifeless body of *Time* magazine's Person of the Century. Harvey had known Albert Einstein only slightly, having once attended the living legend in his New Jersey residence. On their next encounter, Dr. Einstein was lying dead on the morgue table.[8]

Dr. Harvey's autopsy took about two hours. He first opened the torso and found the abdomen full of blood, the result of a fatal aortic blowout. Harvey then made an incision across the scalp, from ear to ear, and peeled the skin downward over Einstein's face. He sawed through the skull, carefully cut the numerous blood vessels and nerves, finally reaching inside to pull out the brain. It looked like all other brains, and Harvey said later that it felt like Jell-O.

Harvey weighed Einstein's brain—exactly 1,230 grams. Most male human brains weigh between 1,200 and 1,600 grams, meaning that the brain that worked out the theory of relativity and set the stage for nuclear fission was on the smallish side—so much for the correlation between brain size and intelligence.

Small brained or not, Einstein was clearly a genius. In that autopsy room, Dr. Harvey pondered the meaning of that term "genius" and marveled at the possibilities: If science could just discover the nature of genius, couldn't we develop more geniuses who could stop war, eliminate hunger, preserve the environment, save the planet?

Thomas Harvey was a Yale-trained pathologist, not a neuroscientist. But he just knew that the science of cytoarchitectonics could somehow unlock the secrets of this unique specimen. Here was a unique opportunity for science to better the world by studying Einstein's brain, the very embodiment of pure intellect.

Dr. Harvey washed up and headed outside to meet the media. He explained that Albert Einstein had suffered from severe arterial disease. Simply put, his aorta had burst and he bled to death. Although Harvey scrupulously avoided the topic, a reporter from *The New York Times* somehow discovered that Einstein's brain—the brain of all brains—was being curated for scientific study.[9]

This was a big problem.

Hans Albert Einstein learned about the proposed study of his father's brain from the newspaper and he was furious. Thomas Harvey had not spoken to anybody about his plan. He had neither family permission nor the legal right to remove and keep the brain for himself. In fact, Einstein had left explicit instructions that his remains (all of them) were to be cremated, with the ashes spread in a secret place. This was done, but without the brain.[10] In an awkward telephone conversation, Harvey later stressed to Hans Albert Einstein the scientific imperative that he preserve the brain and engineer a world-class study. In a controversial and secretive deal, the Einstein family granted a reluctant and retroactive blessing for the study to proceed. Knowing that Albert Einstein had wished otherwise and fearing that a public debate would attract additional unwanted attention, Hans Albert insisted (1) that the results be published only in the scientific literature; and (2) all sensationalism be avoided. Two days later, *The New York Times* reported that Einstein's son had requested scientific study of his father's brain. But Hans Albert was not quoted in the story.[11]

The truth is that Dr. Harvey had misrepresented himself to the Einstein family. His understanding of the human brain was restricted to the postmortem diagnosis of disease, atrophy, or injury. When it came to brain research, Harvey was clearly out of his league. Caught up in the moment, he later acknowledged his "great fortune of being the one, at the right place at the right time. It was the biggest moment in my life."[12]

The family crisis averted, Thomas Harvey began "fixing" the specimen, eventually sectioning Einstein's brain into 240 cubes (many more than usual). Before long, the U.S. Army officially summoned Dr. Harvey to Washington, DC, to attend a conference at the Armed Forces Institute of Pathology. Several of the world's top neuropathologists, convened to formulate a plan for studying Einstein's brain, ordered Harvey to relinquish the brain to those best qualified to conduct the study. In the best tradition of Finders Keepers, Harvey refused, insisting that Einstein's brain was, exclusively, his to possess and control.[13]

When, eventually, Princeton University terminated Dr. Harvey's contract, he once again refused to give up Einstein's brain, triggering a bizarre cross-country odyssey. Harvey moved to the Kansas State Penitentiary, near Leavenworth, jealously guarding his property and keeping the brain close by wherever he moved. Harvey took a job in a biological testing lab and briefly practiced medicine in Weston, Missouri, but lost his medical license for failing a competency exam.

True to his promise, Harvey did his best to minimize publicity, but with little success. The book *Driving Mr. Albert: My Trip across America with Einstein's Brain* tells the loopy story of Dr. Harvey driving a rented Buick Skylark with a Tupperware container in the trunk containing the surviving chunks of Einstein's brain.[14] Enormous publicity has followed since then, including a documentary PBS film and even a 2002 heavy metal tune by Attic of Love called "Stealing Einstein's Brain."

*   *   *   *   *

The strange saga of Albert Einstein's brain embodies, I think, some disturbing parallels to the Kennewick Man/Ancient One controversy, with some significant implications down the road. Let me highlight three key points: (1) the continuing power of Finders Keepers, (2) the enduring importance of the Name Game, and (3) a blind faith in science that sometimes trumps all other concerns.

FINDERS KEEPERS

When a 15th-century conqueror discovered a patch of "unclaimed" land, he declared ownership over the new-found riches, the natural resources, and all things living and inanimate. When Jefferson's Corps of Discovery moved westward to the Pacific, the jointly scientific and commercial enterprise claimed the flora, fauna, rivers, mountains, and the people as U.S. government property (because America was simply wilderness before being "discovered" and defined by Euro Americans). Scientific archaeology laid claim to human bones washing out of the Columbia River, and Thomas Harvey said he owned the brain of Albert Einstein. Each person made these claims because they could (and felt they must)—Finders Keepers.

THE NAME GAME

During the Golden Age of Discovery, European colonial powers coined new terms for their new "discoveries," beginning with Columbus renaming the people and islands of the Caribbean. Lewis and Clark renamed the geography, the flora, and the fauna of the trans–Mississippian West. Archaeologists named the ancient bones Kennewick Man. In each case, the power to name reflects an underlying power to control lands, Indigenous peoples, and histories.

The Name Game played out differently for Thomas Harvey because the famous brain already had a name.[15] In fact, the strange saga of Einstein's brain was all about the name. Two decades after Einstein's death, *Science* magazine tracked down the remnants of his brain, which, by this time, consisted of several dozen brain cubes bobbing in alcohol inside two Mason jars, packed in a wooden cider box and tucked beneath a beer cooler in Harvey's house.[16] When pressed, Harvey explained that he had distributed a dozen sample sets to researchers, but "nothing has been published" from the brain studies and the samples had disappeared.[17]

After the *Science* magazine piece, interest in Einstein's brain skyrocketed. In the mid-1980s, one California research team reported that Einstein's brilliance was due to an elevated number of "glial" cells. Another researcher announced that the patterning of folds inside Einstein's brain accounted for his extraordinary intellect (because of the increased expanse of the cerebral cortex). Still others thought that the Einstein's inferior parietal region was abnormally large, dubbing him a "parietal genius."

As neuroscientists rushed to play the Name Game, they reversed the rules. Without Einstein's name and charisma, this research would have gone nowhere—in popular media or the scientific literature. "Scientists seemed to be vying for [Einstein's brain] like fans stretching to catch a home run ball."[18] Einstein's magical name carried the allure of celebrity and publicity, and those seeking to unravel the secrets of the world's most famous brain became the rock stars of biomedical research. Once news of their research leaked to the press, their phones rang nonstop and some Einstein brain researchers even graced the pages of *People* magazine.[19] Disturbingly, some of this unproven research is still reified in several introductory psychology textbooks.

BLIND FAITH

Christopher Columbus devoutly believed in his God and his king (and queen); his career as conqueror was guided by his faith. Although Thomas Jefferson believed in separating church and state, his blind faith in the New Republic fueled his push to rename and control the trans–Mississippian West.

When Albert Einstein died, American "faith in science became as fashionable as Brylcreem and Hula Hoops," writes Carolyn Abraham.[20] As mainstream America worshipped at the altar of science, the public came to believe that laboratory miracles should just somehow emerge. And in the 1950s, they often they did: The first computer appeared; the first human kidney was successfully transplanted; antibiotics conquered infections (the leading killer of the 19th century); Watson and Crick discovered DNA.

Thomas Harvey kept Einstein's brain because of noble intentions and a blind faith in science to better the human condition. But personal ambition turned this saga into "nonsense, a starry-eyed lunacy."[21] More than fifty years after Einstein's death, science still seeks an explanation for the great man's extraordinary gifts.

The fascination and scientific feeding frenzy over Einstein's brain likely reveals more about us—our assumptions about the brain and our reverence for genius—than about Einstein himself. In fact, scientific research on Einstein's brain has a disturbing downside. A "cult of genius" surrounds the whole enterprise, typically conducted by researchers who "blindly revere his brain as a sacred talisman."[22] Frederick Lepore, prominent neurologist, has wondered aloud if "it would have been better if Harvey had placed Einstein's brain back into the cranial cavity and let it blaze into ashes at the Ewing Crematorium on April 18, 1955."[23]

Infatuated with the materialistic basis of thought, much of modern neuroscience is rooted in a prevailing philosophy that human thought can be defined by brain structure alone.[24] As a result, modern neuroscience veers dangerously close to the phrenology of the 19th century—that long-ago discounted belief in external skull conformation as an accurate reflection of intellectual and emotional faculties. Phrenology is correctly regarded today as an example, par excellence, of yesterday's pseudoscience.

*   *   *   *   *

The unlikely combination of Finders Keepers, the Name Game, some highly questionable ethics, a blind faith (and sometimes arrogance) in the promise of scientific research that trumps all other concerns, a rush for self-promotion, publicity and notoriety, the on-going destruction of the iconic specimen, the resurrection of 19th-century racialism—this disturbing constellation unites the Cult of Einstein's Brain with the controversy over Kennewick Man/Ancient One.

The medical profession continues to wrestle with the bioethical issues surrounding research on cadavers and isolated organs.[25] Under particular scrutiny are investigations that involve living human participants, their remains, cadavers, tissues, biological fluids, embryos, fetuses, and other biological materials, including human DNA and RNA. Each arena requires separate protocols assessing research merit and ethical sensitivity.

The field of anthropology has come a long way from Thomas Jefferson's pronouncement that "the dead have no rights"[26] and the 1989 pronouncement from a respected physical anthropologist that "since all humans are members of a single species ... ancient human skeletons belong to everyone."[27]

When do scientific research priorities override the concerns and rights of individuals (and their families) to control human remains? The answer for contemporary anthropologists is crystal clear, because in June 1998, the American Anthropological Association approved a new code of ethics that states, specifically:

Anthropological researchers have primary ethical obligations to the people, species, and materials they study, and to the people with whom they work. These obligations can supersede the goal of seeking new knowledge and can lead to decisions not to undertake or to discontinue a research project when the primary obligation conflicts with other responsibilities.[28]

As we seek to apply these ethical guidelines to difficult cases like Kennewick Man/Ancient One, perhaps it would be wise, to paraphrase the popular Sierra Club motto, to remember that we are advocating not blind opposition to science, but rather the opposition to blind science.[29]

NOTES

1. This argument is developed at some length elsewhere, in David Hurst Thomas, *Skull Wars: Kennewick Man, Archaeology, and the Battle for Native American Identity* (New York: Basic Books, 2000), especially Chapters 1, 2, and 3.

2. "And out of the ground the Lord God formed every beast of the field, and every fowl of the air; and brought them unto Adam to see what he would call them: and whatsoever Adam called every living creature, that was the name thereof. And Adam gave names to all cattle, and to the fowl of the air, and to every beast of the field … " (Genesis, 2:19).

3. For more on the anthropological implications of the Corps of Discovery, see David Hurst Thomas, "Thomas Jefferson's Conflicted Legacy in American Archaeology," in *Across the Continent: Jefferson, Lewis and Clark, and the Making of America*, edited by Douglas Seefeldt, Jeffrey L. Hantman, and Peter S. Onuf, pp. 84–131 (Charlottesville: University of Virginia Press, 2005).

4. President Jefferson's estate at Poplar Forest continued the theme, displaying a Creek deerskin dress collected by Lewis and Clark at Fort Mandan, painted buffalo robes from the Plains, a Chinook woman's skirt of cedar bark, an Omaha tobacco pouch, and a Crow Indian cradleboard (see Thomas, *Skull Wars*, p. 29).

5. Elsewhere I have termed this "a certain starry-eyed longing for a systematic, if sometimes formulaic approach to the past" (Thomas, *Skull Wars*, p. 241).

6. This theme is developed in more detail in David Hurst Thomas, Foreword, in *Collaboration in Archaeological Practice: Engaging Descendant Communities*, edited by Chip Colwell-Chanthaphonh and T. J. Ferguson, pp. vii–xii (Lanham, MD: AltaMira Press, 2008).

7. The difficult story of the Smith Sound Eskimos is related in Thomas (*Skull Wars*, Chapter 9 and the sources cited therein).

8. The best source on this subject is Carolyn Abraham's *Possessing Genius: The Bizarre Odyssey of Einstein's Brain* (Middlesex, UK: Viking Books, 2001); see also Brian Burrell, *Postcards from the Brain Museum: The Improbable Search for Meaning in the Matter of Famous Minds* (New York: Broadway, 2005).

9. Henry Abrams, Einstein's eye doctor, collected the eyeballs at the autopsy, "Whenever I look at them, in my own mind, I see the greatest person of our time. … I felt like I wanted to continue to be close to him" (Abraham, *Possessing Genius*, p. 63). Einstein's eyeballs are still kept in a safety deposit box in a New Jersey Bank, with a rumored sale in the works (National Public Radio, "The Long, Strange Journal of Einstein's Brain," January 27, 2008 (http://www.npr.org/templates/story/story.php?storyId=4602913).

10. Some years before, a young girl in Geneva had apparently tried to clip a lock of Einstein's hair, as a souvenir. Appalled, Einstein told his family that he wanted to be cremated, "so people don't come to worship at my bones" (quoted in "My Dad Has Einstein's Brain," Carolyn Abraham, *The Guardian*, April 8, 2004).

11. At the time, many thought Harvey's actions were ghoulish. "But to the pathologist a human corpse was a medical tool by which to learn," writes Carolyn Abraham in her book, *Possessing Genius*. "Einstein's brain was the previous raw material of a career-making scientific endeavor. It was the brain of a genius [wrote Harvey] I would have felt ashamed if I'd left it."

12. Abraham, "My Dad Has Einstein's Brain," p. 2.

13. The meeting with army pathologists is described in Abraham, *Possessing Genius*, pp. 88–91. Harvey was apparently transfixed by the presence of greatness. The inept pathologist eventually did distribute a dozen sets of brain sections and slides to his personally selected group of neuroanatomists, urging them to examine "the Rosetta Stone of Genius" for biological differences responsible for Einstein's superior intelligence.

14. Michael Paterniti, *Driving Mr. Albert: My Trip across America with Einstein's Brain* (New York: The Dial Press, 2000).

15. The case of Einstein's brain itself reprises an earlier fixation with curating unusual brains, sometimes with the permission of their owners (such as John Wesley Powell) and sometimes not, as with Ishi (see Orin Starn, *Ishi's Brain: In Search of America's Last "Wild" Indian* [New York: W. W. Norton & Company, 2004]). A. Hrdlička, "An Eskimo Brain," *American Anthropologist*, new series, 1901–, 3(3):454–500, took the extraordinary (and unethical) step of identifying by name the source of the brain being described.

16. Steven Levy, *New Jersey Monthly*, August 1978, describes a "Costa Cider" box and two large Mason jars: "In those were the remains of the brain that changed the world ... anyway, the excitement for me was seeing those little brain-pieces, each the size of a Goldenberg's peanut chew, bobbing up and down in solution."

17. "Editorial: Brain that rocked physics rests in cider box," *Science* 1978(201):696. Harvey eventually moved to North Carolina and gave the remaining brain samples to Dr. Elliot Krauss, a pathologist at the Medical Center at Princeton. "I look at it like I'm the curator" of the brain, said Dr. Krauss in a recent interview by Jeff Milgram, *Princeton Packet* staff writer, August 4, 2000 (http://www.pacpubserver.com/new/news/8-4-00/einstein.html).

18. Abraham, *Possessing Genius*, p. 18.

19. Abraham, *Possessing Genius*, pp. 330–331.

20. Abraham, *Possessing Genius*, p. 79.

21. Brian Burrell, *Postcards from the Brain Museum*.

22. Frederick E. Lepore, "Dissecting Genius: Einstein's Brain and the Search for the Neural Basis of Intellect" (Cerebrum Winter 2001 http://www.dana.org/news/cerebrum/archives.aspx: The Dana Foundation, 2001, http://www.dana.org).

23. Lepore, "Dissecting Genius."

24. "It will always be quite impossible to explain the mind on the basis of neuronal action within the brain, and because it seems to me certain that the mind develops and matures independently throughout the individual's life ... and because a computer (which the brain is) must be programmed and operated by an agency capable of independent understanding" (Lepore, "Dissecting Genius").

25. Gareth D. Jones, *Speaking for the Dead: Cadavers in Biology and Medicine* (London: Ashgate Publishing, 2000).

26. Writing from Monticello on July 12, 1816, Thomas Jefferson penned the words "the dead have no rights," a colorful phrase sometimes cited by some as evidence of his callous, even ghoulish attitude

toward the American Indian. But by examining the wider contexts, we can see that when Jefferson used the words "the dead have no rights," he was not even remotely considering human skeletal remains (see Thomas, "Thomas Jefferson's Conflicted Legacy").

27. Here is the context for this quote:

> I explicitly assume that no living culture, religion, interest groups, or biological population has any moral or legal right to the exclusive use or regulation of ancient human skeletons since all humans are members of a single species. Ancient skeletons are the remnants of unduplicatable evolutionary events which all living and future peoples have the right to know about and understand. In other words, ancient human skeletons belong to everyone. (Douglas Ubelaker and Lauryn Guttenplan Grant, "Human Skeletal Remains: Preservation or Reburial?" *1989 Yearbook of Physical Anthropology* 32:249–287)

28. "Code of Ethics of the American Anthropological Association," approved June 1998 (http://www.aaanet.org/committees/ethics/ethcode.htm).

29. The Sierra Club prominently features its motto on the masthead of its numerous publications: "Not blind opposition to progress, but opposition to blind progress."

CHAPTER 1
PERSPECTIVES ON THE ANCIENT ONE[1]
Heather Burke and Claire Smith

When Judge Gould of the 9th Circuit Court of Appeals described Kennewick Man as "one of the most important American anthropological and archaeological discoveries of the 20th century" (Gould 2004:1584), he was right in more ways than one. The original serendipitous discovery of a skull in the soft sediments of the Columbia River in Washington State in 1996 precipitated a long drawn-out legal battle (*Bonnichsen et al. v. United States*) between eight scientists and a coalition of five tribal groups and became the vehicle for a host of questions critical to the politics of cultural identity, the construction of Indigenous and scientific values, and the role of archaeology in the modern world.

The implications of the Kennewick case have polarized individuals, divided communities, generated a cloud of controversy and media hype, and been spun off into a range of extremist positions, ranging from born-again Vikings to white power racism. In this process, Kennewick Man became the symbol of a battle between "science and religion" and between Native American people and archaeologists over who has the right to control of the past. The ramifications of this controversy have resounded well beyond the United States.

Any of the oldest known skeletal remains on any continent are part of a wider history of the human species, as people moved into and colonized new and often challenging environments. Knowledge of such time periods is a powerful tool—both for science as a means to understand the range and ingenuity of human behavior, and for contemporary Indigenous peoples as a means of codifying their relationships to place over the long term. It was Kennewick's antiquity that precipitated the controversy: The death of a man over 9,000 years ago became an integral part of the origin story for North America and thus far more than just another source of bioanthropological data. Furthermore, Kennewick quickly became part of historically based human rights issues and the complicated history of colonially created tribal communities following the construction of the reservations in the 19th century. As is typical in settler nations, a long history of legally dismantling some tribal nations, restricting the movements of others, and general policies of relocation and reorganization complicated the Kennewick case in ways that prevented the construction of any argument about cultural continuity over the long term and influenced the opinions of judges and the general public alike.

There are two ways in which we can learn from the Ancient One: as a source of data, which many argue makes him extremely valuable, if not unique; and as a cautionary tale—was *Bonnichsen et al. v. United States* the only possible outcome, given the circumstances? Have the scientific benefits to study an archaeological discovery outweighed the damage done to relationships between Native Americans and archaeologists? Although a scientific perspective imbues many of the contributions in this book, it is embraced most directly by C. Loring Brace (Chapter 21), one of the eight plaintiff scientists who has conducted detailed studies on Kennewick Man, along with a team of allied researchers, and Lynn Copes (Chapter 23), both of whom argue for recognition of the positive learning opportunities that Kennewick provides. None of these contributors argue for an archaeology that excludes Indigenous people, or for a science that ignores alternative systems of knowledge when interpreting material remains.

The Kennewick case wasn't the first time that Indigenous values and scientific principles clashed over the reburial of ancient people or the value of oral traditions and it won't be the last. It is almost a truism that the worldviews of Native Americans and other Indigenous peoples differ significantly from those of Western industrialized societies; it is when these come together over issues of stewardship that the colonial legacy that imbues contemporary decision-making becomes exposed. As many of the contributors to this volume contend, the history of archaeology as a discipline reveals it to have been constructed from an Enlightenment perspective and largely practiced within a colonial framework—the goals and purpose of archaeology are absolutely a creation of Western European understandings of the world and reflect, in Steve Russell's words (Chapter 7), "white privilege and ... the identification of science with civilization."

A particularly deep fissure in the case of the Ancient One concerns the competing claims for accessing the past that are represented by scientific and oral history knowledge systems (see contributions by Roger Echo-Hawk [Chapter 41], Steve Hemming, Daryle Rigney, and Christopher Wilson [Chapter 38], and Mary Marchand [Chapter 33]) and the issue of how (or perhaps whether) archaeology will accept the legitimacy of different knowledge systems and resulting repatriation decisions (see Chapter 25 by Laurajane Smith). In that case, as Lynn Meskell (Chapter 34) argues, what will it cost archaeologists to become major players in the call for cultural return and how can our discipline embrace restitution?

As Ouzman (Chapter 39) points out, the case of the Ancient One is not as rare as some people might think. There are more than a dozen human remains dating from a similar period (7,000–10,000 years ago) in the United States that are, or have been, available for study (Fiedel 2004:Table 1) and many others—often much older—from other parts of the world that have been studied with the active cooperation of Indigenous people. Experiences from other situations—particularly those that result in successful working relationships and positive outcomes for all sides—can be both instructive and empowering, especially when it comes to international parallels, such as the Lake Mungo (Australia) or Sara Baartman (South Africa) cases. As George Nicholas, John Jules, and Carrie Dan (Chapter 35) note, the frenzy surrounding Kennewick has obscured many positive collaborative projects and skewed perceptions of the relationship between archaeologists and Indigenous people.

In such a light, it is not possible to discuss the Ancient One without reference to the media hype that surrounded it, transforming it, as Deward Walker, Jr. (Chapter

30) notes, into one of the most publicized anthropological cases in recent U.S. history. The initial misrepresentation of Caucasoid as Caucasian by the media generated a range of claims by a variety of extremist and often highly racist non–Native American groups, which suggested that long before Columbus Europeans must have settled North America. As Jodi Barnes (Chapter 26) contends, such overtly racialized perspectives are connected to wider notions about the legitimate "ownership" of the nation, and the constitution of the white/European self, revealing "a powerful camouflage of unquestioned beliefs" and emphasizing cultural affiliation as something that only *other* people do.

As an ethnic category, "white" becomes the empty norm against which other people are measured. The effects of the media on extremist public perceptions about Kennewick have been both widespread and long lived, a thread that both Michelle Hamilton (Chapter 15) and Ann Kakaliouras (Chapter 9) explore in relation to the World Wide Web. The ease of constant access offered by the web, combined with the unpredictable and unregulated use of content, shifted the meanings of Kennewick far beyond what anyone at the time of discovery in 1996, or actually involved in the dispute, could possibly have envisaged. As one of the enduring threads to the debate, the media's capacity to expand the repercussions of such cases beyond the plaintiffs and defendants into a wider and much more highly politicized realm of public meanings and contemporary identity politics resurfaces in several chapters in this book, especially those by Joel Gilman (Chapter 8), George Nicholas and colleagues, and Steve Hemming and colleagues.

The other enduring thread to Kennewick is NAGPRA—the Native American Graves Protection and Repatriation Act that formed the legal framework within which much of the legal argument was concentrated. The central issue in *Bonnichsen et al. v. United States* was whether the more than 9,000-year-old Kennewick remains were subject to NAGPRA (1990) (25 USC §§ 3001–3011). NAGPRA provides for the immediate repatriation of human remains determined to be Native American to the lineal descendants of those remains, or, if lineal descendants can't be determined, to the tribe on whose land the remains were found or who otherwise have the closest cultural affiliation. NAGPRA defines "Native American" to mean "of, or relating to, a tribe, people, or culture that is indigenous to the United States." In determining the precise meaning of what "is indigenous," the court eventually ruled that it meant, "of, or related to, a tribe, people, or culture that *is presently existing* in the United States." As a result, the trial court in 2002 found that the remains were not subject to NAGPRA's provisions because they could not be determined to be Native American under that definition, and therefore did not have to be returned to the tribal coalition for reburial. In 2004, the 9th Circuit Court of Appeals reaffirmed the trial court's decision, allowing further scientific study of the Kennewick skeleton to proceed.

NAGPRA and *Bonnichsen* raise several interconnected issues relating to cultural property, communal ownership, and cultural heritage. In some respects, the case of *Bonnichsen et al. v. United States* was inevitable, as Thomas F. King (Chapter 16) and James Nason (Chapter 14) argue, both of whom view it as a foregone conclusion from the day NAGPRA was enacted. Grounded as it is in Euro American property law, NAGPRA can only function as a means to determine which party or parties has rights of ownership to ancestors and their property. When there are conflicting interests, the only resolution that NAGPRA can offer is to establish which party takes precedence, making conflict unavoidable in cases such as this. Joel Gilman cites NAGPRA's failure to recognize the interests of multiple groups in the handling of human remains as the main basis for its lack of provision of any statutory mandate for consultation, a situation that tends to preclude cooperation between archaeologists and Indigenous peoples. The nature and scope of such cooperation, including how and whether the interests of archaeologists and Indigenous people can both be served, and how the discipline of archaeology might change as a result of this, is a recurring theme throughout many chapters, particularly those of Michelle Hamilton, Lynn Copes (Chapter 23), Ed Jolie (Chapter 27), and Adam Fish (Chapter 28).

From one viewpoint, Kennewick Man, as one of the oldest human skeletons found in North America, is significant to all humankind because of the scientific information he can provide on the earliest peopling of the Americas, and, by extension, for what this can tell us about the movement of human groups worldwide. Constructing the Ancient One as public property in such a way, however—as with any claim to world heritage—speaks directly to notions of universal stewardship. Governed by technocratic ideals of progress, the formulation of an idea of heritage stewardship originated after World War II and the Hague Convention of 1954 (literally, the Convention for the Protection of Cultural Property in the Event of Armed Conflict). The animating principle of the convention is that damage to cultural property, no matter who it belongs to, damages everyone's cultural heritage "since each people makes its contribution to the culture of the world" (ICOMOS 1954: Preamble).

In this book, the chapter by Ed Jolie points to the concept of the commons as the root notion for stewardship: an older ideal of European (Western) society adopting the role of trustee for a higher public purpose. Any notion of a common heritage highlights a disjunction between the abstract concept and the case-by-case reality of what is deemed to be both worthy and actually capable of protection. Moreover, it must seriously consider the consequences of creating a general property right for all people in materials—especially human remains—with conflicting, as well as deeply religious and philosophical, meanings for specific groups of people.

Many of the contributors to this volume speak directly to these religious and philosophical meanings as they explore the personal, private, and culturally specific values of heritage, in general, and of the Ancient One, in particular. As Walter BigBee (Chapter 17) so eloquently points out, for Native Americans there is no other country in which their cultural traditions can be nurtured and protected. If Indigenous communities are denied access to material culture held in museums, archaeological sites, or private collections, they are unable to use this material to create feelings of common ethnicity or to strengthen notions of kinship. In this light, the importance of the repatriation of human remains comes through clearly in numerous chapters in this book; for all of the tribal coalition members, repatriation is not simply a mechanical act but a vital and sacred connection to a past that has to be held gently in both hands and nurtured from generation to generation. The implications of this for archaeology and archaeologists are manifold.

The collection of chapters in this volume was originally planned as two companion volumes: one that focused primarily on academic responses to Kennewick; the other that presented the viewpoints of Indigenous peoples. The decision to amalgamate the two volumes provided an opportunity to combine a wide range of opinions on the Kennewick debate and to break down an artificial divide between scientists and Indigenous peoples. The chapters are a deliberate and eclectic mix of perspectives: Although there are a number of academic chapters, there are also many personal viewpoints and several in-depth analyses of the range of values that are symbolized by the Ancient One. Many contributions come from established academics; others have been sought from current or recent graduate students or young academics.

Many of the writings are by Indigenous authors, from both inside and outside of the academy, ranging from new graduate students to tribal Elders, for all of whom the Ancient One speaks directly to issues of identity, sovereignty, and belonging. For this reason, all of the tribal coalition papers have been reprinted here exactly as the Elders first wrote or spoke them, with little or no change, since they wish emphatically to be heard in their own words, and without "interpretation." Because the basic issues surrounding the Ancient One are reflected in the political debates of many postcolonial nations, the views of Indigenous people and academics from outside the United States are also important, especially in terms of the international parallels they represent. It is equally vital that the scientific voice isn't lost either, as this is central to our archaeological understandings of the past and the ways in which archaeology is routinely empowered as a discipline to speak for past groups of people.

A number of the chapters were originally published elsewhere but have been reprinted here because of what they contribute to the overall debate. Contributions by Brace, Russell, and Walker are all rewritten versions of original articles published in other venues. Darby Stapp and Peter Jones (Chapter 6) have written short introductory and concluding pieces as "bookends" to their original 2003 article, which provides an in-depth anthropological analysis of the material used by Magistrate Jelderks in coming to his decision in *Bonnichsen et al. v. United States*. The statements by Armand Minthorn (Chapter 4) and Donald Sampson (Chapter 5) were a portion of the original response by the tribes in 1996 to the pending court case. The two key judgments in the case— Jelderks's original 2002 decision and the 9th Circuit Court of Appeals' 2004 opinion—are not in the book because of their length but are available electronically at http://www.friendsofpast.org/pdf/decision-020830.pdf (Jelderks's ruling) and
http://www.ca9.uscourts.gov/coa/newopinions.nsf
- BEC4B164D296BB0188256E78007CB8E3/$file/0235994.pdf?openelement (Court of Appeals).

In short, this edited volume is not a typical collection of academic articles, although many contributions have been written by scholars who are leaders in their fields. Instead, our aim has been to include a diversity of opinions and standpoints on the ever-widening issues surrounding the Ancient One and, in doing so, to reveal some of the fault-lines that fracture modern archaeology.

ACKNOWLEDGMENTS

The long history of this volume means that many people have assisted in one way or another to bring it into being. Adam Fish was instrumental in helping organize the 2005 AAA symposium in which some of the papers in this volume were originally presented and undertook many of the interviews with tribal coalition members that have now become chapters in this book. Guy Moura and Camille Pleasants coordinated the Colville contributions and provided essential feedback.

Although the contents of this volume may seem biased against the scientific perspective on the Kennewick case, we made several efforts to involve the eight main scientists who have studied the skeleton, as well as several others who were instrumental in arguing for the scientific values of further study. Many were understandably reluctant to contribute, given the cloud of controversy that surrounds any mention of Kennewick. In this light, we are especially grateful to C. Loring Brace for his kind and thoughtful contribution to this volume.

NOTE

1. One manifestation of the battle over these human remains is the use of the alternative terms "Kennewick Man," which locates these remains in terms of the contemporary name of a particular place, or "Ancient One," which locates them in terms of Native American lineage and human relationships. In this chapter, we use both terms interchangeably, reflecting our own positions as scientifically trained archaeologists who support Indigenous custodianship of Indigenous human remains.

REFERENCES

Gould, Ronald M. 2004. Appeal from The United States District Court for the District of Oregon John Jelderks, Magistrate Judge, Presiding. 1579 *Bonnichsen V. United States*. Argued and Submitted September 10, 2003—Portland, Oregon. Filed February 4, 2004. Before: Ruggero J. Aldisert, Susan P. Graber, and Ronald M. Gould, Circuit Judges. Opinion by Judge Gould. United States Court of Appeals for the Ninth Circuit.

ICOMOS 1954. Convention for the Protection of Cultural Property in the Event of Armed Conflict. Available online at http://portal.unesco.org/en/ev.php-URL_ID=13637& URL_DO=DO_TOPIC&URL_SECTION=201.html (accessed June 15, 2008).

CHAPTER 2
KENNEWICK: A TIMELINE OF EVENTS, 1996–2007[1]

1996
July 28, 1996
A skull is found in the Columbia River near Kennewick, Washington, by two spectators at the annual hydroplane races. The skull is handed over to the Kennewick police, who search to recover more fragments from the site.

The skull is turned over to the Benton County coroner to determine whether it is associated with a crime scene. The coroner approaches anthropologist James Chatters to assess whether the remains are recent or ancient.

Chatters's initial analysis noting the presence of caucasoid features (a narrow face; a v-shaped mandible with a deep chin; and a long, high, and rounded skull, among other things) and an association with an historic homestead leads him at first to speculate that the skeleton might be European. Chatters eventually determines that the skull isn't recent, but could be either a few hundred or several thousand years old (Chatters 2004).

July 28–August 29, 1996
Under an ARPA (Archaeological Resources Protection Act) permit issued by the Walla Walla District U.S. Army Corps of Engineers (USACE), Chatters finds 350 pieces of bone in the immediate area. This represents almost the full skeleton, including the cranium, which is intact. The skeleton is immediately dubbed "Kennewick Man" by the media.

July 29, 1996
The bones are X-rayed and CAT-scanned. USACE is informed of the discovery because the site is on federal land under its control.

Chatters's continuing analysis reveals that Kennewick man was between forty and fifty-five years old when he died and approximately 170–176 cm tall; he had a stone projectile point embedded in his hip from an old half-healed wound. The projectile is a leaf-shaped, serrated Cascade projectile point, typical of Southern Plateau assemblages from 8500 BP to 4500 BP. Amino acid and stable isotope analysis indicates a heavy dependence on anadromous (migratory) fish in the man's diet. DNA is found intact, but two partially completed extractions are inconclusive.

July 30, 1996

A local newspaper in eastern Washington publishes a story on the discovery, prompting a representative of a local Native American tribe to contact the authorities.

August 5, 1996

At the coroner's request, Chatters sends one bone fragment (a metacarpal) to the University of California, Riverside, to be dated by AMS radiocarbon.

August 19, 1996

Chatters asks UC Riverside to send a sample of the bone to anthropologist David Glenn Smith at the University of California, Davis, for genetic testing.

August 26, 1996

Early analysis reports the metacarpal to be about 8,410 +/- 60 yrs BP, indicating that it was approximately 9,300 calendar years old and thus one of the oldest, well-preserved skeletons in the Pacific Northwest as well as one of the five oldest in North America.

September 2, 1996

Kennewick Man's bones are transferred from the Benton County coroner to USACE.

September 9, 1996

A group of five Native American tribes (the Confederated Tribes of the Umatilla Indian Reservation [CTUIR], the Confederated Tribes of the Colville Reservation, the Yakama Nation, the Nez Perce Tribe, and the Wanapum Band) claims the Kennewick remains under the Native American Graves Protection and Repatriation Act (NAGPRA), a federal law.

September 17, 1996

USACE agrees to the tribal coalition's claim and publishes an official "Notice of Intent to Repatriate" statement as required under law.

Several scientists request permission from USACE to study the skeleton or express alarm over the Notice of Intent. Their requests are denied.

Tribal claimants collect additional bones from the site.

September 24, 1996

USACE publishes the second notice of intent to transfer the skeleton to a coalition of five tribes (NAGPRA requires a waiting period of at least thirty days following the second notice before the remains are repatriated, during which time other claimants may come forward).

September 30, 1996

Timothy Egan publishes a story in *The New York Times*, which transmutes Chatters's use of the term "Caucasoid" into Caucasian, and claims that Kennewick Man "adds credence to theories that some early inhabitants of North America came from European stock" (Egan 1996). Subsequent media stories follow in the *Washington Post, Seattle Post-Intelligencer*, and several other regional newspapers, beginning a wave of controversy.

October 4, 1996

The journal *Science* publishes a news report mentioning the DNA analysis by Smith. USACE orders Smith to stop testing.

October 16, 1996

Eight anthropologists (Robson Bonnichsen, C. Loring Brace, George W. Gill, C. Vance Haynes, Jr., Richard L. Jantz, Douglas Owsley, Dennis J. Stanford, and D. Gentry Steele) file suit in the U.S. Magistrate's Court in Portland, Oregon, to prevent USACE from repatriating the remains, and to allow further study of the remains. Bonnichsen et al. argue that the government has not proven the remains are related to modern Native Americans.

The court issues an order that the scientists must be given fourteen days notice prior to USACE releasing the skeleton.

October 24, 1996

Litigation begins in the U.S. Magistrate's Court.

The Asatru Folk Assembly, a California-based organization following an old Norse religion, also files suit arguing that, if the remains were Caucasian, they (the Asatru) might be culturally affiliated to the remains.

December 1996

The government files a motion to dismiss the scientists' complaint.

1997

February 1997

The court denies the government's motion to dismiss the scientists' and the Asatru Folk Assembly's complaints.

March 1997

Scientists file a motion to be allowed access to study the skeleton. Their study plan includes detailed proposals from seventeen specialists across the country.

March 23, 1997

USACE rescinds its decision to repatriate the skeletal remains. Magistrate Jelderks raises a series of issues concerning the implementation of NAGPRA that he wishes to resolve before making any decision on the fate of the skeletal remains.

April 1997

The government files a motion for judgment in its favor, arguing that study of the skeleton is unnecessary.

June 1997

The court denies the government's motion for judgment and the scientists' motion for immediate study access, but leaves this open to file at a later date.

Magistrate John Jelderks puts the lawsuit on hold. He asks the government to review the law and reconsider whether Kennewick Man should be transferred to the tribal coalition.

July 1997

Concern increases that bones are improperly housed. Reports surface that USACE has allowed tribes to conduct religious ceremonies with the skeleton and that cedar boughs were placed with the bones.

August 1997

Five scientists submit an ARPA request to investigate the discovery site. No permit is granted.

The CTUIR file a competing ARPA request. Their permit is granted to dig ten 1-m^2 square test pits at the discovery site.

August 27, 1997

The Asatru Folk Assembly holds ceremonies at the Kennewick discovery site.

October 1997

USACE admits that five religious ceremonies have been conducted.

USACE hires a conservator, who verifies the presence of ashes and cedar twigs and recommends the bones be stored in sealed containers.

USACE announces a project to study the site.

November 1997

Rep. Doc Hastings first drafts a bill to clarify NAGPRA, requiring, among other things, that cultural affiliation be documented to a much greater extent.

December 1, 1997

Additional research is carried out at the discovery site.

USACE conducts a limited site study. No trenching or test pits are excavated, and coring is limited to five locations. Sediment profiles are limited to 20 cm. Inadequate and conflicting data is obtained, but no report is released until January 1999.

A further bone fragment is found on the beach.

USACE informs scientists of plans to cover the site, ignoring the fact that the site is in the *Federal Register* and therefore NAGPRA applies.

1998

January 1998

Plaintiffs raise concerns that tribes have added bones to the collection on two occasions. USACE access records confirm this.

March 1998

The government reports to the court that portions of both femurs are missing from the collection.

USACE formally enlists assistance in its legal and archaeological review from the Department of the Interior (DOI).

April 1, 1998

USACE gives Kennewick Man to the DOI.

April 6, 1998

USACE covers the site where the bones were found by dumping concrete blocks onto the site, covering it with soil and then planting it with trees. This is against recommendations from USACE scientists to protect the site.

A small box of human and animal bone fragments recovered from the Kennewick site is handed over to the tribes, who rebury the remains with appropriate ceremony.

May 1998

The court issues an order for a hearing to review the adequacy of USACE's curation protocols.

The court orders that the skeleton be moved to a new facility and that plaintiffs be allowed to inspect its condition.

Mediation sessions on curation issues are held in Portland, Oregon.

June 17, 1998

Out-of-court mediation between the parties begins.

July 1998

The U.S. National Park Service (NPS) releases their multiphase study plan.

September 3, 1998

A federal judge orders Kennewick Man moved to the Thomas Burke Memorial Washington State Museum at the University of Washington in Seattle for safekeeping. The court orders that the skeleton be inventoried before it is moved and that two representatives of the plaintiffs may be present.

October 29, 1998

Kennewick Man's bones are transferred to the Burke Museum.

Douglas Owsley (Smithsonian Institution) inventories the skeleton in Richland. The 350 fragments represent one male individual.

James Chatters conducts a condition assessment that shows deterioration of some of the remains (old cracks expanding, new cracks forming).

1999
January 1999

The government reports that the curation of the skeleton has begun at the Burke Museum.

Scientists file analysis documenting the need for more study of the discovery site.

February 27, 1999

A team of federally selected anthropologists working for the DOI presents its preliminary findings based on nondestructive examinations carried out at the Burke Museum.

June 1999

The press reports that Kennewick Man was intentionally buried and that the skeleton displays evidence of red ocher.

July 27, 1999

The National Park Service presents the results of a series of nondestructive studies on: (1) the initial skeletal assessment of the Kennewick remains; (2) the osteological assessment of the skeleton; (3) an analysis of the sediments in which the remains were found; and (4) an analysis of the projectile point embedded in the skeleton.

August 1999

Scientists file a motion requesting immediate response to their 1996 study requests.

The court schedules oral arguments on the scientists' motion for September 14.

September 8–9, 1999

Scholars working for the NPS select bone samples for dating. The government takes 30.3g of bone for C14 dating.

The court hears oral arguments on scientists' motion for immediate response to study request.

Scientists charge that the government mishandled its selection and sampling for C14 dating and assert that the government is engaged in a deliberate misinformation campaign.

The government tells the court that the results of the C14 tests by three laboratories will be released in early to mid-November.

September 21, 1999

The court orders the government to answer scientists' study requests by March 24, 2000.

October 15, 1999

A federal report links Kennewick Man to Asian peoples, not the tribes claiming an ancestral link to the remains and not to Europeans.

The government posts scientific reports to the NPS website.

2000

By 2000, the Kennewick skeleton is being referred to as the Ancient One by members of the CTUIR.

January 12, 2000

The DOI announces C14 results confirming that Kennewick Man is about 9,300 years old.

The DOI announces that Kennewick Man is a Native American. Its interpretation of NAGPRA's intent is that anyone who died on this continent more than 500 years ago is Native American.

The DOI asks the court for six more months to conduct DNA tests.

January 13, 2000

The department continues to study the archaeological, ethnographic, linguistic, biological, genetic, and historical information on Kennewick as well as traditional stories from the CTUIR.

January 14, 2000

The Asatru Folk Assembly withdraws from legal proceedings to claim Kennewick Man.

February 1, 2000

The CTUIR strongly opposes the decision to proceed with DNA analysis, arguing: "Not only does DNA analysis require additional destruction of these human remains, which we oppose, but in our view there is overwhelming scientific evidence that indicates DNA testing can prove nothing more than what they already know, that the remains are Native American" (CTUIR 2000).

February 2000

Scientists ask the court to deny the government's request for six more months to conduct DNA tests.

March 2000

Judge Jelderks allows six months to conduct more DNA tests. He requires monthly status reports, consultation with the plaintiffs, and an answer to the study request by September 24, 2000.

April 2000

The DOI conducts microsampling of bone for DNA tests and taphonomic evaluation to assist in choosing appropriate bones to test. Five scientists are hired (none are plaintiff scientists).

May 2000

DNA tests begin in laboratories at Yale University, the University of Michigan, and the University of California, Davis, over Native American objections.

USACE reports no damage to the Kennewick remains during minor flooding in the Burke Museum collections area.

May 31, 2000

The Yakama Nation from south-central Washington files a motion to intervene as defendants in the lawsuit.

August 8, 2000

DNA tests continue.

Jelderks rules that the Yakama Nation waited too long to enter the legal fight over the custody of Kennewick and denies their request to intervene as defendants.

September 25, 2000

None of the three laboratories sent pieces of the skeleton is able to extract DNA for analysis because of the antiquity and mineralization of the bone.

The DOI completes its examination. Secretary of State Bruce Babbitt announces that the skeletal remains of Kennewick Man should be repatriated because they can be identified as Native American on the basis that geography and oral tradition establish "a reasonable link between these remains and present-day Indian tribe claimants" (Babbitt 2000).

The DOI rules that the bones should be given to the tribal coalition who claimed them as belonging to an ancestor.

Scientists immediately file a request to the court for a status conference.

The Yakama Nation files a request to appear as *amicus curiae*, or friend of the court.

October 2000

Bonnichsen et al. file an appeal against Babbitt's decision.

December 2000

The Society for American Archaeology (SAA) files a request to appear as *amicus curiae*.

2001

January 2001

Scientists file an amended complaint with seven points of concern, as well as a motion requesting raw computer data. The Department of Justice (DOJ) denies the request.

The CTUIR ask the court to put a protection order on the remains.

February 2001

The DOJ files a response to the amended complaint denying plaintiffs' charges.

The court grants plaintiffs' request for raw computer data and denies tribes' request for a protective order.

The court grants SAA's request for *amicus* status.

The court directs the DOJ to provide documents as soon as available and the final amended administrative record by February 19.

May 2001

The National Congress of American Indians are granted request to participate as *amicus curiae*.

Defendants file a Motion to Strike Extra Record Evidence and Declarations; Plaintiffs respond. A government brief filed May 17 asks the court to uphold the decision to repatriate the remains to the tribal coalition and to deny the scientists' issues.

June 4, 2001

The SAA files an *amicus curiae* brief, arguing that the Kennewick remains are indeed Native American under NAGPRA.

June 19, 2001

Oral arguments begin at 10:00 AM in the federal court, Portland, Oregon.

There is a report that the missing femurs may have been found; the FBI takes them into custody and investigates.

July 2001

The FBI drops its investigation.

USACE reports to the court that the femur fragments recovered fit the femur fragments in the collection.

July 26, 2001

J. P. Siofele, Paramount Chieftain Faumuina (a descendant of the first rulers of ancient Polynesia), files a motion with the court to claim the Kennewick remains.

August 2001

The court denies Siofele's motion as untimely.

2002

August 30, 2002

U.S. Magistrate John Jelderks in Portland rules that the bones should be turned over to the eight scientists for study. He rules that the skeleton has not been shown to be Native American and therefore is not subject to the provisions of NAGPRA. Instead, it should be treated as an archaeological resource under the terms of the Archaeological Resources Protection Act, mandating full scientific study and curation in the pursuit of knowledge in the interests of all citizens of the United States.

September 26, 2002
The CTUIR, along with the Yakama Nation, Nez Perce Tribe, and Colville Confederated Tribes, file a motion for post-judgment intervention in the litigation involving the Ancient One.

October 24, 2002
The government files a notice of intent to appeal, and Siofele files an appeal.

October 28, 2002
The tribal coalition files notice that it will appeal the ruling rejecting its request to bury the skeleton.
Scientists file a study plan with the federal attorneys to submit to USACE.

November 2002
The DOI and the tribal coalition files a motion to stay (delay) study of the skeleton and requests an expedited hearing. Scientists file a motion in opposition to DOI and the tribal coalition. The government supports the tribal request for a stay.

December 2002
The tribal coalition files a reply to the scientists' opposition to stay.
Government representatives and scientists continue to communicate on the scientists' study plan.

2003
January 8, 2003
Magistrate Jelderks denies the joint tribal motion for a stay in the case. The stay would have prevented any further study of the remains until the 9th Circuit Court addressed the appeals by the claimant tribes and the U.S. government.

February 12, 2003
The 9th Circuit Court of Appeals grants the joint tribal motion for a stay in the case. The stay keeps the case at status quo, preventing any further study of the remains.

2004
February 4, 2004
The 9th Circuit Court upholds Jelderks's ruling on the grounds that: (1) the plaintiff scientists do have standing to challenge the federal government's application of

NAGPRA to the Ancient One; and (2) the district court's ruling was correct in saying that the record did not support the federal government's determination that the Ancient One is Native American.

The CTUIR Board of Trustees discusses options, but no decision is reached on any further action in the case. The CTUIR meets with other tribes involved in the issue.

April 19, 2004
The 9th Circuit Court of Appeals denies the request for a rehearing of the *Bonnichsen et al. v. United States* decision.

July 2004
The CTUIR Board of Trustees decides not to appeal the case to the U.S. Supreme Court based on financial costs, the uncertainty of whether the Supreme Court would even hear the case, and the risk that an unfavorable Court decision could become law.

September 23, 2004
Senator Ben Nighthorse Campbell (R-CO) first proposes an amendment to NAGPRA that would change the definition of "Native American" in section 108 from that which "is indigenous to the United States" to that which "is *or was* indigenous to the United States" (emphasis added).

2005
April 2005
Senator John McCain (R-AR) proposes the same amendment to NAGPRA.

The Nez Perce, Umatilla, and Yakama Tribes appeal the district court's denial of their motion to intervene in the post-judgment phases of the case.

2006
February 2006
Douglas Owsley announces at the American Academy of Forensic Scientists meeting that Kennewick Man's burial was deliberate.

2007
September 2007
The Affiliated Tribes of Northwest Indians pass a resolution at their annual conference asking that the language proposed in the bill to amend NAGPRA be added to the law. The group represents more than fifty tribes (Affiliated Tribes of Northwest Indians 2007).

October 2007
Congress approves the bill to change NAGPRA to include the words "or was" in the definition of Native American. This is the third time such a change has been

proposed. It would ensure that federally recognized tribes could claim ancient remains even if a direct link to a tribe couldn't be proven.

November 2007

Congressman Doc Hastings (R-WA) proposes a bill opposed to the McCain amendment to clarify that Congress intended NAGPRA only to "apply to human remains or other cultural items that have a special, significant and substantial relationship to presently existing Native Americans." His purpose is to ensure that "scientific inquiry is not extinguished."

NOTE

1. Sections of this timeline have been compiled from information provided at the Burke Museum of Natural History and Culture (http://www.washington.edu/burkemuseum/kman/chronology.php); the Confederated Tribes of the Umatilla Indian Reservation (http://www.umatilla.nsn.us/ancient.html); Friends of America's Past (http:// www.friendsofpast.org/kennewick-man/events/chronology.html); the U.S. National Park Service (http://nps.gov/archeology/kennewick/press.htm); PBS Online NewsHour (http:// www.pbs.org/newshour/bb/science/kennewick/timeline_intro.html); the Smithsonian National Museum of Natural History (http://www.mnh.si.edu/kennewickman/index.html); the Society for American Archaeology (http://www.saa.org/repatriation/KennewickBriefs.html http:// www.saa.org/repatriation/index.html); and the Tri-City Herald's Kennewick Man Virtual Interpretive Centre (http://www.kennewick-man.com/kman/timeline/).

REFERENCES

Affiliated Tribes of Northwest Indians. 2007. Resolution #07-53 Supporting Amending NAGPRA Definition of Native American. 2007 Annual Conference Ocean Shores, Washington. Available online at http://www.atnitribes.org/Resolutions.html (accessed January 9, 2008).

Babbitt, B. 2000. Letter to the Honorable Louis Caldera, Secretary of the Army. Available online at http://www.nps.gov/archeology/kennewick/babb_letter.htm (accessed January 9, 2008).

Chatters, J. 2004. Kennewick Man. In *Northern Clans, Northern Traces: Journeys in the Ancient Circumpolar World*. Smithsonian Institution website, Washington, DC. Available online at http://www.mnh.si.edu/arctic/html/kennewck_man.html (accessed January 9, 2008).

Confederated Tribes of the Umatilla Indian Reservation. 2000. Tribe Opposed to DNA Testing of Ancient One. Press release. Available online at http://www.umatilla.nsn.us/kman5.html (accessed January 9, 2008).

Egan, T. 1996. Tribe Stops Study of Bones that Challenge History. *The New York Times*, September 30, p. A12.

CHAPTER 3
A REVIEW OF STABILITY IN PLATEAU CULTURE AREA BURIAL PRACTICES
RODERICK SPRAGUE

At the request of one of the involved tribes, a summary statement on Plateau burial practices was prepared for use in the Ancient One controversy. The study was based on forty-five years of work in the Plateau of northwestern North America, including the study of archaeological, ethnohistorical, and ethnographic burial patterns. This chapter is based largely on the pertinent literature, as well as extensive, first-hand archaeological fieldwork by me beginning in 1955, and ethnographic fieldwork beginning in 1959. A review of burial practices in the Plateau area reveals the use of earth inhumation to the virtual exclusion of other modes of disposal. The sequence from the rare early prehistoric evidence through later prehistoric, protohistoric, and ethnographic historic periods is unusually stable, with variation limited to minor traits. This pattern is strongly at variance with North America, except for the Great Basin and indicates that the discovery of the Ancient One—if indeed he was intentionally buried—is simply the earliest known example of a long and stable pattern of disposal.

The few known early burials, plus larger numbers of late prehistoric, protohistoric, and historic burials, which are largely primary inhumations, have led to the characterization of the Plateau as an area of relative stability in burial patterns. The protohistoric (*ca.* 1650–1750) and early historic (*ca.* 1750–1835) periods, however, are characterized by rapid change in the minor elements of burial, although not in the general practice of earth inhumation. From approximately 1850 to the present, burial patterns in the Plateau are again characterized by extreme uniformity in major traits, such as earth inhumation, and even in the minor traits, such as container and body orientation or body position. One of the more outstanding features of this final period is the almost invariable orientation of the grave to the east when located outside of Christian cemeteries. This anomalous trait is probably because of the characteristic performance by Plateau nativistic movements of ceremonies in the opposite direction to the dominant Christian population (counterclockwise vs. clockwise, east vs. west).

The burials from Marmes Rockshelter, the oldest Plateau burial site prior to the discovery of the Ancient One, and Rabbit Island, another early site, indicate a pattern of earth inhumation from the earliest times. In the late prehistoric and protohistoric periods, the evidence strongly suggests the continuation of basic earth inhumations. In the historic period, the extended inhumation placed on the back in a rough box predominated to the virtual exclusion of all other forms. The Plateau area is thus characterized by primary inhumation, with centers of ethnographic period cremation followed by inhumation in the far north and on the southern border, and with the addition of archaeological cremation on the lower Columbia River just down river on the western margin of the Plateau.

For a brief time during the late prehistoric period on the Columbia River, and near the location of the Ancient One, bodies were exposed on low structures built across pits. The bodies remained exposed until the structures collapsed, after which the pits were filled in. This practice of exposure followed by inhumation moved up-river from the coast and lower Columbia peoples. The short duration of this variation to burial practices coincided with the introduction of devastating European diseases.

Where the evidence is available, inhumations during all periods were most often placed in sandy areas, usually near the village. Body preparation was rarely more than the dressing of the deceased and the painting of the face. The body was usually wrapped in skin or matting in archaeological examples and in some contemporary reburials, while being placed in a rough box during the ethnographic period. The use of cedar cists, stone cairns, and burned wood in the graves is described ethnographically and inferred archaeologically as a device to discourage digging by coyotes.

Considering the evidence from the Plateau, it is quite likely that the prehistoric pattern in the Plateau was flexed burial on the side, or sometimes on the back, with orientation in any direction but south. With early contact involving the coming of new diseases, new material culture, and new religious concepts, the burial patterns changed rapidly, with the addition of cists, cairns, and fires over the grave, and with rapid changes in flexure, position, and deposition as well as more objects being buried with the deceased. In time, the pattern settled into a dichotomy of extended burials on the back in boxes or coffins that were oriented either to the west for those accepting Christianity, or to the east for those practicing the native religions. Single burials are almost the invariable rule, except for occasional epidemic cemeteries (especially involving children) and mass graves from raids or warfare.

The evidence suggests that the predominant burial pattern of earth inhumation as opposed to other forms is very conservative and not subject to rapid change. On the other hand, the specific details—such as position of the body, the disposal of grave goods, or the form of the container—are traits subject to rapid change. With the traumatic destruction of major portions of the population, the Native people obviously became increasingly concerned with death and burial.

In other parts of North America, the Native American populations have utilized such varied practices as abandonment under brush, in rock clefts, or in sink holes; exposure on platforms, in trees, ossuaries, or elevated canoes; exposure followed by the collection of bones for reburial (bundle burials); defleshing followed by exposure or cremation; burial in pottery vessels; or placement in canoes and directly into springs, rivers, and the surf. In light of these varied traits found even in adjacent areas, the pattern found in the Plateau is surprisingly stable over an extensive period of time. Considering the predominance of this stable pattern of earth inhumation with occasional examples of cremation prior to final inhumation through the whole of the Plateau chronology, it is only logical to consider the apparent extended inhumation of the Ancient One as simply the earliest example of a long period of unusual burial stability. To find any other burial form apart from earth inhumation or cremation followed by inhumation for this individual would clearly be unexpected.

CHAPTER 4
ANCIENT ONE / KENNEWICK MAN: (FORMER) TRIBAL CHAIR QUESTIONS SCIENTISTS' MOTIVES AND CREDIBILITY[1]

DONALD SAMPSON

Most American Indians do not appreciate having the graves of our ancestors disturbed and their remains dissected and studied in the name of science. This practice, generally supported by non-Indian society, has come to the forefront over the past year and a half with the unearthing of a skeleton near present-day Kennewick, Washington. The media and the public have come to know this individual as Kennewick Man.

We have tried to explain to the public and scientists that our religious and cultural beliefs mandate that we rebury the remains of this individual as soon as possible. Many people don't seem to care about, or respect, our religious beliefs. So, rather than present those points again, I will take this opportunity to briefly address some of the scientific issues of this case.

We do not believe the issues surrounding this case are in any manner related to scientific facts. Rather, the issues are the result of an effort of a small group of scientists, through a media campaign, to lay claim to materials which Congress did not intend they have.

In their media campaign, the scientists have led the public to believe they can produce considerable data by studying this individual, including knowledge of the earliest peoples of this continent. In an article published last summer in *The New Yorker* magazine, scientists claim they already know a great deal about Kennewick Man. They think he may have been a fisherman who ate lots of salmon, that he was probably a tall, good-looking man, slender and well proportioned, that he was part of a small band of people who moved about hunting, fishing, and gathering wild plants, that he may have lived in a simple sewn tent or mat hut, and that he may have worn tailored clothing.

The federal court, the Corps of Engineers, and the public should be asking the scientists to demonstrate how they can tell these things. These descriptions of the scientific "knowledge" obtained by the scientists are pure speculation and hypothesis, and do not advance our knowledge of this person, or humankind, a single bit. Almost anyone seeing an old skeleton in that area could have reached the same conclusions without destructive tests like the scientists want to perform.

These scientists are alleging that racial origins can be determined by examining the skeleton. But it is common knowledge among good anthropologists that it is impossible to determine the so-called "race" of an individual. A sample group is needed so that common traits can be determined.

The Kennewick Man remains were examined by Dr. Grover Krantz and there have been indications, using outdated techniques, that the skull has some "Caucasoid" features, some "Native American" features, and a "Negroid" feature. Even following the 19th-century science used by Dr. Krantz, there are three possible origins.

Dr. Krantz is considered primarily as an expert on "Big Foot" or "Sasquatch." From what we understand, his research is regarded by many of his colleagues as far from the mainstream of anthropology.

We also question the credibility and methodology of other scientists involved in the initial studies of Kennewick Man. Why hasn't a detailed report been compiled from those initial studies? Where is the statement of work and description of the methodology used? Were the studies conducted in accordance with the Archaeological Resources Protection Act (ARPA) as they should have been?

The "scientific case" for requiring the U.S. Army Corps of Engineers to allow testing of these remains is, in our viewpoint, shaky to non-existent.

We want the public and scientists to understand that we do not reject science. In fact, we have anthropologists and other scientists on staff, and we use science every day to help protect our people and the land. However, we do reject the notion that science is the answer to everything and therefore should take precedence over the religious rights and beliefs of U.S. citizens.

NOTE

1. Online at http://www.umatilla.nsn.us/kman2.html (last accessed November 11, 2007).

CHAPTER 5
HUMAN REMAINS SHOULD BE REBURIED
ARMAND MINTHORN

In the summer of 1996 a human burial, believed to be about 9,000 years old, was discovered near Columbia Park in Kennewick, Washington. Scientists and others want to study this individual. They believe that he should be further desecrated for the sake of science and for their own personal gain. The people of my tribe, and four other affected tribes, strongly believe that the individual must be reburied as soon as possible.

My tribe has ties to this individual because he was uncovered in our traditional homeland—a homeland where we still retain fishing, hunting, gathering, and other rights under our 1855 Treaty with the U.S. government.

Like any inadvertent discovery of ancestral human remains, this is a very sensitive issue for me and my tribe. Our religious beliefs, culture, and adopted policies and procedures tell us that this individual must be reburied as soon as possible. Our Elders have taught us that once a body goes into the ground, it is meant to stay there until the end of time.

It is not our practice to publicize these types of discoveries, both for the protection of the individual as well as sensitivity to our tribal members. In this case, however, we must take the opportunity this incident has created to help educate the general public about the laws governing these discoveries and what these discoveries mean to us, as Indians. We also hope to give people a better understanding of why this is such a sensitive issue.

The Native American Graves Protection and Repatriation Act (NAGPRA) and Archaeological Resources Protection Act (ARPA), as well as other federal and state laws, are in place to prevent the destruction of, and to protect, human burials and cultural resources. The laws also say that authorities must notify affected tribes and consult with tribal officials on how to handle the discovery, as well as protection and preservation. Our tribe was not properly notified; if we had been, this difficult situation might have been avoided.

Under NAGPRA, tribes are allowed to file a claim to have ancestral human remains reburied. My tribe has filed a claim for this individual, and, when it is approved, we will rebury him and put him back to rest.

In filing this claim, we have the support of the four other tribes that potentially have ties to this individual. These tribes are the Yakama, Nez Perce, Colville, and Wanapum. We share the same religious belief, and traditional practices as well as oral histories that go back 10,000 years.

If this individual is truly over 9,000 years old, that only substantiates our belief that he is Native American. From our oral histories, we know that our people have been part of this land since the beginning of time. We do not believe that our people migrated here from another continent, as the scientists do.

We also do not agree with the notion that this individual is Caucasian. Scientists say that because the individual's head measurement does not match ours, he is not Native American. We believe that humans and animals change over time to adapt to their environment. And our Elders have told us that Indian people did not always look the way we look today.

Some scientists say that if this individual is not studied further, we, as Indians, will be destroying evidence of our own history. We already know our history. It is passed on to us through our Elders and through our religious practices.

Scientists have dug up and studied Native Americans for decades. We view this practice as desecration of the body and a violation of our most deeply held religious beliefs. Today, thousands of native human remains sit on the shelves of museums and institutions, waiting for the day when they can return to the earth and for the day when scientists and others will pay them the respect they are due.

Our tribal policies, procedures, and religious beliefs prohibit scientific testing on human remains. Our beliefs and policies also tell us that this individual must be reburied as soon as possible.

Our religion and our Elders have taught us that we have an inherent responsibility to care for those who are no longer with us. We have a responsibility to protect all human burials, regardless of race. We are taught to treat them all with the same respect.

Many people are asking if there's any chance for a compromise in this issue. We remind them that not only has this individual already been compromised, but our religious beliefs have once again been compromised. Many non-Indians are looking for a compromise—a compromise that fits their desires.

And many non-Indians are trying to bend the laws to fit their desires. NAGPRA was passed by Congress in 1990 to protect Native American burials and set in place a mechanism to have human remains and artifacts returned to the tribes.

We are trying to ensure that the federal government lives up to its own laws and honors our policies, procedures, and religious beliefs. We understand that non-Indian cultures have different values and beliefs than us, but I ask the American people to please understand our stance on this issue. We are not trying to be trouble-makers; we are doing what our Elders have taught us—to respect people while they're with us and after they've become part of the earth.

NOTE

1. Available online at http://www.umatilla.nsn.us/kman1.html (accessed November 11, 2007).

CHAPTER 6

INTRODUCTION TO THE REPRINT OF

AN ANTHROPOLOGICAL PERSPECTIVE ON MAGISTRATE JELDERKS'S KENNEWICK MAN DECISION

DARBY C. STAPP

The article following this introduction first appeared in the *High Plains Applied Anthropologist* (2003, Vol. 23, No. 1:1–16) and was developed in an attempt to infuse anthropology into the Kennewick Man (also known as the Ancient One) legal appeals process. In late 2002, I was becoming increasingly disturbed about Magistrate Jelderks's Kennewick Man decision, which not only gave the suing scientists carte blanche permission to conduct studies on the Ancient One, but also, in my opinion, would enable the scientific community to dictate future decisions concerning virtually all American Indian human remains in collections and inadvertent discoveries. What I found especially disturbing was the magistrate's logic in arriving at his decisions. Much of his reasoning, it seemed to me, was contrary to basic anthropological theory and therefore fundamentally flawed. Yet, despite the baseless reasoning, the anthropological community was largely silent.

As the start of the appeal proceedings grew closer, I got the idea that if several anthropologists, each well versed in one of the subfields, banded together to explicate, in a professional forum, the problems with Jelderks's decision, we might be able to affect the appeals court decisions. The intent was to file an *amicus*, or friend of the court, brief and submit the paper to the court.

My search for fellow anthropologists concentrated on a discussion list moderated by the High Plains Society for Applied Anthropology and a few colleagues who I thought might want to take part. Although some individuals offered ideas, only one indicated that he could make the commitment necessary to produce the paper; that individual was Peter N. Jones.

As we commenced writing, we explored the process for submitting an *amicus* brief. Without going into all of the details, suffice it to say it's not an easy process to submit one; we ultimately had to abandon this idea. As an alternative, in mid-February, Deward E. Walker, Jr. indicated that the *High Plains Applied Anthropologist* would be interested in publishing the article if we could submit it in early March. We did, and the article appeared in the spring 2003 issue. Although the publication could not be entered into the current appeals process, we reasoned that it might have value if the legal proceedings continued.

We are pleased that Claire Smith and Larry Zimmerman liked our piece enough to include it in this volume on Kennewick Man and we hope that it might encourage others to become active in future debates concerning NAGPRA (the Native American Graves Protection and Repatriation Act) and similar laws in other countries. Our original article follows, after which we provide a brief overview of the 9th Circuit Court of Appeals decision, along with our thoughts on that decision.

AN ANTHROPOLOGICAL PERSPECTIVE ON MAGISTRATE JELDERKS'S KENNEWICK MAN DECISION
PETER N. JONES AND DARBY C. STAPP

In 1996, on the banks of the Columbia River, a 9,300-year-old skeleton was found that would become the impetus for the first legal assault on NAGPRA. After the U.S. Army Corps of Engineers (Corps) took possession of Kennewick Man, as he came to be known, they announced their intentions to repatriate the remains to four federally recognized tribes and a nonfederally recognized band that had historically and prehistorically inhabited the region where the remains were found. At this point, eight prominent scientists filed suit in the federal district court of Oregon to prevent the repatriation, demanding to be allowed to study the remains under NAGPRA, the Archaeological Resources Protection Act (ARPA), and their alleged constitutional right to do so. The lawsuit resulted in several hearings that reversed the Corps' decision to repatriate the remains and imposed de facto court oversight of the NAGPRA process. The Corps delegated its responsibility to determine whether the remains were Native American and, if so, whether they were culturally affiliated to any modern-day tribe to the Department of the Interior (DOI).

The DOI then commissioned a series of studies as it attempted to determine cultural affiliation (NPS 2003). These studies were then used by the secretary of the interior to make his September 2001 determination, in which he found the remains to be culturally affiliated with the tribal coalition.

In their filing, the plaintiffs brought seven claims for relief:

- The first claim, brought pursuant to the Administrative Procedures Act (APA), 5 USC §§ 701–706, sought judicial review of defendants' (DOI) decision on remand.
- The second claim alleged several specific violations of NAGPRA.
- The third claim alleged that the defendants (Corps) violated the National Historic Preservation Act (NHPA), 16 USC § 470 et seq., by burying the site where the remains of the Kennewick Man were found.
- The fourth claim alleged that the defendants violated ARPA, 16 USC § 470aa et seq. by failing to maintain the Kennewick Man remains "for the benefit of the American people, failing to make the remains of the Kennewick Man available for scientific and educational purposes, and failing to properly curate the remains to ensure

their long-term preservation as required by an earlier Order of the
District Court for the District of Oregon."
• The fifth claim alleged that the defendants violated the Freedom of
Information Act (FOIA), 5 USC § 552, by failing to respond to
plaintiffs' requests for information.
• The sixth claim, brought pursuant to the Declaratory Judgment Act,
28 USC § 2201, set out plaintiffs' demand for declaratory and
injunctive relief based on violations alleged in other claims.
• The seventh claim, brought pursuant to 28 USC § 1361, sought man-
damus relief in the form of an order compelling defendants to allow
plaintiffs access to the remains of the Kennewick Man "for purposes of study, publication, teaching, and scholarly debate."

After almost five years of legal wrangling, on June 19–20, 2001, Magistrate
Jelderks heard oral arguments on the scientists' assertion that they have the rights to
study the remains. Fourteen months after oral argument, Magistrate Jelderks ruled
that:

• the 9,300-year-old remains were not Native American for the purposes of NAGPRA;
• the remains were not culturally affiliated to the claimant tribes;
• the DOI failed to define the "Identifiable Earlier Group" as required
by NAGPRA;
• the evidence reviewed by DOI was inadequate to show a shared
group identity under NAGPRA; coalition claims were inconsistent
with NAGPRA.

This chapter looks specifically at the anthropology relied on by the court to
throw out the determination that the remains were Native American under NAGPRA
and culturally affiliated to the claimant tribes.

Magistrate Jelderks's 2002 Decision

On August 30, 2002, Magistrate Jelderks announced his decisions in the
Kennewick Man case. His seventy-three-page decision does not neatly correspond
with the claims outlined above but are reviewed below as presented in his decision-
al document.

Magistrate Jelderks's decision was that the secretary of the interior had not
properly demonstrated that the remains were Native American in origin as required
under NAGPRA; therefore, NAGPRA did not apply. This determination paved the
way for the plaintiff's request to study the remains, which the magistrate granted
using authorities found in ARPA (1978).

Given the magistrate's determination that the remains were not Native
American, he deemed it unnecessary to pursue the question of cultural affiliation.
However, citing judicial economy (because he had already reviewed all of the rele-
vant data), Magistrate Jelderks chose to pursue the question concerning cultural

affiliation. On this question, Magistrate Jelderks found that the secretary of the interior's decision was "arbitrary and capricious" and not made by a neutral and unbiased decision-maker (Jelderks 2002:23).

Normally, when a court determines that an agency has made an arbitrary and capricious decision, the magistrate remands the decision back to the agency to try again (Jelderks 2002:69). For example, in a similar case concerning Enola Hill, a sacred site in Oregon, the court's decision made this point clear:

> Courts review agency action under the arbitrary and capricious standard "based on the record the agency presents to the reviewing court." Under this standard, courts do not subject the agency decision to de novo review. Instead, courts "must consider whether the decision was based on a consideration of the relevant factors and whether there has been a clear error of judgment." When an agency decision is based upon expert opinion, the agency has discretion to rely on the reasonable opinions of its own qualified experts, even if the court might otherwise find different views more persuasive. A plaintiff challenging an agency decision on procedural grounds bears the burden of establishing that certain procedures were required under the circumstances, and that those procedures have not been followed. (*Native Americans for Enola v. U.S. Forest Service* 832 F. Supp. 297, 299–300 (D. Or. 1993); [internal citations omitted])

In this case, however, Magistrate Jelderks believed that sending the case back to DOI would serve "no useful purpose" (Jelderks 2002:25). He then took it on himself to determine whether the Kennewick Man remains were culturally affiliated with the tribal coalition, in a fashion acting as a qualified anthropologist. Magistrate Jelderks conducted a review of the information presented to the court and decided that there were not enough data to support a determination of cultural affiliation. He also found that coalitions of tribal claimants violated NAGPRA except in specific cases and determined that the Indian Claims Commission related disposition course as detailed in NAGPRA could not be used.

WAS THE DECISION ARBITRARY AND CAPRICIOUS?

We do not believe that the decision to assign cultural affiliation to the coalition of tribes was arbitrary and capricious. The secretary of the interior based his decision primarily on four lengthy cultural affiliation reports prepared by recognized scholars. One could question the selection of the experts and the approach each took, but each provided enough information to assist in the decision-making process. Moreover, the National Park Service (NPS) obtained additional radiocarbon dates to confirm the age and attempted to get DNA information, despite its own consultants' report that stated that it was not possible to obtain uncontaminated DNA from the remains.

The NPS followed its procedure for determining cultural affiliation and did so in a methodical manner. Following the direction from Congress to use a vast range

of data to make a determination, the secretary considered archaeological, ethnological, biological, oral tradition, and linguistic evidence. Of all the research conducted for the cultural affiliation determination, no evidence was found to directly contradict the proposition that there is a shared group relationship between Kennewick
Man and the tribal coalition. Had the archaeological, oral tradition, or linguistic evidence indicated a cultural hiatus or cultural replacement in the region, cultural affiliation would have been hard to support, but no such hiatus has ever been proposed
and no evidence for it was found for the Kennewick Man analyses. Linguistic evidence suggested a possible link, as did evidence from oral tradition.

Magistrate Jelderks concluded that the DOI's decision regarding cultural affiliation was not reasonably supportable by the analyzed data. However, from an
anthropological understanding of the literature analyzed by the DOI, we believe that
the DOI's cultural affiliation decision is reasonably supportable. Under Section 3 of
NAGPRA and its implementing regulations, the standard of proof is the "preponderance of the evidence." As Secretary of the Interior Bruce Babbitt described in his
letter (2000:4):

> This is a threshold that many scholars hesitate to use for interpretations
> based upon archaeological, anthropological, and historical evidence. The
> determination to be made here is informed by, but not controlled by, the
> evidence as a scholar would weigh it. Instead, the determination for the
> Secretary of the Interior to make is the one that, on the evidence, would
> best carry out the purpose of NAGPRA as enacted by Congress.

Babbitt further stated that the "DOI construes the statute as Indian legislation.
Therefore, any ambiguities in the language of the statute must be resolved liberally
in favor of Indian interests" (2000:2). Although the literature cited in the DOI decision is not exhaustive, it does cover the majority of studies, especially those that are
comprehensive in structure.

Under 25 USC 3002(a)(2)(b), geographical, kinship, biological, archaeological,
anthropological, linguistic, folklore, oral tradition, historical, and other relevant
information and expert opinion must be weighed equally. What this means is that of
the ten categories of possible information, each contributes equally to the decision-
making process and if one category is inconclusive, it should be interpreted as such
and not as supporting or not supporting affiliation. In general, the DOI found that
kinship (direct ancestry) and folklore were not applicable because of the age of the
remains. Instead, the DOI found in favor of the tribes on geographical, historical,
and anthropological (ethnographic) bases and on evidence from oral tradition. The
DOI concluded that linguistic and archaeological evidence is insufficient to support
either affiliation or nonaffiliation. Biological (morphologically based—no DNA
could be extracted from the remains) evidence was found not to favor the tribes.
Thus, the "preponderance of the evidence" (43 CFR 10.14[e]) would support cultural affiliation of the Kennewick human remains to present-day tribes of the Interior
Columbia Basin.

However, Magistrate Jelderks concluded that the DOI's cultural affiliation determination could not be sustained because it:
a) did not adequately determine "an identifiable earlier group" to which the Kennewick Man allegedly belonged, or even establish that he belonged to a particular group, b) did not adequately address the requirement of a "shared group identity," c) did not articulate a reasoned basis for the decision in light of the record, and d) reached a conclusion that is not supported by the reasonable conclusions of the Secretary's experts or the record as a whole. (Jelderks 2002:38)

In forming his conclusion, Magistrate Jelderks relied heavily on the numerous gaps in both the archaeological and biological records in making his claim that the DOI's decision was "arbitrary and capricious" as well as in his own interpretation of the prehistory of the Columbia Plateau (2002:40, 42, 47, 48). However, as is noted in NAGPRA, the criteria for determining cultural affiliation "should not be precluded solely because of some gaps in the record" (43 CFR § 10.14[d]).

Magistrate Jelderks demonstrated a clear lack of understanding of both anthropological theory and American Indian prehistory in the Plateau in his interpretation of what "cultural affiliation" and "identifiable earlier group[s]" are as set out in the NAGPRA guidelines. These guidelines are as follows:

c) Criteria for determining cultural affiliation. Cultural affiliation means a relationship of shared group identity that may be reasonably traced historically or prehistorically between a present-day Indian tribe or Native Hawaiian organization and an identifiable earlier group. All of the following requirements must be met to determine cultural affiliation between a present-day Indian tribe ... and the human remains, funerary objects, sacred objects, or objects of cultural patrimony of an earlier group:
   1) Existence of an identifiable present-day Indian tribe ... with standing under these regulations and the Act; and
   2) Evidence of the existence of an identifiable earlier group. Support for this requirement may include, but is not necessarily limited to evidence sufficient to:
      i) Establish the identity and cultural characteristics of the earlier group,
      ii) Document distinct patterns of material culture manufacture and distribution methods for the earlier group, or
      iii) Establish the existence of the earlier group as a biologically distinct people; and
   3) Evidence of the existence of a shared group identity that can be reasonably traced between the present-day Indian tribe ... and the earlier group. Evidence to support this requirement must establish that a present-day Indian tribe ... has been identified from prehistoric or historic times to the present as descending from the earlier group. (43 CFR § 10.14)

This is confusing language; several anthropologically based ideas are inter-changed with the legal mandates of determining cultural affiliation. However, it can be reasonably comprehended if we understand the word "group" to be a subset of "culture." This is the most parsimonious understanding because it is well known in Plateau ethnography that numerous groups shared a similar cultural identity and epistemology. Taking the NAGPRA statute, Magistrate Jelderks identified the need to define the "earlier group" of which Kennewick Man was a member. Unfortunately, Magistrate Jelderks seemed to be confused by the differences between group and culture. He stated that the secretary of the interior acted "as if there were only one group in this large area during that time. However, the record clearly indicates that as many as 20 highly mobile groups anywhere from 175 to 500 members, may have resided in the region" (Jelderks 2002:39).

Magistrate Jelderks did not understand that these groups composed the Windust/Cascade culture. It is that culture that NAGPRA must mean when it uses the term "group." How do we know this? Quite simply, when dealing with prehis-toric time periods, cultures, not groups, become the scale that can be studied. It would not be reasonable to assume that Congress wanted to require proof at Magistrate Jelderks's group scale, because groups can seldom be identified archae-ologically. The result would mean that precontact human remains would rarely if ever be returned under NAGPRA. To agree with Magistrate Jelderks would again require us to assume that Congress had intended to create "odd or absurd results."

Furthermore, it is also well known from Plateau ethnography that the present-day reservation tribes are a fabricated construction of the federal government; prior to the construction of the reservations, the tribes of the Columbia Plateau were split into many groups that shared a similar cultural identity and epistemology (Walker 1998). Therefore, we can interpret the language above as requiring the existence of an earlier "tribe" (or specific group) that shared a particular cultural identity that can be reasonably traced to the present-day Indian tribe(s) that also share this particular cultural identity, or what may be reasonably attributed to them given cultural change and evolution. NAGPRA states that this must be done by looking at geographical, kinship, biological, archaeological, anthropological, linguistic, folklore, oral tradi-tion, historical, and other relevant information and expert opinion in determining cultural affiliation and identity.

We have conducted a comprehensive review from an anthropological perspec-tive of the documents used in both the DOI's and Magistrate Jelderks's decisions. The review shows that the DOI's decision was not "arbitrary and capricious" in its findings that Kennewick Man is Native American and that cultural affiliation with the defendants can be demonstrated based on a "preponderance of the evidence." The review also demonstrates that Magistrate Jelderks lacked understanding of rel-evant anthropological knowledge of the Plateau area.

ARE THE REMAINS "NATIVE AMERICAN?"

Magistrate Jelderks, following the logic of the plaintiffs, focused initially on the question of whether the remains were Native American. He asked for the NPS's definition of "Native American" and dissected the statute language in an attempt to discover what Congress intended. Although determining whether human remains are Native American is a precursor to invoking NAGPRA, we note that this question has never been, nor is it even today, an issue when confronted with human remains found in North America that are thousands of years old. On this matter, we find that Magistrate Jelderks expended entirely too much energy and, in the end, developed a convoluted logic and unsubstantiated intent of Congress to justify his position that the NPS failed to prove that Kennewick Man was Native American.

Implementation of NAGPRA is by the authority of the NPS. The NPS provided a definition of Native American consistent with current archaeological and anthropological thought. Magistrate Jelderks expressed dissatisfaction over the matter of the 1492 date used in the definition ("any remains dating prior to 1492 are 'Native American' cannot be fairly characterized as 'longstanding'" [Jelderks 2002:27])—again, a misunderstanding of the anthropological data.

The 1492 date has no relevance when it comes to dispositioning the remains of a 9,300-year-old man. Nevertheless, Jelderks fixated on the hypothesis of a person from Africa or Scandinavia finding his way to North America and his remains being assigned as Native American simply because they were found in North America and predate 1492. In the remote case that such an event occurred—and we note that Magistrate Jelderks does not cite any cases where this has occurred (because there are no examples)—we can assure Magistrate Jelderks that justice will be served. The remains and associated context would result in their being assigned as culturally unaffiliated, and they would be treated in an appropriate manner.

Magistrate Jelderks also spent a great deal of time trying to establish what Congress intended. He might have saved time had he consulted anthropologists rather than dissecting sentences and attempting to determine what Congress meant by terms such as "is." Quite simply, Congress's use of the term "Native American" was intended to mean any cultural group living in North America before the settlement of North America by European groups (pre-1492). We know this because that is what virtually all anthropological and archaeological professionals believed in the 1980s; it is what the professional community portrayed to the public and would have portrayed to legislators, and it is still the accepted understanding.

For example, consider a quote from a leading textbook from 1978 by famed archaeologist Jesse D. Jennings. He begins the discussion by talking about how the earliest humans found in the New World were long-headed people and goes through various theories at that time and then concludes:

> Lacking better data, it is therefore taken as a given that the founding New World population was, in fact, Asiatic *Homo sapiens* of Caucasoid-Mongoloid mixture and that the American Indian evolved in the New World in response to a variety of environmental and evolutionary processes. (Jennings 1978:18)

In short, the NPS defined "Native American" appropriately, and its definition is consistent with current anthropological theory. Magistrate Jelderks invented the requirement that a prehistoric skeleton be "proven" Native American, a requirement without foundation. There is no reason to assume that Congress intended that there be such a requirement; institutionalizing such a requirement would result in costly and questionable research that would harm the very remains that Congress passed NAGPRA to protect. As Magistrate Jelderks himself stated (2002:27): "When interpreting statutes, courts do not assume that Congress intended to create odd or absurd results" (*United States v. X-Citement Video, Inc.* 513 U.S. 64, 69–70 [1994] citing *Public Citizen v. United States Department of Justice* 491 U.S. 440, 453–455 [1989]). It would be odd or absurd to assume that Congress wanted all prehistoric burials to be subjected to costly, destructive, and lengthy analyses before being placed under the purview of NAGPRA.

Magistrate Jelderks's conclusions surrounding the "Native American question" indicate that he lacked the anthropological understanding to perform this level of analysis. He stated: "The record would not support a finding that the ancestors of the American Indians were the only people here in prehistoric times, or that only one culture existed throughout prehistoric times. Congress did not create a presumption that items of a particular age are "Native American" (Jelderks 2002:31). In reality, the ancestors of American Indians are the only documented groups known in prehistoric North America; no one suggests there was only one culture, at least not after the Clovis people, *ca.* 1,200 years ago, and Congress did create a presumption that items of a particular age are Native American.

ARE THE REMAINS CULTURALLY AFFILIATED WITH THE TRIBAL COALITION?

In determining that the secretary of the interior's decision was arbitrary and capricious, Magistrate Jelderks found that the secretary did not:

- adequately determine "an identifiable earlier group";
- adequately address the requirement of "shared group identity";
- articulate a reasoned basis for the decision in light of the record;
- reach a conclusion that is supported by the reasonable conclusions of the Secretary's experts or record as a whole. (Jelderks 2002:38)

GEOGRAPHICAL AND KINSHIP EVIDENCE

Geographical and kinship evidence are not applicable in the Kennewick Man case. It is well established that the defendants have resided in the Columbia Plateau for as long as recorded history. Geographical evidence is only used in cases in which the claimants no longer reside in the area of provenance for the item(s) being requested for repatriation under NAGPRA. Similarly, kinship evidence is only used when it is necessary to trace direct lineal descent between a NAGPRA-claimed item and a particular group of individuals. For example, in cases for repatriation of various sacred objects, kinship evidence may need to be demonstrated between the object and the group of individual(s) requesting repatriation.

BIOLOGICAL EVIDENCE

The biological reports cited by the DOI's decision and analyzed by Magistrate Jelderks do not deal with the Plateau specifically but are primarily concerned with the peopling of the Americas and the original populations from whom American Indians are hypothetically derived. These reports conclude that American Indians came from one of three possible geographic regions in Asia (see below). Three sub-categories exist within the biological evidence: (1) dental studies, (2) craniometric studies (morphological analyses), and (3) genetic studies.

DENTAL STUDIES

There are two basic, discrete dental types in Asia: the Sundadonts and the Sinodonts. The Sundadonts are believed to have arisen sometime between 30,000–17,000 years ago in southern Asia. A branch group of the Sundadonts migrated to northeastern Asia and gave rise to the Sinodonts. Turner (1985, 1989) believes that small Sinodont populations migrated to the Americas, most likely in three waves (Greenberg 1987; Greenberg, Turner, and Zegura 1986).

Powell and Rose (1999) conducted an osteological assessment of Kennewick Man for the DOI and found that "Although it is tempting to try to assign Kennewick to either the Sinodont or Sundadont (Turner 1990) patterns, it is simply not possible to attribute the Kennewick individual's dental discrete traits to either the Sinodont or Sundadont groups based on gross morphological observations" (1999:6). This is because Turner's dental patterns are based on relative frequencies of eight key traits based on a large Asian sample, and any individual drawn at random from either the Sinodont or Sundadont groups may exhibit none, some, or all of the characteristics associated with that group.

Powell and Rose also conducted a discrete trait analysis on Kennewick Man's dentition, finding that "Kennewick had a probability of 0.48460 for membership in the Sinodont group, 0.93769 for membership in the Sundadont group" (Powell and Rose 1999:18). This is in congruence with most of the genetic studies that suggest that American Indians began migrating to the Americas between 40,000 and 25,000 years ago. As the Sundadonts moved to northeastern Asia and gave rise to the Sinodonts, it is very likely that many of these Sundadonts/Sinodonts were some of the groups that made their way to the Americas at this time. Thus, the dental evidence, although somewhat inconclusive as to Kennewick Man's cultural affiliation, does support the hypothesis that he is Native American.

CRANIOMETRIC STUDIES

Cranial morphology is a method used by biological anthropologists to measure similarities among crania. Because of the limited sample size (n=25) of skeletons prior to 8,500 BP, craniometric morphological measurements are of very limited scientific value. Although most of these studies claim that Paleoindian skeletons are most similar to south Asian and Polynesian populations, they also note many of the limitations in reaching such conclusions. Steele and Powell (1992:319–320) note "that braincase shape alone cannot be used as a diagnostic character to differentiate all world populations and that dolichocrancy can occur in all geographic populations." They also state:

> We still face the most difficult task of all. Are these distinctive structural features a reflection of subtle differences in the genomes of these earlier populations, or do the differences reflect an adaptational difference, an adaptation accomplished by the plasticity of human growth and development? At present, we cannot accurately answer this question. (Steele and Powell 1992:312–313)

Although the reports cited in the DOI's decision conclude that Paleoindian skeletons are more similar to those of Polynesian and South Asian populations, some found that Paleoindians, "both male and female samples, did not differ significantly from the majority of the samples with which they were compared" (Steele and Powell 1999:110). Others found that their skulls "fall outside the range of any modern population represented by currently available samples" (Jantz and Owsley 1997:79). Finally, as Hackenberger (2000:4) notes: "However, as of yet, no other comparisons with early Northwest specimens have been published with similar statistical techniques."

The human skeleton is one of the most "plastic" morphological aspects of our species. The human skeleton responds to a wide array of environmental, dietary, genetic, life course, and cultural forces to which it is exposed. As Swedlund and Anderson state: "We have volumes of data on how the cranium responds to nutritional, dietary (they are not the same), and environmental forces within the life span, particularly during growth and development" (2003:163). Similarly, and of particular importance to Kennewick Man, comparing crania(um) from one 8,000+ year-old individual to those of modern populations is inherently misleading:

> This is problematic, because a specimen that might date approximately 8,000 years older than its closest reference sample is not only separated by geographic distance but also by considerable temporal distance. We can translate this into very approximate generation times (e.g., 8,000 years/20) and quickly discover that we are talking about a "distance" of approximately 400 generations in which gene flow, drift, mutation, and natural selection have had an opportunity to operate between the specimen and its referents. Add to this environmental plasticity and it is not at all surprising to us that some early Archaic American specimens might plot more closely to Asian, Eurasian, and even European samples. (Swedlund and Anderson 2003:163)

Because of the time span involved in the Kennewick Man situation, the DOI noted that, although the Kennewick crania falls outside any modern group, because of the lack of the number of specimens "the analyses are not particularly robust," and that, "[a]lthough the Kennewick remains do not have a close affinity to any modern group, metric data do suggest an association with the small number of early Holocene human remains" (DOI 2000:21). Therefore, although the evidence is inconclusive as to morphological heritage, it is reasonable to conclude that Kennewick Man and other similar early Holocene human remains such as the Spirit Cave mummy, Gordon Creek woman, and the Marmes burials are Native American.

This conclusion allowed the DOI to proceed with their analysis under NAG-PRA. However, because Magistrate Jelderks lacked a background in general physical anthropological understanding, he misinterpreted this evidence. Magistrate Jelderks concluded that because Kennewick Man's morphological characteristics fall outside of the range of any known population, including contemporary American Indians, the remains must not be Native American as required under NAGPRA. This finding allowed Magistrate Jelderks to dismiss much of the NAGPRA claim and to state that the remains fall under ARPA.

GENETIC STUDIES

Because of the failure to extract, amplify, and analyze any genetic material from the Kennewick remains, only a few genetic reports were cited by the DOI. Most genetic studies done to date locate the ancestral population of American Indians somewhere in Northern Asia or Siberia, in either a single wave of migration (Bianchi et al. 1997; Easton et al. 1996; Merriwether, Rothhammer, and Ferrell 1995) or several waves (Karafet et al. 1997). It should be noted that these genetic studies have many limitations that have been discussed elsewhere (Jones 2002). However, because no genetic material was recovered from the Kennewick remains, this line of evidence is not directly applicable.

Current biological anthropology attributes the origins of Paleoindians to one of three geographic locations in Asia. Dental characteristics show that Paleoindians arose in northern Asia sometime around 20,000 years ago (Turner 1985, 1989). Craniometric analyses tend to show that Paleoindian populations are most similar to Polynesian and south Asian populations morphologically, although some Paleoindian skulls either reside on the extreme of the American Indian range or are not similar to any modern population (Jantz and Owsley 1997, 1998; Owsley and Jantz 1999; Powell and Rose 1999; Steele and Powell 1992, 1994, 1999). Finally, genetic studies presently conclude that the ancestors of modern American Indians were from northern Asia or Siberia (Merriwether, Rothhammer, and Ferrell 1995; Schurr and Wallace 1999). Thus, the current database in biological anthropology tells us that Paleoindians (the ancestors of Kennewick Man as well as present-day American Indians) arose in Asia between 35,000 and 20,000 years ago and made their way to the Americas. However, there is no evidence to support the idea that Kennewick Man and other early Holocene remains found in the Americas are not Native American; in fact, it would seem to support this conclusion.

ARCHAEOLOGICAL EVIDENCE

Like the biological evidence, the archaeological evidence contains numerous gaps in its database. The DOI and Magistrate Jelderks both recognized this fact, although they came to very different conclusions based on it. The DOI noted that although there are "gaps" in the archaeological record, these may not be used solely to construe a lack of cultural affiliation based on NAGPRA guidelines. Furthermore, these gaps are evidence of a lack of knowledge, not of cultural displacement or migration. Magistrate Jelderks, however, interpreted these gaps differently. He concluded that because there are various gaps in the archaeological record, like those in the biological record, there is no evidence of cultural continuity and that cultural displacement or migration may have occurred, even though anthropological theory and current understanding do not support this.

Much archaeological research in the Columbia Basin did not begin until after World War II:

While fieldwork on the Plateau began well before World War II, its real impetus was post-war dam construction, and the resulting River Basin Surveys of the 1950s. The great majority of projects since the 1950s have been related to dams and reservoirs. Within the last 25 years work has expanded out of the canyons and river bottoms. Virtually all of this work is also CRM-related in the form of Forest Service projects, pipeline projects, etc. An impressive body of evidence has built up, but it has significant limitations. Excavations in the canyons, for example, focus on pithouse sites, and on the house pits themselves. We have, therefore, far more information about the contents of the structures than we do for exterior activity areas. (Ames 2000:2)

The nature and basis of CRM (cultural resource management) work is speed and superficiality. Most CRM excavations do not include extensive screening for microbotanical and microzoological remains or other customary methods of site excavation. For example, it is doubtful that if a site contains numerous fish bones CRM excavations would identify them as to species. Furthermore, many smaller, less structurally based sites, such as lithic scatters, pit houses, and temporary campsites that we would expect to find associated with early and middle Holocene time periods, are not usually excavated by CRM work.

Despite a relative lack of thorough, scientific excavations in the Columbia Plateau, regional archaeologists have established an agreed-on cultural chronology that is relatively consistent across the Plateau. Nevertheless, some time sequences used by a few archaeologists can be very confusing and of a microregional nature. The basic time periods used by Ames (2000), Ames et al. (1998), and the DOI (2000) are as follows:

Period IA (11,500–5000/4400 BC)—includes Clovis-type points (many archaeologists term these points Western Fluted [Beck and Jones1997;

Dixon 1999; Grayson 1993]) and is weakly represented. This subperiod is only distinguishable from Period IB by the types of points found; subsistence and mobility patterns are considered the same between these two subperiods.

Period IB (11,500–5000/4400 BC)—includes Windust and Cascade type points. These are the types of points found at a majority of sites during this time; one was found embedded in Kennewick Man. Subsistence orientation emphasizes riverine environments with exploitation of salmon, other fish species, large mammals (including bison), medium-sized mammals (i.e., rabbits), and a wide variety of plant life including camas bulbs and berries (Ames 2000; Ames et al. 1998; Campbell 1985; Cressman 1977; Dixon 1999; Erickson 1990; Galm 1994; Hicks 2000; Jaehnig 2000; Uebelacker 2000). It should be noted that the original report on the Marmes burial by Grover Krantz (1979) concluded that the skeletons from this site did not differ in any determinable way from modern American Indians. This assertion has never been questioned; the Marmes skeletons have not been used, to our knowledge, in any of the biological studies that claim Paleoindians are not related to modern American Indians.

Period II (5000/4400–1900 BC)—includes the Tucannon phase. There are no major differences between Period II and Period I. The differences that can be seen in the archaeological record are the result more of cultural adaptation and technological changes than of cultural population displacement (Ames et al. 1998; Cressman 1977; Dixon 1999; Erickson 1990; Hess 1997; Hicks 2000; Jaehnig 2000; Ubelacker 2000). Subsistence orientation continues with an intensification of uses of salmon and other anadromous fish, but medium-sized mammals (rabbits) are not well represented and seem to fall out of use. Ames (2000:6) construes this as evidence for subsistence patterns being "significantly different than during previous periods," although in Ames et al. (1998) he sees little change between Period I and Period II (Ames fails to define his use of "significantly"). Pithouses are found in the southeastern and south-central areas of the Columbia Plateau by 4000 BC, and some areas exhibit evidence of long periods of occupation. It should be noted that these pithouses occur both in riverine canyons and on the southern uplands, an occupation pattern that is similar to the ethnographic record.

Period III (1900 BC–AD 1720)—According to Ames (2000), this period shows the most change between preceding Periods I and II. There is an intensification of camas and other root exploitation, more exploitation of fish, increased population, evidence of storage pits, and an increase in numbers and sizes of pithouses (Ames 2000). However, many archaeologists (Hicks 2000; Jaehnig 2000) attribute most of these changes to the changing climatic patterns during this time when there were cooler, wetter springs and summers early in the period and then warmer, more modern climate environments toward the end. Although Period II showed some signs of the modern Plateau cultural pattern, such as long periods of occupation of particular riverine and upland sites, this is the period during which most archaeologists believe that the modern Plateau cultural patterns emerged.

Modern Period (AD 1720–present)—This period is covered by the ethnographic literature and continues the patterns established in Period III.

As most archaeologists have noted, as well as Ames and Ames and colleagues (Ames 2000; Ames et al. 1998), there is no evidence in the archaeological record of displacement or migration of any Columbia Basin peoples throughout prehistory. Because of the nature of CRM work that makes it difficult to locate Plateau research reports (Ames 2000; Lyman 1985, 1997), and because of the relative lack of deeply stratified sites that span all time periods, there are various gaps in the archaeological literature, but none of these gaps can be looked at as evidence of cultural displacement or of migration into or out of the Columbia Plateau. Furthermore, there is a preponderance of evidence to support continuing cultural adaptation and technological change. This evidence of continuity includes:

- The exploitation of salmon and other fish species dating back to 11,000 BP and extending to the present (Ames et al. 1998; Cressman 1977; Dixon 1999; Hicks 2000; Jaehnig 2000; Roll and Hackenberger 1998; Schalk et al. 1998);
- Continued exploitation of camas bulbs, berries, and other plant species dating back to 11,000 BP and extending to the present (Ames et al. 1998; Chatters and Pokotylo 1998; Cressman 1977; Green et al. 1998; Gustafson 1972; Hicks 2000; Jaehnig 2000; Roll and Hackenberger 1998);
- Occupation of a central locality around which various groups or bands would move throughout the seasons exploiting various subsistence resources (Ames et al. 1998; Chatters and Pokotylo 1998; Cressman 1977; Dixon 1999; Hicks 2000; Jaehnig 2000; Lohse and Sammons-Lohse 1986; Roll et al. 1998; Uebelacker 2000);
- A progression in lithic technology from stemmed and shouldered lanceolate and notched projectile points during Period IB to stemmed, corner, and side-notched projectile points during Period II to smaller notched projectile points during Period III, although stemmed and corner varieties continue (Hicks 2000; Jaehnig 2000; Leonhardy and Rice 1970; Uebelacker 2000). This progression can be seen as a logical development of projectile points used with atlatls and spears during Period I and Period II to the

development/adaptation of the bow and arrow at the end of Period II and Period III (Dixon 1999). It should also be noted that all projectile point types overlap in time (Hicks 2000);

- Continuing evidence of trade and exchange from 11,000 BP to the present (Erickson 1990; Galm 1994; Hayden and Schulting 1997). This includes the trade and exchange of obsidian from southern Oregon, central Idaho, and British Columbia around Mount Edziza and Anahim (Galm 1994; Fladmark 1985) and Newberry Crater (Connolly 1999), and the use of saltwater shells including Olivella biplicata, Dentalium pretiosum, and fourteen other genera (Erickson 1990). This pattern of trade and exchange increases through time, culminating in the famous trading centers described in the ethnographic literature at such places as the Dalles and Celilo Falls (Hayden and Schulting 1997; Stern 1998).

In our view, and for the reasons given above, the evidentiary gaps in Ames's archaeological study are primarily a result of lack of data and sites and are not necessarily indicative of cultural discontinuity. We have shown above that current understanding of the prehistory of the Plateau supports cultural continuity and continuing adaptation, not discontinuity and/or displacement. As Ames et al. (1998:111) note:

> If there is a cultural manifestation represented during this interval, then, it is clearly transitional in its stylistic elements between the better represented Period IB, and the vastly better represented Period IIIA. Any such entity must also have continued the subsistence orientation of the earlier time and continued a pattern of living that involved ephemeral and shifting, rather than stable, settlements. [We doubt that these settlements were all that ephemeral or shifting.]

LINGUISTIC EVIDENCE

Gaps in the linguistic data are primarily the result of the difficulty in reconstructing languages beyond 4000–5000 years ago. Because of this fact, Magistrate Jelderks dismissed linguistic evidence as supporting neither cultural affiliation nor the designation of Kennewick Man as "Native America" under NAGPRA. However, anthropological understanding comes to a much different conclusion.

Joseph Greenberg (1987) relied on the technique of glottochronology, which examines the rate of retention of a specific list of 200 words, and has determined that slightly more than 80% of this list is retained over 1,000 years. Although Greenberg's designation of three primary language families (Amerind, Na-Dene, and Aleut Eskimo) as ancestral to all contemporary American Indian languages has been contested, many linguists have agreed on his designations of subphyla, including Penutian. Sahaptian (the modern language family of the Nez Perce, Yakama, and other Interior Columbia Basin tribes) is a Penutian language; Ruhlen (1994),

Swadesh (1954), and Hunn (2000) believe that Penutian's ancestral homeland is in southern Oregon and northern California. Likewise, Hunn (2000) and Rigsby (1969) believe that Proto-Penutian was spoken in the Columbia Plateau dating back to as early as 8,000–9,000 years ago.

One of the primary arguments against linguistic affiliation in the plaintiffs' documents is that even if Kennewick Man did speak a Penutian language, it would be unintelligible to modern-day American Indian peoples of the Plateau. This is true for all languages over time, but this does not logically lead to the conclusion that modern American Indian peoples of the Plateau are not linguistically affiliated or descended from Kennewick Man. All languages evolve over time; it can only be reasonably concluded that two peoples are not linguistically affiliated if they speak languages from different phyla. This is not the case in the Plateau, as noted by Hunn (2000), Rigsby (1969), and Ruhlen (1994). Therefore, the preponderance of evidence suggests that the Plateau is the location where Penutian, and subsequently Sahaptian, developed; it can be concluded that prehistoric American Indian peoples of the Columbia Basin spoke an earlier version of either Penutian or Sahaptian.

As we have noted, although there is a lack of evidence for Sahaptian language usage before 2000–4000 years BP, it does not make it improbable that this language, or a proto version of it, was spoken on the Plateau prior to this time. In fact, several linguists and other researchers support the idea that Penutian (the language family encompassing Sahaptian) originated in southern Oregon and that there is no evidence that any other language has ever been spoken in the Plateau (Hunn 2000; Ruhlen 1994; Swadesh 1954). Anthropologically, then, there is no evidence that any other language has ever been spoken on the Plateau and that an early form of Penutian was, therefore, most probably spoken by Kennewick Man and his descendants.

EVIDENCE FROM ORAL TRADITION

Magistrate Jelderks asserted that the DOI inappropriately weighed evidence from oral tradition. We believe this is a misunderstanding of the complexity involved in using oral tradition as evidence (Echo-Hawk 2000; Mason 2000). Because of this difficulty, the DOI covered several pages discussing the merits and drawbacks of using oral tradition in this case. Magistrate Jelderks interpreted this as a "weighing" of the evidence from oral tradition. As we will explain below, evidence from oral tradition is very complex and necessitates a fair amount of coverage to arrive at an appropriate conclusion.

A large body of oral tradition (and mythology) exists throughout the Plateau tribes sharing common creation stories describing a time when the Columbia River was dammed by Monster and how Coyote killed Monster and broke the fish dam to allow salmon to swim up the Columbia River (Clark 1953; Ramsey 1977; Walker and Matthews 1994). Similarly, such oral traditions as "Blood Red Lake" (Clark 1953:72), "How Coyote Made the Columbia River" (Clark 1953, 88), "Legends of Steamboat Rock" (Clark 1953:112), "Origin of the Palouse Fall" (Clark 1953:117; Confederated Tribes of Colville 2000:Part 2c), "The Serpent Monster and Rock Lake" (Colville 2000:Part 2c), and "The Animal People's Race and the Palouse

Hills" (Confederated Tribes of Colville 2000:Part 2c) have all been interpreted as describing the immense glacial floods, lakes, and river channels of the Late Pleistocene and Early Holocene.

We believe that the oral traditions (myths) referring to "nomadic people" and "Stick people," as well as to "rains," do not diminish the weight of the evidence from oral tradition. In the documents cited in the DOI decision, there is no mention of nomadic people or other groups coming into the Plateau or of any groups prior to the modern-day Columbia Basin peoples. There is mention of "Stick people" or "Stick Indians" in the myths, but we believe that the plaintiffs' interpretations of these myths are quite misleading. In *Coyote Was Going There: Indian Literature of the Oregon Country*, compiled by Jarold Ramsey, there is a tale of Stick Indians. As explained in this tale, the Stick Indians were not another group of people but "spirits who live in high gloomy places, like Grizzly Flats (south of Mount Jefferson) and upper Shitike Creek (southwest of Warm Springs Agency)" (Ramsey 1977:85). The mention of rain in the plaintiffs' document can be reasonably bound to the time the Plateau experienced a wetter, cooler climate, around 1900–1000 BC. A large body of oral tradition reasonably describes the late Pleistocene and the major cataclysmic floods that took place during this time. Oral traditions and myths that may describe this time are "Coyote and the Swallowing Monster" (Ramsey 1977), "Creation of the Animal People," "How Coyote Made the Columbia River," "The Origin of Palouse Falls" (Clark 1953), and many others not cited by the plaintiffs or in the DOI's decision.

SUMMARY OF THE CULTURAL AFFILIATION QUESTION

The NPS followed its procedure for determining cultural affiliation and did so in a methodical manner. Following the direction from Congress to use a vast range of data in making a determination, the secretary considered archaeological, ethnological, biological, oral tradition, and linguistic evidence. Of all the research conducted for the cultural affiliation determination, no evidence was found directly to contradict the proposition that there is a shared group relationship between Kennewick Man and the tribal coalition (Figure 6.1). Had the archaeological, oral tradition, or linguistic evidence indicated a cultural hiatus or cultural replacement in the region, cultural affiliation would have been hard to support. But no such hiatus

Knowledge Base	Supporting	Defeating	Neutral
Archaeology			X
Ethnology	X		
Bioanthropology		X (possibly neutral)	
Linguistics			X
Oral Tradition	X		

Figure 1: Evidence for Determination of Cultural Affiliation.

has ever been proposed and no evidence for it was found for the Kennewick Man analyses. Linguistic evidence suggested a possible link, as do oral traditions

In short, the secretary of the interior did not make an "arbitrary and capricious" decision. Magistrate Jelderks may not have liked the decision; he may not have understood it, but that is no basis for ruling that it was arbitrary and capricious.

APPROPRIATENESS OF JOINT CLAIMS

Magistrate Jelderks took exception to the idea that two or more tribes banded together to file a joint claim, except in the most specific of cases. He supported his position by quoting "present-day tribe" language in the law and regulations. This is another example of his lack of anthropological understanding forcing him to attempt to interpret language and the intent of lawmakers. Although we refer today to groups such as the Yakama Nation, Nez Perce, and CTUIR as "tribes," in reality they are assemblies of smaller groups that the U.S. government organized through the treaty or executive-order process. In the past and still today, these groups intermarried on a regular basis (Anastasio 1972). Likewise, they traveled to places to trade and socialize together.

In a very real sense, all of the Plateau tribes are related; therefore, all have a shared group identity with prehistoric Native Americans. Furthermore, it is their shared group way for those tribes with ties to places where remains are found to take the responsibility to care for the remains. And the Palus and Joseph Bands of Nez Perce reside on the Colville Reservation, and some Palus reside on the Yakama Reservation, continuing to share a larger "group identity." In the Kennewick case, the coalition comprises those tribal governments representing people who share culturally continuous links to the area where the Ancient One was laid to rest. This fact may not fit the world as Magistrate Jelderks wants, but it's the way it is.

USE OF THE INDIAN CLAIMS COMMISSION

Magistrate Jelderks reasoned that the DOI was incorrect in relying on Section 3(a)(2)(c) of NAGPRA (25 U.S.C. 3002(a)(2)(c)) as part of its decision-making process. This section of NAGPRA states that, "If the cultural affiliation of the objects cannot be reasonably ascertained and if the objects were discovered on Federal land that is recognized by a final judgment of the Indian Claims Commission or the United States Court of Claims as the aboriginal land of some Indian tribe" the objects can be repatriated using the ICC or U.S. Court of Claims decision as a basis of evidence. As Magistrate Jelderks correctly noted, the defendants acknowledged that the location of the discovery of Kennewick Man has never been subject of a final judgment of the ICC or the U.S. Court of Claims. Because of this acknowledgment by the defendants, Magistrate Jelderks found that the DOI was incorrect in relying on this section of NAGPRA in part of its decision-making process. However, because of Magistrate Jelderks's lack of anthropological understanding concerning the Plateau, he misconstrued the DOI's reasoning behind citing this line of evidence.

The DOI likewise noted that the location of the remains have never been subject to a final judgment of the ICC or the U.S. Court of Claims, but it also noted that the reason for this is because of the importance of the Columbia River for Plateau tribes and their shared use of the river's cultural and natural resources. As Stern (1998), Walker (1998), and many others have noted, the Columbia River was an important shared resource for the Yakama, Nez Perce, Umatilla, Colville, and other tribes. Because all these tribes shared the Columbia River and its natural and cultural resources, an ICC or U.S. Court of Claims final judgment could never be rendered. It is also for this reason that the DOI mentions this line of evidence. All these tribes share a cultural affiliation with the area where Kennewick Man was discovered. It is partly for this reason that they filed a joint claim.

CONCLUSION

It is clear to us that Magistrate Jelderks exceeded his authority legally and intellectually. This is not the first time that Magistrate Jelderks has confused his role in hearing a cultural resource related case. In the Enola Hill case from Oregon, the U.S. Forest Service refused to accept Enola Hill as a Native American Traditional Cultural Property (TCP) and was sued. Magistrate Jelderks heard what is considered the fourth Enola Hill case (*Native Americans for Enola et al v. U.S. Forest Service* [1992]), as explained below:

> Oral arguments for this case were heard in December of 1992. After a short hearing, Magistrate John Jelderks would eventually rule that the Forest Service was in compliance with the law. More importantly, Magistrate Jelderks refused to grant a temporary restraining order preserving the site until the case could be heard on appeal. Issues regarding the validity of Enola Hill as a TCP brought up in the hearings, however, did not escape the Magistrate's attention. Magistrate Jelderks also rules that Enola Hill was not eligible for listing on the National Register as a TCP in his summary judgment released in June 1993. The eligibility of historic properties is not determined in the courts but is solely the responsibility of the Keeper of the National Register, thus it was inappropriate for Jelderks to make such a ruling. Consequently, that point was later vacated on appeal in what could be characterized as the fourth Enola Hill Court case. (Occhipinti 2002:21)

As we have discussed throughout this chapter, Magistrate Jelderks overstepped his legal and intellectual boundary. The DOI made its decision based on the "preponderance of the evidence" as mandated by NAGPRA. Furthermore, as the DOI noted, a decision should be informed by science, but not directed by it. Magistrate Jelderks, however, appeared to conclude that NAGPRA should be directed by science, which defeats the purpose of NAGPRA itself. Although Magistrate Jelderks raised some questions regarding the treatment and judicial processes involved in this case, he presented no evidence to support his decision that the DOI made an "arbitrary and capricious" decision. As we have tried to show from an anthropological analysis of the evidence used in this case, the preponderance of the evidence supports the case that the present-day tribes of the Plateau have a "shared group identity which can reasonably be traced historically or [and] prehistorically" (25 USC § 3001(2)). It is our expectation that the 9th Circuit Appeals Court will overturn Magistrate Jelderks's Kennewick Man decision for similar reasons.

REFERENCES

Ames, K. 2000. *Cultural Affiliation Study of the Kennewick Human Remains: Review of the Archaeological Data.* Washington, DC: Department of the Interior.

Ames, K., D. Dummond, J. Galm, and R. Minor 1998. Prehistory of the Southern Plateau. In *Handbook of North American Indians*, Vol. 12: *Plateau*, edited by D. E. Walker, Jr., pp. 113–119. Washington, DC: Government Printing Office.

Anastasio, A. 1972. The Southern Plateau: An Ecological Analysis of Intergroup Relations. *Northwest Anthropological Research Notes* 6(2):109–229.

Babbitt, B. 2000. Letter from Secretary of the Interior to the Honourable Louis Caldera, Secretary of the Army. Available online at http://www.nps.gov/archeology/kennewick/babb_letter.htm (accessed May 5, 2008).

Beck, C., and G. T. Jones. 1997. The Terminal Pleistocene/Early Holocene Archaeology of the Great Basin. *Journal of World Prehistory* 11(2):161–236.

Bianchi, N., G. Bailliet, C. Bravi, R. Carnese, F. Rothhammer, V. Martinez-Marignac, and S. Pena. 1997. Origin of Amerindian Y-Chromosomes as Inferred by the Analysis of Six Polymorphic Markers. *American Journal of Physical Anthropology* 102(1):79–89.

Campbell, S. 1985. *Summary of Results, Chief Joseph Dam Cultural Resources Project, Washington.* University of Washington: Office of Public Archaeology, Institute of Environmental Studies.

Chatters, J., and D. Pokotylo. 1998. Prehistory: Introduction. In *Handbook of North American Indians*, Vol. 12: *Plateau*, edited by Deward E. Walker, Jr., pp. 73–80. Washington, DC: Government Printing Office.

Clark, E. E. 1953. *Indian Legends of the Pacific Northwest.* Berkeley: University of California Press.

Colville, Confederated Tribes of. 2000. *Native American Graves Protection and Repatriation Act Claim to the Ancient One (aka Kennewick Man).* Nespelem, WA: Confederated Tribes of the Colville Reservation.

Connolly, T. J., ed. 1999. Newberry Crater: A Ten-Thousand-Year Record of Human Occupation and Environmental Change in the Basin-Plateau Borderlands. In *University of Utah Anthropological Papers.* Number 12. Salt Lake City: University of Utah Press.

Cressman, L. S. 1977. *Prehistory of the Far West: Home of Vanished Peoples.* Salt Lake City: University of Utah Press.

Department of the Interior (DOI). 2000. *Human Culture in the Southeastern Columbia Plateau, 9500–9000 BP and Cultural Affiliation with Present-Day Tribes.* Available online at www.cr.nps.gov/aad/ kennewick/encl_3.htm (accessed April 6, 2003).

Dixon, J. 1999. *Bones, Boats, and Bison: Archaeology and the First Colonization of North America.* Albuquerque: University of New Mexico Press.

Easton, R. D., A. Merriwether, D. E. Crews, and R. E. Ferrell. 1996. mtDNA Variation in the Yanomami: Evidence for Additional New World Founding Lineages. *American Journal of Human Genetics* 59(1):213–225.

Echo-Hawk, R. 2000. Ancient History in the New World: Integrating Oral Traditions and the Archaeological Record in Deep Time. *American Antiquity* 65(2):267–290.

Erickson, K. 1990. Marine Shell in the Plateau Culture Area. *Northwest Anthropological Research Notes* 24(1):91–144.

Fladmark, K. R. 1985. *Glass and Ice: The Archaeology of Mt. Edziza. Publication Number 14.* Department of Archaeology, Simon Fraser University, Burnaby, B. C.

Galm, J. 1994. Prehistoric Trade and Exchange in the Interior Plateau of Northwestern North America. In *Prehistoric Exchange Systems in North America*, edited by T. Baugh and J. Ericson, pp. 275–305. New York: Plenum Press.

Grayson, D. 1993. *The Desert's Past: A Natural History of the Great Basin*. Washington, DC: Smithsonian Institution.

Greenberg, J. H. 1987. *Language in the Americas*. Stanford, CA: Stanford University Press.

Greenberg, J. H., C. G. Turner, II, and S. L. Zegura. 1986. The Settlement of the Americas: A Comparison of the Linguistic, Dental, and Genetic Evidence. *Current Anthropology* 27(5): 477–498.

Hackenberger, S. 2000. *Cultural Affiliation Study of the Kennewick Human Remains: Review of the Bio-Archaeological Information*. Washington, DC: Department of the Interior.

Hayden, B., and R. Schulting. 1997. The Plateau Interaction Sphere and Late Prehistoric Cultural Complexity. *American Antiquity* 62(1):51–85.

Hess, S. 1997. Rocks, Range, and Renfrew: Using Distance-Decay Effects to Study Late Pre-Mazama Period Obsidian Acquisition and Mobility in Oregon and Washington. Ph.D. dissertation, Washington State University, Pullman.

Hicks, B. 2000. *Summary of the Southern Plateau/Lower Snake River Archaeological Record: Statement in Support of Affiliation with the Ancient One*. Nespelem, WA: Confederated Tribes of the Colville Reservation, History/Archaeology Department.

Hunn, E. 2000. Cultural Affiliation Study of the Kennewick Human Remains: Review of Linguistic Information. Report prepared for the National Park Service, Department of the Interior, Washington, DC.

Jaehnig, M. 2000. *Establishing Cultural Continuity between Kennewick Man and Modern Columbia Plateau Tribes*. Pendleton, OR: Confederated Tribes of the Umatilla Indian Reservation, Cultural Resources Protection Program.

Jantz, R., and D. Owsley. 1997. Pathology, Taphonomy, and Cranial Morphometrics of the Spirit Cave Mummy. *Nevada Historical Quarterly* 40(1):62–84.

Jantz, R., and D. Owsley. 1998. How Many Populations of Early North Americans Were There? *American Journal of Physical Anthropology* Supplement 26.

Jelderks, J. 2002. Opinion and Order for *Robson Bonnichsen et al. v. United States of America et al.* Civil No. 96-1481-JE.

Jennings, J. D. 1978. *Prehistory of North America*, 2nd ed. San Francisco: W. H. Freeman.

Jones, P. 2002. American Indian Demographic History and Cultural Affiliation: A Discussion of Certain Limitations on the Use of mtDNA and Y Chromosome Testing. *AnthroGlobe Journal*. Available online at http://www.anthroglobe.info/docs/Indian_demography_culture.htm (accessed May 4, 2008).

Karafet, T., S. L. Zegura, J. Vuturo-Brady, O. Posukh, L. Osipova, V. Wiebe, F. Romero, J. Long, S. Harihara, F. Jin, B. Dashnyam, T. Gerelsaikhan, K. Omoto, and M. Hammer. 1997. Y Chromosome Markers and Trans-Bering Strait Dispersals. *American Journal of Physical Anthropology* 102(3):301–314.

Krantz, G. S. 1979. Oldest Human Remains from the Marmes Site. *Northwest Anthropological Research Notes* 13(2):159–174.

Leonhardy, F., and D. Rice. 1970. A Proposed Culture Typology for the Lower Snake River Region, Southeastern Washington. *Northwest Anthropological Research Notes* 4(1):1–29.

Lohse, E., and D. Sammons-Lohse. 1986. Sedentism on the Southern Plateau: A Matter of Degree Related to the Easy and Efficient Exploitation of Resources. *Northwest Anthropological Research Notes* 20(2):115–136.

Lyman, R. L. 1985. Cultural Resource Management and Archaeological Research in the Interior Pacific Northwest: A Note to NARN Readers and the Translucency of Northwest Archaeology. *Northwest Anthropological Research Notes* 19(2):161–168.

Lyman, R. L. 1997. Impediments to Archaeology: Publishing and the (Growing) Translucency of Archaeological Research. *Northwest Anthropological Research Notes* 31(1–2):5–22.

Mason, R. J. 2000. Archaeology and Native North American Oral Traditions. *American Antiquity* 65(2):239–266.

Merriwether, D. A., F. Rothhammer, and R. Ferrell. 1995. Distribution of the Four Founding Lineage Haplotypes in North Americans Suggests a Single Wave of Migration for the New World. *American Journal of Physical Anthropology* 98(4):411–430.

National Park Service (NPS). 2003. Kennewick Man. Available online at www.cr.nps.gov/aad/kennewick (accessed February 19, 2003).

Occhipinti, F. D. 2002. American Indian Sacred Sites and the National Historical Preservation Act: The Enola Hill Case. *Journal of Northwest Anthropology* 36(1):editorial.

Owsley, D., and R. Jantz. 1999. Database[s] for Paleo-American Skeletal Biology Research. In *Who Were the First Americans? Proceedings of the 58th Annual Biology Colloquium, Oregon State University*, edited by R. Bonnichsen, pp. 79–96. Corvallis, OR: Center for the Study of the First Americans.

Powell, J., and J. Rose 1999. Report on the Osteological Assessment of the "Kennewick Man" Skeleton, (CENWWW.97.Kennewick). Washington, DC: Department of the Interior.

Ramsey, J. 1977. *Coyote Was Going There: Indian Literature of the Oregon Country.* Seattle: University of Washington Press.

Rigsby, B. 1969. The Waiilatpuan Problem: More on Cayuse-Molala Relatability. *Northwest Anthropological Research Notes* 3(1):68–146.

Roll, T., and S. Hackenberger. 1998. Prehistory of the Eastern Plateau. In *Handbook of North American Indians*, Vol. 12: *Plateau*, edited by D. E. Walker, Jr., pp. 120–137. Washington, DC: Government Printing Office.

Ruhlen, M. 1994. Linguistic Evidence for the Peopling of the Americas. In *Method and Theory for Investigating the Peopling of the Americas*, edited by R. Bonnichsen and D. G. Steele, pp. 177–188. Corvallis, OR: Center for the Study of the First Americans.

Schalk, R., C. Dillian, S. Hamilon, C. Hodges, D. Olsen, and M. Stratford 1998. *Archaeological Investigations at 450K2A, 450K5, and 450K20 in the Chief Joseph Reservoir.* Honolulu: International Archaeological Research Institute.

Schurr, T., and D. Wallace 1999. mtDNA Variation in Native Americans and Siberians and its Implications for the Peopling of the New World. In *Who Were the First Americans? Proceedings of the 58th Annual Biology Colloquium, Oregon State University*, edited by R. Bonnichsen, pp. 41–77. Corvallis, OR: Center for the Study of the First Americans.

Steele, D. G., and J. Powell 1992. Peopling of the Americas: Paleobiological Evidence. *Human Biology* 64(3):303–336.

Steele, D. G., and J. Powell. 1994. Paleobiological Evidence for the Peopling of the Americas: A Morphometric View. In *Method and Theory for Investigating the Peopling of the Americas*, edited by R. Bonnichsen and D. G. Steele, pp. 141–163. Corvallis, OR: Center for the Study of the First Americas.

Steele, D. G., and J. Powell. 1999. Peopling of the Americas: A Historical and Comparative Perspective. In *Who Were the First Americans? Proceedings of the 58th Annual Biology Colloquium, Oregon State University*, edited by R. Bonnichsen, pp. 97–126. Corvallis, OR: Center for the Study of the First Americans.

Stern, T. 1998. Columbia River Trade Network. In *Handbook of North American Indians*, Vol. 12: *Plateau*, edited by D. E. Walker, Jr., pp. 641–652. Washington, DC: Government Printing Office.

Swadesh, M. 1954. On the Penutiam Vocabulary Survey. *International Journal of American Linguistics* 20(2):123–133.

Swedlund, A., and D. Anderson. 2003. Gordon Creek Woman Meets Spirit Cave Man: A Response to Comment by Owsley and Jantz. *American Antiquity* 68(1):161–168.

Turner, C. G. 1985. The Dental Search for Native American Origins. In *Out of Asia: Peopling of the Americas and the Pacific*, edited by R. Kirk and E. Szathmary, pp. 31–78. Canberra, Australia: Journal of Pacific Prehistory.

Turner, C. G. 1989. Out of Southeast Asia: Dentition and the Peopling of the Pacific Basin and Adjoining Areas. Paper presented at the Circum-Pacific Prehistory Conference, Seattle.

Turner, C. G. 1990. The Major Features of Sundadonty and Sindonty, Including Suggestions about East Asian Microevolution, Population History, and Late Pleistocene Relationships with Australian Aboriginals. *American Journal of Physical Anthropology* 83(3):295–317.

Uebelacker, M. L. 2000. *Cultural Affiliation Determination for the Kennewick Remains: A Critical Review of the Evidence.* Toppenish, WA: Confederated Tribes and Bands of the Yakama Nation.

Walker, D. E., Jr., ed. 1998. *Handbook of North American Indians*, Vol. 12: *Plateau*. Washington, DC: Government Printing Office.

Walker, D. E., Jr., and D. N. Matthews. 1994. *Blood of the Monster: The Nez Perce Coyote Cycle.* Worland, WY: High Plains Publishing.

ADDENDUM:
THE 9ᵀᴴ CIRCUIT'S DECISION ON THE KENNEWICK MAN APPEAL
DARBY C. STAPP AND PETER N. JONES

The U.S. government and four intervener-appellant tribes (the Confederated Tribes of the Colville Reservation, the Confederated Tribes of the Umatilla Indian Reservation, the Nez Perce Tribe, and the Yakama Nation) filed their opening briefs on March 14, 2003 (Mosman 2003; Schlosser and Smith 2003). Ten amicus briefs were also filed, seven in support of the original decision and three supporting the government and joint tribal coalition in their request for reversal. The U.S. government made its final oral arguments on September 10, 2003, stating its reasons for appeal. From the initial filing until the final arguments, there were several briefs and reply briefs filed by the primary parties. All the court documents can be found on the Friends of America's Past website (www.friendsofpast.org). There are many subtle and not so subtle points that the 9th Circuit Court had to address, and we recommend that those with a strong interest in this case read the specific legal documents.

THE 9ᵀᴴ CIRCUIT'S DECISION

The 9th Circuit Appeals Court issued its opinion on February 4, 2004, supporting Magistrate Jelderks on every point (Gould 2004). The claimants presented several different arguments to the 9th Circuit, but the most substantive one concerned Magistrate Jelderks's finding that the government had not shown the remains to be "of or related to a group that is indigenous to the United States" and therefore the remains could not be considered Native American for the purposes of the Native American Graves Protection and Repatriation Act of 1990 (NAGPRA). The 9th Circuit agreed with Jelderks that Congress had intentionally used the phrase "that is indigenous," and therefore a relationship had to be shown with an existing tribe, people, or culture if human remains were to be determined "Native American."

One of the arguments from the government concerned NAGPRA's two-step process. On this point, the 9th Circuit responded:

Despite the statute's language and legislative history, the Secretary [of Interior] argues that the district court's interpretation "improperly collapses" NAGPRA's first inquiry (asking whether human remains are Native American) into NAGPRA's second inquiry (asking which American Indians or Indian tribe bears the closest relationship to Native American remains). The Secretary is mistaken. Though NAGPRA's two inquiries have some commonality in that both focus on the relationship between human remains and present-day Indians, the two inquiries differ significantly. The first inquiry requires only a general finding that remains have a significant relationship to a presently existing "tribe, people, or culture," a relationship that goes beyond features common to all humanity. The second

inquiry requires a more specific finding that remains are most closely affiliated to specific lineal descendants or to a specific Indian tribe. The district
court's interpretation of NAGPRA preserves the statute's two distinct
inquiries. Because the record shows no relationship of Kennewick Man to
the Tribal Claimants, the district court was correct in holding that NAG-
PRA has no application. (Gould 2004:1598–1599)

The 9th Circuit's decision presents findings on various others issues and it is instructive to review the entire decision (Gould 2004).

DISCUSSION

In our original article (Jones and Stapp 2003), we predicted that the 9th Circuit
would overturn Magistrate Jelderks's decisions. We were 180 degrees wrong. None
of the arguments made by the 9th Circuit, however, have caused us to waver from
our original positions, although it has brought to mind a few additional points we
would like to make.

For this discussion, we focus on the primary issue of the appeal: Magistrate
Jelderks's decision that the government had not demonstrated that Kennewick Man
was Native American as defined by NAGPRA, and, therefore, the remains were not
subject to NAGPRA.

In its opening brief, the government argued that, contrary to Magistrate
Jelderks's finding, the Department of the Interior had a reasonable definition of
Native American, that definition being "all tribes, peoples and cultures that were
residents of the lands comprising the United States prior to historically documented
exploration of these lands" (Mosman 2003). Further, the government argued that
Magistrate Jelderks was incorrect when he assumed that determining a set of
remains as Native American would then require mandatory disposition of the
remains to the claimant tribes and preclude further scientific study.

Mandatory disposition is not the inevitable result, the government argued,
because NAGPRA has a two-step process. First, an agency determines whether
remains are Native American to establish if the statute applies; in most cases, this is
a relatively straightforward determination to make. For example, suppose human
remains are discovered inadvertently during a construction project. For the purposes of illustration, let us suppose that the remains are associated with historic artifacts
and the skeletal features are consistent with non-Indian populations known to have
inhabited the area. The remains would be determined not to be Native American and
NAGPRA would not be invoked. The remains would be removed and the agency
would determine the best disposition for them.

On the other hand, let us suppose that human remains are unearthed along with
stone tools and other aboriginal items, and that the skeletal features are consistent
with those typically associated with Native Americans. In this case, the agency
would determine the remains to be Native American, NAGPRA would be invoked,
relevant tribes notified, project activities in the immediate area would cease for thirty days, the remains would be protected in place, and the agency, in consultation

with the tribes and others, would determine the best way to proceed.

Then the cultural affiliation process, a much more arduous process, would begin. The process is quite detailed, with specific actions and schedules to be followed, and we refer the reader to the NPS website for details (http://www. cr.nps.gov/nagpra/mandates/index.htm). In general, an announcement of the remains would be published in local papers, and if a group could demonstrate that, by a preponderance of the evidence (using geographical, kinship, cultural anthropological, archaeological, biological, linguistic, oral tradition, and historical evidence) they are culturally affiliated with the remains, the remains would be repatriated to them following notification in the *Federal Register.* If no group could demonstrate cultural affiliation to the satisfaction of the agency, and with the concurrence of the NPS NAGPRA coordinator, then the remains would not be repatriated; the remains would be considered unaffiliated and retained by the agency until the NPS finalizes its procedures on the treatment of unaffiliated remains.

In its appeal, the government argued that the existing NAGPRA process was reasonable and consistent with congressional intent. It would not be reasonable to suggest, as Magistrate Jelderks did, that extensive studies be conducted to demonstrate that the skeletal remains bear some relationship to "a *presently existing* tribe, people, or culture to be considered Native American" (Mosman 2003:31–35, emphasis added). To require such analyses at the initial stage of discovery would require burdensome studies, expense, and time delays for the responsible agency, which is clearly contrary to what Congress intended.

As discussed above, the 9th Circuit disagreed (Gould 2004). How the court's "first inquiry," which only requires a "general finding" that a significant relationship to a presently existing tribe, people, or culture is supposed to be conducted is not explained. That they think a general finding of a significant relationship can be made indicates a fundamental misunderstanding of human skeletal biology, archaeology, and anthropology. For example, in reaching its conclusion that no evidence existed that Kennewick Man was Native American, the court cited the following points:

- During the initial discovery, local coroners thought the remains were of European, not Native American, descent.
- Later testing by scientists demonstrated that the cranial measurements and features of Kennewick Man most closely resemble those of Polynesians and southern Asians, and that Kennewick Man's measurements and features differ significantly from those of any modern American Indian group living in North America.
- The empirical record was insufficient to establish cultural continuities or discontinuities and that major changes occurred in lifestyle from 9,000 years ago to the emergence of the Plateau culture 2,000–3,000 years ago.
- There was very little evidence of burial patterns during the 9,500–8,500-year period, and significant temporal gaps exist in the mortuary record for other periods.

- The linguistic analysis was unable to provide reliable evidence for the 8,500–9,500-year period.
- A possible relationship was shown from oral history evidence, but the court found that oral histories change rapidly, and 9,000 years is too long a period to bridge with oral history alone.

Note that, in making these points, the court cited the NPS studies, which took years and several hundred thousand dollars to complete. Furthermore, we believe the 9th Circuit misinterpreted several of the studies' conclusions, similar to the misinterpretations of Magistrate Jelderks as we discussed in our original article.

WAS THE CORPS HASTY IN MAKING A NATIVE AMERICAN DETERMINATION?

When faced with the need to make a timely determination on whether Kennewick Man was Native American, and therefore whether NAGPRA needed to be invoked, what did the Corps know? They knew the remains dated to about 9,000 years ago, a time in which the Plateau had been settled for thousands of years by people who many scientists believed were the ancestors of present-day tribes. Chatters himself had gone on record in 1989 stating that Cascade people were ancestral to present-day Plateau peoples (Chatters 1989).

The Corps knew that Kennewick Man was found in the heart of Indian Country on the Columbia River, where tribes say they have lived since "time immemorial." The Corps knew that the molars were ground down, a hallmark characteristic of pre-contact Native American burials in the region. And, finally, they knew that a stone projectile point, an item commonly linked with prehistoric peoples in the region, was found in the hip. Was this not sufficient information on which to make a general finding that there was a significant relationship to a presently existing tribe, people, or culture in the region? Apparently not.

THE IMPLICATIONS OF THE COURT'S DECISIONS

We could debate many of the findings, as we did in our original article, but what is the point? The case is over; it will not be appealed to the Supreme Court. In retrospect, the government and tribes may never have had a chance. When District Court Judge Gould wrote that Kennewick Man "is one of the most important American anthropological and archaeological discoveries of the 20th century" (Gould 2004:1584), the 9th Circuit Court's bias became clear; it valued Kennewick Man for its scientific value and would evaluate all evidence and arguments from that perspective. Never mind that NAGPRA does not use anthropological or archaeological significance as a criterion against which to judge the disposition of remains.

The implications of the decision of District Court of Oregon and the 9th Circuit Court are far-reaching. From a land manager's perspective, inadvertent discoveries of human remains will now be dictated by the funding available to conduct the studies required to determine whether the remains have a significant relationship to a presently existing tribe, people, or culture. When discovered in a construction setting, a determination will rarely be able to be made in the ground and therefore the agency will not be able to invoke NAGPRA. There will be nothing illegal about removing human remains and continuing the construction while studies are conducted. If the results come back as "Native American," then the appropriate notifications can be made and consultation begin.

Consider also the nonconstruction inadvertent discovery situation, such as a burial washed out of an eroding river bank. Again, the remains will need to be removed for detailed study before NAGPRA is invoked. The remains will go into storage until funding for studies is allocated in annual budgets, and, as all those working in cultural resource management know all too well, funding for such endeavors is on the decline. Because the remains are only subject to ARPA until NAGPRA is enacted, there will be little cause for the agency to commit funds for a NAGPRA determination. As a result of this decision, the United States has now reversed the trend of taking Native American human remains out of government ownership and possession and has reinstituted the trend toward acquisition and storage of human remains—the exact situation that NAGPRA was enacted to correct.

KENNEWICK MAN AS A PRECEDENT-SETTING CASE

Kennewick Man was not a straightforward case; he was a bit of an oddity. Although the remains were characteristic of other remains from that time period, as we wrote in our original article, they were not typical of more recent native remains. There were prehistoric artifacts found in association with the remains, but there were also many historic-era artifacts. This was not one of the simple determinations described earlier. It is instructive to review what happened and what might have happened under other circumstances.

When the coroner took the cranium to James Chatters for a determination of whether the remains represented a modern-day crime scene or an archaeological specimen, the crime scene was immediately ruled out. As indicated in his notes from that first hour, Chatters believed the remains represented either a historic white male or a 5,000-year-old prehistoric person. Once that determination was made, the coroner no longer had jurisdiction under Washington State law. Chatters, however, continued working on Kennewick Man, claiming the coroner did have jurisdiction and began recovering the remaining parts of the skeleton from the river and analyzing them. The Corps, which then had to issue an ARPA permit retroactively, with no research design and no tribal consultation, received regular selective updates from Chatters on matters concerning the remains.

Unbeknownst to the Corps, Chatters proceeded to make a time-consuming, complex, potentially damaging plaster cast of the cranium, presumably because he recognized the potential scientific significance. He then arranged to have a complex facial reconstruction conducted by a novice, using speculative formulas. Then, under the authority of the coroner's office (which, as stated earlier, had no authority), he sent a bone for radiocarbon dating and DNA analysis. When the date of 8700 BP came in verbally, this information was kept secret while Chatters made plans to send the remains to the Smithsonian Institution. When the date was confirmed in writing a week later, announcements were made and the Corps stepped in to take control of the situation, as it should have done the first day. The Corps insisted that the Benton County sheriff's office go to Chatters's home, where he had been keeping the remains, and secure them until the Corps could make arrangements to take possession. At this point, the Corps was upset, tribes were outraged, and Chatters was livid. Not a good platform from which sound and thoughtful decision-making can occur. The Corps invoked NAGPRA, and the rest is history.

Consider, however, what might have happened had the Corps taken immediate possession of the remains as soon as it was determined that there was no crime scene. They would have been faced with a situation of conflicting information about whether the remains were Native American or Euro American. Discussions likely would have proceeded with Chatters, who clearly had a strong interest from the scientific side, and local tribes, which were interested in whether he was an ancestor. It is difficult to ascertain where we would have gone from there, but that would have been a platform from which thoughtful, respectful negotiation and decision-making could have occurred.

The Corps may have been hasty in assigning cultural affiliation to the tribal coalition, but it was reasonable when it made the determination that the remains were Native American and invoked NAGPRA. The Kennewick Man NAGPRA process went awry because Chatters pursued his own agenda and hoodwinked the powers that be, not because something was wrong with NAGPRA. Because the Corps trusted Chatters and did not take possession of the remains, as is typically done on Corps lands, Kennewick Man went off on a bizarre and convoluted journey, which has ended with NAGPRA being gutted and now unable to effect the disposition of the majority of Native American human remains, as Congress intended.

REFERENCES

Chatters, J. C. 1989. The Hanford Cultural Resources Management Plan. Richland, WA: Pacific Northwest National Laboratory.

Gould, R. M. 2004. Appeal from The United States District Court for the District of Oregon John Jelderks, Magistrate Judge, Presiding. 1579 Bonnichsen V. United States. Argued and Submitted September 10, 2003—Portland, Oregon. Filed February 4, 2004. Before: Ruggero J. Aldisert, Susan P. Graber, and Ronald M. Gould, Circuit Judges. Opinion by Judge Gould. United States Court of Appeals for the Ninth Circuit.

Jones, Peter N., and Darby C. Stapp. 2003. An Anthropological Perspective on Magistrate Jelderks, Kennewick Man Decision. High Plains Applied Anthropologist 23(1):1–16.

Mosman, M. W. 2003. Opening Brief for the Federal Appellants. In the United States Court of Appeals for the Ninth Circuit No. 02-35994 District Court No, 96-1481JE (D. Or.) Robson Bonnichsen, C. Loring Brace, George W. Gill, C. Vance Haynes, Jr., Richard L. Jantz, Douglas W. Owsley, Dennis J. Stanford and D. Gentry Steele, Plaintiffs-Appellees, V. United States of America, et al., Defendants-Appellants, and Confederated Tribes of the Colville Reservation, Nez Perce Tribe, Confederated Tribes of the Umatilla Indian Reservation, Confederated Tribes and Bands of the Yakama Nation, Defendants-Intervenors-Appellants on Appeal from the United States District Court for The District of Oregon.

Schlosser, T. P., and R. R. Smith. 2003. Appellant Tribes' Opening Brief in the United States Court of Appeals for the Ninth Circuit. Robson Bonnichsen, C. Loring Brace, George W. Gill, C. Vance Haynes, Jr., Richard L. Jantz, Douglas W. Owsley, Dennis J. Stanford and D. Gentry Steele, Plaintiffs-Appellees, V. United States Of America, et al., Defendants-Appellants, and Confederated Tribes of the Colville Reservation, Nez Perce Tribe, Confederated Tribes of the Umatilla Indian Reservation, Confederated Tribes and Bands of the Yakama Nation, Defendants-Intervenors-Appellants on Appeal from the United States District Court for The District of Oregon Honorable John Jelderks. Nos. 02-35994 & 02-35996 (Companion Appeals) Related case DC 96-1481JE (D. Or.). March 14, 2003.

CHAPTER 7

LAW AND BONES AND WHAT THE MEANING OF "IS" IS[1]

Steve Russell

Pawnee historian James Riding In (1992) calls it "imperial archaeology"—the proposition that European "discovery" of the Americas conferred the right to, not only the soil, but also the bodies of the people buried in that soil. This attitude toward Indian graves manifested itself early on, famously in the graverobbing excursion from the *Mayflower* (Mourt 1622:33–34) and the "scientific" excavation of an Indian burial mound by Thomas Jefferson (1743–1826:223–226). The origins of this disrespect for the dead are not immediately obvious because it did not extend to European dead.

For the Spanish in the desert Southwest, cemeteries were *campo santo*—holy ground—but the United States inherited most of its legal traditions from English common law. The great compiler of the common law, William Blackstone, addressed the property status of burials as follows:

> (T)hough the heir has a property in the monuments and escutcheons of his ancestors, yet he has none in their bodies or ashes; nor can he bring any civil action against such as indecently at least, if not impiously, violate and disturb their remains, when dead and buried. The parson indeed, who has the freehold of the soil, may bring an action of trespass against such as dig and disturb it: and, if any one in taking up a dead body steals the shroud or other apparel, it will be a felony; for the property thereof remains in the executor, or whoever was at the charge of the funeral. (Blackstone 1979, vol. 2:429)

In a discussion of the crime of larceny, Blackstone used burials to demonstrate the requirement that there be a property interest before there can be a theft:

> This the case of stealing a shroud out of a grave; which is the property of those, whoever they were, that buried the deceased: but stealing the corpse itself, which has no owner, (though a matter of great indecency) is no felony, unless some of the gravecloths be stolen with it. (Blackstone 1979, vol. 4:236)

Although human remains were clearly not considered property in English common law (Bernard 1979:16–17; Price 1991:21), graves were not entirely without protection. Blackstone's "parson" had the power and the duty to keep the sanctity of the place where most people were buried—the churchyard—and the ecclesiastical courts would provide a remedy against disturbers of the dead (Price 1991:21).

Most of the United States never had ecclesiastical courts with secular authority, and the practice of burying the dead outside of churchyards was not confined to Indians. Small community cemeteries, slave cemeteries, and family cemeteries are found down many rural roads, and the markings of these cemeteries often failed to survive the community, the institution of slavery, or the family as an economic enterprise. Even some churchyards probably became unmarked cemeteries when Spanish missions failed and the missionaries were recalled to what is now Mexico.

Because of burial practices so different from those of England, common law in the United States came to vest responsibilities toward the dead in next of kin rather than with Blackstone's "parson" or Bernard's "ordinary" (Bernard 1979:13). U.S. common law is in complete agreement with English common law in recognizing no property interest in a corpse (Leming 2003:§§ 3, 5; Surette 2002:§ 2); but with no ecclesiastical authority over burial places, American courts looked to families to protect the repose of the dead. Responsibilities toward the dead became connected to what the U.S. cases call a "quasi property right" in the next of kin.

> Interest in a corpse came to be accepted as a bundle of legal rights inhering in the next of kin or other person charged with the duty and right of burial and preservation of the remains. These rights did not depend upon a finding or a holding that there is a conventional property right in a corpse, or that the remains have monetary value. The bundle of rights includes that of holding and protecting the body until it is processed for burial, cremation or other lawful disposition, and carrying out the burial or other last rites; and the right to the undisturbed repose of the remains in grave, crypt, niche, urn, or elsewhere sanctioned by law. Unlawful violations of these rights constitute actionable wrongs. (Bernard 1979:17)

These rights are far from absolute, and in any clash between the interests of the dead (regardless of who may be asserting those interests) and the interests of the living, presently extant persons prevail. The dead may be disturbed, for example, by the government's exercise of the power of eminent domain (Bernard 1979:4), or by the necessity to exhume a body to determine facts that affect the rights of the living (*Gray v. State* 1908; Leming 2003:§ 10; Surette 2002:§§ 53–58). Still, repose of the dead is an important value that can only be overcome by some specific and weighty countervailing interest proved in the process of securing a court order for disinterment (Leming 2003:§§ 50–51; Surette 2002:§§ 7, 9). Judge (later Justice) Cardozo stated the American rule: "The dead are to rest where they have been laid unless reason of substance is brought forward for disturbing their repose" (*Yome v. Gorman* 1926:129). If there is a continuum of reasons for allowing disturbance of the dead, it appears to begin with the immediate needs of living persons (forensic disinterment and eminent domain cases) and proceed to more abstract needs (medical education and research) (Iverson 1990), but stop well short of idle curiosity or personal profit.

In the Native American Graves Protection and Repatriation Act (NAGPRA) (25

U.S.C.A. § 3001–3013, 2001), Congress located archaeology and physical anthropology on a part of the continuum that does not justify disturbing the dead if the disturbance would offend certain living persons. The living persons who have standing under NAGPRA to claim control of human remains and funerary objects are, in order of priority, lineal descendants of the deceased, the tribe on whose lands the deceased was discovered, the tribe that has the closest cultural affiliation with the deceased, or the tribe that has been recognized as aboriginally occupying the area in which the deceased was discovered by a final judgment of the Indian Claims Commission or the U.S. Court of Claims.

Three observations are in order about this last congressional priority, the tribe aboriginally occupying the area in which "the deceased" (note the human being language) was discovered. First, and from the Indian point of view, substantial parts of the United States have never been "recognized ... by a final judgment of the Indian Claims Commission or the United States Court of Claims" as Indian land. This is an accident of legal history, not a reflection that North America was to any degree *terra nullius*. Second, this is exactly what the 9th Circuit Court later scorned as "a tenuous, unknown, and unproven connection, asserted solely because of the geographical location of *the find*" (*Bonnichsen et al. v. United States* 2004:977, emphasis added—note the *non*-human being language). Finally, this direction from Congress is some indication that repatriation was intended to proceed in virtually all cases.

The discussion of protecting burials in the ground slips seamlessly into a discussion of repatriation, because the two cannot logically be separated. If a looter is prosecuted for desecrating a grave, human remains and funerary artifacts will usually come into the possession of agents of the government. At some point when the lawsuit is over, some disposition will have to be made, referring to some stated or unstated standard for when reburial is appropriate. The same is true for salvage archaeology. After a careful documentation of inadvertently discovered human remains, the reburial question arises.

The American Indian repatriation movement is about civil rights, and NAGPRA is its fruit (Harjo 1992; Strickland 1992; Thornton 1998:394–403). Reburial should occur, Indians claim, because that is generally what the dominant culture does with human remains. To except Indian remains is to except Indians from common humanity. Dead human bodies have historically been used to accomplish the political ends of the living (Cantwell 1990), and the political end here is that Indians be afforded "equal concern and respect in the design and administration of the political institutions that govern them" (Dworkin 1977:180).

NAGPRA simply accommodates cultural reality in allowing Indian tribes to claim the same next-of-kin status that Catholics might claim if a Spanish mission cemetery was disturbed, or that African Americans might claim if a slave cemetery was disturbed, a cultural reality that has been hidden behind archaeology's scientific pretensions. European burials in this country are not disturbed without permission of next of kin or a court order. If they are disturbed by accident, they are documented (or not) and reinterred.

The history of archaeological imperialism is well known to most readers of this volume and need not be repeated here (Bieder 1992; Fine-Dare 2002:47–114; Thomas 2000; Thornton 1998), except to note that history as the political impetus behind NAGPRA: (Native American Grave and Burial Protection Act: Hearing on S.1021 and S.1980 before the Senate Select Committee on Indian Affairs, 101st Cong., 2d Sess., 1990; Protection of Native American Graves and the Repatriation of Human Remains and Sacred Objects: Hearings on H.R. 1381, H.R. 1646, and H.R. 5237 before the House Committee on Interior and Insular Affairs, 101st Cong., 2d Sess., 1990; Trope and Echo-Hawk 1992). Opposition to NAGPRA comes in the classic guise of imperial science—we know what is best for you because we as scientists represent all of humanity (Meighan 1992)—and in the slightly different claim that scientific (credentialed) graverobbing is superior to recreational (uncredentialed) graverobbing, therefore Indians should join with the credentialed to thwart the uncredentialed (Mallouf 2000). To the occupants of the robbed graves or their next of kin this distinction is elusive.

Whether the dead have "rights" is more a question of moral philosophy than law (Bahn 1984), however, the Anglo American legal tradition teaches "a widely shared belief that there are ethical constraints on actions that involve the dead" (Fisher 2001: 558). It is part of our social contract that "if some action would result in harm or benefit for a now-dead person, then this is one of the normatively relevant considerations that needs to be taken into account" (Fisher 2001:567). Historically, there have been ethical constraints on actions that involve the dead, except for dead Indians, and harm to a dead person is a normatively relevant consideration unless the dead person was Indian. The purpose of NAGPRA was to change all that by redefining dead Indians from "archaeological resources" (16 U.S.C. § 470bb (1), 2000) to deceased human beings.

Once dead Indians are people, the issue becomes: Who has standing to represent their human interests? NAGPRA uses the unfortunate language of ownership (25 U.S.C. § 3002, 2001), making Indians the only human beings about which American law recognizes a property interest since the ratification of the Thirteenth Amendment legally abolished chattel slavery. Gerald Vizenor (1976:62–82) has suggested that the thorny issue of repatriation might be easier to work out among living persons if bones—like the rivers and trees of Justice Douglas's famous dissent in *Sierra Club v. Morton* (1972:741)—had standing to sue. Vizenor has reached, no pun intended, the spirit of the issue, but he may be too optimistic about the ability of courts to follow his discourse.

The response of science in congressional debates and now in the courts has been to introduce age as a proxy for race. This substitution did not succeed during the drafting of NAGPRA, but it has succeeded in the so-called Kennewick Man case (*Bonnichsen et al. v. United States* 2004). In the first paragraph of the opinion, the dead Indian at issue is framed as scientific data, "one of the most important American anthropological and archaeological discoveries of the late twentieth century" (357 F.3d at 966). Even though the scientists are the plaintiffs, the Indians appear to have the burden of proof because "in the absence of a conclusive determination of cultural affiliation, the (Indians) cannot establish that permitting Plaintiffs-scientists to study the Kennewick Man's remains offends their religious views or customs" (357 F.3d at 968, note 8). "NAGPRA" admits the court, "was enacted with two main goals: to respect the burial traditions of modern-day Indians and to protect the dignity of the human body after death" (357 F.3d at 973). The latter goal is conspicuously missing from the opinion. The standing of the scientists, unlike the standing of the Indians, did not significantly trouble the Circuit Court of Appeals or the trial court.

Studies are an "open sesame" for graves, at least when the graves contain Indians:

> Although the results of these studies might be of interest to the general public, plaintiffs are not asserting a mere general grievance or interest that is shared by the world at large. The plaintiffs have asserted a personal interest in this controversy. They propose to personally conduct tests on the remains, and to analyze the results of those tests. This (*sic*) data will then be used to further their ongoing research. That is sufficient nexus to confer standing. ... In addition, I note that the results of plaintiffs' research likely will be published in various scientific journals and could advance their professional careers. (*Bonnichsen et al. v. United States* 1997:634–635, citations omitted)

Echoing the characterization of Indians as book burners in the repatriation debates, the trial court opined:

> Plaintiffs' contention is that to the trained eye the skeletal remains *are* analogous to a book that they can read, a history written in bone instead of on paper, just as the history of a region may be "read" by observing layers of rock or ice, or the rings of a tree. Plaintiffs are not asking the government to conduct the tests and publish the results. Plaintiffs simply want the government to step aside and permit them to "read that book" by conducting their own tests. (*Bonnichsen et al. v. United States* 1997:646, emphasis in the original)

What is lacking in these opinions, both trial and appellate, is any scintilla of humanity. It's as if NAGPRA never happened, as the judges frame the inquiry the way the scientific community wants it framed. Dean Rennard Strickland (1992:176) was too optimistic when he wrote that "(t)he enactment of NAGPRA brought to an end almost five hundred years of conflict about culture." Age is back as a proxy for race, and one reading of the appellate opinion is that any remains lacking cultural context that antedate the founding of the United States in 1789 are now back to the status of archaeological resources rather than human beings (357 F.3d at 976), contrasting "indigenous to the United States" with "in the area that now constitutes the State of Hawaii" and drawing the conclusion that therefore ancient Hawaiians are protected by the plain language of NAGPRA whereas ancient Indians are not).[2]

These opinions are of a piece with what I have called in another context (Russell 2004) "the jurisprudence of colonialism," a jurisprudence the United States has in common with other colonial societies (Seidemann 2004).

But, wait, weren't those judges merely following The Law? Well, no. Because I am a judge myself, perhaps I have more license that other scholars to give short shrift to such nonsense. Judge Jerome Frank (1930:390) described the process as well as anyone:

> The process of judging, so the psychologists tell us, seldom begins with a premise from which a conclusion is subsequently worked out. Judging begins rather the other way around—with a conclusion more or less vaguely formed; a man ordinarily starts with such a conclusion and afterwards tries to find premises which will substantiate it. If he cannot, to his satisfaction, find proper arguments to link up his conclusion with premises which he finds acceptable, he will, unless he is arbitrary or mad, reject the conclusion and seek another.

This is so partly because "(w)e may try to see things as objectively as we please. Nonetheless, we can never see them with any eyes except our own" (Cardozo 1921:13). I have some idea of the judges' attitudes about the privileging of science because my education is similar to theirs, and I note that one of the appellate judges in *Bonnichsen* literally wrote the contemporary book on legal thinking (Aldisert 1989). Scientific discourse is privileged in describing the bones at issue in *Bonnichsen* but also *sub silencio* in the absence of any critical examination of what sketchy plans the scientists put forward. Indians must justify themselves; science is self-justifying. The court construed NAGPRA with discourse from the days prior to NAGPRA: "It seems to be tacitly assumed that archaeologists have the right to do almost anything in the name of scholarship" (Bahn 1984:127).

The flip side of privileging science is how the opinions recirculate old race narratives (Baez 2002): Indians standing in the way of human progress, motivated by archaic ideas and mysticism. The Indians' tribal stories "are just not specific enough or reliable enough or relevant enough ..." and "... the record as a whole does not show where historical fact ends and mythic tale begins" (357 F.3d at 979). The racism is certainly unconscious (Lawrence 1987:328–344), but apparent to any Indian who has been patronized or called "Chief."

Slam-dunk cases do exist, so it is fair to ask whether the hegemonic narrative adopted by these judges was the only rational one available to them. Not only were there robust competing narratives, there is plenty of reason to think that the Congress that passed NAGPRA would have preferred a different result (Trope and Echo-Hawk 1992):

> The unanimous support for the law in Congress reflects an acknowledgement that the Constitution and all prior property laws, the common law and legislation, were not being afforded to tribes and Native American individ-

uals. NAGPRA does not create any new rights for tribes or Native Americans. Rather, it applies the common law of property, enjoyed by all others in the United States, and extends those rights to disenfranchised tribes and Native Americans, Native Hawaiians and members of Alaska Village corporations. (Hutt 2004:546, citations omitted)

It is fair to say that there was no shortage of intellectually respectable paths to a different result in *Bonnichsen* (Flood 2002; Hutt 2004; Tsosie 1999). After the fact, Cherokee scholar S. Alan Ray (2006) eviscerated the *Bonnichsen* opinion. Writing in the *Temple Law Review*, Ray took no prisoners, and it's hard to marginalize him for his ethnicity, given the quality of his analysis by mainstream standards.

The appellate opinion in *Bonnichsen* construes the NAGPRA definition of "Native American"—"of, or referring to, a tribe, people, or culture that *is* indigenous to the United States"—to mean a *presently existing* tribe, "presently" meaning since 1789. Under that narrow definition of "Native American," it is not entirely clear how any individual set of human remains found without artifacts can be Native American and therefore subject to NAGPRA—regardless of age. Bones without associated artifacts cannot be connected to a particular tribe except by geography and oral traditions.

The 9th Circuit Court seems to have some inkling of the absurdity they have unleashed when they hedged the precedential value of *Bonnichsen*: "We do not foreclose the possibility that, in any other statute, Congress's use of the present tense, in the context of a different statute, with different statutory language, structure, and purposes, could implicate a time period other than the present" (357 F.3d at 973, note 16). This sounds like the mother of all result-oriented decisions—*Bush v. Gore* (2000:109)—where the Supreme Court warned that "(o)ur consideration is limited to the present circumstances."

Although the *Bonnichsen* court has given fair notice that their opinion should not be taken too literally, it does contain alarming implications for NAGPRA in general, not just the disposition of Indians who are both dead and ancient. Scientists who want to slice and dice have legal standing, and Indians who want to rebury may not. We are still the done to rather than the doers. We have no control over the discourse about us, legal or scientific (Crawford 2000), despite the fact that, so far, all the scientific enterprise has gained by its imperial disregard of common decency is a self-serving farrago of anachronistic fictional narrative and speculation (Chatters 2001) and a lionization of the perpetrators by Jeff Benedict (2003), a popular author famous for feeding another source of anti-Indian sentiment: casino gambling (Benedict 2000).

NAGPRA has been gutted over the question of what the meaning of "is" is. In 2004, Ben Nighthorse Campbell (R-CO), the only American Indian in the U.S. Senate, offered an amendment to NAGPRA to change "is" to "is or was," which the legislative history of NAGPRA would show was the intent in the first place. Upon Campbell's retirement, the amendment has been sponsored by John McCain (R-AZ), whose state contains a lot of Indian country. The National Congress of

American Indians has endorsed the change from "is" to "is or was" for the civil rights legislation that it is, and same parties have chosen sides that clashed in the original debate over NAGPRA. The debate over "is," which is really the pre-NAGPRA debate about age as a proxy for ethnicity, has continued in every congressional session since 2004. It is much easier to stop legislation than to pass it, so the forces of scientific grave-robbing have an advantage in addition to the ones conferred by white privilege and by the identification of science with civilization.

The passage of NAGPRA was, for Indians, an emotional high like the destruction of the Death Star in the original *Star Wars* movie. Another reason for good feelings is that Indians are no longer entirely alone, as non-Indian archaeologists come to realize that they can do science with human dignity (Klesert and Powell 2000; Thomas 2000; Thoms 1998; Zimmerman 1990, 2000). However, in spite of the splendid victory that is NAGPRA and the growing influence of dissenters within the imperial ranks, the Kennewick litigation and the subsequent contretemps in Congress are forceful reminders of what Suzan Shown Harjo (1992) calls our "unfinished agenda." The empire has struck back, and the civil rights clock has been reversed until Congress instructs the courts on what the meaning of "is" is.

NOTES

1. An earlier version of this chapter appeared as "Law and Bones: Religion, Science, and the Discourse of Empire," in *Radical History Review*, vol. 99, p. 214.

2. Although the 9th Circuit opined that remains relating to tribes not extant in 1789 are not Native American within the meaning of NAGPRA, it would be more consistent with the purposes of the law to hold that remains prior to 1492 *are* Native American within the meaning of NAGPRA, a position stated by an *amicus* brief in an apparent "parade of horrible" argument against the Indians (357 F.3d at 977, note 21).

REFERENCES

Aldisert, R. J. 1989. *Logic for Lawyers: A Guide to Clear Legal Thinking.* New York: Clark Boardman Company.

Baez, B. 2002. Affirmative Action, Hate Speech, and Tenure: Narratives about Race, Law and the Academy. New York: Routledge Falmer.

Bahn, P. G. 1984. Do Not Disturb? Archaeology and the Rights of the Dead. *Oxford Journal of Archaeology* 3(2):127–139.

Benedict, J. 2000. Without Reservation: The Making of America's Most Powerful Indian Tribe and Foxwoods, the World's Largest Casino. New York: HarperCollins.

Benedict, J. 2003. No Bone Unturned: The Adventures of a Top Smithsonian Forensic Scientist and the Legal Battle for America's Oldest Skeletons. New York: HarperCollins.

Bernard, H. Y. 1979. *The Law of Death and Disposal of the Dead.* Dobbs Ferry, NY: Oceana Publications.

Bieder, R. E. 1992. The Collecting of Bones for Anthropological Narratives. *American Indian Culture and Research Journal* 16(2):21–35.

Blackstone, W. 1979 [1765]. *Commentaries on the Laws of England.* London: University of Chicago Press.

Bonnichsen et al. v. United States, 969 F.Sup 628 (D.C. Oregon 1997).

Bonnichsen et al. v. United States, 357 F.3d 962 (9th Cir. 2004).

Bush v. Gore, 531 U.S. 98 (2000).

Cantwell, A-M. 1990. The Choir Invisible: Reflections on the Living and the Dead. *Death Studies* 14(6):613–628.

Cardozo, B. 1921. *The Nature of the Judicial Process.* London: Yale University Press.

Chatters, J. C. 2001. *Ancient Encounters: Kennewick Man and the First Americans*. New York: Simon & Schuster.

Crawford, S. J. 2000. (Re)Constructing Bodies: Semiotic Sovereignty and the Debate over Kennewick Man. In *Repatriation Reader: Who Owns American Indian Remains?*, edited by D. A. Mihesuh, pp. 211–236. Lincoln: University of Nebraska Press.

Dworkin, R. 1977. *Taking Rights Seriously*. London: Duckworth.

Fine-Dare, K. S. 2002. *Grave Injustice: The American Indian Repatriation Movement and NAGPRA*. Lincoln: University of Nebraska Press.

Fisher, J. 2001. Harming and Benefiting the Dead. *Death Studies* 25(7):557–568.

Flood, M. A. 2002. "Kennewick Man" or "Ancient One"?—A Matter of Interpretation. *Montana Law Review* 63(1):39–90.

Frank, J. 1930. *Law and the Modern Mind*. New York: Brentano's.

Gray v. State, 114 S.W. 635 (Tex. Crim. App. 1908).

Harjo, S. S. 1992. Native Peoples' Cultural and Human Rights: An Unfinished Agenda. *Arizona State Law Journal* 24(1):321–328.

Hutt, S. 2004. If Geronimo Was Jewish: Equal Protection and the Cultural Property Rights of Native Americans. *Northern Illinois University Law Review* 24(3):527–562.

Iverson, B. A. 1990. Bodies for Science. *Death Studies* 14(6):577–587.

Jefferson, T. 1743–1826. Notes on the State of Virginia. Available online at http://etext.lib.virginia.edu/toc/modeng/public/JefVirg.html (accessed May 18, 2005). University of Virginia Library Electronic Text Center, Charlottesville.

Klesert, A. L., and S. Powell 2000. A Perspective on Ethics and the Reburial Controversy. In *Repatriation Reader: Who Owns American Indian Remains*, edited by D. A. Mihesuh, pp. 200–210. Lincoln: University of Nebraska Press.

Lawrence, C. R., III. 1987. The Id, the Ego, and Equal Protection: Reckoning with Unconscious Racism. *Stanford Law Review* 39(2):317–388.

Leming, T. L. 2003. Dead Bodies. In *American Jurisprudence* 2d, vol. 22A. St. Paul, MN: West Group.

Mallouf, R. J. 2000. An Unraveling Rope: The Looting of America's Past. In *Repatriation Reader: Who Owns American Indian Remains?*, edited by D. A. Mihesuh, pp. 59–73. Lincoln: University of Nebraska Press.

Meighan, C. 1992. Some Scholars' Views on Reburial. *American Antiquity* 57(4):704–710.

Mourt, George 1971 [1622]. Mourt's Relation: Journal of the Plantation at Plymouth. Boston: J. K. Wiggin.

Price, H. M., III 1991. *Disputing the Dead: U.S. Law on Aboriginal Remains and Grave Goods*. Columbia: University of Missouri Press.

Ray, S. Alan 2006. Native American Identity and the Challenge of Kennewick Man. *Temple Law Review* 79(1):89–154.

Riding In, J. 1992. Without Ethics and Morality: A Historical Overview of Imperial Archaeology and American Indians. *Arizona State Law Journal* 24(1):11–34.

Russell, S. 2004. The Jurisprudence of Colonialism. In *American Indian Thought*, edited by A. Waters, pp. 217–228. Oxford: Blackwell Publishing.

Seidemann, R. M. 2004. Bones of Contention: A Comparative Examination of Law Governing Human Remains from Archaeological Contexts in Formerly Colonial Countries. *Louisiana Law Review* 64(3):545–588.

Sierra Club v. Morton (405 U.S. 727 1972).

Strickland, R. 1992. Implementing the National Policy of Understanding, Preserving, and Safeguarding the Heritage of Indian Peoples and Native Hawaiians: Human Rights, Sacred Objects, and Cultural Patrimony. *Arizona State Law Journal* 24(1):175–191.

Surette, E. C. 2002. Dead Bodies. In *Corpus Juris Secundum*, vol. 25A. St. Paul, MN: West Group.

Thomas, D. H. 2000. Skull Wars: Kennewick Man, Archaeology, and the Battle for Native American Identity. New York: Basic Books.

Thoms, A. V. 1998. Beyond Texas' Legacy: Searching for Cooperation without Submission. *Texas Forum on Civil Liberties and Civil Rights* 4(1):41–52.

Thornton, R. 1998. Who Owns Our Past? In *Studying Native America: Problems and Prospects*, edited by R. Thornton, pp. 385–413. Madison: University of Wisconsin Press.

Trope, J. F., and W. R. Echo-Hawk 1992. The Native American Graves Protection and

Repatriation Act: Background and Legislative History. *Arizona State Law Journal* 24(1):35–77.

Tsosie, R. 1999. Privileging Claims to the Past: Ancient Human Remains and Contemporary Cultural Values. *Arizona State Law Journal* 31(2):583–677.

Vizenor, G. 1976. *Crossbloods: Bone Courts, Bingo, and Other Reports*. Minneapolis: University of Minnesota Press.

Yome v. Gorman, 152 N.E. 126 (N.Y. Ct. App. 1926).

Zimmerman, L. J. 1990. Reflections on the Issues: Implications for the Scholarly Disciplines. *Death Studies* 14(6):629–639.

Zimmerman, L. J. 2000. A New and Different Archaeology? In *Repatriation Reader: Who Owns American Indian Remains?*, edited by D. A. Mihesuh, pp. 294–306. Lincoln: University of Nebraska Press.

CHAPTER 8

KENNEWICK MAN, THE NATIVE AMERICAN GRAVES PROTECTION AND REPATRIATION ACT, AND THE WORLD ARCHAEOLOGICAL CONGRESS: A MATTER OF HERITAGE LAW

JOEL B. GILMAN

The controversy over the disposition of the Kennewick remains that culminated in the U.S. 9th Circuit Court of Appeals decision *Bonnichsen et al. v. United States*[1] illustrates why archaeologists need to learn more about law and why lawyers need to learn more about archaeology. The emerging field of heritage law seeks to integrate the study of heritage values with the study of law as a values-negotiating mechanism and provides useful tools with which to tease out nuances of legal reasoning and intention in the context of heritage issues.

In this chapter, I will consider the original purpose of the Native American Graves Protection and Repatriation Act (NAGPRA)[2] as interpreted by the court in *Bonnichsen* and the arguments presented by the World Archaeological Congress (WAC) in supporting an amendment to NAGPRA proposed by former U.S. Sen. Ben Nighthorse Campbell (R-CO) that seeks to overturn *Bonnichsen*.[3] I contend that there is a need to ground such debates as much on an understanding of the applicable legal framework as on the contemporary archaeological ethics that WAC has worked so diligently to promote. Finally, I argue that the interests of both archaeologists and indigenous people would be better served through respectful consultation and cooperation on the appropriate handling of ancient remains.

I should note at the outset that my perspective will be at odds with the positions argued by most of the writers in this volume. My defense of the *Bonnichsen* decision is based on its resolution of a complex legal dispute arising within a matrix of conflicting social and cultural values. Although sometimes derided as "definitional sleight-of-hand," the decision, in fact, reflects a nuanced consideration of congressional intent.

THE DISPUTE

The U.S. Court of Appeals for the 9th Circuit's final ruling in April 2004 appears to have resolved the legal dispute over the disposition of the Kennewick remains. No doubt the archaeological and heritage debates over whether Native American claims to the Ancient One should supersede archaeological interests in these ancient remains will continue for years to come. However, those debates will be well served by an understanding of the reasons for the court's interpretation of Congress's intent in drafting NAGPRA.

Much criticism has been directed at the court's conclusion that NAGPRA's definition of "Native American" only includes existing indigenous tribes, peoples, and cultures. Sen. Campbell's amendment would change the definition to remove this qualification. In endorsing the amendment, the WAC (2004) stated: "The purpose of the amendment is to ensure that human remains are assumed to be Native American if they pre-date the documented arrival of European explorers. This change is consistent with the spirit of the original NAGPRA legislation and is simple good sense."

WHAT THE COURTS ACTUALLY SAID

Whether or not the amendment is indeed "simple good sense," there is much evidence to suggest that the amendment's purpose is not at all "consistent with the original intent of Congress." The trial court in *Bonnichsen* pointed to other phrases in the statute to support its conclusion:

> NAGPRA defines "Native American" as "of, or *relating* to, a tribe, people, or culture that *is* indigenous to the United States." ... [U]se of the words "is" and "relating" in the present tense requires a relationship to a presently existing tribe, people, or culture. This is consistent with the Act's definition of the term "sacred objects" as meaning "ceremonial objects which *are* needed by traditional Native American religious leaders for the practice of traditional Native American religions *by their present day adherents.*"[4]

Seidemann (2003) argues that NAGPRA was never meant to apply to ancient human remains. "To the contrary, what is abundantly evident from the legislative history is that Congress was especially concerned with reparations for the wrongs committed against Native Americans since A.D. 1492" (Seidemann 2003:166).

To the *Bonnichsen* court, the intent behind NAGPRA was not simply to repatriate all indigenous remains to Native American groups, but rather to ensure that remains are repatriated to identifiable lineal descendants, or, if no such descendants can be located, to a cultural group having a demonstrable affinity with the remains. It was accepted that some remains could not be repatriated given the difficulty of establishing the identity of lineal descendants or cultural affinity:

> Congress's purposes would not be served by requiring the transfer to modern American Indians of human remains that bear no relationship to them. Yet, that would be the result under the [U.S. secretary of interior's] construction of the statute, which would give Native American status to any remains found within the United States regardless of age and regardless of lack of connection to existing indigenous tribes. The exhumation, study, and display of ancient human remains that are unrelated to modern American Indians was not a target of Congress's aim, nor was it precluded by NAGPRA.[5]

It is unfortunate that the court's ruling came in the context of an on-going media circus. When the skeleton was first examined by forensic anthropologists, the cranio-facial features were reported to appear more like contemporary European features than Native American. News coverage of a "9,000-year-old white guy" in

North America quickly overshadowed the significance of finding *any* remains that old in North America. Only eleven sets of remains that old have been found, and the Kennewick remains are by far the most complete and well preserved (Chatters 2000). However, the media focus quickly shifted to the fantasy of identifying a "pre-Indian" civilization in the Americas. The Asatru Folk Assembly in northern California filed papers with the trial court, claiming the remains were their ancient Nordic ancestor (Malcomson 2000). Much ignorant speculation that should never have seen the light of day was given inordinate coverage, recalling the 19th-century Mound Builder Myth—that a highly advanced (by European standards) civilization predated Native American occupation of the Ohio River valley (Southerton 2004:23).

It is even more unfortunate that news coverage summarized the court's decision as stating that the remains were not Native American, which, of course, is absurd. As noted above, what both the trial court and the court of appeals concluded was that the remains did not fall within NAGPRA's specific definition of "Native American" in that they were not identifiable as having lineal descendants or cultural affinity with any existing Native American group and thus did not come within NAGPRA's mandate to repatriate them. Sen. Campbell's proposal and the WAC endorsement seem directed more toward this media interpretation of the court's decision, rather than toward the decision itself.

In support of its position on the Campbell amendment, WAC (2004) argued that, in other countries, repatriation statutes have not interfered with scientific research. "In Australia, for example, there is on-going scientific research on human remains from Lake Mungo, some of which have been recently re-dated to around 60,000 years" (WAC 2004). This statement neglects to mention that the 60,000-year-old Lake Mungo remains, originally discovered in 1969, were available for scientists to study for twenty years before it was suggested they be repatriated, and even following repatriation they are still available for research (Smith and Burke 2003:186).

In contrast, anthropologist James Chatters had less than two months to study the Kennewick remains before they were sequestered pending the outcome of the legal dispute (Chatters 2000). The handling of the Lake Mungo remains is hardly an argument for the Campbell amendment. It is ingenuous to suggest that amending NAGPRA to effectively overturn the *Bonnichsen* ruling would not interfere with scientific research. Indeed, the trial court in *Bonnichsen* noted, "[I]t is undisputed that if the Tribal Claimants gain custody of the remains, they will prohibit all further scientific study and documentation of the remains, whether by Plaintiffs or by other scientists."[6]

REPATRIATION LAW IN THE UNITED STATES AND AUSTRALIA

An important element of heritage law is that it is international in scope, and comparisons between the laws of different jurisdictions are central. The Kennewick controversy offers insights in this regard. In comparing the Campbell amendment to "similar legislation in other countries," the WAC press release may have meant

Australia's repatriation statute, the Aboriginal and Torres Strait Islander Heritage Protection Act 1984 (Commonwealth) (ATSIHPA). However, this comparison overlooks important differences between NAGPRA and ATSIHPA.

Whereas under the Campbell amendment NAGPRA would mandate the immediate repatriation of newly discovered indigenous human remains and funerary objects to the claimant with the closest affinity, ATSIHPA includes no such mandate. Rather, it confers on the responsible federal minister the duty to consult with interested groups—both indigenous and scientific—as to the best approach to handling newly discovered remains, and allows the minister discretion in deciding how to proceed.[7] Thus, the Australian statute contemplates a high degree of cooperation and consultation, instead of mandating a specific outcome.

NAGPRA, however, makes no provision for such consultation and cooperation. As written, NAGPRA provides a mechanism first to determine whether human remains are Native American, and, if so, then second to determine to which Native American group they should be returned. The Campbell amendment seeks to mandate the outcome of the first decision for all human remains predating 1492. Once the second decision has been made, there is no statutory mandate for consultation or cooperation as to the further handling of the remains. Instead, it is solely at the receiving group's discretion to decide how the remains will be handled.

Consider how the Kennewick remains might have been handled under the Australian statute. The federal agency would consult—one hopes in good faith—with all interested parties and perhaps delay repatriation for a reasonable period of time during which respectful research might be conducted, the particulars of which would be determined through negotiation among the interested parties. Indigenous groups would participate fully in that research and advise on the proper handling of the remains. On completion of the research, the ultimate disposition of the remains could be arrived at by further negotiation, not as a mandated statutory outcome.

CONCLUSION

Because NAGPRA provides no statutory mandate for consultation—indeed, the administrative record introduced at trial reveals the outright hostility of the Department of Interior toward the scientists' repeated requests to study the remains[8]—the scientists were compelled to file suit. The major failing of NAGPRA is not its definition of "Native American" but that, once human remains are deemed to be outside the statute's purview—the result in *Bonnichsen*—Native Americans have no right of participation. After the 9th Circuit's final ruling, the tribes unsuccessfully petitioned the district court for the right to participate in decisions on how the remains were to be handled and studied.[9]

Unlike the Australian statute, NAGPRA does not recognize the interests of multiple groups in the handling of human remains, once the two questions posed by NAGPRA are resolved. Instead of debating the statute's definition of "Native American," the interests of both archaeologists and indigenous people would be better served by requiring consultation on the appropriate disposition of ancient remains, recognizing that both indigenous peoples and Western science have a legitimate interest in them.

NOTES

1. 217 F.Supp.2d 1116 (D. Or. 2002); *affirmed*, 367 F.3d 864 (9th Cir. 2004).

2. 25 USCA §§ 3001–3011.

3. S.2843 §14. The bill expired at the close of the 108th Congress. Sen. Campbell did not stand for reelection in 2004. The definition amendment was reintroduced in March 2005 as Sec. 108 of S. 536, the Native American Omnibus Act of 2005, by Sen. John McCain (R-AZ). Following hearings in July 2005, the definition amendment was removed from the bill. The bill was reintroduced in 2007 as S. 2087, with the amendment to the definition restored.

4. 367 F.3d 864, 876 (citations omitted; emphasis in the original).

5. 367 F.3d 864, 876 (citations omitted; emphasis in the original).

6. 217 F.Supp.2d 1116, 1122.

7. ATSIHPA §§ 20(2), 21P.

8. 217 F.Supp.2d 1116, 1122–1130.

9. *Bonnichsen et al. v. United States* (No. Civ. 96-1481 JE; Decided Dec. 15, 2004).

REFERENCES

Chatters, J. C. 2000. The Recovery and First Analysis of an Early Holocene Human Skeleton from Kennewick, Washington. *American Antiquity* 65(2):291.

Malcomson, S. L. 2000. The Color of Bones. *The New York Times*, April 2.

Seidemann, R. M. 2003. Time for a Change? The Kennewick Man Case and Its Implications for the Future of the Native American Graves Protection and Repatriation Act. *West Virginia Law Review* 106(Fall):149.

Smith, C., and H. Burke 2003. In the Spirit of the Code. In *Ethical Issues in Archaeology*, edited by L. Zimmerman, K. Vitelli, and J. Hollowell-Zimmer, pp. 177–197. Walnut Creek, CA: AltaMira Press.

Southerton, S. G. 2004. *Losing a Lost Tribe: Native Americans, DNA, and the Mormon Church*. Salt Lake City: Signature Books.

World Archaeological Congress (WAC). 2004. Media release: *World Archaeological Congress Supports NAGPRA Amendment* (October 20).

CHAPTER 9
KENNEWICK MAN: A VIRTUAL POLITICAL OBJECT "UNDER CONSTRUCTION"

ANN M. KAKALIOURAS

Discovered by accident and pulled from the bed of the Columbia River in southern Washington in 1996, the 9,200-year-old Kennewick Man skeleton is perhaps the most publicized set of human skeletal remains in recent American history. The remains and the conflict over their disposition have been featured in such widely read publications as *Newsweek* (Begley and Murr 1999) and *The New Yorker* (Preston 1997) and profiled on PBS's *NOVA*" and *60 Minutes*.[1] As one of the oldest skeletons ever to be found on the North American continent, Kennewick Man has come to occupy the position of a so-called First American in the media, as well as in academic and public policy spheres (e.g., Bonnichsen 1999; Owsley and Jantz 2003). Although the national coverage of the controversy has waxed and waned over the last decade, Kennewick Man's presence on the Internet has been both a constant and dynamic feature of his "virtual" existence on the U.S. political stage.

In this chapter, I suggest that the World Wide Web, as the site where Kennewick Man is most frequently experienced, encourages the production, duplication, and spread of both textual and graphical representations of the skeletal remains that are distinct products of Euro American political imaginations and scientific sensibilities.[2] The web representations of Kennewick Man as a Caucasian—or as a so-called European ancestor—threaten modern Native Americans' inclusion in American ancient history. Further, the prevailing influence of physical anthropological discourse in U.S. society—that skeletal remains are fundamentally scientific objects—limits Native American peoples' dialogic participation in narratives of the ancient history of the Western Hemisphere, a history that now includes Kennewick Man as an integral actor.

KENNEWICK MAN ONLINE

Numerous stories about the Ancient One/Kennewick Man have already been told from diverse cultural and political angles (e.g., Downey 2000; Thomas 2000). Here, I will add just another small piece to the Kennewick narrative with an analysis of some of the effects produced by representations of Kennewick Man on the Internet. The actual Kennewick skeleton continues to reside at the Burke Museum in Seattle, where the remains have been curated for a decade. On the World Wide Web, however, one can access approximately 100,000 sites that contain information about Kennewick Man.[3] Three categories of sites generally deal with the find: newspapers that publish their content online, so-called virtual museums or interpretive centers, and white supremacist websites.

The virulently racialized representations of Kennewick Man at white national-ist and white supremacist sites are of particular interest to me here. They reflect white supremacist anxieties over the changing racial make-up of the United States and attempt to construct an exclusively "white" American ancient history.[4] Marsha Michie (2000) has established that the Internet is a comfortable home to a large and diverse network of racist organizations, which can now transmit their message to constituents easily and relatively anonymously. She has also shown how the Internet encourages a kind of standardization of language and techniques of representation across the white supremacist network, where images, phrases, and terms are bor-rowed from one place for reuse in others.

Kennewick Man's pattern of representation on white supremacist websites is an example of the kind of uniformity of expression the Internet helps to construct. His lifeway and potential cultural position are narrated in a remarkably consistent fash-ion. Depicted as an ancient European trapper or frontiersman, Kennewick Man is distanced from characteristics that denote Indianness in the American imagination. His individuality is highlighted, and he is not presented as a part of a so-called trib-al group. Furthermore, terms that anthropologists have used to denote "pre-modern" people, such as "hunting and gathering" and "small-scale society," are not applied to descriptions of Kennewick Man's cultural context at these websites.

The representations of Kennewick Man on a diversity of white supremacist–themed websites act in opposition to a North American ancient history where Native Americans played a prominent role. Such depiction is accompanied by claims that so-called Caucasians were the original inhabitants of the United States. Moreover, in this view, modern Native people represent those who displaced and victimized Kennewick Man and his imagined European relatives. Native Americans are represented as colonizing hordes who took over land originally belonging to a white Kennewick Man. The devastating human consequences of the more recent colonization of the Americas in the 16th century are, of course, never mentioned. These sites, therefore, aim to invalidate Native American political agency and claim America as a white-first and white-only nation. Modern Native people are thus cast as the descendants of ancient savage criminals by white supremacists—an "Indian" victory over Kennewick Man was justly avenged by the Europeans who were to fol-low. A recent quote from a site hosted by the Stormfront White Nationalist Community starkly illustrates this pattern: "The natives were a Johnny Come Lately. Have you ever heard of the Kennewick Man? ... [T]he Kennewick Man was a member of the Caucasian race. So we were here first, our people were ethnically cleansed by the arrival of the natives from Asia, and we came back and took it back" (Stormfront White Nationalist Community 2007).

CONSTRUCTIONS AND (FACIAL) RECONSTRUCTIONS ON THE WEB

Although racist websites are admittedly an extreme illustration of the ways in which Kennewick Man is represented, there is one image that most websites, regardless of place on any political spectrum, have adopted. That image is the facial reconstruction made by Dr. James Chatters and sculptor Thomas McClelland. The

process through which a cast of the Kennewick skull came to take on this very specific set of facial characteristics is described by Chatters on Nova's "Mystery of the
First Americans" website (Chatters 2000). Chatters and McClelland used a technique called "the Gerasimov School" of facial reconstruction or approximation.
This technique is different from a more generalized style commonly used in forensic science that produces a rather flattened, featureless image. As Chatters describes
it, the Gerasimov technique entails the sculptor crafting each facial muscle out of
clay and placing them in anatomical position on the facial bones, thus producing a
more specific and individualized reconstruction. In what Chatters calls "The
American School"—the more generalized technique—the artist works directly on
the skull and does not produce the muscles separately.

This seemingly objective attention to morphological detail used in producing
Kennewick Man's facial reconstruction produces an effect—but perhaps not the
intended reality—of representational accuracy, one reminiscent of what Timothy
Mitchell, borrowing from Heidegger, terms "certainty of representation" (1988:7).
Mitchell, in describing the "political certainty" of Europe in the age of Orientalism,
states: "Exhibitions, museums and other spectacles were not just reflections of this
certainty, however, but the means of its production, by their technique of rendering
history, progress, culture and empire in 'objective' form" (Mitchell 1988:7).

In terms of Kennewick Man's face, the careful placement of wrinkles atop the
more specific muscular substructure is meant to correspond with the original osteological age determination of the skeleton as an older male.[5] The scar on his forehead
mirrors a traumatic lesion on the frontal bone itself. Also, the NOVA website allows
the user to manipulate the sculpture and focus on whatever detail one wishes to
highlight. This representation of the skull produces its own authority through a scientific certainty not mediated by repeated observations or peer review. The scientific process used here, however, only ineffectively masks any individual or cultural
perceptions informing Kennewick Man's placement in a larger morphological heritage.

Chatters and McClelland, therefore, have artfully created objectivity through
their "certainty" that their process of construction and the eventual form of
Kennewick Man's face should mirror that of someone who looks European and
therefore not someone who looks Native American. Whether these modern ethnic
"looks" have any actual correspondence to patterns of ancient American morphology, or more pointedly, to ancient cultural linkages, are critical questions that remain
uninvestigated. One is asked only to receive this reconstruction as made.
Furthermore, this image is the only widely available facial reconstruction from the
skull that has been produced in the last decade, and there is little indication that
alternative images will replace the popularity of the original "re"-construction.

Moreover, on the World Wide Web, images of the skull and this facial reconstruction are in a position of representational equivalency, from the BBC (Murcott
1999) all the way to the white supremacist sites. The next step in this process is to
substitute an even more specific image for the facial reconstruction, one that
emerged in the popular press soon after it was released. Inserting Patrick Stewart as

a shorthand replacement for the facial reconstruction next to a cast of the Kennewick skull is an expected, if ethnically unfortunate, visual leap (Figure 9.1). An identity for Kennewick Man that is representationally distant from that of Native Americans is, therefore, achieved through this facial reconstruction. The copying and pasting of this image to website after website has succeeded in producing a very specific "Caucasian" Kennewick Man.[6]

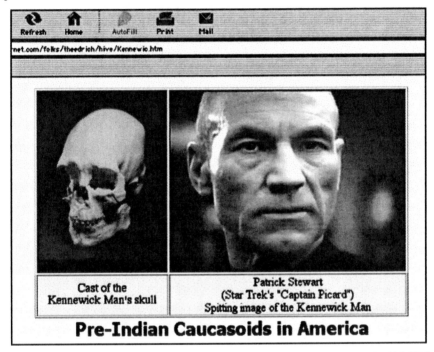

Figure 9.1: Screenshot of Patrick Stewart and the Kennewick/Ancient One cranium (Colin, Son of Theedrich, 2000). Reproduced with permission of the website owner.

Native American people, however, are not absent from the Internet. Rhonda Fair (2000) documented an extensive network of tribal websites that show a diverse range of Native self-representation. Also, the Confederated Tribes of the Umatilla (2007), one of the Native claimants of Kennewick Man, have posted a series of position papers on their website on the Kennewick controversy. The Umatilla and many other tribes, though, do not experience skeletal remains as objects that can be "refleshed" and reimagined as living people. The World Wide Web, then, as a constructed social space, does not provide a context where the Native people involved in the case choose to visually represent Kennewick Man, or the Ancient One.

Though an image of Kennewick Man as a Native American person does exist on the web, at the Burke Museum's website (Burke Museum of Natural History 2007), his back is turned and his features are left to be constructed in the imaginations of the viewing subjects. That space is already occupied, however, by the face

produced by anthropology. This face is for those who are accustomed to constructing lives and identities for skeletal remains. The networked experience of
Kennewick Man, thus, is specifically for Euro Americans, who, by our scientific
authority, continue to put skin on Native American bones. As museums and interpretive centers become even more "virtual," the question then becomes: Who will
represent Native American people in an ancient American history that includes
Kennewick Man?

ACKNOWLEDGMENTS

Thanks to Stacey Langwick, panel organizer and chair of "Experience and the Making of Political
Actors," at the 2000 American Anthropological Association Annual Meeting, where I presented a version
of this chapter (Kakaliouras 2000). Thanks also to Lesley Bartlett, Anne Marie Choup, and Rachel
O'Toole who read multiple drafts of the original paper and urged me to publish it years ago.

NOTES

1. The *NOVA* broadcast was adapted into an interactive website (NOVA 2000) and the *60 Minutes* spot
aired on CBS on October 25, 1998.

2. I shall refer to the Ancient One as "Kennewick Man" to underscore the effectiveness of his representation as "Caucasian." I do not, however, personally subscribe to the idea that the name Kennewick Man
is any more accurate than the appellation Ancient One.

3. This general figure comes from a keyword search for "kennewick +man" at http://www.google.com,
accessed on December 18, 2007.

4. For example, see http://newnation.org/NNN-kennewick-man.html and http:// www.stormfront
.org/forum/showthread.php/history-white-race-434271p2.html.

5. A recent article in *Time Magazine* (Lemonick and Dorfman 2006), however, includes an update to
Kennewick Man's face and age determination; he is pictured on the cover looking more Native
American, and he may have been in his late thirties, instead of in his fifties, as Chatters originally
claimed.

6. But see Thomas (2000:xxv) for another individualistic and perhaps plausible vision of Kennewick
Man as Chief Black Hawk.

REFERENCES

Begley, S., and A. Murr 1999. Who Were the First Americans? *Newsweek*, April 26. Available
    online at http://www.newsweek.com/id/88135 (accessed April 17, 2008).
Bonnichsen, Robson 1999. An Introduction to Who Were the First Americans? In *Who Were the
    First Americans?*, edited by R. Bonnichsen, pp. 1–24. Proceedings of the 58th Annual
    Biology Colloquium, Oregon State University. Center for the Study of the First Americans,
    Oregon State University, Corvallis.
Burke Museum of Natural History. 2007. Kennewick Man—Burke Museum. Available online at
    http://www.washington.edu/burkemuseum/kman/ (accessed December 17, 2007).
Chatters, J. 2000. Meet Kennewick Man. In NOVA's Mysteries of the First Americans. Available
    online at http://www.pbs.org/wgbh/nova/first/kennewick.html (accessed December 18,
    2007).
Confederated Tribes of the Umatilla 2007. Ancient One/Kennewick Man. Available online at
    http://www.umatilla.nsn.us/ancient.html (accessed December 16, 2007).
Colin, Son of Theedrich 2000. Pre-Indian Caucasoids in America. Available online at
    http://www.harbornet.com/folks/theedrich/hive/Kennewic.htm (accessed September 10,
    2000).
Downey, R. 2000. *Riddle of the Bones: Politics, Science, Race, and the Story of Kennewick Man.*

New York: Copernicus.

Fair, R. S. 2000. Becoming the White Man's Indian: An Examination of Native American Tribal Websites. *Plains Anthropologist* 45(172):203–213.

Kakaliouras, A. M. 2000. The Construction of a Political Object: The Case of Kennewick Man. Paper presented at the 99th Annual Meeting of the American Anthropological Association, San Francisco, November 15.

Lemonick, Michael D. and Andrea Dorfman 2006. Who Were the First Americans? *Time Magazine*, March 5. Available online at http://www.time.com/time/magazine/article/ 0,9171,1169905,00.html (accessed December 18, 2007).

Michie, M. 2000. White Pride World Wide: Whiteness on the Internet and the Resurgent Politics of Supremacy. Unpublished ms. on file at the University of North Carolina, Chapel Hill, Anthropology Department.

Mitchell, T. 1988. *Colonising Egypt*. Berkeley: University of California Press.

Murcott, T. 1999. Bid to Clear up Kennewick Mystery. BBC News. Available online at http://news.bbc.co.uk/2/hi/science/nature/283327.stm (accessed December 16, 2007).

NOVA. 2000. The Face of Kennewick Man. Available online at http://www.pbs.org/ wgbh/nova/first/kennewickvr.html (accessed December 18, 2007).

Owsley D. W., and R. L. Jantz 2003. Kennewick Man—A Kin? Too Distant. *In Claiming the Stones/Naming the Bones: Cultural Property and the Negotiation of National and Ethnic Identity (Issues and Debates)*, edited by E. Barkan and R. Bush, pp. 141–161. Los Angeles: Getty Research Press.

Preston, D. 1997. The Lost Man. *The New Yorker*, June 16, pp. 70–81.

Stormfront White Nationalist Community. 2007. Re: Not Much to Celebrate. Available online at http://www.stormfront.org/forum/showthread.php?p=4668944 (accessed December 18, 2007).

Thomas, D. H. 2000. *Skull Wars: Kennewick Man, Archaeology, and the Battle for Native American Identity*. New York: Basic Books.

Chapter 10
Are These My People?
Guy F. Moura

One frustrating and disappointing aspect of the Ancient One controversy for me, a white, Euro American anthropologist, is the behavior of the "plaintiff scientists." No matter how the public or judiciary justify to themselves that the Ancient One is not a Native American and not affiliated with the claimant tribes, the plaintiff scientists made statements and supported positions that, by training and practice, they know are false, untrue, or unethical. They were unrelenting in their position, no matter how many studies and tests were done on the human remains and in the face of conclusions by the secretary of the interior that the remains were Native American and affiliated with the claimant tribes. Interior's decisions were based on expert findings and a preponderance of the evidence. What happened to cultural relativism and emic perspective? What happened to the professional ethics of the American Anthropological Association, the World Archaeological Congress, and the Register of Professional Archaeologists?

How can the Ancient One not be a Native American? The Native American Graves Protection and Repatriation Act (NAGPRA) definition of Native American is "of, or relating to, a tribe, people, or culture that is indigenous to the United States." The Ancient One and associated artifact come from a place and time well documented archaeologically as being part of the established Native American sequence in the United States (thus, an indigenous culture). Both the time identified through radiometric means for the human remains and the projectile point found in the skeleton are from local archaeological sequences with recognized regional settlement and subsistence practices. The Ancient One's community was from the area; they were not some far-wandering nomads.

Legal sophistry employed by plaintiffs' attorneys was a mechanism the scientists allowed to move forward. An example of the chicanery applied in the case includes debates over what the meaning of "is" is in the NAGPRA definition of "Native American," and questions such as "Are Viking sites Native American?" or "Are 100,000 year old sites Native American?" just because they predate 1492. A determination of Native American is not simply a question of being pre-Columbian. Viking sites contain artifacts from a culture that is not indigenous to the United States. Sites 100,000 years old have not been identified in the United States or, at least, are not accepted by the broader professional community; nor would they contain artifacts of an indigenous culture if the artifact assemblage mirrored coeval assemblages found in Asia or Europe. Many argue there were no *Homo sapien sapiens* 100,000 years ago. When, and if, authentic 100,000-year-old sites with distinctive artifact assemblages are found in the United States, then it may be time to address questions of ethnicity; until such sites are discovered and documented, it is a moot question.

Not one of the scientists stated they believed the Ancient One to be Caucasian, but they allowed public opinion to hold that belief and they allowed court arguments to foster such an interpretation. The public relations campaign waged by the scientists, their associates, their legal representatives, and affiliated avocational organizations was unprofessional, misleading, disingenuous, and borders on racism. The tribes did not fight a public relations war out of respect for the person whose remains we call the Ancient One and in adherence to tribal cultural beliefs.

Having worked with, studied under, been acquainted with, or studied the works of, the plaintiff scientists, I doubt they believe that "Kennewick Man" is Caucasian, Polynesian, south Asian, or Ainu. After all is said and done, how could any 9,000-year-old human remains found in the Columbia Basin of Washington State be other than native to America, or Native American? The scientists' actions subvert the intent and purpose of NAGPRA. The conflict and controversy engendered by this debate polarized Indian and non-Indian communities in the Northwest and across the nation. We are in jeopardy of returning to that time when there was no respect for the culture and people indigenous to this country; a time when Indians were second-class citizens, their ancestral remains commodities and burials desecrated for the personal gain or aggrandizement of a few greedy and ambiguous people. This level of disrespect for people and human remains goes against all I have been taught since coming to work on the Colville Reservation and all I was taught in becoming an anthropologist. It is shameful. Next, they may want to gather skulls from battle-fields again.

CHAPTER 11
A VOICE MUST BE HEARD
RECHANDA LEE

A 9,300-year-old skeleton discovered off
the shore of the Columbia River is now
subject to be studied
No longer possessing the title of human
his remains are left without a voice.
In the background there remains
small echo cries, a scream for
REPATRIATION.
As the story begins with a question
of who was this person
This epic story unfolds as
scientists are trying to unlock his secrets,
attempting to link pieces to solve a complex puzzle
BUT, a puzzle with missing pieces cannot be solved
Only when those missing pieces are taken into
consideration can the puzzle be answered.

For many years, American Indians have been classified as objects of study, as
walking beings with no knowledge to determine who they are as peoples. Evidently
a struggle remains, as tribal groups attempt to protect their ancestral peoples from
desecration and exploitation. The missing piece of the puzzle is not only the voice
from the ancestral remains, but also from the existing, living, and flourishing tribes
of today. For centuries, scientists have been studying American Indians for their
own personal gain; at present, archaeologists are given the privilege of studying
archaeological resources for the common interest and professionally gathering
information for future benefit, and the tribes, once again, become the subjects of
study.

The American Indian people believe they do not need archaeologists telling
them about their history, because from their perspective they already know it
through oral tradition passed on to them from their elders and through their religious
practices. In this respect, all American Indian tribes "want the sciences that are supposed to serve humanity to serve all of humanity equally, and to serve the dignity of
all people equally" (Jemison 1997:59). The Kennewick Man case has brought more
strife to the American Indian community because now the Indians have to fight for
their identity and prove they are the descendants of the first peoples who occupied
North America.

This case raises the question of identity and what it might mean to be an American Indian in North America. What scientists fail to realize is that the erroneous interpretation of Kennewick's remains challenge the American Indian way of life; everything that provides a structure for, and forms, their identity. Traditional histories are important to the American Indian community because they provide people with a sense of identity and lineage linked to their respected communities; they explain how they became peoples of the land and where they have come to reside. But these traditional histories are also being subjected to questioning as scientists try to link all human races to Africa.

Although the field of anthropology has developed ethics in relation to humans, a gap remains regarding cultural sensitivity and understanding. As a painting can easily become blurred and distorted, archaeologists can sometimes get caught up in the discovery of resources from the past and they tend to forget about ethical principles. As Roger Anyon and colleagues have noted: "Archaeologists are interested in learning about the past. Native Americans are interested in maintaining the cultural traditions they inherited from their ancestors who lived in the past" (1997:83–84). There are clearly two different perspectives, and there is a lack of understanding as scientists cannot grasp the concept of "sacredness," and American Indians cannot grasp the concept of "eagerness" to learn all, no matter what the cost.

Through the concept of race, archaeologists are trying to make sense of the world; however, one must be aware that such efforts could be mistaken for inventing things through imagination and irrationality. Different factors should be taken into consideration when examining the Kennewick case. Morphology should not be a guide to an individual's ethnicity, but interestingly enough on the scientific spectrum, morphology supposedly provides a face to the mystery of our past.

Sometimes morphology can be an illusion, as Edward Curtis's photographs from the 1900s clearly demonstrate: a group of Alaskan Arctic women with "Asian features"; a young Kootenai woman from Idaho and a San Juan Pueblo man from New Mexico, whose features are more "European"; and a Shoalwater man from Washington with heavy facial hair (Burke Museum 2004). A European person tends to have a narrower head and heavy facial hair, and we see in Curtis's photos that some American Indians do not possess morphological features that are necessarily "Indian"; rather, they have morphological features that are more European or Asian. Therefore, morphology is not a reliable guide to determine one's ancestry or race because geographical variations and environmental factors cause humans to adapt differently to their surroundings. It is one thing to characterize the gene pool of early Americans as diverse and possibly indicative of complex population histories; it is quite another to ascribe decontextualized, biological race to an isolated skull based on qualitative and somewhat subjective features (Swedlund and Anderson 1999:571).

Moreover, the Kennewick case is nothing more than an ideological interpretation of "an active component in the struggle between the powerful and the powerless, rather than a consequence of technological and social change" (McGuire 1988:473). It has become a political issue in the context of ownership and determining what is correct, in the sense of who were the first Americans and the rights and privileges supposedly associated with this inheritance. Indeed, Kennewick has become a political issue for members of the scientific community as they strive for fame and the discovery of knowledge that they might, or will, never find the answer to. For the American Indian community, Kennewick remains a social issue because their beliefs and identity are constantly being challenged.

The Kennewick case, in my opinion, has brought much strife to the American Indian community. Once again, we must fight to gain recognition of who we are as peoples. Anthropology and the scientific fields need to interact with the local community to understand their perspectives and their culture. Within the Kennewick case, there is a lack of respect for the American Indian community and a feeling of domination or power within the scientific community. There should be a mending of differences, as we all need to be ethically just. The scientific community needs to show consideration for all American Indian communities and let their voices be heard.

REFERENCES

Anyon, R., T. J. Ferguson, L. Jackson, L. Lane, and P. Vicenti. 1997. Native American Oral Tradition and Archaeology, Issues of Structure, Relevance, and Respect. In *Native Americans and Archaeologists, Stepping Stones to Common Ground*, edited by N. Swidler, K. E. Dongoske, R. Anyon, and A. S. Downer, pp. 77–87. Walnut Creek, CA: AltaMira Press.

Burke Museum of Natural History and Culture. 2004. *Native American Views*. Available online at http://www.washington.edu/burkemuseum/kman/native_american_views.htm (accessed December 29, 2007).

Jemison, P. G. 1997. Who Owns the Past? In *Native Americans and Archaeologists, Stepping Stones to Common Ground*, edited by N. Swidler, K. E. Dongoske, R. Anyon, and A. S. Downer, pp. 57–63. Walnut Creek, CA: AltaMira Press.

McGuire, R. H. 1988. Dialogues with the Dead. In *Recovery of Meaning: Historical Archaeology in the Eastern United States*, edited by M. P. Leone and P. B. Potter, Jr., pp. 435–480. Washington, DC: Smithsonian Institution Press.

Swedlund, A., and D. Anderson. 1999. Gordon Creek Woman Meets Kennewick Man: New Interpretations and Protocols Regarding the Peopling of the Americas. *American Antiquity* 64(4):569–576.

CHAPTER 12
RESPECT AND HONOR
JOHN ELI SIROIS

As a member of the Okanagan and Wenatchi Tribes of the Confederation of the Colville Indian Reservation, I have a distinct view of the need to return the Ancient One to rest. The teachings of our people have strict guidelines to follow for the ones who have passed on before us. We take earnest care in respecting their remains so as not to disturb their spirit or their resting place. Elders, grandparents, and ones who have passed on receive the utmost in respect and care according to our traditional values. Unfortunately, our recent history has forced our culture to deal with an unfamiliar and unpleasant task of reburying ancient (and not so ancient) relatives, because of encroachment from outside forces. Road projects, bridges, dams, and other public actions have forced our people to move gravesites, unearth our loved ones, and relocate them to another area out of the way of contemporary uses.

When a community member passes, the immediate family and community take extreme care of that individual. It is a matter of respect and honor that these individuals receive the greatest care and attention on their final journey to what some Elders refer to as the "Happy Hunting Grounds." Tools, items, trinkets, and such are sometimes included with these loved ones for their journey to the other side. The grounds where our ancestors are buried are considered sacred. The possible molestation of these areas or gravesites is forbidden and audacious. According to custom, any disturbance needs immediate remediation to restore the person and site to a restful state. Without the remediation/restoration of order, chaos and social unrest will occur and affect the entire community.

These beliefs drive the Confederated Tribes of the Colville Indian Reservation to push for the immediate reburial and restoration of the Ancient One to a peaceful site. While scientists and courts debate the ties of this Ancient One to one ethnic group or another, social unrest and chaos will wreak havoc on our communities.

It is odd that scientists would pursue this Ancient One for study. What are their motives in studying this person? Do they want to establish a tie that Caucasoid people lived here thousands of years ago, in some desperate attempt to assert an Indigenous right and denigrate existing Indigenous rights and relationships to this land? Do they seek prestige that academic accolades may bring? What further confounds me as a person educated in the dominant society is that these scientists would run roughshod over federal regulations, Indigenous rights, and common decent respect to attain the accolades they so desire. When one looks at the surface of this "discovery," it is clear that these scientists did not even follow their own professional protocols and procedures. Moreover, it is appalling these scientists have not been reprimanded and stripped of their credentials in the archaeology field.

Over the course of the last few hundred years, academics have poured into Indigenous communities to document, preserve and catalog this "disappearing" Indigenous knowledge. Assuming their scientific methods are far superior to that of Indigenous knowledge, academics fail to realize that their own bigoted beliefs blind them to a body of knowledge developed over thousands of years. The only difference between Indigenous knowledge and scientific knowledge is that Indigenous knowledge developed over thousands of years of applied scientific method, whereas Western science is but a few hundred years old. Indigenous people had the ability to study and find ways to survive based on their surroundings and on what nature provided. Nature gives life and we humans live in this system. It seems that contemporary science seeks to remove humankind from nature, as some sort of objective separate recorder/documenter of the natural system. Indigenous knowledge recognizes, embraces, and respects that intertwining relationship of knowledge and nature. Contemporary science lacks that ability and in many ways justifies the inappropriate acts of exhuming dead bodies to study them for possible supporting evidence of their theories.

As stated before, reburial and repatriation are new concepts to our ways, but our Elders have developed and adapted ceremonies to address these kinds of situations. We, as a tribal community, take great pride and care in the manner in which we return our ancestors to safe resting places. Our applied scientific method or traditional ways have always included adaptation for survival. If we found a new way to accomplish a task that took fewer resources and was less damaging to the entire system, then we incorporated the idea to pass along to other generations. With this spirit for innovation, we can continue our traditional ways and respect our ancestors. Given the diversity of "belief ways" or religions, the Confederated Tribes of the Colville Indian Reservation incorporate and invite all religions to participate in our ceremonies in a respectful manner.

Looking at contemporary society on the Colville Indian Reservation, it has challenges and social ills that stem from past abuses. These past abuses need to be healed for a more healthy community to arise. With the Ancient One still above ground, the hearts of the Colville Tribes will always feel the hurt inflicted on this person and all other ancestors who were forcibly moved from their resting places to make room for foreign actions. The people of the Plateau and all other tribal nations have sacrificed thousands of acres of land to live in peace. We have freely volunteered to serve in the armed forces to protect all Americans' homelands. We now are being asked to sacrifice our religious ways and the protection of our ancestors. If the courts decide that our interests are not as important as some scientists' claim for academic accolades, then they will continue the injustices perpetrated on Indigenous people. At some point, these wrongs toward Indian people must stop. We, as Indian people, will always take care of our ancestors and pray for their pro-

tection. If the Ancient One is not repatriated, Indigenous people will just keep pray-
ing and fighting for the safe return of our elder. Losing is not an option.

In the future, tribes, federal agencies, academic institutions, and scientists
need to improve existing cultural resource protection laws to reflect all of the communities involved. It should be the goal of all parties involved to increase the
understanding and lessons learned of future discoveries about our ancestors.
Respect and empathy are huge components that need to be interjected into this
whole process.

The dominant society needs to understand how Indigenous people feel about
this situation of the Ancient One. What if the tables were turned and the Colville
Tribes' History and Archeology Department wanted to test a theory of European
descendants and Manifest Destiny? If we Indigenous people, as scientists, decided
to dig up several graves at Arlington National Cemetery because knowing the
genetic make-up of individuals who fought and killed Indian people may hold a
missing link in how Indian people could communicate with U.S. society today, is
it our academic right to conduct these scientific tests on Arlington gravesites to
prove our theory? Why is it now acceptable to allow these scientists to hold our
ancestor above ground to test their theories? Indigenous people, because of our
beliefs, would never conduct such a venture, but having empathy toward another
group is such a powerful tool to bring about cross-cultural understanding and
respect. Communication, empathy, respect, and common sense need to be applied
to improve how we "discover" things, how we begin to understand our surroundings, and how we are connected to that reality.

Incorporating these ideals into our everyday lives will help us deal with issues
before they make it to court. These ideals appeal to a higher ethical standard or
conduct for all in our communities. It may be a tough assignment for humanity, but
to handle the challenges before us, we must embrace these ideals with our collective might. To survive, we must all adapt to our environment to balance the system
in which we live and are intertwined.

CHAPTER 13
THE ANCIENT ONE
HARVEY MOSES, JR.

The whole ordeal of the Ancient One is just another injustice, another act of inhumanity, and a swipe at the inherent sovereignty of the American Indian(s) that has been happening since 1492.

Studying our ancestry is not going to do the scientists (European descendants) any good. If they want answers about our (American Indians') past, present, or future, they need to come and talk to us. To study our ancestry for the sake of modern humanity is an oxymoron. Their kind slaughtered our ancestors with their armies and with their diseases. If they want to see what makes them the way they are (Pilgrims), let them (scientists) go to Europe and study their ancestors' remains.

CHAPTER 14
OWNING INDIANS: NAGPRA REDUX[1]
JAMES D. NASON

PREFACE

What follows is only tangentially about the legal issue concerning Kennewick Man, or the Ancient One, although he does come into it. It is really about two other, related, issues. First, it is about U.S. legal culture, the history of the origins of that culture as it relates to Native Americans, and the way that legal culture figured in the lawsuit concerning the Ancient One. Second, this chapter focuses on the emergence of the Native American Graves Protection and Repatriation Act (NAGPRA) and what it has meant and might mean for the ownership, control, and/or disposition of Native American human remains in America. These two issues come together in the consideration of ancient Native American human remains in a way that highlights distinct cultural differences between Native American and Euro-American cultures, including attitudes about legal culture in the United States. In the end, there appears to be an irreconcilable gulf between these cultural perspectives, one for which a compromise is difficult to imagine without further significant social and legal changes.

AMERICAN COLONIALISM, AMERICAN LAW

All laws are created in response to a community's concerns about specific societal issues. They are framed within the cultural values and related biases of that community and therefore reflect not only that particular community's culture but, more specifically, the manner in which those who develop the language of the laws choose to interpret their culture at that moment in time. This process thus illustrates changes over time in social attitudes and cultural values as they emerge in a community. In culturally diverse societies, laws are even more than otherwise conditioned by complex issues of political dominance, subgroup interaction and interdependence, economic factors, religious suasion, and other considerations. In the contemporary world, all of this occurs in an often postcolonial environment, where not all members of the broader community are, in fact, equal under the law in a de facto if not a de jure sense.

This perspective on law, and on the changing nature of law in any one society, is what is generally meant by the phrase "legal culture." This cultural aspect of a legal system refers to the social attitudes and the cultural products of those attitudes that are represented by laws based in sociocultural mores, emerging from culturally embedded legislative processes, and subsequently applied by equally contextualized enforcement.[2] America's legal culture and the history of this legal culture, often mirroring the broader history of the nation, reflect all of these points. It is also a history sometimes marked by abrupt and significant changes in law and underlying legal principles in response to equally significant changes in the social and political climate.

In 1857, for example, seven of the nine justices on the U.S. Supreme Court, including Chief Justice Roger B. Taney, were staunch supporters of slavery. In the infamous Dred Scott case, they ruled that no slave or free African American could become a citizen or bring suit in federal courts and that the United States could not bar slavery in any of its territories. Yet, after the cataclysmic events of the Civil War, the U.S. Congress enacted the Thirteenth Amendment to the Constitution, which summarily abolished slavery or any other form of noncriminal involuntary servitude.

In the course of only eight years, slavery, formerly a fundamental legal right, became no longer legal. This remarkable change in law did not, however, affect a legal culture in which other racist laws subsequently saw to it that African Americans, along with other people of color in America, were denied equal protection under the law and pragmatically denied many of the benefits of citizenship, with all of the socioeconomic consequences such treatment entailed. Legal culture—the social and cultural values of the dominant element in a society as seen in laws and legal institutions—does not, then, necessarily change with the passage of even very significant laws.

The manner in which the United States, as a nation, developed from its first colonial period and has dealt with Native Americans throughout its history exemplifies the evolution of many of the legal principles and attitudes that have formed U.S. legal culture. This history is one in which the changing relationships between Euro-Americans and Native Americans were linked with the emergence of Euro-American laws that affected every aspect of Native American life and culture from the 15th century onward.

The first 400 years of European and subsequent U.S. colonialism in America were characterized by the widespread extinguishing of Native American governments, laws, and legal principles and the imposition of European legal systems. Indeed, the initial colonial Spanish legal system of the *encomienda*, based so firmly in the concept of *terra nullius*, provided Spanish conquistadors and later colonists with complete authority over all resources of granted lands, including the native population.

This history is so well known that we need not dwell on the initial legal attitude that Native Americans were not even human beings, their later legal elevation to human but slave status through the efforts of Bartolome de Las Casas in the early 1500s, or the decimation to the point of extermination of the early Native American victims of these legal practices. It is, however, relevant to note at least briefly that the transition from the *encomienda* system to the *repartimiento* and, ultimately, to peonage, did little to change the involuntary servitude of Indigenous peoples. These legal shifts did not actually change the operative legal culture in many places in the New World or the actual status quo of the Indigenous population.[3]

English and French colonial regimes in North America were similarly based on legal ideals that first emerged during the Crusades: that "discovered" lands were property of the Crown; that indigenes held no title to any of those lands; and that European rights, laws, and customs were superior to those of any non-Christian savages who might otherwise inhabit those lands. The essentials of colonialism were all present in U.S. history during the centuries of settlement and expansion that followed discovery and exploration. Early European and later U.S. colonizers increasingly dominated all natural resources, the labor to exploit those resources, and the markets to profit by those resources; in the process, they imposed their own religious, linguistic, political, and sociocultural values and institutions on Native Americans.

It is hardly necessary to point out the ways in which Euro-American laws became the law of the land, were arbitrarily forced on Native Americans, and structured the systematic takeover and attempted destruction of Native American society, land tenure, and culture. In this history, Native Americans were most often regarded as obstacles to an inevitable and enviable Euro-American "progress." As obstacles, prominent Euro-American leaders at different points in time believed that Native Americans needed to be cajoled and dealt with, controlled and geographically curtailed, militarily punished and exterminated, or forcibly absorbed into emerging U.S. society as second- or third-class persons dwelling on the legal, social, economic, and political fringes of U.S. life. Any of the contemporary treatises on this history can amplify these points in detail.

What concerns us here are a few salient points about the history of the status of Native Americans in U.S. law and the nature of the key legal doctrines that have affected this status. All of the doctrines that require our attention are from the 19th century and represent the legal findings of Chief Justice John Marshall. The first, and in some ways most essential, doctrine deals with the absolute power of Congress and its authority to deal with Indian affairs, a perspective derived from the constitutional provision concerning the regulation of commerce. The second doctrine held that Native American governments were dependent nations under the superior sovereignty of the U.S. government, that Native American land tenure rights were extinguished by the original European rights of discovery, and thus that Native American governments had only limited sovereignty as might be provided for by treaty or other acts of Congress. The related third doctrine derived from the second and made it clear that Native Americans were to be considered as wards of the U.S. government, which would exercise considerable control over Native American life and livelihoods in its role as trustee of Indian welfare and resources.

All of these have continued to be fundamental to the manner in which succeeding courts have adjudicated issues that involve the relationships between the federal government and Native American nations. Their influence in practical terms over

Native Americans cannot be overestimated. They provided the basis for the expansion of the reservation system, the imposition of forced relocations, reductions in, or eliminations of, in-trust lands held by treaty, the mandatory removal of Indian children to boarding schools, the attempted conversions to various forms of Christianity, the oversight and control of federal agents over all land transactions, the loss of any Native American government control over lands that were instead deeded individually to tribal members, control over how and under what circumstances tribal resources could be utilized, and, ultimately, attempts to terminate Native American governments and disestablish reservations.

The effects of early European colonialism in America and the subsequent imposition of U.S. legal culture on Native Americans probably cannot ever be completely understood, if only because of their complex and vast impacts. We can say, for example, that the demographic analyses of precontact Native American population decline is on the order of 98%, but that hardly conveys the actual human meaning of such a holocaust—except to marvel at today's strength and vitality of Native American communities. We can say that Native Americans went from a precontact period in which they were the sole inhabitants and sovereigns over these lands to a condition by the 1930s where they only retained some limited degree of sovereignty or ownership over less than 2% of all lands in the United States.

There were also important changes taking place in U.S. law and, ultimately, in U.S. legal culture that affected Native Americans during the 20th century. Before 1879, for example, Native Americans were not considered to be persons in U.S. law and essentially had no individual rights. Although the 1919 American Indian Citizenship Act was a singularly ineffective mechanism designed only to "award" honorably discharged Indian veterans of World War I, the subsequent Indian Citizenship Act of 1924 did provide universal citizenship to all Native Americans by fiat. This congressional act was not so much a benefit sought by Native Americans as another piece of the ongoing legislative effort to assimilate Indians into U.S. culture. It came fifty-nine years after the abolition of slavery in 1865 and the subsequent granting of legal, if not actual, civil rights to African Americans.

Other notable events in the shifting attitudes of Congress toward Indians in the 20th century included the 1930s Indian New Deal and its centerpiece, the Indian Reorganization Act, which effectively restored tribal governments with mechanisms for new tribal constitutions and tribal governments. These were, of course, strictly to be based on American models of democratic government. At the same time, government decrees again granted religious freedom to Indians, despite opposition from Christian groups and others. Later termination policies were overturned with new laws for tribal self-determination, including expanded tribal powers over Native American children and their education.

A number of late 20th-century legal decisions better defined the separation of tribal jurisdiction and autonomy against the intrusion of the states and lesser governments and have upheld the validity of treaties and provided for new enforcement of original treaty provisions. But other legal decisions have also further impinged on Native American religious rights, including a Supreme Court ruling in 1988 that a congressional act, the American Indian Religious Freedom Act, was not law but policy.[4] This was, among many other things, a reminder that Congress may propose what is law, but it is the courts that ultimately dispose on legislation.

U.S. laws are primarily based on English common law principles and have in some ways been conditioned by Euro-American experience in America, especially dealings with Native Americans. They are written in English, with all of the cultural understandings and nuances that inherently apply to the chosen words, which, in turn, reflect a Euro-American worldview. They are, moreover, interpreted by a judiciary in a manner that is also embedded in this same legal cultural context. To put it another way, U.S. laws applied to Native American issues—what they actually say and how they say it—are, in many instances, widely at variance with Native American social, legal, and cultural values. This is, in fact, a key point in what follows.

AMERICAN ARCHAEOLOGY, NATIVE AMERICANS, AND THE LAW

Other important changes in 20th-century U.S. legal culture and laws have dealt with archaeological activity, especially the manner in which archaeological activities impact Native Americans. In contrast to many European nations, the United States was late in passing federal legislation to protect its national archaeological resources and other cultural heritage. The first such law for archaeological resources was the Antiquities Act of 1906 (P.L. 59-209, 16 USC 431). This was enacted in response to a growing need to control archaeological activity on federal lands or lands otherwise controlled by the federal government (e.g., Native American tribal lands). It instituted the first permit requirements for excavations, as well as fines and imprisonment for violations, and further required that recovered materials be preserved in museums.

Congress was uninterested as to whether Native Americans wished to see their buried ancestors, sacred objects, and other funerary materials dug up and placed in museums or governmental agencies, and there were, of course, no provisions for Native American approval, oversight, or control over any part of this process. Nor, for that matter, was any Native American consulted about the designation of Native American human remains—the bodies of ancestors—as archaeological resources, like potshards or flint scraps.

In 1906, living Native Americans were not citizens, had limited rights, and, as "wards" of the government, were subjected to every kind of government policy designed to eradicate their culture. And, although living Native Americans were not subject to slavery in 1906, dead Native American bodies could be, and were, owned through the Antiquities Act. They were disposable property, just like all other inanimate debris from former lives taken from ancient and historic Native American homes and sites. By law this was not desecration, but rather Science, and therefore inherently good. Desecration, and the laws prohibiting it, was something that applied to other, non-Indian, human remains. Native American human remains were not, in this sense, human at all but just things, otherwise known as "archaeological resources" used for the benefit of non–Native American scholars and the further advancement of Science. This was not a professional ethical dilemma. Indeed, there were no anthropological ethical codes that addressed any concerns of this kind.

Actual enforcement of the Antiquities Act was sketchy or nonexistent, particularly in the western United States, and illegal excavations were commonplace in a public arena where there was little or no support for the law itself. By the time this illegal activity had become devastatingly widespread, the penalties provided for in the Antiquities Act were so minor they hardly constituted a significant deterrent, given the fabulous increases in market value for illicitly obtained archaeological materials.

This sad state of affairs came to a head in 1974, when a case involving a successful prosecution of the law was appealed and the court of appeals ruled that the Antiquities Act was unconstitutionally vague and therefore could not be applied (Friedman 1985). Congress attempted to solve this problem with the passage of the Archaeological Resources Protection Act of 1979 (ARPA) (P.L. 96-95, 16 USC 470). Using more precise language, ARPA reinstituted permit requirements and greatly expanded penalties for violation to protect archaeological resources located on federal lands or lands controlled by the federal government (Indian lands). As before, Native American human remains were lumped together with bottles, baskets, weapons, and so on as "archaeological resources" and were eligible to be kept by any eligible institution, not just museums.

ARPA is not simply a better crafted version of the Antiquities Act of 1906, and there are important differences between it and its predecessor, notably the inclusion of Indian tribal concerns and authority in several key ways. Under ARPA, Indian tribes must be notified prior to any archaeological research proposed for their lands and the tribe must approve the permit for such work, setting forth whatever terms and conditions they regard as appropriate. Additionally, Indian tribes must approve of any proposed disposition or exchange of archaeological resources removed from their lands. Indian tribes and tribal members themselves are not automatically required to have permits for excavations on tribal lands; it is understood that tribes can develop their own archaeological protection laws to address those and other concerns. In other words, tribal sovereignty with respect to what occurs on tribal lands resurfaced in ARPA. This reflected the changes that had occurred in tribal status and federal-tribal relationships since the 1930s, particularly after the 1960s. Stronger tribal governments, better legal representation, the growth of tribal economies, the public impact of Indian activism, and the passage of laws related to self-determination (e.g., the Indian Self Determination Act of 1975) were all key elements in the advances made by tribes during this period, and these advances influenced government policy and congressional legislation.

ANTHROPOLOGISTS, MUSEUMS, AND NAGPRA

Although other federal legislation concerning Native Americans and archaeological work was enacted between 1935 and 1990, the most important was NAGPRA in 1990 (P.L. 101-601, 25 USC 3001-13). In many respects, NAGPRA is the most important cultural heritage law ever enacted in the United States. It is also, as others have pointed out (Echo-Hawk 2002; Malaro 1998; Mihesuah 2000; Nason

1997), four different kinds of law. It is a law that reaffirms and further defines Native American tribal sovereignty with respect to its provisions for cultural heritage. It is in part criminal law, with provisions against trafficking in protected cultural materials. It is administrative law, because it sets forth procedural steps that must be taken. Finally, and perhaps most importantly, it is significant civil rights law, because it provides legal protection to Native American human remains equal to that of all other Americans, and in so doing, was believed by many to change the previous legal status of all those human remains as property.

NAGPRA establishes legal protections for Native American archaeological sites and their contents, including human remains, on tribal and federal lands, and provides mechanisms for the automatic involvement of tribes in making decisions about those sites and cultural materials. NAGPRA makes it illegal to traffic in Native American human remains and designated cultural objects. NAGPRA required museums, federal agencies, and other educational institutions directly or indirectly receiving federal support, to provide summaries and inventories of their relevant holdings to tribes by 1993 and 1995, respectively. NAGPRA requires that those same agencies and institutions continue to consult with tribes regarding their collections. More significantly, NAGPRA also requires the expeditious repatriation of Native American human remains and designated cultural objects by those agencies and institutions when a tribe demonstrates cultural affiliation and makes a request, with few exceptions, including an agency or institution proving that it has right of possession.

In other words, NAGPRA mandates the necessity for agencies and institutions to undertake very specific actions, with deadlines, for Native American cultural materials in their possession so that repatriation of these human remains and cultural materials can take place, while also protecting and involving tribes in decisions about archaeological materials found on tribal or federal land and prohibiting, generally, any commercial dealing in any of these cultural materials. NAGPRA is obviously a complex law in many respects, and a very significant one.

We can legitimately ask why such a law was needed, much less passed, in the context of U.S. legal culture. As Marie Malaro, the Smithsonian's former chief counsel, has pointed out: "[T]he law is a clumsy tool to resolve conflicts based on cultural differences" (Malaro 1998:114). As we'll see, these "cultural differences" were such that the Euro-American institutions owning Native American human remains—actively supported by anthropological organizations and individuals— had few or no intentions of considering Native American requests for the repatriation and reburial of those bodies prior to NAGPRA's passage. Moreover, it was quite clear that those same scholars and institutions felt that their cultural beliefs in this regard were superior and that the cultural beliefs of Native Americans about their dead merited little consideration. Under these circumstances, and with decades of Native American frustration over this and countless other issues, it is hard to imagine how, ultimately, legal action could have been avoided. This all becomes obvious when we consider how the law was passed.

Given the central role of Native Americans in this legislation and the goals that

Congress intended for it, NAGPRA is a startling turnaround from the earlier Antiquities Act, when Native Americans had no say in anything, much less the right to maintain their own cultural heritage. This is not because of some sudden epiphany on the part of countless members of Congress. This law came about because of a nationwide Native American movement to correct a dreadful wrong represented by decades of extensive private and scholarly collecting of Native American bodies and objects, widespread private and federally supported archaeological work, and the inherently racist nature of postcolonial American laws like the Antiquities Act. Prior to NAGPRA's passage, Congress had at least briefly examined the discriminatory actions of federal agencies toward Native American religious practices and beliefs, and had passed the American Indian Religious Freedom Act (AIRFA) in 1978. In this same period, Congress also passed other legislation giving tribal governments greater control over their affairs.

NAGPRA arose out of this changing political and legal climate through the dedicated efforts of groups like the Native American Rights Fund, American Indians Against Desecration, tribal governments, and other organizations and individuals, including the North American Indian Museums Association (NAIMA). Their actions included demands that state governments enact burial site protection and repatriate human remains from state-held collections. In 1981, foreshadowing many key details of the ultimate nature of NAGPRA, NAIMA issued its "Suggested Guidelines for Museums in Dealing with Requests for Return of Native American Materials" (NAIMA 1981:38–39).[5]

All of these prior actions and circumstances were important, but there were events that even more directly precipitated direct tribal demands to Congress for the repatriation of Native American human remains. One of these was the presentation in 1987 by the secretary of the Smithsonian Institution of their human remains holdings before the Select Committee on Indian Affairs. The prompt Native American response to this was a request for the appropriate reburial of all of these human remains, including those that could not be specifically identified by tribe (U.S. Senate 1990). It was also pertinent that, by the late 1980s, a majority of states had passed laws to protect Native American burial sites and/or require the repatriation of human remains and grave materials in state collections to tribes. Could Congress ignore a problem so widespread that a majority of states had acted on it, particularly in the face of direct appeals for action to key members of Congress?

THE BATTLE OVER NAGPRA

The ensuing debates over a national repatriation law and the ultimate passage of NAGPRA clearly demonstrated the lines of cultural demarcation between Native American scholars, lawyers, and tribal leaders and non–Native American academics, associations, and institutions. They unequivocally showed the willingness of a majority of the latter to argue at the start against Native American civil rights with respect to human remains and Native American cultural rights with respect to sacred objects, patrimonial objects, and objects removed from graves.

For others, it was a sad reflection on the state of "anthropological ethics," if only because it highlighted the disdain with which many anthropologists viewed Native American concerns in the face of their own efforts to continue to own Native American bodies. Later anthropological and museological organization statements about a possible national repatriation law implied that Native Americans were essentially ignorant or disrespectful of the considerable values of these collections of bodies and objects and of the importance of Science itself.

Museum-based anthropologists and administrators, represented primarily by the American Association of Museums (AAM), provided a statement to Congress in 1987 and later generated a policy statement in 1988 that set forth its opinions on repatriation (AAM 1987, 1988). Like the statement of the American Anthropological Association (AAA), it essentially argued that Science was good, collections were important, Native American human remains would be treated with respect, illegally acquired materials could be repatriated on request, but scientific values should be weighed against Native American interests for all other requests.[6] At the same time, major public media exposés about the status of Indian burial grounds, looting, and the treatment of graves as "archaeological resources" effectively presented a counterpoint that complemented Native American representations to Congress.

It was in this context that Congress passed the National Museum of the American Indian Act at the end of 1989, which not only established the Smithsonian's new museum, but also dealt directly with the repatriation of Native American human remains and designated cultural objects from Smithsonian collections. At the same time, Congress deliberated repatriation bills introduced into the House of Representatives by Morris Udall (D-AR) and into the Senate by Daniel Inouye (D-HI) and John McCain (R-AR) (see U.S. Senate 1990). Despite intense lobbying against many of the provisions of these bills by the AAA, the Society for American Archaeology (SAA) and the AAM, along with other anthropological organizations, it was clear by late 1990 that Congress was, in fact, going to pass repatriation legislation. The strategies employed in the lobbying by the AAM and their impact on Congress convey volumes about their issues with NAGPRA and how they approached it.

In a special report presented at a major museum association meeting in October 1990—just one month before final passage of NAGPRA—Daniel Monroe and Walter Echo-Hawk outlined what had happened.[7] At that time, Monroe was the AAM's special representative to Congress on repatriation and Echo-Hawk was a key Native American representative from the Native American Rights Fund. The significance of their remarks, given what others have said about the law's passage and congressional intent, bears repeating at some length. Monroe noted that AAM conflicts with Native Americans over repatriation had been based on six key assumptions: (1) scientific rights of inquiry superceded all other rights, including human rights, if these were in conflict; (2) museums held a high moral ground and were seen as morally correct in maintaining human remains for study; (3) museums placed a high priority on preserving collections; (4) Indian cultural materials were fundamentally like all other ownable art; (5) museums could accurately interpret

Native American materials without Native American involvement; and (6) museums were seen by the federal government as fundamentally good institutions incapable of doing wrong.

Relying on these assumptions, AAM's reactions to the introduction of proposed NAGPRA legislation went through four phases:

- In phase one, repatriation was viewed with considerable alarm as a threat to control over collections. It was widely believed that Indians simply didn't understand museums and their goals, and any requests for repatriation were met with confusion and fear. This was true despite earlier pleas in the literature to carefully consider the dreadful relationships (or lack thereof) that existed between Indians and museums and the legitimate concerns of Native Americans (see Ames 1987; Bassett 1986; W. Echo-Hawk 1989; Hill 1980; Nason 1973).
- In phase two, the introduction of legislation led to a major effort to create policy guidelines in the belief that this would happily remove the lawmakers' concerns and the legislation would go away.
- In phase three, with legislation nearing completion, museum representatives began the difficult process of attempting a dialog on repatriation with Indian representatives, which led to the shocking realization that Indians might be right. But the failure of AAM to act, even as it began to come to grips with its assumptions about this issue, led to increased legislative action.
- Finally, in phase four and facing impeding legislation, AAM realized that its political objections had had no influence on Congress and that the museum perspective was increasingly considered by Congress to be retrogressive and entirely lacking in moral standing or leadership. AAM realized that its assumptions would be challenged and that it would lose any role in the process leading to passage of NAGPRA.

These assumptions, and the arguments based on them by AAM and other groups like the SAA, as well as individuals, centered on some basic values about the nature of science, its fundamental good and importance, and the necessity of not placing any restrictions on scientific inquiry, the ethical stance of museums and anthropologists—"We are ethical professionals who know best"—and the willingness of museums to talk to individual Indian groups about specific cases.

Other perspectives emerged from various quarters, including that it was inappropriate for one group (Indians) to tell everyone else what should be studied, that modern-day Indians were not religious in any traditional way, that Indians only wanted things back so they could sell them, that real Science should otherwise not be shackled by the religious views of a minority group, and that tribes today couldn't establish affiliation with older cultural materials anyway.

Native Americans, in their turn, flipped several of these arguments on their head (e.g., that non-Indians had no right to dictate to Indians what they should think about their ancestors' bodies or sacred objects or that Indians should be guided by a Euro-American construct about Science). Others expressed the opinion that much of the research had failed to benefit Native Americans, that some museums had barred Native Americans from even entering collection areas, that Native Americans did maintain traditional values with respect to human remains and sacred materials, and that Native Americans did not, in fact, recognize any artificial cut-off date in their relationships with ancient remains and cultural materials.

In the last moments before the passage of NAGPRA, AAM and Native American representatives met daily, often for as long as ten to fourteen hours a day, in an attempt to reach consensus. AAM recognized that the legislation was going to pass and that the choice then was either to try for a partnership with Native Americans or to have no role whatsoever in the final wording of the legislation. During these negotiations, the AAM had six goals: to exclude this legislation from use by any other domestic or foreign group; to limit museum liability in the case of good faith repatriations when there were conflicting claims; to establish a review committee procedure for resolution of conflicts; to try to reduce inventory costs in a short time period; to clarify concepts of cultural affiliation, sacred, and associated burial objects; and to develop equitable standards of burden of proof for the ownership of cultural objects.

The outcome of these discussions is obvious in the final legislation passed unanimously by Congress and signed into law by the president on November 23, 1990. Tribal goals as outlined by Walter Echo-Hawk were met, as were many museum goals for clarification on the issues outlined by Daniel Monroe. Archaeologists did not succeed, however, in removing oral history and expert testimony from the list of valid evidence to be used to establish cultural affiliation, or in placing a time limit on the antiquity of remains subject to the law. Instead, both prehistoric and recent remains were to be given equal protection under the law:

> Once remains are shown to be those of a Native American, they are absolutely protected. There is no requirement that the remains must have been associated with an actual burial. There is no age requirement, and therefore prehistoric and recent remains are afforded equal protection. (memorandum from Keith Kintigh, Gary Kingman, Walter R. Echo-Hawk, and Jack F. Trope to the Senate Select Committee on Indian Affairs, September 12, 1990; in Hutt 1992:143–144)

To what extent was this law a compromise between the interests of museums, scholars, and Native Americans, a perspective suggested by SAA representatives and others (see, for example, National Park Service [NPS] 1998:25)? Bearing in mind that all laws are in some ways compromises, this was hardly the perspective of key representatives like Monroe and Echo-Hawk. In the final analysis, initial museum and anthropological opposition against the passage of any repatriation law was ignored in Congress's unanimous approval of NAGPRA, and NAGPRA's final structure benefited from the input and negotiations that had taken place between

Native Americans, museums, and anthropological representatives. As one jurist who has dealt extensively with archaeological law later commented, NAGPRA was "drafted from the Native American perspective" (Hutt 1992:142).

For the first time since U.S. colonial and postcolonial control over Native Americans, the bodies of Native Americans were afforded the same civil rights as those of all other Americans and could not arbitrarily be owned as property by institutions without the express approval of Native Americans. This was not a religious issue, except insofar as all laws against desecration and owning dead bodies are ultimately based on religious values common to humankind. The lingering issue, of course, had to do with how one interpreted congressional intent with respect to establishing claims for those Native American bodies.

IRRECONCILABLE DIFFERENCES

Strident opposition to the law continued after NAGPRA's passage—especially among some archaeologists and physical anthropologists who felt that their fields, if not their careers, were threatened by the loss of these "data." These scholars remained convinced that they should be able to continue to own Indian bodies. Others in the same museum and scholarly communities that had so vigorously tried to prevent NAGPRA's passage now sought to find ways to reach accords with Native Americans, who were suddenly "peers" in this arena to a degree that had rarely before been true, much less widely desired. This included new programs for cooperation and Native American inclusion in museums and professional societies. At the same time, some organizations, including the SAA, for example, continued to lobby their positions on the law through the regulatory process. These efforts, which continue today, represent what some of us believe to be irreconcilable differences with respect to Native American perspectives on human remains. This is quite clear with respect to the general issue of "unidentified human remains" and related cases such as "Kennewick Man" or Spirit Cave.

The law is crystal clear with respect to Native American human remains where lineal descendants are known—they must be repatriated expeditiously on request. It is equally clear in all cases where cultural affiliation can be demonstrated by a preponderance of evidence, including oral history and expert testimony.[8] This means that most Native American human remains are, and should be able to be, repatriated on tribal request, because in most cases ample evidence exists to reasonably connect those remains to contemporary tribal groups, as the law outlines.

But there are other cases in which this is not so, and in some of those the law has been interpreted by the responsible federal agency to favor repatriation. For example, in cases in which a tribal group is no longer federally recognized but still exists, the remains of their ancestors can be repatriated to another related tribe that is recognized or to the nonrecognized group providing other federally recognized tribes in the same area concur. This is also the case in which a tribe has become virtually extinct. Joint claims by more than one tribe can also be made, so that a consortium of tribes can justifiably claim otherwise "culturally unidentifiable" human remains from a given area (NPS 2007).

In all of these instances, the law has been interpreted so that these "unidentifiable" human remains are, in fact, repatriated or disposed of to a tribal community, and these resolutions have been driven by the foundational principles embedded in NAGPRA: respect for the dead and the primacy of tribal rights in making decisions about those dead. But beyond these are cases in which the antiquity of human remains has led to serious disagreements about their relationship to contemporary tribal communities, and, for that matter, about whether they should be regarded as Native American at all. This was, of course, one aspect of the now infamous Kennewick Man case.

In this case, about which so many hundreds of pounds of ink and thousands of pounds of paper have been expended, the presiding magistrate finally ruled that he thought ARPA and not NAGPRA should have been the applicable law. This was related to his belief, contrary to the anthropological evidence presented by the government, that no reasonable relationship could be established between those human remains and the claimant tribes.

A far more troubling portion of his decision was the idea voiced by others that these remains were not Native American at all (thus NAGPRA couldn't apply in any event) because Kennewick Man didn't look like modern Indians. This often-repeated speculation is essentially archaeological racial profiling and was decidedly odd as some respected physical anthropologists had already noted that those remains looked similar to other ancient remains from that period in time, and that none of these ancient remains were morphologically like modern peoples (Powell and Stone 1999). Joseph Powell and J. A. Rose, the first physical anthropologists to carefully examine these remains, said in their report:

> Thus it is possible that the term "Native American," when used in a biological context, is irrelevant when applied to ancient human remains because founder populations did not exhibit the pattern of morphological and metric variation seen among late Holocene populations in the Americas. However, such a situation does not completely rule out the possibility that these remains might be biologically ancestral to modern American Indian populations. ... Much of the interpretation of the biological affinity of [the] Kennewick results depends on the subjective opinions and assumptions about the rate of morphological change possible during the last 10,000 years. ... (Powell and Rose 1999:9)

In the Kennewick Man case, this disturbing judicial observation about morphology (originally introduced by some anthropologists, with the companion idea that Kennewick Man was Caucasoid) would mean that anyone seeing examples of European medieval armor in museums would have to conclude that the wearers of that armor could not possibly be related to any modern Europeans, as the average height, shape, and build of those armor wearers is so dramatically different from that of modern Europeans. And this significant morphological change took place over the course of only a few hundred years in Europe—not the thousands of years involved in these Native American cases. Indeed, morphology in connection with "race"—itself a repudiated sociopolitical construct rather than "science"—is deservedly suspect. As the physical anthropologist Jonathan Marks pointed out in this case:

> The "Caucasoid" Kennewick Man ... has been the subject of extensive heated correspondence. ... To call it "Caucasoid" is to connote aspects of ancestry, not simply morphology; it directly suggests that America was settled by Europeans and that those now called "Native Americans" are actually less "native" than they think. This is a strongly political statement requiring an exceptional level of validation. ... [The] "racial" variation in cranial form of prehistoric Native Americans is well attested from earlier studies. ... Other material similar to Kennewick ... also appearing "Caucasoid" and with a very old date, nevertheless has mitochrondrial DNA markers characteristic of American Indians, just as we should suspect. So what is the point of racializing these remains? It serves only to clothe 21st-century issues like NAGPRA in the conceptual apparatus and vocabulary of the 19th century. (Marks 1998:1, 4)

Equally discouraging is seeing the same morphological argument crop up in the Spirit Man case (Rose 2000), which perhaps suggests an attempt to make this notion part of the legal culture in the United States, where morphological racial profiling is a daily occurrence. Although these points are perhaps moot now, it is interesting to note that some archaeologists have since argued that Magistrate Jelderks overstepped his legal and intellectual boundaries in the Kennewick Man case, misunderstood NAGPRA's essential nature, and ignored relevant data that did, in fact, support the initial repatriation decision, just as others have applauded it for upholding the rights of science (Jones and Stapp 2003).

There are valid and interesting anthropological arguments about the relationships between ancient remains and modern tribal communities, or rather about how and what kinds of data might be applied in such cases. But unlike ARPA, NAGPRA was not fundamentally about the scientific status of Native American human remains but rather about their civil rights status. We should remember that NAGPRA does not require "scientific certainty."

Some scholars would obviously like to see Science reintroduced as the superior value system in these cases, as they continue to reiterate the same arguments that Congress heard in 1989 and essentially rejected. This attitude is reflected by the SAA litany presented at meetings of the NAGPRA Review Committee, which suggests that NAGPRA was intended to be a balance between the "legitimate" interests of science, museums, and tribes, and that the law is not really about reburial, a perspective echoed by the American Association of Physical Anthropologists (AAPA). These views, like those on beauty, are in the eye of the beholder, but to argue seriously that Congress did not intend NAGPRA's passage to provide Native Americans with the right to recover and rebury their dead would appear to be an attempt at historical revisionism that would make any Stalinist-period Soviet historian proud.

Such a position argues that Native Americans only have rights to claim human remains that can be proven to be related and should only be able to do so in a context in which oral history, tribal cultural perspectives on what it means to be "related," and the indigeneity of the pre-European occupants as Native Americans is not relevant. The law does indeed ask that cultural affiliation be reasonably established, and here, of course, the catch is, and remains, "reasonable to whom?" Clearly, what seems perfectly reasonable to Native Americans is anathema to many anthropologists.

Other old and tired arguments also crop up in pronouncements made by some anthropologists about cases like Kennewick Man or Spirit Cave, including the idea that repositories like museums exist only to serve the interests of researchers, which both ignores all modern museological theory and practice and is simply too silly and ill-informed to take seriously, or the notion that museums must care for the heritage of all Americans (or the world) and that this should include Native American bodies. We all know that these dissentions are actually about ancient Native American human remains, their Native American status, and the ability of contemporary tribes legally to establish a relationship with them. Because these points rest on cultural perspectives about the world that are quite different, they are worth exploring further.

"CULTURALLY UNIDENTIFIABLE" NATIVE AMERICAN HUMAN REMAINS

These varied cultural perspectives, and the propaganda that surrounds them, continue to be played out in public deliberations regarding "culturally unidentifiable" Native American human remains and the NAGPRA regulations that would apply to them (see, for example, NPS 1995, 1997a, 1997b, 1998, 2007). Because this is a complex issue for which a conclusion was not reached when NAGPRA was first drafted, Congress left this task to the NAGPRA Review Committee. This committee, made up of three members nominated by tribes, three members nominated by museum and scientific organizations, and one nominated by all of these, was specifically charged in the law with the responsibility to recommend "specific actions for developing a process for disposition of such remains" (P.L. 101-601, Section 8(4)c(5)). In 1995, the committee requested comments on their draft recommendations on this issue. In this draft, the members of the original committee stated their belief that the general principles of NAGPRA applying in cases where affiliation could be established should also provide the primary guidance when a connection between human remains and associated funerary objects and a contemporary tribe could not definitely be established. Their unanimous recommendation is worth noting in full:

[S]uch remains and objects, no matter how ancient, are nevertheless Native American, and they should be treated according to the wishes of the Native American community. *Ultimately, decisions about what happens to the*

*remains of Native American individuals from anywhere in the United States
and associated funerary objects should rest in the hands of Native
Americans.* These decisions can and should be informed by anthropological, archaeological, historical, folkloric, biological, linguistic and spiritual
evidence, and non Native Americans can and should be consulted when
appropriate in the decision making process. However, the final decision
should be made entirely by Native American people. (NPS 1995; emphasis
in the original)

This recommendation specifically and clearly applied to cases like Kennewick
Man as well as to other cases in which no original burial location was known, and
it was just as specifically opposed by the usual parties. As proposed, it reflects
Native American viewpoints about their universal and unending relationships with
Native American dead and the inherently sacred nature of those remains as well as
the intent of Congress that Native American human remains be treated with respect
and subject to repatriation or other disposition in accord with tribal requests. These
viewpoints have led some to characterize the resulting dissentions as "religion vs.
science," thus revealing the obvious difficulty some non-Indians have in grasping
the differences between what is religion and what is sacred, which also became a
problematic issue in the framing of what might or might not be NAGPRA-eligible
"sacred" objects. Religion vs. Science may make good press, but it seems a discouraging comment on the cultural understanding of some anthropologists. We can speculate that it is related to the distinctive cultural barrier that exists in contemporary
Western culture between the natural and supernatural worlds, a barrier not recognized in Native American cultures.

Subsequent drafts of proposed regulations on this matter have been produced
since 1995. The most recent draft regulation on the disposition of culturally unaffiliated human remains has, as did its predecessors, several key points: (1) human
remains must be treated with the utmost respect, no matter their status; (2) disposition should ultimately be a tribal decision; and (3) different reasonable solutions for
disposition exist because of different circumstances (NPS 2007:58583–4).

In accord with legislative intent, the Review Committee has recommended that
culturally unidentifiable human remains be subject to tribal disposition in accordance with the area where those human remains were found, or were later located,
and that reinterment of Native American human remains should occur in accord
with state or other law should no tribal group wish to accept control over them (NPS
2007:58589). The SAA repudiates these fundamental points in promoting its agenda that this is an illegal broadening of NAGPRA's intentions (EurekaAlert 2007).
They also appear to want to deny any agency or museum the right to repatriate these
remains and objects even if they wish to do so, despite the fact that this is a specific right provided to them in the law (P.L. 101-601 Section 11(1)(A)). The SAA's
position is fundamentally mirrored by the AAPA (AAPA n.d.; SAA 2004).

It is not clear when, or if, this regulation will be finally issued, or what challenges it will face. It is not clear whether proposed legislative changes to NAGPRA

will clarify the original intent of Congress, or what challenges that clarification will then face. What is clear is that opposition to the repatriation and/or disposition to Native Americans of Native American human remains, and specifically "culturally unidentifiable" human remains, represents thus far an irreconcilable difference between Native Americans and some academics and their organizations. It is also entirely possible that the outcome of this matter may well depend on the state of U.S. legal culture at the time, when and if this matter is adjudicated.

NAGPRA Redux

In 1987, Michael Ames, a noted Canadian anthropologist and museum director, asked an intriguing question, which he followed up with some salient thoughts:

> How are anthropologists and museums responding to the increasing efforts by Indian peoples to take charge of their own cultural identities? Indians are no longer willing to be treated as resource banks. ... They protest against the treatment of their heritage as a commodity. The notion that scholars carry with them everywhere the privilege of academic freedom that endows them with the right to study anyone anywhere "for the sake of science" is increasingly being challenged by others. ... As Indian intellectuals regain control over their own images and their own destinies, they will claim as well their right to provide the answers. It will be wise to listen carefully, even if we might not always agree, because the growing intellectual autonomy of Indigenous peoples will have considerable impact on how anthropologists and their museums in the future deal with the "the natives." ... The white man's interpretation of North American history will also be transformed. Europeans in North America, perhaps feeling the lack of an ancient history and a distinctive New World culture of their own, have been inclined to appropriate Indian history—"our native heritage" and "our native peoples," as they say in polite circles. (Ames 1987:15, 18)

Some archaeologists have voiced similar concerns. In an article aptly titled "The Past as Power," Bruce Trigger (1985) commented at length on the "acrimonious confrontations" that surrounded archaeological work on burial sites and that Indian claims for the sanctity of those sites were seen as unreasonable by archaeologists, as those claims encompassed all such sites, not just those associated with a group's recent past. He observed that:

> Indians who have rejected the work of most archaeologists as inimical to their own interests and aspirations have evaluated the history and current state of archaeology more accurately than archaeologists themselves have done, and ... their acceptance of the discipline requires many archaeologists to overcome their own continuing indifference and bad attitudes with respect to native peoples. (Trigger 1985:31–32)

In a similar vein, Deward Walker, Jr., has written about the open opposition of the SAA and the Smithsonian Institution to NAGPRA, and the "historic disinterest" of anthropologists in key Indian issues. He also expressed the hope that Native American challenges for change in the discipline would succeed, preventing the real possibility that anthropology will become an "irrelevant exercise conducted by academic pedants" (Walker 1994:43). These thoughtful expressions of concern force us to consider the nature of anthropological ethics and of the role of values in science.

Just 100 years ago, Native Americans had no rights as citizens and precious few civil rights and were firmly under the control of a colonial administration that was determined to change them in every respect. The government knew that it was right and that its actions were moral and good. Governmental policies and laws were deeply embedded in a legal culture that relegated Native Americans to third-class status, marked by poverty and a massive population loss. Indeed, many scholars of that period had pronounced that Native Americans would shortly be a "vanishing race," and this belief spurred efforts to research and collect Native American heritage and their bodies (see, for example, Kehoe 2006:570; Nason 1996:360).

This research was carried out by scholars who believed that it was their right and their duty to probe, dig, record, measure, and otherwise obtain all the information and make use of all of the collections that could be obtained from living and dead Native Americans. This was, of course, Science, and it was intended for the future benefit of coming generations of scholars, as well as the larger public who would be educated and entertained by the assembled exotica. Science was good; Science was Progress; and Science was right and moral. This was certainly the dominant view of Science within Euro-American society and had been for some time.

Historians of science have noted that science and scientific attitudes were deeply embedded in the cultural values of Euro-American societies and Western culture (see, for example, Deloria 1995; Pyenson and Sheets-Pyenson 1997; or Tuomey 1996). Yet, it is not always remembered by those who work as scientists that this cultural foundation is, in fact, value laden. In his comments on this, Abraham Maslow, a past president of the American Psychological Association, remarked: "The classical philosophy of science as morally neutral, value free, value neutral is not only wrong, but is extremely dangerous as well. It is not only amoral, it may be antimoral as well" (Maslow 1971:20). In a recent publication that dealt with a scientist's responsible conduct in research, the National Academy of Sciences spoke to the issue of values:

> Other kinds of values also come into play in science. Historians, sociologists, and other students of science have shown that social and personal beliefs—including philosophical, thematic, religious, cultural, political, and economic beliefs—can shape scientific judgment in fundamental ways. (National Academy of Sciences 1995)

This point is illustrated by Charles Lyell, whose views of geological change were influenced as much by his personal religious views as by his geological observations. Less benign historical examples can be seen in the "science" of anthropological phrenology in the 19th century and its applications, or the more dreadful later "science" of Nazi-inspired eugenics. These were accepted by some scientists at the time as valid because they fit with a set of values that were held by those individuals. Science is not, in other words, value free, and those values that most critically affect science are cultural ones. Groups of scientists sharing the same cultural perspective will tend to view science and its values in the same way. What does this tell us about the scientific values or research ethics associated with the large-scale collecting of ancient and modern Native American bodies, and the status of those bodies, until NAGPRA, as property?

Whatever personal qualms might have afflicted some, there were no professional ethics in anthropology 100 years ago, or in the museum field, and certainly no one thought there was anything improper about owning Native American bodies. Many anthropologists who researched and collected in Native American communities were deeply sympathetic to the plight of those they studied, and some of the data that were acquired, like some of the objects they were given in trust, were intended for safekeeping, or to help non–Native Americans better understand Native Americans. In other cases, this was absolutely not true and the relationship between scientist and community was hardly one of trust. Some keepers of sacred and patrimonial objects destroyed those objects rather than see them alienated to museums.

The lack of ethical standards in anthropological research changed markedly with the adoption in 1971 of the Principles of Professional Responsibility by the AAA (AAA 1971). In the very first lines of its first section, it states that:

In research, anthropologists' paramount responsibility is to those they study. When there is a conflict of interest, these individuals must come first. Anthropologists must do everything in their power to protect the physical, social, and psychological welfare and to honor the dignity and privacy of those studied.

This seems fairly clear, especially when reinforced by later admonitions to use every effort to cooperate with those being studied and to try to anticipate the consequences of research and publication on those being studied. Anthropologists were well aware of the antipathy that Native Americans felt toward the disinterment of the dead and what they viewed as the desecration of burial sites. In light of this opposition, we might have expected such research to have been stopped or to have been done only with the consent of the affected communities. Similarly, the continuing maintenance of many thousands of Native American human remains in government repositories and museums was rarely viewed with anything less than deep distress by Native Americans.

How, then, in light of those ethical statements within AAA, was the collection and ownership of Native American bodies seen as ethical? The answer is, I think, complex. First, it is worth pointing out that none of these ethical codes are enforceable, but rather are comments for guidance. Second, archaeologists had their own organization, and its ethical code expressed no such sentiments. Indeed, the SAA's current code of ethics, adopted in 1996, focuses on the archaeologist's role and duty in protecting the archaeological record and, in doing research, to "promote public understanding" for "the benefit of all people," while also urging members to consult in good faith with affected groups (SAA 1996:5, 17). And in this, as in the original opposition to many aspects of NAGPRA, the concern of anthropologists has also been to "ethically" uphold their rights as scientists to carry out research as they see fit, as this is also perceived to be an ethical duty to the profession, if not also to humankind. Other current archaeological ethical statements appear to take a very different approach to this matter. In the first code of ethics of the World Archaeological Congress, for example, members are urged:

3. to acknowledge the special importance of Indigenous ancestral human remains, and sites containing and/or associated with such remains, to Indigenous peoples; and
4. to acknowledge that the important relationship between Indigenous peoples and their cultural heritage exists irrespective of legal ownership. (World Archaeological Congress 2006)

Other rules say that:
2. members shall negotiate with and obtain the informed consent of representatives authorized by the Indigenous peoples whose cultural heritage is the subject of investigation; and
5. members shall not interfere with and/or remove human remains of Indigenous Peoples without the express consent of those concerned. (World Archaeological Congress 2006)

Using these standards, no Native American human remains would be excavated, much less removed to a repository or a museum, without the consent of the community—unless, of course, you choose to dispute who is or is not an Indigenous person (viz. Native American), which we have seen arise in the case of some ancient American remains. This once more brings us back to cultural values and cultural perspectives about the past and the present.[9]

NAGPRA was intended to resolve the fundamental civil and human rights issues surrounding the ownership of Native American human remains as property by government agencies and educational institutions. In passing this law, Congress heard, in its deliberations on various bills, a wide variety of perspectives on the issues involved from all sides. Facing what appeared to be virtually inevitable, groups like the AAM, the AAA, and the SAA presented statements that voiced varying degrees of support, although these were couched in careful terms and with limits on what repatriation should mean (see, e.g., AAM 1988). Similarly, representatives of some of these organizations have stated that, in this penultimate moment if not before, they and their organizations supported the law's passage and contributed to the final wording of various sections of the law (e.g., Kintigh 1994). Perhaps so, although the general momentum toward passage was as clear as the law's primary intent, despite the imperfect details of some of its wording. The devil lies in those details, as we have seen, as well as in the cultural perspectives, legal and otherwise, that are brought to bear in considering those details.

Native Americans are not opposed to archaeological work, despite whatever other calumnies are sometimes uttered. In their testimony to Congress in 1989, Native American witnesses stated that: "they did not object to the study of human remains when there is a specific purpose to the study and a definitive time period for the study. The Native American witnesses did object, however, to museums retaining human remains without a clear purpose ..." (U.S. Senate 1990:5). In fact, many tribes have their own professional archaeological operations, hire non-Indian archaeologists, and carry out their own professional archaeological work. But it is also true that tribes wish to play, as they did when they lobbied in support of NAGPRA, the final decisive role in decisions about "archaeological resources" that concern them first and foremost.

These decisions have been, are now, and always will be based on Native American perspectives about their place in the world, their connectedness to the remains of ancestors, the sacred nature of those remains, and the view that Native Americans have always been the Indigenous peoples of these lands. Even the government believed that "Native American" meant the people and cultures Indigenous to this land (P.L. 101-601, Sec. 2(9)). What, then, does Indigenous mean? What is the time limit on deciding whether someone born here "before the historical arrival of Europeans" is Indigenous, and thus Native American? Native Americans obviously believe that all of the ancient peoples of this land are Native American, and thus ancestors. Archaeologists and physical anthropologists do not believe this perspective is valid, because it cannot as yet be scientifically demonstrated to be so, despite the common-sense aspect of what it means to be Native American. And the consequences of this are that the question of ancient remains continues to be a property issue—who can legally own and control Native American bodies? Who can destroy Native American bodies in the name of Science? Are these not questions based on irreconcilable differences of cultural perspective? If the legal answer to these questions is that non–Native Americans can collect, own, and destroy Native American human remains, and do so summarily without consent from Native Americans, then we are really talking about a kind of slavery, the involuntary ownership of Native American bodies who are owned as property and entirely subject to the will of the owner. In 1989, at the beginning of the debates about NAGPRA, a seminal article by Vine Deloria, Jr., referred to this as "A Simple Question of Humanity," and began by asking: "Are American Indians human beings?" (Deloria 1989:1). As it turned out, this is still not an idle question if our ancestors' bodies can simply be "resources" for Science.

Native American human remains should not be kept as serfs in an anthropological scientific kingdom. Native Americans should do whatever they can legally to prevent this abuse of their fundamental human rights and U.S. civil rights from continuing. In the current legal culture in the United States, there seem to be only a few options that might capture the attention of anthropologists. Native Americans could, for example, consider a moratorium on any new archaeological or anthropological research of any kind on tribal lands or in tribal communities, except, of course, for their own projects staffed by their own personnel. Native Americans with the necessary resources could consider buying the land on which sites are located to prevent excavations except on their own terms. Native Americans could begin to step up the request rate for repatriation and demand more prompt action for those requests. Native Americans could demand that the federal government insist on prompt compliance to NAGPRA by those agencies that are still stonewalling, as well as demanding that fines be levied against those museums that have remained recalcitrant or silent about their NAGPRA obligations. And Native Americans could step up their own legislative and regulatory lobbying to ensure that their voice is heard and action taken. I personally hope that draconian and costly actions like these will not be required to resolve this issue, but the cultural gulf that separates Native Americans and many non-Indian scholars and their organizations in this matter seems, at least now, to be too great to bridge.

It is not possible to say when, or if, U.S. laws and legal culture will come to grips with the issue of owning Native American bodies, or whether anthropologists will ever reach an accord with Native Americans. In voicing his hope that Native Americans and anthropologists will become collaborators in a common endeavor, Deward Walker said that anthropologists would have to shake off their conviction "that Native Americans are not so important for what they *are* as for what they *were*" (Walker 1994:43; emphasis added). Nor is it obvious that American legal culture will come to recognize that Native American cultural values about the past and about their dead should have an equally valid place alongside Euro-American cultural and scientific values. However soon, or if, this may occur, it is not soon enough—it is time to recognize that Euro-American cultural values, especially those inextricably embedded in Western science, are just that, and are fundamentally different—but not better than—Native American culture and values. It is time to let all of our people go.

NOTES

1. This is not, at least in the usual sense, a formal academic chapter. Although there are some citations that are intended to clarify some points for readers, I have made no attempt to write at length and in great detail, much less exhaustively cite every historical fact, event, or process mentioned. Most, if not all, of these are too well known and too widely available in the standard literature to cause confusion or pose a mystery to those who wish to explore them further. This is, then, a perspective on the meaning of those facts and processes, what they represent in this human rights issue, and the history and contexts that have informed that perspective. Two other words of caution: At one time, archaeology was considered a part of anthropology. In some contexts, I refer to anthropologists in this more inclusive sense; in others, where it is relevant to do so, I specifically refer to archaeologists. In the same sense, I refer most often to Native Americans as the most inclusive term (i.e., including Native Hawaiians and Arctic peoples); in others I use the term Indian, or American Indian, as it may be more relevant there to do so.

2. The concept of legal culture can be explored in a number of publications, including Nelken (1997) or Nelken and Feest (2001).

3. Even the abolition of peonage in Mexico in 1915 actually did little to immediately alter the status of

the peons or their conditions of servitude for some years thereafter; in places like Brazil, predatory actions against the Indigenous population have continued to this day.

4. This decision on the American Indian Religious Freedom Act (AIRFA) (P.L. 95-341, 42 USC 1996), arose in *Lyng v. Northwest Indian Cemeteries Assn* (485 U.S. 439 [1988]). AIRFA's intent was to restate that it was the policy of the United States to protect and preserve Native American "access to sacred sites, use and possession of sacred objects, and the freedom to worship through ceremonials and traditional rites." Although AIRFA apparently created greater abuses against Native Americans by some federal agencies in some instances and was ultimately relegated to the judicial scrapheap, many of its essential elements were restated in Executive Order Number 13007, Indian Sacred Sites, issued by President Clinton in 1996.

5. In this context, it is important to remember that, before NAGPRA, most museums could not voluntarily repatriate human remains. This was because human remains were regarded as important collection elements (i.e., property), and as property might be considered assets that could not be alienated because of the legal standing of museums. This legal standing, a result of laws of incorporation or government status, forbade institutions as public trusts from giving away assets.

6. The AAA's statement read, in part:

> Individuals and communities have valid concerns ... about the treatment and disposition of human remains that may conflict with valid research and educational interests. A balance must be struck between [these] interests in each situation and the concerns of different cultures ... Human remains are to be treated with respect. Respect can include careful curation and a recognition that valuable anthropological, historical, and medical information can be obtained through analyses. (AAA n.d.)

7. These data are taken from nearly verbatim notes of the oral presentations presented on October 26, 1990, by Daniel Monroe and Walter Echo-Hawk at the annual meeting of the Western Museums Association in San Jose, California. Their report began with Echo-Hawk presenting a Native American historic overview of the issues, followed by Monroe's presentation of the assumptions behind AAM's opposition to repatriation and the AAM's negotiating goals. Echo-Hawk then discussed Native American goals and they both ended with a presentation of the basic provisions in NAGPRA.

8. There was a clause introduced that could delay repatriation should research be considered indispensable and when the outcome would be of major benefit to the United States, but this is unlikely to be a frequent occurrence and thus is largely a moot point.

9. Within the museum field, no code of ethics existed in this country prior to 1925, and the 1925 code effectively said nothing memorable about collecting (AAM 1925). After NAGPRA, the revised code of ethics for the AAM notes, aside from some standard museological considerations, that "the unique and special nature of human remains and funerary and sacred objects is recognized as the basis for all decisions concerning such collections," which leaves a vast realm for creative interpretation by any number of lights (AAM 2000).

References

American Anthropological Association (AAA). n.d. Statement of the American Anthropological Association Commission on the Treatment of Human Remains. Washington, DC: American Anthropological Association.

American Anthropological Association (AAA). 1971. Principles of Professional Responsibility. Available online at www.aaanet.org/stmts/ethstmnt.htm (accessed November 30, 2007).

American Association of Museums (AAM). 1925. *Code of Ethics for Museum Workers.* New York: AAM.

American Association of Museums (AAM). 1987. Statement submitted to the Senate Select Committee on Indian Affairs on S. 187 The Native American Cultural Preservation Act. February 20. Washington, DC: AAM.

American Association of Museums (AAM). 1988. *Policy on Repatriation of Native American*

Ceremonial Objects and Human Remains. March 1. Washington, DC: AAM.

American Association of Museums (AAM). 2000. *Code of Ethics for Museums 2000.* Washington, DC: AAM.

American Association of Physical Anthropologists (AAPA). n.d. AAPA Position Statement. Available online at www.physanth.org/positions/cuhr.htm (accessed March 16, 2006).

Ames, M. M. 1987. Free Indians from Their Ethnological Fate: The Emergence of the Indian Point of View in Exhibitions of Indians. *Muse* 5(1):114–119.

Bassett, C. A. 1986. The Culture Thieves. *Science* 86 7(6):22–29

Deloria, V., Jr. 1989. A Simple Question of Humanity: The Moral Dimensions of the Reburial Issue. *Native American Rights Fund Legal Review* 14(4):1–12.

Deloria, V., Jr. 1995. *Red Earth, White Lies, and the Myth of Scientific Fact.* New York: Scribner.

Echo-Hawk, R. 2002. *Keepers of Culture: Repatriating Cultural Items under the Native American Graves Protection and Repatriation Act.* Denver: Denver Art Museum.

Echo-Hawk, W. 1989. Sacred Material and the Law. In *The Concept of Sacred Materials and Their Place in the World*, edited by G. H. Capture, pp. 67–81. Cody, WY: Buffalo Bill Historical Center.

EurekaAlert 2007. Proposed federal rule threatens 2 decades of established law (3 December 2007). Available online at www.eurekalert.org/pub_releases/2007-12/bki-pfr120307.php (accessed December 5, 2007).

Friedman, J. L., ed. 1985. A History of the Archaeological Resources Protection Act: Laws and Regulations. *American Archaeology* 5(2):82–119.

Hill, R. 1980. Indians and Museums: A Plea for Cooperation. *Council of Museum Anthropology Newsletter* 2(7):42–43.

Hutt, S. 1992. Illegal Trafficking in Native American Human Remains and Cultural Items: A New Protection Tool. *Arizona State Law Journal* 24(1):135–150.

Jones, P. N., and D. C. Stapp. 2003. An Anthropological Perspective on Magistrate Jelderks' Kennewick Man Decision. *High Plains Applied Anthropologist* 23(1):1–16.

Kehoe, A. B. 2006. *North American Indians: A Comprehensive Account.* Englewood Cliffs, NJ: Prentice-Hall.

Kintigh, K. W. 1994. Reply to Randy McGuire and Deward Walker re NAGPRA. Available online at www.native-net.org/archive/nl/9312/0166.html (accessed February 8, 1994).

Malaro, M. C. 1998. *A Legal Primer on Managing Museum Collections.* Washington, DC: Smithsonian Institution Press.

Marks, J. 1998. Replaying the Race Card. *Anthropology Newsletter* 39(5):1, 4–5.

Maslow, A. 1971. *The Farther Reaches of Human Nature.* New York: Viking.

Mihesuah, D. A., ed. 2000. *Repatriation Reader: Who Owns American Indian Remains?* Lincoln: University of Nebraska Press.

Nason, J. D. 1973. Finders Keepers? *Museum News* 51(7):20–22.

Nason, J. D. 1996. Museums. In *Native America in the Twentieth Century*, edited by M. B. Davis, pp. 359–363. New York: Garland.

Nason, J. D. 1997. Beyond Repatriation: Issues of Cultural Policy and Practice for the 21st Century. In *Borrowed Power: Essays in Cultural Appropriation*, edited by B. Ziff and P. Rao, pp. 291–312. New Brunswick, NJ: Rutgers University Press.

National Academy of Sciences. 1995. *On Being a Scientist*, 2nd ed. Committee on Science, Engineering, and Public Policy, National Academy of Sciences, National Academy of Engineering, Institute of Medicine. Washington, DC: National Academy Press.

National Park Service (NPS). 1995. Draft Recommendations Regarding the Disposition of Culturally Unidentifiable Human Remains and Associated Funerary Objects. NAGPRA Review Committee, National Park Service, U.S. Department of the Interior (May 16, 1995), Washington, DC.

National Park Service (NPS). 1997a. Notice of Draft Principles of Agreement Regarding the Disposition of Culturally Unidentifiable Human Remains. National Park Service, U.S. Department of the Interior. Federal Register 64(1201):33502–33504. June 23, 1999.

National Park Service (NPS) 1997b. Recommendations Regarding the Disposition of Culturally Unidentifiable Native American Human Remains. National Park Service, U.S. Department of the Interior. Federal Register 65(111):36462–36464. June 8, 2000

National Park Service (NPS). 1998. Native American Graves Protection and Repatriation

Review Committee Meeting Minutes, Fifteenth Meeting, June 25–27, 1998, Portland, Oregon. Available online at www.nps.gov/history/nagpra/REVIEW/meetings/ RCMIN015.htm (accessed November 28, 2007).

National Park Service (NPS). 2007. Native American Graves Protection and Repatriation Act Regulations—Disposition of Culturally Unidentifiable Human Remains. *Federal Register* 72(199):58583.

Nelken, D., ed. 1997. *Comparing Legal Cultures*. Hants, UK: Dartmouth Publishers.

Nelken, D., and J. Freest, eds. 2001. *Adapting Legal Cultures*. Oxford: Hart Publishing.

North American Indian Museums Association (NAIMA). 1981. Suggested Guidelines for Museums in Dealing with Requests for Return of Native American Materials. In Directory of North American Indian Museums and Cultural Centers. Simon Brascoupe, ed., pp. 38-39. Niagara Falls, NY: NAIMA.

Powell, J. F., and J. A. Rose. 1999. Report on the Osteological Assessment of the "Kennewick Man" Skeleton (CENWW.97.Kennewick). U.S. Department of the Interior, National Park Service Archeology Program. Available online at www.cr.nps.gov/archeology/kennewick/powell_rose.htm (accessed November 28, 2007).

Powell, J. F., and A. Stone. 1999. Kennewick Man on Trial: Physical Anthropology. Lecture at the University of Washington, October 23, 1999, on Kennewick Man, hosted by the Burke Museum. Videorecording.

Pyenson, L., and S. Sheets-Pyenson. 1997. *The Norton History of Science in Society*. New York: Norton.

Rose, M. 2000. Spirit Cave and Kennewick. *Archaeology On Line*. Available online at www.archaeology.org/online/news/kennewick5.html (accessed March 10, 2006).

Society for American Archaeology (SAA). 1996. SAA Principles of Archaeological Ethics. *SAA Bulletin* 14(3):5, 17.

Society for American Archaeology (SAA). 2004. Critical Issues: NAGPRA. Available online at www.saa.org.repatriation/lobby/legalReview.html (accessed March 16, 2006).

Trigger, B. 1985. The Past as Power: Anthropology and the North American Indian. In *Who Owns the Past?*, edited by I. McBryde, pp. 11–40. Melbourne, Australia: Oxford University Press.

Tuomey, C. 1996. *Conjuring Science: Scientific Symbols and Cultural Meanings in American Life*. New Brunswick, NJ: Rutgers University Press.

U.S. Senate. 1990. U.S. Senate Report 101-473, September 26, 1990, Providing for the Protection of Native American Graves and the Repatriation of Native American Remains and Cultural Patrimony. Washington, DC. Available online at www.cr.nps.gov/nagpra/MANDATES/US_Senate_Rpt_9-26-90.htm (accessed March 16, 2006).

Walker, D. E., Jr. 1994. Anthropologists and Native Americans. In *Native America in the Twentieth Century*, edited by M. B. Davis, pp. 41–44. New York: Garland.

World Archaeological Congress. 2006. *First Code of Ethics*. Available online at www.wac.uct.ac/za/archive/content/ethics.html (accessed March 22, 2006).

Chapter 15
Colonizing America: Paleoamericans in the New World
Michelle D. Hamilton

The protracted legal saga and subsequent 2004 court decision to permit analysis of the Kennewick skeleton has ongoing implications that highlight the continuing conflict between tribal peoples and anthropologists. For the scientific community, Kennewick Man represented the opportunity to analyze one of the oldest skeletons found on the North American continent. For American Indians, the battle symbolized a test of their legal right to control their own cultural and biological patrimony, including their ancestral dead. This disparity in perspective reveals why future access to ancient American skeletons will likely continue to be determined by federal courts, and not by cooperative agreements between tribal peoples and anthropologists.

The Paleoamerican Paradigm

Some specialists are now considering the possibility that different colonizing groups from Asia and possibly Europe are required to account for the biological, cultural, and linguistic diversity found [in the New World]. Many specialists believe that the future of First Americans research must focus on exploring the validity of this new paradigm. (Robson Bonnichsen, quoted on PBS website 2000)

Kennewick Man and other ancient remains are of importance to the scientific community because they lend insight toward understanding the earliest peopling of the Americas. Based on the physical appearance of Kennewick Man and other ancient American skeletal remains, some biological anthropologists have proposed a new scenario for the migration of humans into North America that removes American Indians as the New World's first inhabitants and replaces them with an older, unspecified population (e.g., Jantz and Owsley 2001; Owsley and Jantz 2001). They argue that the earliest humans on the North American continent share no biological continuity with modern American Indians and demonstrate phenotypic traits more similar to non-specific European, Indo-European, or Eurasian groups. Based on cranial measurements of approximately thirteen ancient American human remains dated older than 7,000 years (including Kennewick, Spirit Cave, Browns Valley, Pelican Rapids, Lime Creek, and Wizards Beach), proponents of this new theory argue that the earliest humans to inhabit the continent were not ancestral to American Indians and that there is no direct ancestor-descendant relationship (see Jantz and Owsley 2001). Because this theory is imprecisely defined in both the academic and public arenas, in this chapter it will hereafter be referred to it as the "Paleoamerican Paradigm."

The initial designation of Kennewick Man as "Caucasian" and the speculation regarding his possible European origin has had unfortunate consequences. The anthropologist who first examined the remains initially believed the skeleton was of an historic individual, based on the "presence of Caucasoid traits, [and] lack of definitive Native-American characteristics" (Chatters 1997:9). This pronouncement, combined with a subsequent facial reconstruction that looked uncannily like *Star Trek*'s Patrick Stewart, immediately caught the imagination of the public, where the message ultimately received was that "Whites" were the first people to settle the Americas. Although anthropologists did not specifically claim that Kennewick Man was Caucasian, his ancestry is posited as something other than American Indian, usually in the direction of a putative European population. A sampling of speculation on the origins of the first Americans shows the avoidance of the term "Caucasian," but still arguing for a non–American Indian origin:

> It is absurd to argue about whether ... Kennewick Man is Caucasian. The answer to that question is not informative. But if we can ascertain that Kennewick is more similar to contemporary European populations than to any others, that tells us something. (Richard Jantz, quoted in Owsley and Jantz 2001:570)

> Initial studies have shown that the craniometric pattern departs from contemporary American Indians, often in the direction of European[s]. (Jantz and Owsley 2001:146)

> The scientists have never said, "Kennewick Man is not Native American." He could be. Or he might not be. (Douglas Owsley, quoted on PBS website 2000)

> [I]n terms of its closest classification, [Spirit Cave] does have a "European" or "Archaic Caucasoid" look. (Preston 1997:75)

Other anthropologists offered contrasting viewpoints on the practice or implication of characterizing Kennewick Man as European or Caucasian:

> I really do object to saying there is such a thing as a Caucasoid trait. ... You can find changes in cranial size just within certain groups that lived in the same area. [In using the term Caucasoid to describe Kennewick Man] the hands of the anthropological clock had just been put back 100 years. Kennewick Man has become a textbook example of why race science is bad science. (Alan R. Goodman, quoted in Thomas 2000:115)

> The use of the term Caucasoid really is a red flag, suggesting that whites were here earlier and Indians were here later, and there's absolutely no reason to think that. (Donald K. Grayson, quoted in Thomas 2000:117)

> I don't think this will change our view of Native American ancestry. The fact

that Kennewick Man doesn't look to some like a Native American ... doesn't mean anything" (David J. Meltzer, quoted on the Burke Museum website 2008).

This transformation in thinking about the origins of founding American populations is apparent in recent academic literature, where the term "Paleoindian" is rapidly being replaced by "Paleoamerican." Although the term "Paleoamerican" is not new, having been used interchangeably with Paleoindian since the 1960s (i.e., Bryan 1965), what *is* new is the assertion that Paleoamerican now excludes American Indians (i.e., Bonnichsen and Turnmire 1999; Lepper and Bonnichsen 2004). As Owsley and Jantz (2001:567) state: "[Early skulls] especially fall outside the range of American Indian populations and are so different that it may be more correct to refer to them as Paleoamerican rather than Paleoindian as many do."

Taken in a broader historical context, this new "geographical" naming shift has legal, cultural, and social consequences, as highlighted by Watkins (2004:61):

> The change in terminology may have no impact on the study of early populations in North and South America, but the change certainly carries with it political implications since, by replacing "Indian" with "American," it illustrates the political aspects of naming. ... If the naming of a geographic feature carries with it such power, imagine the power of being able to name the culture that used that geography.

THE CRANIOMETRIC EVIDENCE

How did researchers arrive at the conclusion that Kennewick Man and other ancient American remains are not representative of ancestral American Indian populations? A series of cranial measurements were taken on the skulls and then statistical analyses performed to compare those measurements against those of eight historic American Indian groups (as well as twenty-six non–American Indian groups worldwide). Similarities in shape were found with the modern European samples but not with the modern American Indian samples, while three of the ancient skulls "provide evidence for the presence of an early population that bears no similarity to the morphometric pattern of recent American Indians" (Jantz and Owsley 2001:146). Researchers are in essence arguing that comparing the measurements of the ancient and modern skulls shows that the ancient skulls more closely resemble modern Europeans, inferring that the first people to arrive in the Americas were not related to American Indians but to a different unspecified population.

However, critics argue that what is reflected in the ancient American skeletal record is not indicative of colonization of the Americas by early European ancestors, but by the ancestors of American Indian populations who no longer resemble their descendant populations due to influences of chronology, evolution, environment, and adaptation (Van Vark, Kuizeng, and Williams 2003). Some of the criticisms of the Paleoamerican Paradigm include the following five points.

1. Craniometric analyses are descriptive studies—there are no underlying models or theories to explain what is being observed. So, although such analyses are able to describe the ancient skulls as different from those of modern American Indians, they cannot provide an explanatory mechanism to articulate why this is so. Without an underlying causal framework, the Paleoamerican Paradigm is not open to hypothesis testing or falsification. Because the model has no explanatory power, it is difficult to refute the following observation: "Even if the early people don't look like modern Indians, it's possible they are ancestral to today's Native Americans" (Joseph Powell, quoted in Wilford 1999:4).

2. A related critique is the utilization of craniometric methodology to make inferences about ancient and modern American populations. By the 18th century in America, craniometrics were used almost exclusively to promote a view of European superiority, especially as compared to American Indians. This soon paved the way for political legislation, such as enforced removal, and social agendas, such as Manifest Destiny, to play a large part in the destruction of formerly intact American Indian cultures. This is not to deny that craniometric and morphometric techniques are not capable of providing descriptive information, but their use as a typological seriating device to categorize human populations may carry underlying racial overtones. In 1935, Aleš Hrdlička warned anthropologists against an overreliance on cranial shapes to make inferences about the past:

> One of the greatest faults and impediments of anthropology has always been and is largely to this day, in spite of ever-growing evidence to the contrary, the notion of the permanence of skull types, and their changeability only through racial mixtures and replacements. It is time that this attitude be replaced by more modern and rational views on the subject, based on the steadily increasing knowledge of biological laws and processes. ... (Hrdlička, quoted in Powell 2005:214)

3. A significant but unknown component not satisfactorily addressed by the Paleoamerican Paradigm is the point at which American Indian cranial morphology over the last 10,000 or so years assumed its modern form, and what evolutionary processes and environmental constraints (at both the macro and micro levels) work to shape the human cranium over time. Researchers promoting the Paleoamerican Paradigm state that "when comparing early skulls with available modern populations, we note that most of them fall outside the normal range of recent population variation" (Owsley and Jantz 2001:566). This point is important because it is at the crux of the debate—comparing the shape of ancient human skulls to modern humans may be akin to comparing apples to oranges. Anthropologist David Hurst Thomas summarizes it this way:

> In North American Indian populations (and, indeed, human populations worldwide), there has been a distinct tendency for skulls to become

more globular ("rounder") and less robust over the last 10,000 years. This being so, no experienced physical anthropologist should be surprised that the Kennewick skull has a longer, more robust face than recent Native Americans. (Thomas 2000:116)

4. Another consideration not explained by the Paleoamerican Paradigm is the influence that pressures such as genetic drift, demographic growth, and sexual selection had on the cranial and skeletal morphology of the earliest Americans and to what degree these evolutionary forces changed the physical appearance of ancient Americans. Anthropologist Joseph Powell argues:

> There is a huge amount of variation among the first Americans. ... Much of that is genetic, and it comes from the fact, I think, that these first Americans had very small colonizing populations, and they have a great degree of genetic variation due to genetic drift. (Joseph Powell, quoted on *National Geographic* News website 2005)

If left unaddressed, one of the underlying tenets of the Paleoamerican Paradigm must become that American Indians are an evolutionarily static group whose biology is fixed throughout time, and not subject to the same evolutionary processes as all other human groups.

5. Craniometric analysis by other researchers indicates that ancient New World remains have an overall skeletal morphology and pattern most similar to modern Southeast Asians and not Europeans (Neves and Hubbe 2005; Powell and Neves 1999). Even definitive Paleoindians (those known to be ancestral to certain American Indian groups) are unlike modern American Indian and European samples and show little or no evidence of a European component in craniofacial variation (Powell 2005).

KENNEWICK MAN IN THE PUBLIC ARENA

The confusion over the racial attribution of the earliest Americans persists. The simplified message promulgated to the mainstream press—that Europeans were the first people on this continent—prompted public headlines in publications such as the *Washington Post* to proclaim: "Skeletons Suggest Caucasoid Early Americans" (Rensberger 1997), and the popular science magazine *Discover* to announce on its cover: "Europeans Invade America: 20,000 B.C." (Wright 1999). This theory has also found a very accepting audience among a segment of the population more than ready to embrace the underlying racial implications. Numerous white supremacist and nationalist groups point to research on Kennewick Man, Buhl Woman, Spirit Cave Man, Wizard's Beach, and others as proof of the inherent superiority and primacy of the white race (Figure 15.1). Many of their positions on the ancestry of Kennewick Man are similar to those promulgated in the mainstream press:

The reasons for the American Indian sensitivity over the issue are obvious—proof that Whites—even if only in small numbers—walked the continent of North America before the Amerinds themselves would undermine the latter's claim to be the original "Native Americans." For the sake of political correctness, much valuable scientific data is being suppressed. (A. Kemp, on March of the Titans website 2006)

[Kennewick Man's] skull isn't an Indian skull at all, but is the kind of skull that white people have. ... Suddenly, the Indians who have been claiming a

The Spirit Cave Mummy, Nevada, USA :
Physical Evidence of Whites in North America, 7000 BC.

Alongside: An artist's impression of the Spirit Cave Mummy at the time of its discovery. Discovered in 1940, but only analyzed racially in 1994, this 9,000 year old mummy was discovered in a cave in the modern day state of Nevada, USA. The skeletal structure is clearly that of a White male - putting Whites on that continent either prior to, or simultaneous with, the originally Mongoloid Amerind population.

Below: A reconstruction of the face of the Spirit Cave Mummy, based on a cast of the skull, showing the various stages used in the reconstruction process (As published in Newsweek, US edition, 26 April 1999). The Spirit Cave Mummy was the first - but not the last - ancient White remains found in America and has forced a rethink on exactly who are "Native Americans".

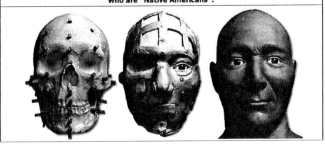

KENNEWICK MAN - WHITE RACIAL TYPE

Above The skull of a 9,000 year old White racial type discovered in North America: Kennewick Man, found in the Kennewick River in Washington State, USA. Artifacts found in the surrounding area suggests he was part of a larger community. Right: A reconstruction of the face of Kennewick Man, based on the skull. The features are clearly not American Indian and show clear White characteristics.

Above: The skull of Wizards Beach Man: one of the White skeletons to have been discovered on the North American continent, all dating from before 7000 BC.

Figure 15.1: Webpage images discussing the Spirit Cave Mummy, Kennewick Man, and others as reflecting "clear White characteristics" (March of the Titans website 2006).

moral high ground because "they were here first," have a rival. (H. Millard, on New Nation News website 2000)

The question of the peopling of the Americas is acknowledged as a complex issue, but anthropologists must ensure that the meaning they convey is not simplistically reduced to "Europeans arrived in the Americas first," because in the eyes of the lay public and mainstream press this is the message received and currently accepted as fact. With this brief sketch of some of the complexities inherent in the conflict over the study of ancient American skeletal remains, I now turn to the perspectives of a tribal community to elucidate their positions on Kennewick Man, their ancestral dead, and their continuing conflict with anthropologists.

AMERICAN INDIAN PERSPECTIVES

In partial response to the Paleoamerican Paradigm, and in an effort to avoid triggering another battle over ancient skeletons that may be discovered in the future, some tribal authorities have turned to legal remedies to avoid a repeat of the Kennewick Man outcome. Since 1990, federal cultural resource laws have changed the academic and scientific landscape of American bioarchaeology, and American Indian tribes are finding that a number of these laws are of great utility in their efforts to protect tribal resources, especially human remains. Two of the most powerful tools in their arsenal are the Native American Graves Protection and Repatriation Act (NAGPRA) and Section 106 of the National Historic Preservation Act. The ratification of NAGPRA was a defining (and restricting) event for the discipline of bioarchaeology, and the increasingly successful utilization of Section 106 by federally recognized sovereign tribes is resulting in further legal limitations on the collection of data from both American Indian skeletal remains and mortuary site settings.

I will examine the implications of the Kennewick Man court case for the relationship between anthropologists and American Indians by focusing on an example from the Eastern Band of Cherokee Indians, a federally recognized sovereign tribe based in North Carolina with an active Tribal Historic Preservation Office. As the former Section 106 Officer for the Eastern Band of Cherokee Indians, I have been able to learn first-hand about the tribe's perspectives in dealing with anthropologists, repatriation issues, and the Kennewick Man court judgment.

Like most North American Indian tribes, the Eastern Band of Cherokee Indians have a strong cultural ethos regarding mortuary behavior, with traditionally defined and clearly elucidated restrictions about the treatment of the dead. Cherokees oppose anthropological studies on American Indian skeletons; this opposition stems from a complicated avoidance proscription based on cultural theories of pollution and corruption as well as a deep conviction that it is degenerate activity to disturb the dead. These principles make up the Cherokee philosophy regarding mortuary treatment and, in turn, influence their attitudes toward anthropological research. The Cherokee perception of corpses and their potential to influence the living are not necessarily representative of other tribal people's views, but a generalized American Indian sentiment can be distilled from the core of their belief—that the ancestral dead are not to be disturbed.

THE EASTERN BAND'S RESPONSE TO THE KENNEWICK JUDGMENT

NAGPRA was intended as legislation that would provide American Indians with a legal mechanism to claim and repatriate affiliated tribal remains. As an article of cultural legislation that deals with Native American dead, NAGPRA has been employed for the benefit of tribal interests all across North America. But, as in the Kennewick Man case, tribes are finding that NAGPRA is not a perfect law, and in Cherokee experience, not without serious flaws.

Russell Townsend, the tribal historic preservation officer for the Eastern Band of Cherokee Indians, identifies the main failing of NAGPRA from a tribal viewpoint. This involves the contested process of ascertaining cultural affiliation, which proved to be the linchpin in the Kennewick Man court case that ultimately permitted scientists to study the remains and denied the tribes the right to rebury them:

> If a tribe cannot prove cultural affiliation, then the repatriation request cannot be successfully made. ... In the list of NAGPRA guidelines there are no directions on how to discern cultural affiliation beyond broad categories such as direct lineal descent or geographic region. In this sense, establishing direct lineal descent beyond a time when birth certificates become commonplace is difficult. ... Scientists define cultural affiliation based on ceramic traditions, settlement patterns, mortuary patterns, craniometrics, material culture, and landscapes. Each of these areas becomes more tenuous as one moves back in time. Tribes utilize language, landscape, parentage, behavioral culture, and specialized material culture to establish cultural affiliation. Again, these criteria are best suited to examination of only the recent past. (Townsend, personal communication 2005)

The Kennewick Man court proceedings were closely monitored by the Eastern Band of Cherokee Indians. The results further spurred the tribe to protect its dead by avoiding triggering NAGPRA entirely during the course of federal undertakings, via prearranged Memoranda of Agreement and Memoranda of Understanding initiated under Section 106 consultations that addressed the treatment of human remains prior to their possible discovery. The Tribal Historic Preservation Office of the Eastern Band of Cherokee Indians has used this technique to great effect, forming cooperative agreements with multiple federal, state, and local agencies, as well as with other tribes to ensure that, in the case of inadvertent human remains discoveries, NAGPRA is *never* activated, circumventing scientific study and research entirely. Avoidance or reburial occurs without ever determining cultural affiliation beyond "American Indian." This model is increasingly being utilized by other sovereign tribes as well, working in cooperation with each other to present federal agencies with a unified front when dealing with issues of avoidance, repatriation, and reburial.

THE FUTURE OF PALEOAMERICAN STUDIES

The recent debate over the remains of Kennewick Man ... has done little to foster a reconciliatory relationship, rather it has probably done more to polarize the issues. (Society for American Archaeology, on Burke Museum website 2008)

In the wake of the Kennewick Man court ruling, scientists have now completed their studies on the skeletal remains, hopeful that the data gathered will illuminate what is known about the earliest human migrations to the North American continent. Tribal people have begun to reassess the utility of NAGPRA and are now turning to alternative legal measures to restrict scientific access to skeletal remains. These new shifts in tribal practices are a challenge to the discipline of anthropology, increasing by orders of magnitude as more federally recognized tribes and tribal historic preservation offices exercise growing control over their cultural, historical, and biological landscapes.

In 2007, tribal groups, enraged by the Kennewick Man outcome and continued appropriation and retention of their dead, were instrumental in introducing an amendment to NAGPRA that alters the current definition of Native American from "of or relating to, a tribe, people, or culture that is indigenous to the United States" to an all-encompassing "of or relating to, a tribe, people, or culture that is or was indigenous to the United States." If this bill passes, it will effectively render all human remains dated before 1492 as Native American, leading to further decreases in opportunities to study any ancient American remains. It is ironic that in winning the Kennewick Man decision, anthropologists may ultimately end up with a pyrrhic victory. Now on notice, tribes will avoid activating NAGPRA by ensuring a priori nondisturbance of human remains under Section 106 and mounting legal challenges and amendments to NAGPRA. It is likely that anthropologists may not be cognizant of the subtle shaping of their own discipline by these new tribal imperatives, all in direct response to the outcome of the Kennewick Man case.

REFERENCES

Burke Museum website. 2008. Kennewick Man on Trial. Available online at http://www.washington.edu/burkemuseum/kman/anthropologists.php (accessed April 21, 2008).

Bonnichsen, R., and K. L. Turnmire. 1999. *Ice Age People of North America*. Corvallis: Oregon State University Press.

Bryan, A. L. 1965. *Paleo-American Prehistory*. Pocatello: Idaho State University Press.

Chatters, J. C. 1997. Encounter with an Ancestor. *Newsletter of the American Anthropological Association* 38(1):9–10.

Jantz, R. L., and D. W. Owsley. 2001. Variation among Early North American Crania. *American Journal of Physical Anthropology* 114(2):146–155.

Lepper, B. T. and R. Bonnichsen. 2004. *New Perspectives on the First Americans*. College Station, TX: Center for the Study of the First Americans.

March of the Titans website. 2006. A History of the White Race. Available online at http://www.white-history.com (accessed April 21, 2008).

National Geographic News website. 2005. Americas Settled by Two Groups of Early Humans, Study Says. Available online at http://news.nationalgeographic.com/news/2005/12/1212_051212_humans_americas_2.html (accessed April 21, 2008).

Neves, W. A., and M. Hubbe. 2005. Cranial Morphology of Early Americans from Lagoa Santa, Brazil: Implications for the Settlement of the New World. *Proceedings of the National Academy of Sciences* 102(51):18309–18314.

New Nation News website. 2000. Starlog: Remains of Captain Beamed down to the Planet of the Apes 9,000 Years Ago Found: Bury Him Fast before Anyone Catches on. Available online at http://www.newnation.org/NNN-kennewick-man.html (accessed April 21, 2008).

Owsley, D. W., and R. L. Jantz. 2001. Archaeological Politics and Public Interest in Paleoamerican Studies: Lessons from Gordon Creek Woman and Kennewick Man. *American Antiquity* 66(4):565–575.

PBS website. 2000. NOVA's *Mystery of the First Americans*. Available online at http://www.pbs.org/wgbh/nova/first (accessed January 2007; site has since been retired by PBS).

Powell, J. F. 2005. *The First Americans: Race, Evolution, and the Origin of Native Americans*. Cambridge: Cambridge University Press.

Powell, J. F., and W. A. Neves. 1999. Craniofacial Morphology of the First Americans: Pattern and Process in the Peopling of the New World. *Yearbook of Physical Anthropology* 110(S29):153–188.

Preston, D. 1997. The Lost Man. *The New Yorker*, June 16, pp. 70–81.

Rensberger, B. 1997. Putting a New Face on Prehistory: Skeletons Suggest Caucasoid Early Americans. *The Washington Post*, April 15, p. A1.

Thomas, D. H. 2000. *Skull Wars: Kennewick Man, Archaeology, and the Battle for Native American Identity*. New York: Basic Books.

Van Vark, G. N., D. Kuizeng, and F. L. Williams. 2003. Kennewick and Luzia: Lessons from the European Upper Paleolithic. *American Journal of Physical Anthropology* 12(2):181–184.

Watkins, J. 2004. Becoming American or Becoming Indian: NAGPRA, Kennewick and Cultural Affiliation. *Journal of Social Archaeology* 4(1):60–80.

Wilford, J. N. 1999. Archaeology and Ancestry Clash over Skeleton. *The New York Times*, November 9, p. F4.

Wright, K. 1999. The First Americans. *Discover Magazine* 20(February):52–62.

CHAPTER 16
THE LAW IS AN ASS:
A PERSPECTIVE ON THE ANCIENT ONE
THOMAS F. KING

My perspective on the Ancient One is a rather distant one, because I live on the opposite side of the North American continent (in Maryland), and because I really don't have a dog in the fight over him. It's informed, though, by many years of practice trying to resolve disputes over more or less ancient people, places, and things under Section 106 of the National Historic Preservation Act—including quite a few involving American Indians and ancestors—and intense interaction over several years in the 1980s with a remarkable advocate for ancestors' rights—the late Jan Hammil, who ran an offshoot of the American Indian Movement called American Indians Against Desecration.

I've recounted elsewhere (King 2002:105–106) how Jan taught me that the reason for getting the ancestors back into the ground was not to respect the rights of their descendants, but to respect *the ancestors themselves*—whoever's ancestors they might be—and to allow them to continue their journey to the spirit world, wherever and whatever that might mean. This was a revelation to me, because like most archaeologists—and clearly like the authors of the Native American Graves Protection and Repatriation Act (NAGPRA)—I'd always thought about the matter in terms of property rights. You own the bones of the people to whom you can show a relationship, I reasoned, but you don't own anybody else's. Jan pointed out the fact—which should have been obvious to me, the descendant of Confederate warriors—that at least since the Civil War in the United States, nobody owns anybody else. The dead, she argued, own *themselves*, and are *themselves* entitled to respect. And it sure as hell wasn't respectful to interrupt their journey to the afterworld by digging them up and putting them in boxes on a laboratory shelf.

Now, I obviously could have been argumentative and said that preserving the ancestors' bones for scholarly research is perfectly respectful—science being a noble calling, after all, performed for the good of all humankind. But I had to admit that the ancestors probably would not agree. They, after all, surely got buried with the expectation that they'd stay buried and return to the soil. And I remembered trying to make a traditional community in Yap[1] understand that we really had to excavate ancestral remains to make way for a new airport—how utterly incomprehensible it had been to them that we could commit such an offense to the dignity of the dead.

Or I could have said that I don't believe that the ancestors, being dead, actually give a damn, and that my Judeo-Christian/secular morality trumped Jan's Indigenous morality because—well, because I had the power. But as a lifelong Liberal and proud of it, I wasn't inclined to say that.

In fact, as a practitioner of Section 106 review, which is all about consultation, negotiation, compromise, and recognizing differing values and priorities, I saw a lot of sense in what Jan said. The ancestors coalesced in my mind into a very important interest group that deserves a place at the table—at the head of the table, even— when we're negotiating about what to do with their remains. But not the *only* interest group; there are other legitimate interests, too—notably the interests of science and the future that it purports to represent. Because, yes, science must purport to represent the future—albeit, usually, only by implication—because if science isn't good for learning things that will inform the future, things that will be in some sense relevant to the future, then it's surely good for nothing at all.

This all brings me, finally, to my perspective on the Ancient One, or Kennewick Man, or whatever else you choose to call him—the ancestor[2] who washed out of the Columbia River bank back in 1996. I can best lay out my perspective in terms of what I think we living people should have done when he emerged from the ground—what would have been done in what I envision to be the best of all possible worlds.

In that world, that alternative universe, everyone would accept the invitation of the Judeo-Christian God in Isaiah 1:18, to "reason together." That means everyone—the Army Corps of Engineers, the tribes, the physical anthropologists, the neo-Vikings, or whoever was interested. They might start by asking themselves what the Ancient One himself would most likely prefer to be done with his remains; but it might be more efficient to take it as given that he wanted to stay in the ground and get on along the spirit trail, after all, that's where he'd been, and presumably what he'd been doing, before the river got into the act.[3] So the beginning assumption might be that, unless there was a really, really good reason to do otherwise, respect for the Ancient One's presumed wishes would require that he be put back in the ground, and the discussion could then turn to how, where, and when to put him there.

But, of course, in this case there *would* be—in the eyes of some of the consulting parties—good reason to do otherwise. The physical anthropologists would argue that he ought to be kept out of the ground for the sake of what science could learn from him. OK, the tribes might then ask, show us what you're talking about. What do you think can be learned from him, and frankly, why should we give a damn? What is it about your scientific research that makes it worth disrespecting this ancestor? And violating our cultural traditions, and in our belief putting yourselves and us at risk of spiritual injury? "Well ..." the scientists would say, and then they'd set out their rationale—what they thought they might be able to learn, or what future scholars might be able to learn—from the Ancient One's remains. The tribes might well say that the scientists were blowing smoke, and not from a sacred pipe. Others at the table might ask about compromise; is there some middle ground to be found? The discussions would continue.

In the end, there might be agreement about what to do, but it's likely that often someone would have to break an impasse—consider all the points made by the various parties and make a decision. Who would that be? Maybe the Corps of

Engineers, as the agency with responsibility for the land, but it would be better, I think, to have some independent, representative body do it. Something like the NAGPRA Review Committee, but making its decision not based on who has legal rights to the bones, but on *what they concluded best represented the broad interests of the public*—living, dead, and not yet born—and on the persuasiveness of the arguments put forth around the negotiating table. Whatever the decision, everyone—including the Ancient One—would have been given as fair a hearing as could be given.

That, I think, is what would happen in a better world, if we had a better law. But we don't have such a law. Instead, in NAGPRA, we have a law that forces the disputants to argue about who has rights in the dead—who owns the Ancient One. That seems to me to be about as disrespectful of the poor guy as anyone can possibly be, and it offends me as a policy wonk because I don't think it results in rational, balanced, public-interest decisions. In NAGPRA we have a deeply flawed law that guarantees needless conflict and irrational decisions and under which the conflict over the Ancient One and the way it's been "resolved" thus far were inevitable. I think we ought to have a better, wiser, more respectful way of deciding how to treat the remains of people like the Ancient One when they appear in our world.

NOTES

1. An island group in Micronesia, now one of four states comprising the Federated States of Micronesia.

2. Understanding that he may not have been anyone's biological ancestor; he may have died without offspring. But in Jan Hammil's broad definition of the term, he was certainly an ancestor, a predecessor, and exactly whose ancestor he was, if anyone's, is irrelevant—though not, of course, under NAGPRA.

3. Of course, one could also argue that eroding out of the riverbank was part of the journey to the spirit world, and therefore the bones should go back into the river.

REFERENCE

King, T. F. 2002. What's Really Wrong with NAGPRA. In *Thinking about Cultural Resource Management: Essays from the Edge,* edited by T. F. King, pp. 103–111. Walnut Creek, CA: AltaMira Press.

CHAPTER 17
MY MOTHER MARRIED A WHITE MAN
WALTER BIGBEE

The white men brought Manifest Destiny. With it came slaughter, disease, starvation, and theft of our land. The Civil War made the U.S. military unequaled in strength. Like an atom bomb, a fury was unleashed on the remnants of my people. Genocidal practices reduced the Bison and Comanche Nations to a small reservation in the Indian Territory. Defeated, a once proud and vibrant culture was displaced and reduced to homeless prisoners in their own country.

As famine raged in Ireland, an influx of refugees created a demand for what remained of Comanche land. By an act of Congress, our reservation was divided and each adult was allotted a 160-acre parcel. The remaining land was then opened for homesteading.

Comanche children were forced into boarding schools where policies of cultural genocide were brutally enforced. Young adults returned from school without the cultural knowledge to perpetuate their communities as they once were. My grandfather, like so many victims, converted to Christianity and alienated my mother from traditional culture.

Mom's generation were the first Indians permitted to attend public school. Their worldview was further broadened by the advent of television. Enticed into the "American dream," mom eloped with my white father when she was fifteen.

I was four in 1962 when Dad earned his doctorate and took us to live in Ethiopia. I now realize the profound influences of that experience. In those years, my fundamental worldview and social intuitions were established. Being ethnic people of color, we blended in well and got along with the Ethiopians. I often wondered why other Americans kept distant as aggressive observers.

In anticipation of the next hunt or fishing trip, I daydreamed of growing up to be like the nomadic Bushmen. I was drawn into neighboring farm villages by an intuitive bond. Other times, I wandered to the barns to ride horses and learn of the animals. We had to grow and prepare much of our food. We enjoyed being outside and devised toys and games. I am blessed to have experienced subsistence living and the wisdom of tribalism. They have given me a tangible sense of what it was to roam free on the prairie like my ancestors.

I never contemplated being Indian until the American school was to perform a Thanksgiving Day pageant. Being of color, I was selected to be one of the Indians who would feed then dance for the Pilgrims. This was a first glimpse into my tragic history and the repressions of my future.

Leaving Africa and being thrust into suburban America was a devastating culture shock. People were distinctly white or distinctly black and there wasn't any brown. Being Indian was an enigma to them as well as to me. Alienated, I longed for the familiar in Africa and found solace in hunting, fishing, riding, and camping.

The late 1960s brought the civil rights movement, hippy-ism, and "Indian Power!" With social revolution, the world began to sympathize with Indigenous suffering and Native Americas were granted self-determination. Many Native American people from across the country lived in the Washington, DC area. There were festivals, powwows, protest marches, social gatherings, and other cultural events. We had language classes, and I immersed myself in books and learned arts and crafts. With enlightenment came the awareness that my heritage was no longer a way of life; it was something we did on weekends, holidays, or otherwise as scheduled activities.

Delving into self-awakening, I hit another harsh reality. There are distinctions beyond tribal affiliation and blood quantum. Not raised in a Comanche community and devoid of Comanche mentors, I lack the stereotypical attributes needed to validate my heritage. Lacking ritual capacities, I often can be merely a passive observer. The stigma of "urban half-breed" has tormented my existence and, much like the product of the boarding school, I approached my heritage with apprehension and humiliation.

Nonetheless, I devote my life to filling this void by living in part as my ancestors did through subsistence activities and the self-taught construction of cultural objects. As a child who witnessed the impact of Euro American imperialism on the Third World and then grew up to find myself a victim of this as well, any joy I feel continues to be overshadowed by an inescapable sadness. My past has been ripped from my existence and I'm often denied the function of a shared identity. I suffer a "generational trauma": enduring and not wanting to be in one world, while having limited access to the other. I'm surrounded by constant repressive reminders of dominant societies' insatiable desire to remake other cultures into the likeness of themselves.

My parents, my photography career, and my personal quest have taken me to many Third World and Native American communities. Museums, archaeological sites, and culture centers are integral to this experience as they offer a plethora of otherwise lost information. Yet these venues are also dismal reminders.

Culture centers are remarkable in the way they offer opportunities to participate in the rich cultural diversity of the world. Invariably, they exhibit the commonality of a shared and tragic colonial history.

I realize that Native American publishing is an essential tool linking communities to displaced resources. Unfortunately, I have also encountered non-Native publishing, which, under the pretext of sensitivity, profits from a willingness to perpetuate stereotypes.

Museums with Indigenous staff tend to have a proactive recognition of the sacred relationship between cultures and their heritage. With this they are making great strides to involve Native People in designing and implementing projects that make Native American communities the primary beneficiaries of their collections.

I served six years with a group of Native American advisors for an archaeological research center where I encountered passive declarations of sensitivity, bolstered by token gestures of Native American involvement. Suggestions that living descendants must be the primary benefactors of their work were answered with diplomatic rebuttals. In one debate, the advisors were held powerless as the CEO claimed the research center could do whatever it wanted. Through many debates, I repeatedly presented reminders of our tragic past and the responsibility the center bears. Unable to refute this, some staff questioned whether archaeology was an appropriate venue to address these issues. During more intense debates, certain staff resorted to questioning my character and motives.

With rightful ownership being the major issue, archaeological practices continue to be a profane form of colonization, protected by colonial law that justifies the desecration of our ancestors and the pilfering of artifacts for the sole benefit of Western science and ideals. As such, archaeology is an incorrigible act of attrition.

In this struggle, Kennewick Man has become an important artifact to Western authorities in their efforts to prove the land bridge theory. Although this may be the result of well-intentioned scientists, this theory has also been misconstrued to dilute Indigenous creation beliefs in an attempt to exonerate Manifest Destiny. In actuality, Kennewick Man exposes a tragic irony in self-righteous Western ideals. The United States, having created Native American Graves Protection and Repatriation Act laws in an attempt to bring him justice, cannot negotiate his fate under these laws because it has annihilated his descendants and rendered his heritage extinct.

People of other ethnicities can live securely in a melting pot, knowing their culture is being nurtured and perpetuated in a mother country. It's very different for Native Americans, because there are no other lands to retreat to. This heightens our concern with safeguarding our culture for future generations. This is relatively uncomplicated if traditions and rituals are still intact; however, it becomes nearly impossible to accomplish when unique cultural resources have been stolen or destroyed. Fortunately, there is a multitude of material culture in museums, archaeological sites, and private collections. Yet, with limited or no access to these materials, communities are denied the mutual use of this material to create feelings of common ethnicity and notions of kinship. Thus, repatriation of these resources becomes a major dilemma for Native communities.

A respected traditional leader once told me that before Western colonization, Native Americans were not faced with its associated atrocities and, because our cultural progress has been profoundly disrupted, we have yet to gain the necessary rituals and ceremonies to forgive them their crimes.

CHAPTER 18
WHOSE FAMILY?
NEGOTIATING STEWARDSHIP OF THE
ANCESTORS
PEI-LIN YU

Like many of us, I first heard about Kennewick Man, or the Ancient One, from the popular press. The Columbia River seemed very far away. I was in graduate school, surfing a wave of new information and struggling to master new skills. One of these was conducting research (i.e., investigating a problem in a way that is understandable to others). An important research technique is applying knowledge from a separate, but relevant, frame of reference to a problem (Binford 1983, 2001). As it turns out, two of the most important lessons I've learned about Kennewick Man and the Native American Graves Protection and Repatriation Act (NAGPRA) process didn't come from graduate school, *Newsweek*, or even a training course (although they familiarized me with some issues). I learned most about NAGPRA by going to places where people have never heard of it.

In the Chinese countryside three years ago, my father and I walked up a green hill to a tiny museum. We'd come to visit the remains of "Lantian Man," an ancient being over 500,000 years old. A small, brilliantly painted ancestor shrine housed a smiling bronze bust of Lantian Man (or Woman), and slate tablets describing the significance of this venerable ancestor. Casts of his fossilized bones reposed in a glass case inside the museum; the real ones, kept in a vault in Beijing, tell us how long he lived, what he ate, and how athletic he was. Although Lantian Man is too old to trace to a lineal descendant or particular ethnic group, he belongs to all Chinese families, including mine. China is apparently eager to invite the rest of the world to see him. Lantian Man taught me the value of collective custody, honoring one's ancestors, and willingness to learn from them.

Years before and thousands of miles away on the plains of Venezuela (Yu 1997), I helped deliver a stillborn baby girl in a small shelter made of branches interwoven with grass. Had the baby survived, I would have been her "little mother," as I belonged to the family system of her village. Because I delivered the baby, it was my duty to bury her. Her mother, grandmother, and grand-aunt told me exactly how to prepare her body. I followed the burial instructions very carefully, and the family helped me by singing the proper songs. The Pumé women taught me the burden and honor of implementing procedures on the behalf of families.

As a federal archaeologist, I have worked with the Confederated Tribes of the Colville Reservation, the Spokane Tribe of Indians, and the National Park Service to implement NAGPRA for burials found on federal lands at Lake Roosevelt on the upper Columbia River. Now at California State University at Sacramento, I am responsible for conducting the NAGPRA process for thousands of Native American burials that hold silent vigil in the university's repository. Many Californian tribes are potential claimants, and we will be speaking with all of them. Although NAGPRA's procedures are laid out in the regulations, Kennewick Man shows us that the context of their application is not always clear.

The consultation process may lead down paths that are costly in time, money, and human emotions. As we walk these paths together, I am mindful of the lessons from that best frame of reference for NAGPRA: the outside world. I credit other people with the best of motives and try to hold myself to the highest standards of integrity, impartiality, and clarity. I document everything I do. And I remember to bring life experience, including my understanding of family, to the table.

REFERENCES

Binford, L. R. 1983. *In Pursuit of the Past*. New York: Thames and Hudson Press.
Binford, L. R. 2001. *Constructing Frames of Reference*. Berkeley: University of California Press.
Yu, P-L. 1997. *Hungry Lightning: Notes of a Woman Anthropologist in Venezuela*. Albuquerque: University of New Mexico Press.

CHAPTER 19
COMMENTS REGARDING
THE ANCIENT ONE

BARBARA FRIEDLANDER ARIPA

The creator gave us the land to take care of; as caretakers we are not fulfilling our inherent responsibilities or exercising our inherent rights. We can't "own" the land, it's here for all to use. Our people never had specific boundaries until the U.S. government set boundaries for us—and had we been asked to establish our tribal boundaries, we could not have done so due to intertribal marriage and kinship.

Several years ago, in 1996, as culture committee secretary, I was contacted about the "Ancient One" (human remains) being found along the Columbia River. The Colville Confederated Tribes (CCT) were informed of the possibility of a lawsuit regarding the possession or ownership of the remains for reburial purposes. Immediately, elders were contacted to journey from Nespelem to Kennewick to pray over the site of recovery.

Elders and members of the Palus and Nez Perce Longhouse journeyed to Kennewick, Washington, to the site of discovery. The Seven Drum people prayed for the Ancient One. My prayer was "to the creator to forgive this disturbance of our Elder One, prayers for the people who didn't know the wrong they were doing to our Elder, and to be able to return the Ancient One to his final resting place, and forgiveness for being moved again."

The specific site was near Kennewick, WA, in Columbia Park. There was a lot of controversy concerning the remains. Several tribes were claiming ownership. Eventually, five tribes came to a cooperative agreement to regain the remains for reburial. There were other groups of people, archaeologists, and various other organizations, who claimed the Ancient One was a descendant of non–American Indian people. There was much controversy over the remains. The tribes requested that the Burke Museum be caretakers of the remains. The tribes' coalition retained an outside attorney to assist our legal staff in representing them in federal court. CCT funds were dedicated to the trial. Eventually, the courts determined that the Ancient One was to be turned over to the archaeologists for additional testing. The tribes appealed the case and testing was temporarily on hold.

The last appeal failed, the court determined that the tribes do not have a claim and the archaeologists will be allowed to resume full blown testing, which will (undoubtedly) set a precedent as to the future of the Native American Graves

Protection and Repatriation Act (NAGPRA) findings for other old remains that may be in storage and will not be returned to tribes for reburial. This court decision is not right; when and how could a non-Indian have traveled to our country and ended up with one of our arrows stuck in him?

Since time immemorial, aboriginal Native American Indians' inherent spiritual ties to the land for food gathering (fishing, hunting, root gathering) have been perpetual. Tribes have ancient prayers handed down for each and every part of their life, dealing with all natural resources. Tribes have spiritual ties to the land, lakes, and rivers. There are prayers especially for the water—a prayer of Thanksgiving, for nourishing Mother Earth and all her inhabitants; prayers for the fish—a prayer for fishing, as the Salmon Chief and fishermen prayed for salmon for everyone; a prayer by the women for drying salmon; prayers for gathering roots and berries. There are prayers for every aspect of our lives.

The future of NAGPRA is endangered. It is a law to preserve and protect tribes' historic and ancient artifacts, human remains, and to return remains to tribes. Therefore, the court decision will affect the future of all tribes as to the return of artifacts and the reburial of other remains not yet delivered to tribes. The reburial processes of different tribes vary; the Colville tribes' prayer for these remains is spiritual, not only for the remains but also for the community and people involved. The withholding of other remains in repositories/facilities will affect the healing process of tribes when they have knowledge of burial sites that are disturbed and remains are not taken care of. The Colville Confederated Tribes' culture and traditions are that the dead are to return to Mother Earth for burial—to return to dust, to Mother Earth.

I had attended a meeting to support Joanna Leith, then culture committee chairperson in Kennewick, with the other tribes and Dr. McManamon. We were having lunch; several of the tribes were discussing a strategy to fight for the remains. Some stated they should have the remains as they were the aboriginal/treaty owners; others disagreed—they were the owners. On and on—finally, I remarked that the government was pulling the tribes apart; we must stand together as one, and speak with one voice, not several and against each other. We are Indian people and must stand as one body, not fight against one another.

Many years ago, I was told by my grandmother, Nellie Moses-Kamiakin, that this specific area was Palus territory. Kamiakin lived in the Palus; this was his aboriginal homeland. The Palus camped and fished in this area. Historians and archaeologists have discovered through research that the Palus are the aboriginal inhabitants. Today, members of the Palus are enrolled with all of the five tribes claiming affiliation with the Ancient One: the Confederated Tribes of the Colville Reservation, Nez Perce Tribe, Confederated Tribes of the Umatilla Indian Reservation, Yakama Nation, and Wanapum Band.

FUTURE OUTLOOK FOR THE ANCIENT ONE

Regardless of present circumstances, the remains need to be in the ground. Just as long as the Ancient One is reburied on Indian-owned land, which is our desire, it would be acceptable for prayers by the five coalition tribes. Tribally, Palus rights should be made known to the government and all tribes concerning the river use: fishing, camping, spiritually.

During the Hanford Project,[1] the Department of Energy was required to take responsibility for cultural resources under its jurisdiction. Prehistoric and anthropological statements were to be reviewed by the tribes; the Wanapum, Nez Perce, Yakama, and Umatilla were contacted regarding the "draft manuscript." The U.S. government claimed that the Palus and Wanapum refused to make a treaty and move to reservations; they continued to live in and use their aboriginal lands. The government and archaeologists maintain that the Palus tribe is extinct. Not so, there are many of us living.

Tats ka low wit, lem'limt

NOTE

1. The Hanford site, located near Richland, Washington, was used for atom bomb construction during World War II. It subsequently became a nuclear power generator and is now a waste clean-up site. The cultural resources assessment and management program for the development took place between 1987 and 1989.

CHAPTER 20
AN INTERVIEW WITH ADELINE FREDIN[1]

When we began to legislate for the recognition of Native American civil and human rights, it was something brand new to Native American people. Existing laws did not recognize that we were alive, except to say, "The ancient people are no longer here." The federal government acted as though Native American people were extinct. For years, the tribes felt like they could not do anything and thought maybe science is right. When Native American people began to recognize that science and law were wrong, many hard feelings began between Native American people and the scientific community.

Tribes throughout the nation felt like the U.S. government needed to recognize their civil, human, and inherent rights. This is why we began a national movement to have human remains recognized as central to Indigenous people. Tribes got together throughout the nation and informed the government and public we were not extinct, dead, or gone; our ancestors had a right to come home, not be in the Smithsonian Institution, and not be dissected by science. We had to unite and come together and understand that anything that affects one tribe affects all Indian nations. Eventually, we were successful in getting the Native American Graves Protection and Repatriation Act (NAGPRA) passed and recognition of our human and civil rights. We succeeded, but the Ancient One was mishandled and it was clear from the beginning that the Ancient One was more of an ambition of the scientists.

If tribes in Connecticut, New York, and Florida lose, so do the Colville. Whenever you affect one tribe's law or legal rights, you affect every tribal nation. This is how federal law works. The importance of this case goes beyond Native America. Indigenous people from Australia, South Africa, and South America contacted the Colville with phone calls and letters concerned that if the U.S. government is going to treat us as if we did not have any civil or human rights, then they, too, will be harmed. For Native Americans and Indigenous people throughout the world, it is important that the Colville win back the Ancient One. If the Colville lose the Ancient One, we lose for everybody else, big time.

Without consultation, science has no right to study Native American human remains. Had the scientists treated the tribes as if they have sovereign rights to make up their own legal agreements regarding scientific research, this would not have gone to court. The scientists asked themselves: "How can I be recognized? What can I get out of this?" They did not care if they affected the relationship between Indian country and science. Jim Chatters's ambition set a pattern. You can't blame him by himself, because that selfishness existed in the scientific community. You can't mix ambition and ignorance. That selfish ambition started with Chatters, caught the other scientists, and influenced the federal agencies. If they had sat down and consulted with the tribes it would have been different. We have always said that we could have come out with a win-win situation. Now we just have to start over again and make sure that we go back and clear up the mistaken decisions by the federal agencies.

The tribes have a right to understand their history. If it is through scientific research, so be it. The Colville Tribe was open to nondestructive scientific research of the Ancient One. Native American and scientific knowledge can work in a productive relationship, but it depends on the archaeological project and the tribal historic preservation officer. In the end, human rights trump scientific rights. Rather than giving the opportunity to science to decide humans' destiny, science needs to be watched.

The Jelderks court did not consider Native American peoples' historic records and stories important. It is unfortunate that, because the U.S. government came in here and used Indian place names, such as the "Okanagan," "Wenatchees," and "Wanapums" to describe the people rather than the normal description the Indian people had for their clans, such as the spider, frog, and lizard people, many Native Americans' abilities to identify who they are and who their ancestors were was destroyed and their true names disappeared. Nevertheless, some of that information did survive. And we can reach back to ancestral stories through pictographs and different natural and archaeological features.

Our tribal affiliation packets submitted to the court prove that we can trace our ancestry through stories and legends, back to people and places. We had information that Dr. Francis McManamon, chief archaeologist of the National Park Service, dumped our tribal packets. Had we known, we could have had the Department of Justice and Walter Echo-Hawk, Native American Rights Fund attorney, intervene. Jelderks did not see the tribal packets. We tried to get some of our contacts in Washington, DC, to physically take the tribal packets, but it was too late. Some of the attorneys and others involved knew that this judge had already made up his mind. He painted our knowledge as a bunch of hearsay, fantasy.

If the Ancient One is not Native American, then he must be somebody. How can they tell that he is not Indigenous? Is he carrying a driver's license? If he is Native American but not Indigenous, then who do they think they are? If the planned DNA tests prove that he is Native American and they say he is not Indigenous, then they have to prove it. But if the DNA comes back and does not tie the Ancient One to Native American people, then we do not care what they do with the Ancient One.

This issue must be settled here and now. We have a situation with which we must deal. The federal agency was wrong in doing what they did and the tribes have to go back to that federal agency and accuse them of violating federal law. They had no business allowing any individual to intervene that was not part of the agency or from the tribe. The law is very specific; it says you contact the tribe. We cannot wait for another opportunity—for the national interest and Indigenous people everywhere—the tribes need to get back in there and clean this one up.

Federal law states tribes and THPOs[2] have the power to repatriate our ancestors; that is the basis of our claim. Before THPOs, but in preparation for them, we established Section 106 of the National Historic Preservation Act, NAGPRA, and the American Indian Religious Freedom Act. We laid it all out ahead of time. We did not want the state to tell us how we should behave. We had a right to do it ourselves. We did everything we could, looking at state and federal laws, even redrafting some state law to let the tribes have the final say.

When we were drafting the laws, archaeologists would say, "This is what you do when you come on human remains." The tribes were like, "No, this is what you do when you come on human remains." And the archaeologists would rebut, "But, this is what the law says." The tribes replied, "We are going to change that law." If the Ancient One had been uncovered without us first laying everything out years ahead of time, the tribes would have no say.

The scientists' motivation is pure selfishness. They do not even care about their fellow scientists. The relationship between the tribes and the general ideas of cultural resources management has been damaged. Did they care? No.

Once there were some white archaeologists in Navajo country who had done everything by the book. Around the rim of a canyon were these little piles of rocks. The archaeologists thought they were ceremonial and religiously significant. The Indian people who were there watched the archaeologists. Later on, one of the older Indians went to the younger archaeologist and said, "Come here let me show you something." It was night, they went out there, and he said, "Turn that rock over." It was luminous. He said, "When it is dark and you can't see the edge, you turn the rocks over and you know where the edge is." The scientist would never have known; he would have walked over the edge. Archaeologists need to share their investigations with Native American people because sometimes it is not mysterious, it is simple common sense.

Colville tribal members first started doing archaeology at Chief Joseph Dam on the Columbia River in 1978. But when the excavations began, there were no Indian people working on the sites. We went to the colonel of the U.S. Army Corps of engineers (USACE) and said, "We have a lot of Indian people out of work and they know how to use a shovel." They hired forty-seven tribal members and they did a good job. We got a call later from Washington, DC. They wanted to know how the Colville people could work cooperatively with the USACE. We told them, "It is difficult to labor with the federal government, you can't expect it, or demand it. You gotta work at it." We were one of the first tribes to do so in the nation. We were then the first in Indian Country to have an archaeological ordinance, a tribal repository, and an archaeology department. We were a model for many tribes. We helped encourage Indian people to know that it is possible to learn something positive about themselves through archaeology. Though for the most part they resented it, archaeologists found out that working with Native Americans gave them another way of looking at archaeology.

Another way we can mobilize for the future is to professionally organize traditional cultural properties (TCP) information so that it can be integrated into professional research. In that way, traditional practices and customs can become part of the investigation. A TCP expert asks Native American people what an "archaeological" feature is and we get a different answer.

On Wells Dam, also on the Columbia River, professional archaeologists went along the shore and saw these rings of rocks that were neither hearths nor baking ovens. They did not know what they were. A tribal member, Sleepy Cleveland, was sitting up in his house on a bluff above the Columbia River and he saw the archaeologists walking in a row recording these little rock circles. He shared with his company that he was told that was where the young boys did their puberty ceremonies. And that gave a whole new meaning to what was happening at that period of time at that particular site and why it was important to Native American people. Integrate traditional, social, and behavioral information into your investigations. That will be easier once professional archeologists begin to share information with Indian people.

THPOs could help prevent a future Ancient One through contract archaeology. When I was a THPO, though it had never had been done before by a tribe, I knew we could get contracts for archaeology work along the Columbia River. When we started getting contracts we knew we could invest Native American information into the archaeological investigation and that is what we did.

Integrate all your information, all your knowledge—sovereignty, trust responsibilities, human rights, civil rights, and science. There are not that many people who know how to integrate all of it. Archaeologists are still looking through that one small window. Isn't it lonesome looking through that one little window? The scientists demand that the Ancient One only be handled scientifically. They don't want to broaden their view through their window; they just want to make it much stronger. When brighter, more sensitive, humane people get involved in archaeology, we will avert another Ancient One disaster. The younger generations as well as the grandparents need to look to the 7th generation. When I go toes up, I am going to be able to say, "I looked ahead to the 7th generation. I gave my life to protecting Native Americans rights, of being proud of who we are."

NOTES

1. Interviewed by Adam Fish, January 20, 2005.

2. THPOs are Tribal Historic Preservation Oficers.

CHAPTER 21
EXPLORING THE
KENNEWICK CONNECTION

C. LORING BRACE, NORIKO SEGUCHI, AND MARY L. BRACE

The discovery on July 28, 1996, of one of the oldest and best-preserved human skeletons in the Western Hemisphere set off what came close to being a decade-long stalemate between those who assumed it was an ancestor—the "Ancient One" as some claimants were calling it (Powell 2005)—and those who suspected that it was sufficiently different from its Native American claimants that it should not be turned over to them without a thorough test to find out its actual relationships.

When the photograph taken in 1996 by Dr. James C. Chatters, the first trained anthropologist to handle the Kennewick skeleton, was printed in a widely distributed public source (Egan 1996), those of us who have worked on most of the samples listed in Table 21.2 immediately felt that it had a striking similarity in form to that of the crania of the Ainu of northern Japan. This led a number of us to ask the U.S. Army Corps of Engineers (Corps) for the opportunity to test our suspicions in quantitative fashion. The Corps never answered or acknowledged our requests.

When another Chatters photograph of the Kennewick cranium was prominently displayed in the June 16, 1997 issue of *The New Yorker* magazine (Preston 1997), that feeling was reinforced. Here we reproduce that picture (Figure 21.1) and also show one of a recent Ainu cranium (Figure 21.2) to document the resemblance. The Kennewick specimen is nearly 10,000 years older and clearly more robust, but a comparable reduction in robustness while maintaining a similarity in form has occurred in all parts of the world where *in situ* continuity can be documented (Brace 2005; Brace and Tracer 1992). The Ainu, then, cannot have given rise to Kennewick, but there is no reason why the ancestors of the Ainu could not have been the ancestors of the Kennewick individual as well. It has long been realized that the ancestors of the Ainu were the prehistoric Jomon of the Japanese archipelago and the coast and islands to the north and northeast (Hudson 1999; Koganei 1903, 1927, 1937). The Early Jomon, then, could very well have represented the ancestors of Kennewick and possibly other early inhabitants of the Western Hemisphere as well.

The Kennewick find was made in the shallows of a body of water connected with the Columbia River near the town of Kennewick, close to the southern edge of the State of Washington, in the American Pacific Northwest (Chatters 1997). The

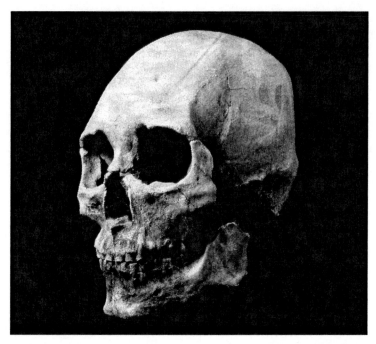

Figure 21.1: Kennewick, from Preston, 1997, with permission from Conde Nast.

actual site was on land under the control of the Army Corps of Engineers, and not very far from Richland, Washington, the site of the Hanford nuclear reactor that had played a role in the creation of the nuclear bombs dropped on Japan at the end of World War II. Radioactive material had been dumped locally adjacent to Native American property, and the U.S. Army was anxious to avoid drawing attention to the area. Because of this, they wanted to appease the local Native Americans, so they supported the latters' wish to gain possession of the Kennewick remains, which they wanted to bury unstudied in a secret place (Egan 1996). A group of eight scientists sued the U.S. government for access to the skeleton in order to carry out such a study and to find out to whom it was actually related. It was estimated that after four years, the defendants had spent $2 million in trying to quash the scientists' aspirations (Chatters 2001).

There was a bill framed by Congress in early April 1998 to forbid the burial of the Kennewick site, but it was not finalized before the two-week Easter recess. Before Congress could reconvene and pass it, the Corps used helicopters to dump more than a million-and-a-half pounds of gravel, boulders, logs, and dirt on the area where the skeleton had been found (Morell 1998). Finally, thousands of trees were planted in the newly constructed terrace (Miller 1999). To the complaint that the burial of the site was to prevent anyone from finding out anything more (Laswell 1999), the assistant attorney general, Environment and Natural Resources Division, Washington, replied that this had been done to ensure that the site would be available

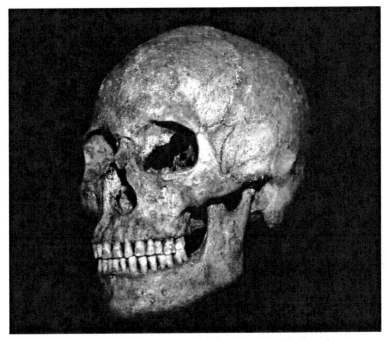

Figure 21.2: Ainu male, University of Tokyo, Museum of Anthropology.

for future study and not washed away by spring floods (Schiffer 1999). The site, however, was on the southern shore of Lake Wallula (Morell 1998). This lake was behind a dam, there is no current there and no danger from spring flooding (Morell 1998), and, because of the government-sponsored interment, no hope of a subsequent refinding of the site for systematic archaeological testing. All told, it has to count as a massive governmental cover-up (Miller 1999). After nearly a decade of their suit, the scientists were finally given access to the Kennewick skeleton at the Burke Museum in Seattle, Washington, late in February 2006. This is a preliminary report on the findings of one part of that group.

TESTS OF POPULATION AND INDIVIDUAL RELATIONSHIPS

The first thing we did to test the possible relationships between the population samples we wished to compare was to convert the battery of measurements made on the Kennewick specimen and the individual skeletal samples studied into Z-scores (Brace, Brace, and Leonard 1989). This meant that we were able to combine both male and female data without having to be concerned about the sex-related differences in sheer body size in the dimensions of the specimens measured (Brace and Hunt 1990). The measurements used are listed in Table 21.1; the populations compared with the numbers of females and males in each are listed in Table 21.2. The R- or Relationship-Matrix technique, originally applied to testing genetic elements (Harpending and Jenkins 1973), has been adapted for use on quantitative traits

Table 21.1: Craniofacial measurements used in this study.

Kennewick (mm)

1.	Nasal Height	(Martin No. 55)[1]	55.00
2.	Nasal Bone Height	(Martin No. 56 [2])	23.00
3.	Piriform Aperture Height	(Martin No. 55 [1])	37.00
4.	Nasion Prosthion Length	(Martin No. 48)	76.00
5.	Nasion Basion	(Martin No. 5)	110.00
6.	Basion Prosthion	(Martin No. 40)	113.00
7.	Superior Nasal Bone Width	(Martin No. 57 [2])	14.00
8.	Simotic Width	(Howells 1973)	9.20
9.	Inferior Nasal Bone Width	(Martin No. 57 [3])	15.32
10.	Nasal Breadth	(Martin No. 54)	25.05
11.	Simotic Subtense	(Howells 1973)	3.04
12.	Inferior Simotic Subtense	(Brace and Hunt 1990)	7.40
13.	Fronto Orbital Width Subtense at Nasion	(Woo and Morant 1934)	16.66
14.	Mid-Orbital Width Subtense at Rhinion	(Woo and Morant 1934)	20.19
15.	Bizygomatic Breadth	(Martin No. 45)	140.00
16.	Basion Bregma	(Martin No. 17)	139.53
17.	Basion Rhinion	(Brace and Hunt 1990)	116.00
18.	Width at 13 (Fronto Malar Temporalis)	(Brace and Hunt 1990)	106.50
19.	Width at 14 (Mid-Orbital Width)	(Woo and Morant 1934)	60.29

[1] Martin numbers are from Martin (1928).

(Relethford and Blangero 1990). R-Matrix values for samples from the different populations can be compared by the neighbor-joining procedure (Saitou and Nei 1987), which produces web-like trees (Huson and Bryant 2006) where the distances between the groups being tested are proportional to the relationship each has with each other, as indicated by the values of the variables measured. The statistics supporting those results are reported in Brace et al. (Forthcoming).

THE KENNEWICK DENTITION

The initial realization that Kennewick did not really resemble those who were claiming it as an ancestor led to the suggestion that it had "Caucasoid" features and may have been the remains of an early European-derived settler in the American Northwest (Chatters 1997). To be sure, the Ainu have often been said to have Caucasoid traits (Gjerdman 1926; Kodama 1970; Vallois 1967; von Baelz 1901). It is true that, like Kennewick, the pre-19th-century European settlers in the Western Hemisphere all had edge-to-edge bites (Brace 1977), but virtually none ever showed the degree of wear visible in the Kennewick dentition. The teeth are so heavily worn that few of them will yield reliable measurements of the mesial-distal or

Table 21.2: Samples used in this study with N for females and males.

Sample	# of females	# of males	Total
Ainu	23	33	56
Aleut	15	17	32
Atayal	14	22	36
Athabascan	23	19	42
Blackfoot	17	15	32
Borneo	5	7	12
Buhl	1	0	1
Buriat	14	12	26
Burma	15	21	36
Bushman/Hottentot	3	9	12
China Bronze	16	45	61
Chukchi	7	12	19
Chumash	35	36	71
Contra Costa (SF Bay)	10	15	25
Delaware	7	6	13
Eskimo	63	77	140
Tierra del Fuego	7	15	22
Great Lakes	7	8	15
Haida	24	25	49
Heilongjiang	8	10	18
Hopi	5	7	12
Indian Knoll	19	22	41
Japan	100	217	317
Java	1	4	5
Jomon	6	3	9
Kennewick	**0**	**1**	**1**
Lagoa Santa	2	3	5
Maryland	12	14	26
Mexico	34	42	76
Mississippian	30	25	55
Mongol	21	29	50
Mongol Bronze	25	29	54
Neolithic China	9	21	30
North Australia	6	12	18
North China	24	38	62
Patagonia	4	9	13
Peru	29	26	55
Polynesia	87	74	161
Port au Choix	10	8	18
Sepik River New Guinea	4	6	10

Table 21.2: Continued
Samples used in this study with *N* for females and males.

South Asia	20	31	51
South Australia	13	16	29
South China	43	84	127
Snake River	8	6	14
Spirit Cave	0	1	1
Sudan	5	10	15
Tennessee Archaic	10	19	29
Thai	27	37	64
West Africa	51	54	105
West Europe	111	152	263
Windover	17	15	32
Wizards Beach	0	1	1
Sum Total			2,412

buccal-lingual dimensions. The upper-right and lower-left third molars lacked occluding partners for a long enough time that occlusal wear was not extreme, but two third molars simply do not provide us with a basis for inferring anything about TS, the summary tooth size statistic (Brace 1980).

When the eight-point wear-rating scale proposed by B. H. Smith (1983) is used, the results are shown in Table 21.3. A score of 8 is recorded when wear has gone down below the lowest reach of crown enamel. As can be seen in Table 21.3, over twenty teeth are rated at 7 and 8, which are the two most extreme degrees of wear on the scale. When one considers Europe, one has to look well back into the Pleistocene to find comparable degrees of dental wear—something that is never approached in the edge-to-edge occlusion of the first European settlers in the Western Hemisphere. Although the degree of wear is comparable to that of the "fern-root plane" in the Maori dentition (Taylor 1963), the form is very different. Instead of pushing the tooth over on its side so that the buccal surfaces of the lower molar crowns and roots and the comparable lingual surfaces of the upper molars function as the occlusal plane, the teeth are largely worn straight down with the roots remaining vertical, although as is shown in Figure 21.3, the lingual wear on P^2, M^1, and M^2 show the first stages in what has been reported as the "fern-root plane." The result is highly reminiscent of the kind of wear seen in Eskimo dentitions prior to their switchover to the use of canned foods as they became acculturated (de Poncins 1941; Waugh 1937). This is clearly shown by the image of mandibular tooth wear illustrated in Figure 21.4. The form of the wear on the anterior teeth looks very much like that caused by leather working on the Eskimo dentition. The extraordinarily "Eskimoid" maxillary-mandibular occlusal wear pattern is clearly shown in Figure 21.5.

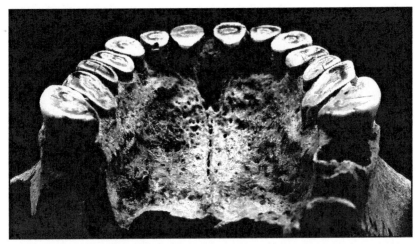

Figure 21.3: Kennewick maxillary dentition.
Photograph taken by Chip Clarke at the Burke Museum, University of Washington, Seattle,
under the direction of Douglas Owsley, Smithsonian Institution, Washington, DC.

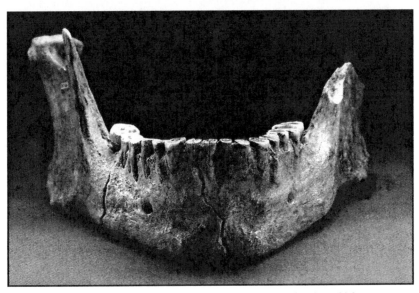

Figure 21.4: Kennewick mandibular dentition; see credits for Figure 21.3.

KENNEWICK CRANIOFACIAL DIMENSIONS
TESTED AGAINST ASIAN AND PACIFIC SAMPLES

When the R-Matrix values for the Asian and Pacific groups listed in Table 21.2 and the Kennewick individual are treated by the neighbor-joining procedure (Saitou and Nei 1987) and plotted as web-like trees (Huson and Bryant 2006), Kennewick is always at the end of a long twig. This is because it is simply an individual specimen

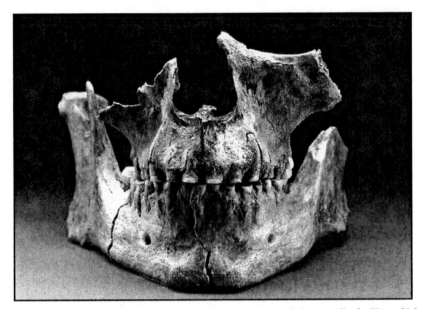

Figure 21.5: Kennewick maxillary and mandibular dentitions occluded; see credits for Figure 21.3.

	L	R		L	R
I^1	7	7	I_1	8	8
I^2	7	8	I_2	8	8
C	6	7	C	7	6
P^1	8	8	P_1	7	7
P^2	8	8	P_2	6	6
M^1	8	8	M_1	7	7
M^2	7	7	M_2	6	7
M^3	3	—	M_3	—	4

Table 21.3: A tooth-by-tooth wear rating for Kennewick using
the Smith (1983) eight-point tooth-wear scale.

with single figures and no standard deviation for each variable, whereas all the other twigs are for groups with mean dimensions and common variance (the raw data results are reported in Brace et al. Forthcoming). Even so, the ties remain consistent, even when the nature of the other samples is completely changed. The Kennewick individual is always on the same twig as the Ainu of Japan and Polynesians, no matter what combination of other groups is used. The Ainu, for their part, are clearly the descendants of the prehistoric Jomon of the Japanese archipelago (Brace and Nagai 1982; Fitzhugh 1999; Hudson 1999), although the Ainu have been historically identifiable as such for somewhat less than 2,000 years.

As of 150 years ago, the Ainu were to be found from the northern Japanese island of Hokkaido to Sakhalin Island off the coast of Manchuria and the Kurile island chain north of the southern part of the Siberian peninsula of Kamchatka (Fitzhugh 1999). Because of the limited amount of archaeological research at the northeastern edge of Asia, the traces of the Ainu's Jomon ancestors are much more difficult to identify. It is generally accepted that the Jomon were descended from the sea mammal–eating Late Pleistocene inhabitants of the eastern coast of Asia and farther west (Zhushchikovskaia 2005), but whether they had come north from Southeast Asia (Hanihara 1991) or south from Siberia (Kozintsev 1993) has been a continuing subject of debate (Fitzhugh 1999; Hudson 1999). Some of the characteristics of their Ainu descendants may provide clues concerning that possible area of origin. First, the Ainu have the lightest average skin color of any of the inhabitants of Asia, which argues against a tropical ancestry (Harvey and Lord 1978). Next, the beards and body hair that occur in abundance among the Ainu (Hutchinson, Gregory, and Lydekker 1902) are less likely among tropical people.

Furthermore, average tooth size, tooth by tooth, is significantly smaller than that of anyone else in Asia (Brace, Brace, and Leonard 1989; Brace and Nagai 1982). This also suggests that they had descended from people who had lived for a long time in the north "temperate" zone during the last glaciation, where cooking was obligatory simply to eat food that was regularly frozen. This was why the earliest and most pervasive degree of human dental reduction occurred throughout the north temperate zone of the Old World (Brace 2005).

The initial Jomon period of Japan has a calibrated date of 16,500 years ago and is associated with one of the oldest pottery-making traditions in the world (Habu 2004; Lapteff 2006). That, in turn, was preceded, as was the case at the western edge of the Old World, by a prolonged reliance on earth oven cookery (Brace 1976). The consequences of the effect of the "neutral theory" for both the eastern and western populations were a comparable amount of dental reduction in the northernmost inhabitants (Brace 2005). According to the neutral theory, amino acid substitutions occur at a constant rate and many might be neutral (Kimura 1968; Ohta and Aoki 1985; Ohta and Kimura 1971).

If selection for a given trait is reduced or suspended, then amino acids affecting the construction of the trait in question will not be disadvantageous, even though most of those affecting that construction would lead to a reduction of its size (Brace 2005). We suggest that this, rather than Southeast Asian origins—sundadonty (Turner 1989)—is why incisor shoveling is also markedly less evident in the Jomon, Ainu, and early North American dentition than in that of most of the living inhabitants of East Asia.

It has been suggested that the Jomon gave rise to the peoples who moved out into the Pacific and settled the islands of Oceania (Brace, Brace, and Leonard 1989; Brace and Hunt 1990; Brace and Nagai 1982; Brace and Tracer 1992), although such a possibility has also been vigorously denied (Pietrusewky 2005, 2006a, 2006b). This is consistent with the picture presented in the dendrograms in Brace et al. (Forthcoming) and the Mahalanobis D^2 figures shown in Table 21.4. If this is what happened, then it means that the Jomon spoke an Austronesian language. Although we have no direct evidence concerning what kind of language they spoke, we should be able to get some hints on that score from the language spoken by their direct descendants, the Ainu of Hokkaido. Although Ainu has been treated as a linguistic isolate (Laufer 1917), the complete lack of voiced consonants or surds, the presence of a vigesimal number system (Laufer 1917; Sternberg 1929), and more than seventy word parallels between Ainu and "Malayo-Polynesian" (Gjerdman 1926) suggest that the Ainu language must have been derived from proto-Austronesian (Murayama 1992).

Table 21.4: D^2 figures between the major groups used in Table 21.2 and the Kennewick individual.

	Ainu	Bering	Heilong	Jomon	Kenn	Tahiti	Hawaii	NZ	Marq	E. Asia
Ainu	0.00									
Bering	14.88	0.00								
Heilong	19.29	13.94	0.00							
Jomon	8.24	15.78	26.90	0.00						
Kenn	16.70	38.05	45.47	34.68	0.00					
Tahiti	11.78	16.04	18.29	19.41	26.76	0.00				
Hawaii	5.75	10.75	16.74	9.00	26.73	8.44	0.00			
NZ	6.41	17.95	18.90	13.98	26.54	14.30	4.62	0.00		
Marq	10.00	10.36	15.36	16.40	26.76	7.69	5.32	7.32	0.00	
E. Asia	12.70	8.80	9.89	13.80	36.36	12.23	7.56	11.55	7.43	0.00

The fact that Japanese itself, although basically an Altaic language (Murayama 1972), has been called a *Mischsprache* (a mixed-speech), because a very large portion of its basic vocabulary is of Malayo-Polynesian origin, suggests a long-time contact with an Austronesian-speaking people (Murayama 1976). And, indeed, the Japanese came from the mainland into an island archipelago that had long been inhabited by a non-Japanese-speaking people who could be identified as one of the main sources from which the Austronesian-speaking peoples arose. The Ainu language itself could be called a *Mischsprache* because of the overwhelming long-term influence of a more powerful Altaic-speaking people (Ohno 1970).

KENNEWICK TESTED AGAINST WORLDWIDE SAMPLES

When Kennewick is tested against a worldwide set of human craniofacial samples (see also Brace et al. Forthcoming), again Kennewick lies on a twig with the Ainu and Polynesians. In this plot, the Jomon sample is in another cluster with a 300–1,700-year-old sample from Contra Costa County in San Francisco Bay (Cook and Heizer 1962) and the 8,200–9,500-year-old Lagoa Santa sample from southeast central Brazil (Neves et al. 2003). Other twigs in the cluster that includes the Jomon are the Haida from the North American northwest coast, and Tierra del Fuego and Patagonians from the southern end of South America, as well as other North American samples. The case can be made that the Jomon inhabitants of the northeast coast of Asia were an important source for the first inhabitants of the Western Hemisphere. It is also quite clear that, despite over a century and a quarter of claims to the contrary (de Quatrefages 1881; Dewar 2002; Neves and Hubbe 2005; Neves, Hubbe, and Piló 2007; Neves and Pucciarelli 1991; Neves et al. 2003; Rivet 1908, 1925; Ten Kate 1885; Verneau 1903), neither Africans nor Australians played a recent role in acting as a source for the first Americans. One thing that Brace et al. (Forthcoming) make quite clear is that the long-term claims for a probable Melanesian or Australian source for the over 9,000-year-old Lagoa Santa people of southeastern Brazil are not supported by a comparison of the relevant samples (Seguchi et al. 2006).

THE SETTLING OF THE NEW WORLD

We suggest that the Jomon could very well represent the population from which the Western Hemisphere was initially settled, and it could well be the seagoing capabilities of those people that made this possible. It has been noted that watercraft capable of formidable oceanic voyaging were present in prehistoric Japan (Aiken, Ames, and Sanger 1986). It is reasonable to assume that the craft manufactured by the Ainu that allowed them to engage in offshore whaling and swordfish catching were simply a perpetuation of what their Jomon forebears had been making. The Ainu canoe, built of planks sewn to a dugout bottom piece (Iwasaki-Goodman and Nomoto 1999), was made by essentially the same technique as that used on the American northwest coast (Ohtsuka 1999), the southern California coast (Hudson 1976), Chile (Lothrop 1932), and down past the Strait of Magellan to the west coast of Patagonia (Cooper 1917).

There have been suggestions that the style of construction of the sewn-plank canoe was brought to the Western Hemisphere by Polynesians (Graebner 1913; MacLeod 1929). Given that the ancestors of the inhabitants of the northeast coast of Asia were in place long before there was anyone in Polynesia, however, and that the Jomon could well have made a major contribution to the ancestry of the Polynesians, there is a better chance that Jomon boat-making skills were what enabled the Polynesians to reach their various islands long after the time that the same kinds of boats brought people to Beringia and down the full extent of the west coast of the New World (Fladmark 1983).

Finally, another kind of watercraft may also have been brought to the New World from roots in the Old, namely the birch bark canoe. Americans tend to think of the birch bark canoe as stereotypically associated with the Native Americans along the Canadian-American border, which, indeed, is the case (Roberts and Shackleton 1983). However, it is also present in Siberia, Manchuria, and down into Hokkaido at the northern end of Japan where the Ainu used it for inland stream navigation (Deguchi 1992; Nishimura 1931). Presumably, like the plank canoe, the Ainu inherited it from their Jomon ancestors. The Ainu also tapped the sugar maple, *Acer saccharum*, every spring so that they could make maple syrup (Keira and Keira 1999). Again, this is an activity that they almost certainly inherited from their Jomon ancestors, and one can infer that when those of northeast Asian ancestry moved from Beringia down the ice-free corridor between the Laurentide and Cordilleran ice sheets after 11,000 years ago (Dixon 1999), they brought both the birch bark canoe and the tradition of manufacturing maple sugar with them to spread across the woodlands of southern Canada and the northern United States.

In summary, when the craniofacial dimensions of the 9,300-year-old Kennewick specimen are compared to ancient and recent human craniofacial samples from both sides of the Pacific Ocean, it is clear that Kennewick is more closely related to the earliest inhabitants of the Western Hemisphere than those early entrants are to its immediate pre-Columbian residents. Not only that, Kennewick clearly ties more closely to the recent Ainu of Japan and coastal northeast Asia and to their evident ancestors—the prehistoric Jomon—than to any other population. The Jomon, as the direct descendants of the Paleolithic inhabitants of northeast Asia, have an antiquity greater than that of the first inhabitants of the New World.

The planked-canoe technology that the Ainu inherited from their Jomon forebears allowed them to make use of deep-sea mammals and fish and it also provided the capability of the Jomon to spread across the coast of Beringia and down the western edge of the Americas more than 12,500 years ago, on the one hand, and, more recently, out into Oceania as the first inhabitants of Polynesia, on the other. With the melting of the Late Pleistocene glaciers providing an ice-free corridor between the North American Laurentide and Cordilleran ice masses, Jomon-derived people, aided by the use of birch bark canoes, could come from the Beringian north and spread south and east across the swamp-lake-and-stream country to the south of the melting glaciers. Craniofacial data clearly show that subsequent entrants into the Western Hemisphere did not have the same Asian roots as the first, or Jomon-derived, arrivals.

Kennewick cannot be made to stand for these first Old World immigrants to the Western Hemisphere, nor can he be implicated as one of the bearers of the plank canoe, the birch bark canoe, or the maple syrup–making traditions of the New World, but he can certainly be recognized as the direct descendant and morphological representative of the people who were responsible for that and so much more.

ACKNOWLEDGMENTS

For access to the material used in the work reported here, we are grateful to the curators and managers of the collections in: Academia Sinica in Taipei, Taiwan; University of Alabama Museums, Moundville, Alabama, Department of Anthropology; American Museum of Natural

History, Division of Anthropology, New York; Anyang Museum, Henan, People's Republic of China; Ban Po Museum in Xian, People's Republic of China; Bernice P. Bishop Museum, Honolulu, Hawaii; Burke Memorial Museum, University of Washington, Seattle; Central Washington University, Ellensburg, Washington, Department of Anthropology; College of Traditional Chinese Medicine in Chengdu, People's Republic of China; Dickson Mounds Museum, Lewistown, Illinois; Duckworth Laboratory, Cambridge University, Cambridge, England; Erindale College, Mississagua, Ontario, Canada; Fudan University, Department of Biology, Shanghai, People's Republic of China; Gadja Mada University, Laboratory of Physical Anthropology, Yogyakarta, Indonesia; Field Museum, Department of Anthropology, Chicago, Illinois; Fowler Museum, University of California Los Angeles, Los Angeles, California; Indiana University Laboratory of Bioanthropology, Bloomington, Indiana; the Hearst Gymnasium basement and the Lowie Museum, University of California Berkeley, Berkeley, California; Illinois State Museum, Springfield, Illinois; Indiana University, Bloomington, Indiana, Laboratory of Bioanthropology; the Institute of Archaeology in the Chinese Academy of Social Sciences in Beijing and the Institute of Vertebrate Paleontology and Paleoanthropology, Beijing, People's Republic of China; the Institute of Archaeology, Mongolian Academy of Sciences, Ulaanbaatar, Mongolia; the Institute of Zoology, Copenhagen, Denmark; Istituto di Antropologia, Florence, Italy; Kyoto University Laboratory of Physical Anthropology, Kyoto, Japan; the Kyushu University Medical School, Department of Human Anatomy, Fukuoka, Japan; McClung Museum, University of Tennessee, Knoxville, Tennessee; Memorial University, St. Johns, Newfoundland, Canada; Musée de l'Homme, Paris; Museum of Anthropology, University of Michigan, Ann Arbor, Michigan; Museum of Anthropology, Tokyo University, Tokyo; the Nagasaki University Medical School, Department of Anatomy, Nagasaki, Japan; the Nanning Medical College, Guangxi-Zhuang Autonomous Region, People's Republic of China; Natural History Museum, London; Nevada State Museum, Carson City, Nevada; Ohio State Museum, Ohio Historical Society, Columbus, Ohio; Peabody Museum of Archaeology and Ethnology, Harvard University, Cambridge, Massachusetts; University of Porto Laboratory of Anthropology, Porto, Portugal; the Prince Philip Dental Hospital, Hong Kong; Rochester Museum & Science Center, Rochester, New York; the Sapporo Medical College, Department of Anatomy II, Sapporo, Japan; the Sirirai Hospital, Bangkok, Thailand; Smithsonian Institution, National Museum of Natural History, Department of Anthropology, Washington, DC; William S. Webb Museum of Anthropology, University of Kentucky, Titusville, Kentucky; and the Windover Laboratory, Titusville, Florida.

REFERENCES

Aikens, C. M., K. M. Ames, and D. Sanger. 1986. Affluent Collectors at the Edges of Eurasia and North America: Some Comparisons and Observations on the Evolution of Society among North-Temperate Coastal Hunter-Gatherers. In *Prehistoric Hunter Gatherers in Japan: New Research Methods*, edited by T. Akazawa and C. M. Aikens, pp. 3–26. Bulletin 17. Tokyo: The University Museum, the University of Tokyo.

Brace, C. L. 1976. Tooth Reduction in the Orient. *Asian Perspectives* 19(2):203–219.

Brace, C. L. 1977. Occlusion to the Anthropological Eye. In *The Biology of Occlusal Development*, edited by J. A. McNamara, Jr., pp. 179–209. Monograph No. 7, Craniofacial Growth Series. Ann Arbor: Center for Human Growth and Development, University of Michigan.

Brace, C. L. 1980. Australian Tooth Size Clines and the Death of a Stereotype. *Current Anthropology* 21(2):141–164.

Brace, C. L. 2005. "Neutral Theory" and the Dynamics of the Evolution of "Modern" Human Morphology. *Human Evolution* 19(1):19–38.

Brace, C. L., M. L. Brace, and W. R. Leonard. 1989. Reflections on the Face of Japan: A Multivariate Craniofacial and Odontometric Perspective. *American Journal of Physical Anthropology* 78(1):93–113.

Brace, C. L., and K. D. Hunt. 1990. A Non-Racial Perspective on Human Variation: A(ustralia) to Z(uni). *American Journal of Physical Anthropology* 82(3):341–360.

Brace, C. L., and M. Nagai. 1982. Japanese Tooth Size, Past and Present. *American Journal of Physical Anthropology* 59(4):399–411.

Brace, C. L., N. Seguchi, A. R. Nelson, P. Q. Feng, and M. L. Brace. Forthcoming. The

Connection of the Kennewick Palaeoindian Specimen, and the Sources of the Original Inhabitants of the New World. In D. L. Owsley and R. L. Jantz, eds. Title not yet fixed. College Station: Texas A&M University Press.

Brace, C. L., and D. P. Tracer. 1992. Craniofacial Continuity and Change: A Comparison of Late Pleistocene and Recent Europe and Asia. In *The Evolution and Dispersal of Modern Humans in Asia*, edited by T. Akazawa, K. Aoki, and T. Kimura, pp. 439–471. Tokyo: Hokusen-Sha.

Chatters, J. C. 1997. Encounter with an Ancestor. *Anthropology Newsletter* 38(1):9–10.

Chatters, J. C. 2001. *Ancient Encounters: Kennewick Man and the First Americans*. New York: Simon & Schuster.

Cook, S. F., and R. F. Heizer. 1962. Chemical Analysis of the Hotchkiss Site (CCo-138). *University of California Archaeological Survey* Report No. 57, pp. 1–25.

Cooper, J. M. 1917. Analytical and Critical Bibliography of the Tribes of Tierra del Fuego Adjacent Territory. *Bureau of American Ethnology Bulletin* 63, 233 pp.

Deguchi, A. 1992. Nihon no Dento-teki Senpaku no Keifu (The Ocean Cultures of Asia and Japan). In *Umikara Mita Nihon Bunka (The Japanese Culture from an Ocean/sea Perspective)*, edited by T. Obayashi, pp. 485–519. Tokyo: Shogakkan.

de Poncins, G. 1941. *Kabloona*. New York: Reynal and Hitchcock.

de Quatrefages, A. 1881. L'Homme Fossile de Lagoa-Santa (Brésil) et Ses Descendants Actuels. *Comptes Rendus des Séances de l'Academie des Sciences* 93(22):882–884.

Dewar, E. 2002. *Bones—Discovering the First Americans*. Toronto: Random House.

Dixon, E. J. 1999. *Bones, Boats and Bison: Archeology and the First Colonization of Western North America*. Albuquerque: University of New Mexico Press.

Edgar, H. J. H., E. A. Jolie, J. F. Powell, and J. E. Watkins. 2007. Contextual Issues in Paleoindian Repatriation: Spirit Cave Man as a Case Study. *Journal of Social Archaeology* 17(1):101–122.

Egan, T. 1996. Tribe Stops Study of Bones that Challenge History. *The New York Times*, September 30, p. A12.

Fitzhugh, W. W. 1999. Introduction. In *Ainu: Spirit of a Northern People*, edited by W. W. Fitzhugh and C. O. Dubreuil, pp. 8–26. Los Angeles: Arctic Studies Center, National Museum of Natural History, Smithsonian Institution, University of Washington/Perpetua Press.

Fladmark, K. R. 1983. Times and Places: Environmental Correlates of Mid-to-Late Wisconsin Human Population Expansion in North America. In *Early Man in the New World*, edited by R. Shutler, Jr., pp. 13–41. Beverly Hills, CA: Sage.

Gjerdman, O. 1926. Word Parallels between Ainu and Other Languages. *Le Monde Oriental* 20:29–84.

Graebner, F. 1913. Amerika und die Südseekultures. In *Ethnologica im Auftrage des Vereins zur Förderung des Städtischen Rauten-strauch*, Vol. 1, edited by W. Foy, pp. 43–66. Cologne, Germany: Joest-Museums für Völkerkunde.

Habu, J. 2004. *Ancient Jomon of Japan*. Cambridge: Cambridge University Press.

Hanihara, K. 1991. Dual Structure Model for the Population Structure of the Japanese. *Japan Review* 2:1–33.

Harpending, H., and T. Jenkins. 1973. Genetic Distance among Southern African Populations. In *Methods and Theories of Anthropological Genetics*, edited by M. H. Crawford and P. L. Workman, pp. 177–198. Albuquerque: New Mexico Press.

Harvey, R. G., and J. M. Lord. 1978. Skin Colour of the Ainu of Hidaka, Northern Japan. *Annals of Human Biology* 5(5):459–467.

Hudson, D. T. 1976. Chumash Canoes of Mission Santa Barbara: The Revolt of 1824. *The Journal of California Anthropology* 3(2):5–15.

Hudson, M. J. 1999. Ainu Ethnogenesis and the Northern Fujiwara. *Arctic Anthropology* 36(1):73–83.

Huson, D., and D. Bryant. 2006 Application of Phylogenetic Networks in Evolutionary Studies. *Molecular Biology and Evolution* 23(2):254–267.

Hutchinson, H. N., J. W. Gregory, and R. Lydekker. 1902. *The Living Races of Mankind*. London: Hutchinson & Company.

Iwasaki-Goodman, M., and M. Nomoto. 1999. The Ainu on Whales and Whaling. In *Ainu: Spirit of a Northern People*, edited by W. W. Fitzhugh and C. O. Dubreuil, pp. 222–226.

Los Angeles: Arctic Studies Center, National Museum of Natural History, Smithsonian Institution, University of Washington/Perpetua Press.

Keira, M., and T. Keira. 1999. Village Work: Gender Roles and Seasonal Work. In *Ainu: Spirit of a Northern People*, edited by W. W. Fitzhugh and C. O. Dubreuil, pp. 234–239. Los Angeles: Arctic Studies Center, National Museum of Natural History, Smithsonian Institution, University of Washington/Perpetua Press.

Kimura, M. 1968. Evolutionary Rate at the Molecular Level. *Nature* 217:624–626.

Kodama, S. 1970. *Ainu: Historical and Anthropological Studies*. Sapporo, Japan: Hokkaido University Medical Library Series 3, Hokkaido School of Medicine.

Koganei, Y. 1903. Über die Urbewohner von Japan. *Globus* 84(7):101–106.

Koganei, Y. 1927. Zur Frage der Abstammung der Aino und ihre Verwandtschaft mit anderen völkern. *Anthropologischer Anzeiger* 4(3):201–207.

Koganei, Y. 1937. Zur Frage des "Südlichen Elementes" in Japanischen Volke. *Zeitschrift für Rassenkunde* 5(2):123–130.

Kozintsev, A. G. 1993. Ainu Origins in the Light of Modern Physical Anthropology. *Homo* 44(2):105–127.

Lapteff, S. 2006. Relationships between Jomon Culture and the Cultures of the Yangtze, South China, and Continental Southeast Asia. *Japan Review, Journal of the International Research Center for Japanese Studies* 18:249–286.

Laswell, M. 1999. The 9,400-Year-Old Man, the White House Keeps Trying to Bury Him. *The Wall Street Journal*, January 8, p. W11.

Laufer, B. 1917. Vigesimal and Decimal System in the Ainu Numerals. *Journal of the American Oriental Society* 37(3):192–208.

Lothrop, S. K. 1932. Aboriginal Navigation of the West Coast of South America. *Journal of the Royal Anthropological Institute of Great Britain and Ireland* 62(July–December):229–256.

MacLeod, W. C. 1929. On the Southeast Asian Origins of American Culture. *American Anthropologist* 31(3):554–560.

Martin, R. 1928. *Lehrbuch der Anthropologie in Systematischer Darstellung*, Vol. 2, *Kraniologie, Osteologie*. Jena, Germany: Gustav Fischer Verlag.

Miller, J. J. 1999. Remains of the Day: Politics Buries a Key Archeological Find. *National Review* 51(4):31–33.

Morell, V. 1998. Kennewick Man's Trials Continue. *Science* 280(5361):190–192.

Murayama, S. 1972. Review of *Japanese and Other Altaic Languages* by Roy Andrew Miller. *Monumenta Nipponica* 27(4):463–467.

Murayama, S. 1976. The Malayo-Polynesian Component in the Japanese Language. *Journal of Japanese Studies* 2(2):413–431.

Murayama, S. 1992. *Ainugo no Kigen (The Origin of the Ainu Language)*. Tokyo: Sanichi Shobo.

Neves, W. A., and M. Hubbe 2005. Cranial Morphology of Early Americans from Lagoa Santa, Brazil: Implications for the Settlement of the New World. *Proceedings of the National Academy of Sciences U.S.A.* 102(51):18309–18314.

Neves, W. A., M. Hubbe, and L. B. Piló. 2007. Early Holocene Human Skeletal Remains from Sumidouro Cave, Lagoa Santa, Brazil: History of Discoveries, Geological and Chronological Context and Comparative Cranial Morphology. *Journal of Human Evolution* 52(1):16–30.

Neves, W. A., A. Prous, R. González-José, R. Kipnis, and J. Powell. 2003. Early Holocene Human Skeletal Remains from Santana do Riacho, Brazil: Implications for the Settlement of the New World. *Journal of Human Evolution* 45(1):19–42.

Neves, W. A., and H. M. Pucciarelli. 1991. Morphological Affinities of the First Americans: An Exploratory Analysis Based on Early South American Human Remains. *Journal of Human Evolution* 21(4):261–273.

Nishimura, S. 1931. The Kaniwa-Bune or Birch-Bark Canoe. In *A Study of Ancient Ships of Japan*, Vol. 8, pp. 197–248. Tokyo: The Society of Naval Architects.

Ohno, S. 1970. *The Origin of the Japanese Language*. Tokyo: Kokusai Bunka Shinkokai Okada.

Ohta, T., and K. Aoki, eds. 1985. *Population Genetics and Molecular Evolution: Papers Marking the Sixtieth Birthday of Motoo Kimura*. Tokyo: Japan Scientific Societies Press.

Ohta, T., and M. Kimura 1971. On the Constancy of the Evolutionary Rate of Cistrons. *Journal of Molecular Evolution* 1(1):18–25.

Ohtsuka, K. 1999. *Itaomachip*: Reviving a Boat-building and Trading Tradition. In *Ainu: Spirit of a Northern People*, edited by W. W. Fitzhugh and C. O. Dubreuil, pp. 374–376. Los Angeles: Arctic Studies Center, National Museum of Natural History, Smithsonian Institution, University of Washington/Perpetua Press.

Pietrusewsky, M. 2005. The Physical Anthropology of the Pacific, East Asia, and Southeast Asia: A Multivariate Craniometric Analysis. In *The Peopling of East Asia: Putting Together Archaeology, Linguistics, and Genetics*, edited by L. Sagart, R. Blench, and A. Sanchez-Mazas, pp. 201–229. London: Routledge-Curzon.

Pietrusewsky, M. 2006a. The Initial Settlement of Remote Oceania: The Evidence from Physical Anthropology. In *Austronesian Diaspora and the Ethnogenesis of People in the Indonesian Archipelago*, edited by T. Simunjuntak, I. H. E. Poojoh, and M. Hisyam, pp. 320–347. Jakarta: Indonesian Institute of Sciences, LIPI Press.

Pietrusewsky, M. 2006b. A Multivariate Craniometric Study of Prehistoric and Modern Inhabitants of Southeast Asia, East Asia and Surrounding Regions: A Human Kaleidoscope? In *Bioarchaeology of Southeast Asia*, edited by M. R. Oxenham and N. Tales, pp. 59–90. Cambridge: Cambridge University Press.

Powell, J. 2005. *The First Americans: Race, Evolution, and the Origin of Native Americans*. Cambridge: Cambridge University Press.

Preston, D. 1997. The Lost Man. *The New Yorker* 72(16):70–81.

Relethford, J. H., and J. Blangero. 1990. Detection of Differential Gene Flow from Patterns in Quantitative Variation. *Human Biology* 62(1):5–25.

Rivet, P. 1908. La Race de Lâgoa Santa chez les Populations Précolombiennes de l'Équateur. *Bulletins et Mémoires de la Société d'Anthropologie de Paris* V^e série, Vol. 9, pp. 209–274.

Rivet, P. 1925. Les Origins de l'Homme Américain. *L'Anthropologie* 35:293–319.

Roberts, K. G., and P. Shackleton 1983. *The Canoe: A History of the Craft from Panama to the Arctic*. Camden: International Maine Publishing Company.

Saitou, N., and M. Nei. 1987. The Neighbor-Joining Method: A New Method for Reconstructing Phylogenetic Trees. *Molecular Biology and Evolution* 4(4):416–425.

Schiffer, L. J. 1999. We're Protectin' Them Dry Bones. *The Wall Street Journal*, January 29, p. A15.

Seguchi, N., H. Umeda, A. R. Nelson, and C. L. Brace. 2006. Do Early South Americans Show Biological Similarity to Australians? Lagoa Santa in Odontometric and Craniometric Perspective. *American Journal of Physical Anthropology*, Supplement 42, p. 162.

Seguchi, N., H. Umeda, A. R. Nelson, and C. L. Brace. Submitted. Do Early South Americans Show Biological Similarity to Australians? *Anthropological Science*.

Smith, B. H. 1983. Dental Attrition in Hunter-Gatherers and Agriculturalists. Unpublished Ph.D. Dissertation in Anthropology, University of Michigan, Ann Arbor.

Sternberg, L. 1929. The Ainu Problem. *Anthropos* 24(5, 6):755–799.

Taylor, R. M. S. 1963. Cause and Effect of Wear of Teeth: Further Non-Metrical Studies of the Teeth and Palate in Moriori and Maori Skulls. *Acta Anatomica* 53(1–2):97–157.

Ten Kate, H. 1885. Sur les Crânes de Lagoa-Santa. *Bulletin de la Société d'Anthropologie de Paris* 3e série, Vol. 8, pp. 240–244.

Turner, C. G., II 1989. Teeth and Prehistory in Asia. *Scientific American* 26(2):88–96.

Vallois, H. V. 1967. *Les Races Humaines*, 7th ed. Paris: Presses Universitaires de France.

Verneau, R. 1903. *Les Anciens Patagons, Contributions à l'Étude des Races Précolumbiennes de l'Amérique du Sud*. Monaco: Imprimerie de Monaco.

von Baelz, E. von. 1901. Menschen-Rassen Ost-Asiens mit specieller Rücksicht auf Japan. *Verhandlungen der Berliner Gesellschaft für Anthropologie, Ethnologie und Urgeschichte* 33(19):166–190, 202–207, 245–249, 393–394.

Waugh, L. M. 1937. Influence of Diet on Jaws and Face of the American Eskimo. *Journal of the American Dental Association* 24(10):1640–1647.

Zhushchikovskaia, I. S. 2005. *Prehistoric Pottery-Making of the Russian Far East*. Translated and edited by R. L. Bland and C. M. Aikens. Oxford: Archaeopress.

CHAPTER 22
KENNEWICK MAN
AND ASSESSMENTS OF "RACE" USING A
VARIETY OF RESEARCH METHODS
KRISTI A. GRINDE

Within the past few decades, especially with the advent of new scientific techniques for the assessment of "race" in skeletons, the use of craniometry—the determination of "race" by the outward appearance of the skull—has somewhat fallen by the wayside. However, several research studies have still used this method of analysis to draw conclusions about the origin of Native Americans in the New World, from Fueguians and Peruvians to Kennewick Man (Chatters 2000; Frisancho and Baker 1970; Hernandez, Fox, and Garcia-Moro 1997). Craniometry has been used in such cases, either because of a lack of access to more in-depth information on the individual, or because some still believe that a basic "racial" distinction can be made from the cranial features alone to allow for accurate assessment of an individual's ethnic affiliation.

The reasons for a decline in its use stem from its application during the Nazi regime in Germany to show the apparent superiority of some races over others (Jorion 1982). During this time, cranial variation was used not only to support the assumption that there were indeed clear differences in the features of the skulls of various groups or "races" of people, but also that those features could then be used to prove either the superiority or inferiority of those groups. Earlier, craniometry had been used to define the major "races" of the world, separating Europeans from Asians, Australians, and sub-Saharan Africans. However, these classifications did not take into account the Native American populations, who generally did not fit into any of the other categories, nor did it consider the variations that occur within one large group of people, such as the differences that have been noted between the Japanese, Chinese, Koreans, and Mongols, all of whom have been neatly categorized into the Asian group (Lahr 1996).

The use of craniometry in recent years has mainly been used to determine why certain features, such as facial flatness, are present in one group of people, while completely missing, or only minimally pronounced, in another with whom the first group have been directly associated (Rothhammer and Silva 1990). Research into large collections has shown that one reason for these differences lies in the variation of geography and climate between relatively close areas (Rothhammer and Silva 1990). These circumstances account for most of the observable diversity in cranial formation, and, as such, "races" are no longer distinguishable based on craniometrical analysis because the area in which a group of people live plays a larger part (on a considerable timescale) in the development of the cranium than their apparent ethnic or "racial" affiliations.

For these reasons and others, scientists have made an effort to develop and employ new techniques to analyze the origins and migrations of human populations. Some of these studies have included the use of new genetic information, such as mitochondrial DNA (mtDNA) to determine the genetic history of an individual along the maternal line (Torroni et al. 1994). Essentially, two people can be genetically linked to another by the variation, or lack thereof, between their two sets of mtDNA (talkorigins.org 2004; see Foley 2003). The greater the similarity between the two sets, the more closely related the two individuals are, despite any outward appearances—including their cranial measurements—which may appear completely different. Such genetic information has been used to differentiate the various groups of Native Americans who migrated to the New World (Bonatto and Salzano 1997). Typically, they are divided into four major blood haplogroups, each of which denotes a different familial origin, although they have all been traced back to similar groups in Asia, leading to the conclusion that Native Americans did indeed arrive across the Bering Strait from Asia into the New World (Merriwether, Rothhammer, and Ferrell 1995; Smith et al. 1999).

Nonmetric traits, which are genetically inherited bone and dental markers that normally cannot be altered by the environment, are considered much more effective in accurately determining the familial group to which an individual belongs (Turner 1971, 1983). Nonmetric analysis has been used not only to ascertain different family groups clustered within archaeological cemeteries but also to determine the levels of variance within a specific group of people and thus how much variation in trait expression is visible, so still useful as a tool for familial association (Birkby 1982; Brothwell 1965). For instance, five markers may distinguish one group of people, but within that group a person may express only three of the five traits. That is why nonmetric analysis has been criticized by some researchers, whereas others indicate its usefulness in combination with other information, such as genetic analysis for familial association (Brothwell 1965; Parker Pearson 1999).

Very recently, stable isotope analysis has been used to ascertain the origin and migration of individuals. This essentially involves taking a tooth and extracting a small amount of it to calculate the levels of certain elements that have formed within the structure. Certain isotopes, such as strontium, reflect the geology of an area, so that the levels found in the tooth can be matched to a certain location (Dupras and Schwarcz 2001; Montgomery et al. 2003; Price, Manzanilla, and Middleton 2000). If that individual's isotope levels varied widely from others in the same assemblage, or from the local geology in which they were buried, then they can be confirmed as migrants into the area, rather than locals. Steps can then be taken to determine which area their levels correspond to and thus where they originated. Although this method is useful for small movements of people, it does have limits, because, unlike the other methods mentioned, it cannot be used to determine where the familial origins of the individual lie. However, in the case of discoveries such as Kennewick Man, isotope analysis can be useful in determining his patterns of movement and whether he derived from an area near where he died or from an entirely different location; so, it can be used as a starting point for his "racial" or ethnic affiliation.

Each method of analysis has its advantages, as well as its flaws, and it is only with a combination of such analyses that an accurate picture can be drawn of the movement of the individual during his or her lifetime, as well as his or her ancestral origins and "racial" affiliation, if such a term can be used. It is obvious that distinct "races" do not really exist, scientifically speaking, but are simply variations on a theme and it is with this knowledge that researchers can better define who an individual is and where he or she comes from.

REFERENCES

Birkby, W. H. 1982. Biosocial Interpretations from Cranial Nonmetric Traits of Grasshopper Pueblo Skeletal Remains. In *Multidisciplinary Research at Grasshopper Pueblo, Arizona*, edited by W. A. Longacre, S. J. Holbrook, and M. W. Graves, pp. 36–41. Anthropological Papers No. 40. Tucson: University of Arizona Press.

Bonatto, S. L., and F. M. Salzano. 1997. Diversity and Age of the Four Major mtDNA Haplogroups, and Their Implications for the Peopling of the New World. *American Journal of Human Genetics* 61(6):1413–1423.

Brothwell, D. R. 1965. *Digging up Bones: The Excavation, Treatment and Study of Human Skeletal Remains*. London: Trustees of the British Museum.

Chatters, J. 2000. The Recovery and First Analysis of an Early Holocene Human Skeleton from Kennewick, Washington. *American Antiquity* 65(2):291–316.

Dupras, T. L., and H. P. Schwarcz. 2001. Strangers in a Strange Land: Stable Isotope Evidence for Human Migration in the Dakhleh Oasis, Egypt. *Journal of Archaeological Science* 28(11):1199–1208.

Foley, J. 2003. Fossil Hominids: Mitochondrial DNA. Available online at http://www.talkorigins.org/faqs/homs/mtDNA.html (accessed April 17, 2008).

Frisancho, A. R., and P. T. Baker. 1970. Altitude and Growth: A Study of the Patterns of Physical Growth of a High-Altitude Peruvian Quechua Population. *American Journal of Physical Anthropology* 32(2):279–292.

Hernandez, M., C. L. Fox, and C. Garcia-Moro. 1997. Fueguian Cranial Morphology: The Adaptation of a Cold, Harsh Environment. *American Journal of Physical Anthropology* 103(1):103–117.

Jorion, P. 1982. The Downfall of the Skull. *RAIN* 48(February):8–11.

Lahr, M. M. 1996. *The Evolution of Modern Human Diversity: A Study of Cranial Variation*. Cambridge: Cambridge University Press.

Merriwether, D. A., F. Rothhammer, and R. E. Ferrell. 1995. Distribution of the Four Founding Lineage Haplotypes in Native Americans Suggests a Single Wave of Migration for the New World. *American Journal of Physical Anthropology* 98(4):411–430.

Montgomery, J., J. A. Evans, D. Powlesland, and C. A. Roberts. 2003. Continuity or Colonization in Anglo-Saxon England? Isotope Evidence for Mobility, Subsistence Practice, and Status at West Heslerton. *American Journal of Physical Anthropology* 126(2):123–138.

Parker Pearson, M. 1999. *The Archaeology of Death and Burial*. College Station: Texas A & M University Press.

Price, T. D., L. Manzanilla, and W. D. Middleton. 2000. Immigration and the Ancient City of Teotihuacan in Mexico: A Study Using Strontium Isotope Ratios in Human Bone and Teeth. *Journal of Archaeological Science* 27(10):903–913.

Rothhammer, F., and C. Silva. 1990. Craniometrical Variation among South American Prehistoric Populations: Climatic, Altitudinal, Chronological and Geographic Contributions. *American Journal of Physical Anthropology* 82(1):9–17.

Smith, D. G., R. S. Malhi, J. Eshleman, J. G. Lorenz, and F. A. Kaestle. 1999. Distribution of mtDNA Haplogroup X among Native North Americans. *American Journal of Physical Anthropology* 110(3):271–284.

Torroni A., M. T. Lott, M. F. Cabell, Y. S. Chen, L. Lavergne, and D. C. Wallace. 1994. MtDNA and the Origin of Caucasians: Identification of Ancient Caucasian-Specific Haplogroups, One of Which Is Prone to a Recurrent Somatic Duplication in the D-loop

Region. *American Journal of Human Genetics* 55(4):760–776.

Turner, C. G. 1971. Three-rooted Mandibular First Permanent Molars and the Question of American Indian Origins. *American Journal of Physical Anthropology* 34(2):229–242.

Turner, C. G. 1983. Dental Evidence for the Peopling of the Americas. In *Early Man in the New World*, edited by Richard Shutler Jr., pp. 147–157. London: Sage.

CHAPTER 23
ANCESTORS, ANTHROPOLOGY, AND KNOWLEDGE

LYNN COPES

I was never a dinosaur-crazy five year old. It wasn't until I was fifteen, working as a counselor at a summer science camp, that my charges' infectious enthusiasm introduced me to the appeal of digging in the dirt for old bones. Perhaps because the excitement for digging things up hit during my adolescence, when feelings of self-importance are often magnified, my experiences quickly transformed from an enthusiasm for dinosaurs to one for fossil hominins and human evolution.

Paleoanthropology has since been my academic focus and personal passion, but fortunately, as an undergraduate, my studies have concentrated more broadly on general anthropology. I say "fortunately," because I have truly developed as a scholar of humanity (and isn't that what all anthropologists strive toward?) by learning from the often contentious past that all areas of the discipline have had with Indigenous peoples. It hasn't been a comfortable process of discovery—one tends to take personally any criticism of one's beloved field, whether justified or not—but I feel more prepared to enter the profession of paleoanthropology having at least begun to investigate these issues.

My first experience with the Native American Graves Protection and Repatriation Act (NAGPRA) occurred at the American Museum of Natural History, New York, where I work in the "skull room," which houses nearly 10,000 human crania from all over the globe. The wealth of information and number of stories revealed by those bones is truly staggering. The effects of altitude and latitude, cultural practices, sexual division of labor, disease, and diet, among other things, are all reflected in an individual's skeletal system, and these remains are treated with the utmost respect for the precious information they can reveal. The problem with the collection is the means by which it was obtained—mainly through robbing graves across the world. It cannot be denied that many physical anthropologists and archaeologists of past generations behaved in morally reprehensible ways to obtain their collections. The excuse that it was done in the name of science is unacceptable. I fully agree that, despite the immense scientific value of skeletal material collections, they should be returned to the cultures from which they came, if requested. This seems the only way to attempt to mend a relationship that for years accepted disrespect and the abuse of power as the status quo.

The deliberate worldwide grave robbing conducted by anthropologists for the purpose of collecting is just one example of past mistakes that left deep and lasting damage that future scholars have been left to repair. NAGPRA, although far from perfect, seems to be a valuable start to repairing relations between non-Indigenous anthropologists and those whose culture was exploited for so long. Breaking down the artificial division between the two groups is also essential—it is difficult to find an anthropologist who will defend the actions of past generations, nor are all Indigenous peoples of one mind regarding the study or repatriation of human remains. I am hopeful that the coming years will see a dramatic increase in the numbers of Indigenous anthropologists, museums, and study centers focusing on Indigenous perspectives and research and knowledge regarding biological and cultural information about all of humanity.

That said, the paleoanthropologist in me balks at the controversy of Kennewick Man. I don't feel that this material should fall under NAGPRA's guidelines. This individual lived so long ago that there is no possibility of determining his direct biological or cultural descendants. He was likely not intentionally buried, nor was he intentionally dug up for the purpose of research. His bones came to the surface in much the same way they were buried—naturally. A specimen this old is truly an ancestor of us all. I understand that by asserting that the bones should belong to no individual or group (or rather, that they belong to us all as a collective species), I must defend science's "right" to study them. It seems as if the controversy is a no-win situation: A group of people desire his reburial with as intense a desire as another group wishes him to remain the object of study.

I think the issue reveals more about the past history of contentious relations between the two groups than it does a desire on either part to prevail in this particular argument. I cannot deny that Indigenous groups have been sorely abused by the field of anthropology, yet I also cannot logically conceive of any biological or cultural connection between a specific group of living people and a man who died 9,500 years ago. In the face of such intense and emotional controversy, I can only propose a compromise. The bones should remain objects of scientific inquiry, but under the supervision of workers chosen by the Indigenous groups so that proper standards of respect can be assured. These researchers would work closely with the Indigenous populations to make sure that the questions asked when examining the remains are relevant to modern groups. This general practice of respectful treatment and relevant inquiry is something that all anthropologists strive to maintain whenever they study human remains, but is especially important in a case like this.

In the end, I can only hope that all individuals can examine their own personal beliefs and desires, while avoiding getting stuck in stereotyped mindsets determined by the larger group. At the heart of the discipline of anthropology is the truly noble goal of creating a more complete picture of humanity, past and present, for the purpose of its future betterment. Anthropologists who can only see the world through the lens of their own cultural upbringing can never hope to achieve this goal, but modern science has accomplished much good for the world and cannot be given up completely.

CHAPTER 24
AN INTERVIEW WITH JOE PAKOOTAS[1]

The Palus are one of the twelve Confederated Tribes of the Colville Reservation. Palus' traditional territory includes the area where the Ancient One was discovered. Knowing the ancestry, stories, legends, and significance of the area, it is important that the Colville tribes maintain this fight for the Ancient One.

The scientists wanted to do intrusive studies on the Ancient One. Our spiritual teachings told us we did not want the studies to be done in the manner they were planned. The Colville Confederated Tribes were forced to utilize attorneys, council, and staff to protect that site and the Ancient One himself.

Early on, we thought that the federal government was going to pull the five defendant tribes together and decide on a course of action for repatriation. It was wonderful, we thought, we were going to come together and do the reburial in a cooperative manner. But it did not happen that way. Each one of the five tribes jumped in with their feet first, claiming the Kennewick area was in their territory; the inner fighting set us back. The Colville, Yakama, Umatilla, and Nez Perce are always fighting over territory and that is how the federal government likes it. We are always fighting over the ceded territories, and we had to first get those arguments out of the way.

If the Ancient One is not repatriated, it is going to greatly affect the Colville and all Indian people. There are sites being found almost daily in Indian country and, depending on the age of the sites, this court's decision is going to determine if those remains can be repatriated. This will weaken the Native American Graves Protection and Repatriation Act (NAGPRA) and negatively affect our culture.

There are many different sites throughout our traditional territories that will be impacted. Scientists wanted to do studies of the Clovis site by Wenatchee, Washington, but it was stopped by NAGPRA and the Archaeological Resources Protection Act and other legislation and laws that are in place. The Ancient One court proceedings may have convinced some people that NAGPRA is not justifiable. Now, they believe they can initiate studies to clarify or verify some of the theories important to the scientific community.

Scientists do not know if the Ancient One is Caucasian. They are guessing that he is Caucasian and they are using him to validate their theory on the land bridge, that we came from Asia, that we are not indigenous or native to this country. Knowing their intent, it is really difficult to deal with the scientific community.

The name Dr. Chatters keeps coming up in this area and he is a great scientist; he has done good work in Indian country, but recently I think the Native communities have lost their faith in him. Who do we trust anymore? We now have our own tribal staff of archaeologists who have the heart and the interests of the Native Americans in their minds and that is who we are trusting.

The most important thing for anyone working in Indian country is to understand the local communities in which they are living. Nowadays, in most universities, some training in cultural competency is necessary. Knowing and understanding some of the history and the religious aspects of the community is required. Cultural competency training for archaeologists may help alleviate the problem we have in archaeologists not understanding the authenticity of our spirituality.

Universities are becoming interested in Native American cultures and all people of color because of our growing populations. We may be able to enact positive change through the teaching of law and cultural education. In 2008, the Washington State Bar will have some Indian law on their bar exam. Tribal courts are going less by state or federal law and more by Indian law, cultures, traditions, and how we deal with people. With Indian law being taught in universities, the courts are going to understand our culture.

The state of Washington is looking at cultural competency in the education field to work not only with Native Americas but also with the Hispanic community—in fact, all communities of color. If this training is not now available in all universities, maybe future students will seek out interactions with other cultures. These interactions are going to be very important in how they work with and are received by the local people. The Colville tribe has an agreement with the University of Washington (UW) so that their students can come to our reservation and understand our businesses. We have also embraced medical students from UW so that they can understand our communities and how the federal government deals with the tribes. This education goes both ways. It would be excellent to expand that to archaeological students in local universities. The battle over the Ancient One is going to inspire more of these collaborations.

We recently purchased a site on the Okanogan River that was traditionally used for salmon fishing. Pictographs and pithouses are on the site. Central Washington University (CWU) would like to establish an anthropological research station there. So the university is interested in learning and working with us and is willing to understand more from the Natives' perspective, more toward the actual living culture of the Native peoples and communities, not solely from the scientific or academic perspective. We encourage this partnership.

Hopefully, we can start to work with the archaeology departments at UW, CWU, and local community colleges. Society is changing now and the plaintiff scientists are the old guard, they do things by their book; what we need to do is basically *rewrite that book*. We are going to do it with young innovative archaeologists and insightful professors at universities.

Before this case, young archaeologists did not understand the cultural importance of the Ancient One or other Native American burials. If you just come out of college and have not been in Indian country before, you may not understand our culture. This is a national and international case, so students throughout the world are seeing the importance we as Native Americans place on the remains of our ancestors. Change is occurring. The archaeological community is weighing in: either they want to be *amicus*, friends of the court, or they want to support us monetarily in the fight, so this case has brought up the young archaeologists who want to do the right thing. Eventually, Indian people and young archaeologists are going to collaborate and protect the laws that are in place on behalf of the Indian people.

NOTE

1. Interviewed by Adam Fish, January 12, 2005.

THE PRACTICE OF ARCHAEOLOGY (AND ARCHAEOLOGISTS)

CHAPTER 25
GOVERNING KENNEWICK

LAURAJANE SMITH

Conflicts over control of the Kennewick human remains are very revealing about the role archaeological knowledge and expertise plays in state-mediated attempts to regulate or "govern" certain social problems. One way of looking at the Kennewick conflict is to understand it in terms of the legitimacy—and therefore the power and authority—given to certain forms of knowledge. The ability to control the meaning and value of human remains, as well as "possess" the actual remains, is a significant statement of power. Archaeologists should note that this works two ways—not only for Indigenous communities, but also for the archaeological community (see Byrne 2004; Lahn 1996; Smith 2004a).

It is important to recognize that any struggle over the possession of human remains is tied up with issues of social and cultural identity. Consequently, the question of who has the "right," or authority, to make pronouncements about Indigenous cultural identity, either past or present, becomes a key issue. Archaeologists need to recognize that their identity is also inextricably tied up in this debate, as the legitimacy of archaeological disciplinary identity itself, and the validity of dominant theoretical values and norms, is called into question. In other words, Kennewick cannot be reduced simply to a "science versus religion" conflict, as it has been in the media, nor can it be understood only as an issue of ethics. These sorts of characterizations misunderstand the consequences of the debate, both for Indigenous peoples and archaeologists, and ignore the complex networks of discourses and power relations within which Indigenous and archaeological knowledge move.

Rather than focus on Indigenous interests, which are discussed powerfully elsewhere in this volume, I want to discuss the consequences this debate has for archaeological knowledge and identity. In particular, I want to illustrate exactly what it is that archaeologists have gained in the Kennewick conflict and what it is that I think they may have lost. I believe that the various court "victories" of the plaintiff archaeologists in the Kennewick case are pyrrhic, in that significant opportunities for theoretical growth, development, and public engagement have been missed and denied.

To understand my position, it is important to recognize that archaeological knowledge and expertise is not just about another interest group in debates over the disposition of human remains. Rather, archaeologists hold a special position in this debate because of the way governments and bureaucracies use archaeological knowledge to help them make sense of, and regulate, certain social problems. Archaeological knowledge may be understood as a "technology of government"— a body of knowledge the state deploys to help policymakers understand certain demands and claims based on appeals to the past.

The American state is confronted by a range of demands for social, cultural, and economic justice by Indigenous groups, who argue for the legitimacy of their political claims on the basis of their sovereignty and rights as Indigenous peoples. Being able to define cultural identity on the basis of appeals to the past often underlines the political legitimacy of wider American Indian claims to land, civil rights, and social justice. To make sense of these demands, governments and their bureaucracies call on a range of experts and forms of expertise to help them define and comprehend these claims and translate Indigenous cultural claims into knowledge systems understood by policymakers, bureaucrats, senators, and so forth. One of the areas of expertise—or technologies of government—drawn on is archaeology. Here, the role of archaeology and the way it is, and can be, mobilized in this process has been institutionalized through the procedures and legal frameworks that underline cultural resource management (CRM).

CRM regulates the use, value, and meaning given to a range of cultural objects and places and provides clear procedures through which archaeological knowledge and expertise may be called on and deployed. In these processes, fraught sociocultural conflicts that rest on, or intersect with, understandings of the past are reduced and reapprehended as "merely" technical issues of site management or preservation.

The U.S. CRM process and legislative base, established in the 1970s, mobilized processual theory to lend it scientific gravitas. The rhetoric of archaeological science and professionalization that dominated much of this theoretical literature was key in demonstrating—through archaeological lobbying for cultural resource legislation and policy—the utility of archaeology as a technology of government. The "commonsense" view of science embedded in the discipline at this time found synergy with bureaucratic understandings and cultural expectations about the legitimate nature of knowledge.

Thus, conflicts over the disposition of objects and the management of sites and places are part of a wider process in which governments and their agencies confer, withhold, or otherwise regulate claims to political and cultural legitimacy. Archaeology benefits in this process by having its authority as a discipline continually underlined and reinforced through its role as a technology of government, and, through CRM, its access to the discipline's database maintained. It is important to stress that this is not a static set of relationships. Archaeological expertise and authority will themselves be marginalized by more powerful economic interests in CRM, and, in certain political contexts, Indigenous knowledge may be granted greater legitimacy than archaeological pronouncements. The mobilization of archaeology will thus not *always* mean that archaeological wishes are upheld, but nonetheless its deployment in helping policymakers understand and regulate certain problems or conflicts ensures an overall primacy in knowledge claims over the past.

We can see this process played out in the implementation of the Native American Graves Protection and Repatriation Act (NAGPRA) and the Kennewick case.

NAGPRA has often been characterized as legislation aimed primarily at benefiting Indian interests. However, a more critical approach reveals NAGPRA to be a piece of legislation designed to formalize negotiations between the state, American Indians, and archaeologists. It reinforces the role of archaeology as a technology of government and provides more precise guidelines for the deployment of archaeological and other expert knowledge in pronouncements over cultural identity and translating Indigenous knowledge claims into bureaucratically meaningful contexts.

In 2000, Bruce Babbitt, secretary of the interior, legitimized the knowledge of the Confederated Tribes of the Umatilla Reservation by determining that the Kennewick remains were Indian and subject to NAGPRA. Babbitt's determination, made in the context of a sympathetic Democratic administration, acknowledged and affirmed the legitimacy of Indigenous oral history and traditions. This determination never really undermined the authority of archeological governance. Rather, Babbit simply chose not to deploy archaeological knowledge at that time or in that case. Nonetheless, it *was* perceived by some in the discipline to have delegitimized, not only archaeological knowledge, but also the discipline's identity as an objective and authoritative science. Given that the case had become so *very* public, the sense that it *did* pose a threat to archaeological authority became real.

It is noteworthy that it was archaeologists and anthropologists—self-identified as objective scientists—who not only ensured that the case remained public but also mounted the court challenge. A consequence of the subsequent court determinations that supported the scientific claims of the plaintiffs, and the very public publication of these determinations, was a reinforcement of the authority and legitimacy of scientific archaeology. The courts reasserted the role of archaeology as a technology of government, and, in so doing, reaffirmed the central place of processual theory and its values within the archaeological discipline. Moreover, the interests of bioarchaeology were publicly placed on the archaeological agenda.

The arguments I have made in terms of archaeological governance, and the nature and significance of both NAGPRA and Kennewick, are expounded elsewhere (Smith 2004b). The point I wish to stress here is that the various so-called victories of the plaintiffs have further enhanced the authority of archaeological governance. Rather than being a cause for celebration, this has very negative and concrete consequences for both Indigenous peoples and archaeologists. It is extremely unfortunate that Kennewick was not returned to the Umatilla, both as a mark of respect for Indigenous cultural knowledge and as a matter of social justice.

Attempting to make sense of Indigenous knowledge claims, which are based on entirely different epistemological understandings of the past, through appeals to archaeological expertise denies the legitimacy of Indigenous knowledge and subsequently undermines the political legitimacy of Indigenous interests in wider political negotiations with governments and their policymakers. The whole process of archaeological governance disallows any acceptance of *difference*—rather, all things must be understood through the lens of archaeological science. I am not suggesting that Indigenous knowledge must always be accepted at face value, nor must it always take precedence over archaeological knowledge. Rather, I am suggesting that as a baseline we accept that it is legitimate for different knowledge systems to coexist, and, moreover, acknowledge and understand the extended political and cultural consequences that will occur when one knowledge system is given greater authority and legitimacy over another.

In addition, archaeological theory and practice are also regulated and "governed" in the processes I have described. The discourse of archaeological science must continually be invoked if the utility of archaeology as a technology of government, and thus archaeological access to its data, is to be maintained. Critical theoretical debate will never really advance in such a context. Indeed, any concrete and public challenge to processual theory will be constrained by the need to maintain the discourse that assures the authority and legitimacy of archaeology in the eyes of the state. Thus, what archaeology has lost in the Kennewick case is an opportunity publicly to overthrow, not only the regulatory role it has over Indigenous knowledge claims, but also its *own* governance and regulation, and thus expand the opportunities for theoretical debate and public engagement.

The discipline needs to risk undermining its state-sanctioned authority and develop new, creative ways of asserting the public relevance and utility of archaeological knowledge and interpretation. Continually rehashing the old scientistic claims to archaeological expertise stifles disciplinary development and impacts on the political negotiations between various interests and the state. This is not to say that archaeologists should be shy in engaging with and even challenging other interpretations of the past (for instance, creationist views, racist views, or derogatory views of women—see Schadla-Hall [2004])—nor should archaeologists shrink from actively participating in negotiations over the political legitimacy of some interests and interest groups. Rather, I am arguing that archaeology must become politically more sophisticated and understand the role its knowledge plays outside of disciplinary boundaries—only by understanding this and actively using this understanding to engage or disengage with various social and cultural issues can the discipline really start to claim a legitimate sense of "stewardship of the past."

REFERENCES

Byrne, D. 2004. Archaeology in Reverse: The Flow of Aboriginal People and Their Remains through the Space of New South Wales. In *Public Archaeology*, edited by N. Merriman, pp. 240–254. London: Routledge.

Lahn, J. 1996. Dressing up the Dead: Archaeology, the Kow Swamp Remains and Some Related Problems with Heritage Management. In *Issues in Archaeological Management*, edited by L. Smith and A. Clarke, pp. 25–31. Brisbane, Australia: Tempus Publications, St Lucia, University of Queensland.

Schadla-Hall, T. 2004. The Comforts of Unreason: The Importance and Relevance of Alternative Archaeology. In *Public Archaeology*, edited by N. Merriman, pp. 255–271. London: Routledge.

Smith, L. 2004a. The Repatriation of Human Remains—Problem or Opportunity? *Antiquity* 78(300):404–413.

Smith, L. 2004b. *Archaeological Theory and the Politics of Cultural Heritage*. London: Routledge.

CHAPTER 26
KENNEWICK MAN/ THE ANCIENT ONE: CRITICAL WHITENESS AND THE PRACTICE OF ARCHAEOLOGY

JODI BARNES

Archaeologists are rarely implicated in the representation and struggles of living peoples because their subjects are often presumed to be dead and buried. Yet, as many archaeologists move toward a more politically responsible and engaged practice that recognizes that other communities and groups have equally legitimate claims to stewardship (e.g., Derry and Malloy 2003; Dongoske, Aldenderfer, and Doehner 2000; Kerber 2006; Loring 2001; McDavid and Babson 1997; Shackel and Chambers 2004; Swidler et al. 1997; Watkins 2003), the connections between contemporary communities and ancient cultural property have increasingly become an issue. Critical whiteness, as both a category of analysis and a mode of antiracist practice, provides a lens through which to examine the Kennewick Man case and to recognize different standpoints, power, and politics in the practice of archaeology.

Many archaeologists may see themselves as "color blind," yet archaeological practices tend to lead to the "conscious racialization of others," although not necessarily the "conscious racialization of the white self" (Frankenberg 1997:6). White skin privilege is the underlying research assumption for many scholars of critical whiteness studies. It includes the analysis of how white skin both signifies and underwrites various kinds of social, political, and economic advantages in the United States (Rasmussen et al. 2002). For me, a white woman, the reality of white privilege is disconcerting. Yet I cannot deny that my identity as white confers status, privilege, and power. I had been taught about racism as something that puts others at a disadvantage; I had not been taught to see its corollary, white privilege, as something that puts me at an advantage (McIntosh 1988).

For many archaeologists, white skin privilege is one of the primary places in which knowledge is situated. It influences the practice of archaeology, engagement with the communities in which we work, and our questions and concerns. It has also influenced the way in which the Kennewick Man case has been viewed. This privilege needs to be acknowledged and challenged (Blakey 1994, 1996; Epperson 2004; Orser 2004). The lived assumptions embedded within the practices of archaeology are based in a powerful camouflage of unquestioned beliefs—that the white archaeologist is "unmarked and unremarkable, universal and representative" (Bérubé 2001:235). These ideas are rooted in colonial discourse and a Western scientific purview, both embedded in whiteness.

RACE AND AMERICAN ARCHAEOLOGY

Race is a social construction with real effects that can be seen in the development of American archaeology. Archaeologists, confronted with their own impassioned, class motivated idea of race and wrapped in the protective cloak of "unimpassioned science," perpetuated racial bigotry in the name of archaeology (Orser 2004). The Euro American stereotype that portrayed America's native peoples as being inherently unprogressive was an important factor in archaeology's development (Thomas 2000; Trigger 1980). An element of Indian imagery was required to make the concept of the United States work (Thomas 2000). The westward experience was portrayed as a foreclosing event, an inevitable advance from low to high, from simple to complex, and in more senses than one, from "Indian" to "American." In this "progress"—this proof of "America"—the profoundest role was reserved, not for the abundance of land, but for the fatal presence of the Indian. "Civilization" required a "savagery" against which to distinguish itself. Archaeology became a way to document the course of American culture from one evolutionary stage to the next—from "Indian" to "American"—and, in the process, validate the doctrines of progress and Manifest Destiny (Thomas 2000).

This continued as archaeologists became more interested in cultural chronology, treated prehistoric data typologically, and ignored the connection between the data and living native peoples (McGuire 1997; Trigger 1980). A profession of mostly non–Native American archaeologists tends to see time as having a distancing effect, wherein archaeologists write about a different people than those who are around us today (Hantman 2004; McGuire 1989). This distancing effect allows archaeologists to talk about the Kennewick Man case in terms of cultural affiliation and repatriation rather than engaging American Indians in a dialog about reburial and the practices of archaeology.

CRITICAL WHITENESS AND THE PRACTICE OF ARCHAEOLOGY

Scholars of critical whiteness have critiqued whiteness as invisible and unmarked (e.g., Frankenberg 1994, 1997); as "empty" (e.g., Roediger 1994); as structural privilege (e.g., Massey and Denton 1994); as primarily violence and terror (e.g., hooks 1992); as the institutionalization of European colonialism (e.g., Alexander and Mohanty 1997); and as antiracist practice (e.g. Aal 2001; Kivel 1996). I consider critical whiteness to be a form of antiracist practice, which attempts to deconstruct and counteract the hegemony of whiteness. Because whiteness is rooted in colonialism and has ramifications for contemporary research, it is a way to examine archaeological practices that are often seen as the unmarked and unremarkable—ideas about science, history, and the nation.

Ruth Frankenberg (1997) argues that the notion of race is linked to ideas about legitimate "ownership" of the nation, with "whiteness" and "Americanness" tightly connected. "Whiteness" as a location of racial dominance is linked with "Americanness" as a location of cultural dominance or normativity within the United States. White/European self-constitution is fundamentally tied to the discursive production of others. Through this construction of alterity along racial and cultural lines, American Indians are conceived as fundamentally different from, and inferior to, white Europeans. Americanness and whiteness tend to be constructed as similarly normative, empty, and as excluding of communities of color and white ethnic groups (Frankenberg 1994).

KENNEWICK MAN/THE ANCIENT ONE

When the human remains now known as Kennewick Man or the Ancient One were found, it was argued that the remains could be those of a European settler because of physical features such as the shape of the skull and facial bones. Although a Cascade phase point dating from 9000 to 4500 BP was recovered from the hip, it was argued that the remains had characteristics inconsistent with any American Indian remains previously documented in the region (*Bonnichsen et al. v. United States* 2003). The skull shape and facial features were described as "Caucasoid." From the beginning, the popular press misused and confused the word "Caucasoid" (as a descriptive term applied to certain biological features associated with European racial designations) with "Caucasian" (a culturally defined racial type). And almost overnight, the location of the proposed founder populations for American Indians was magically transformed from the steppes of northeast Asia to the Caucasus region of southeast Europe—from "Mongolian" to "Caucasian," from "brown" to "white" (Watkins 2001:149). With several tribes[1] filing claims to Kennewick Man, science faced the possibility of losing one of the "founder populations" of North America. Watkins (2001:150) argues that the fact that "the skeleton was not related to *any* recent human groups, especially any American Indian groups, made it more difficult to justify repatriating it to any particular Indian group and easier to justify continued study."

The Kennewick Man case demonstrates how archaeology situates whiteness against nonwhiteness without critically examining science and therefore legitimizes the power that science confers over the history of the nation. The archaeologists invested in the Kennewick Man case see it as a way to "shed light on the origins of humanity in the Americas" (*Bonnichsen et al. v. United States* 2003), portraying the nation's history as empty and using science as a way to fill our past. Many archaeologists argue that "[t]here is enormous public interest in understanding the original peopling of the Americas and the history of Native American groups" (Society for American Archaeology Board of Directors 2000).

Kennewick has not been repatriated because scientists maintain that it is in the best interest of the public for the remains to be studied. Yet American Indians seem to be excluded from this interpretation of public because it is up to them to prove their stake in the past. Rather than putting the pressure on the scientists to prove their rights to the human remains, white scientists place the responsibility on the Indians to prove their legitimacy. Science is given the normalized position with jurisdiction and authority.

With archaeologists in the position of authority over the past, their "scientific interests in human remains and cultural items" (Society for American Archaeology

Board of Directors 2000) are associated closely with "ownership" of the past. They are seen to be able to offer truth "about our nation's and, indeed, our human heritage" (Society for American Archaeology Board of Directors 2000). However, these ideas about legitimate ownership of the past are closely linked with whiteness, Americanness, and who is considered knowledgeable about the past. "Meanwhile, the repressed memory of the brownness of the original residents of the land ... forms another crucial dimension of the story" (Frankenberg 1997:6) of America, yet the privilege of whiteness influences who gets to tell it.

In Conclusion

Our knowledge is always situated in social and political contexts. White perspective is the perspective most often held by Euro Americans and the institutions they construct and dominate; it is not the product of skin color, but of culture and experience (Brown et al. 2003:56). Because archaeology has traditionally been a Euro American endeavor, it functions within a white perspective. Archaeological discourse refers to how archaeology is done and who is allowed to do it. Discourse is a place where power relations are exercised and enacted (Fairclough 1989). "Power *in* discourse" (Fairclough 1989) is related to the powerful participants—the white archaeologists—controlling and constraining the contributions of nonpowerful or less powerful participants, American Indians, descendant and geographic communities, and other contemporary actors.

If archaeology is to live up to its potential as a meaningful social science, archaeologists must be able to investigate the historical nature of race and racialization in important and insightful ways (Orser 2004), including examining the practices of our discipline. We cannot ignore how whiteness affects power structures among archaeologists, including equity and diversity within the profession and involving communities of color in the archaeological process. Archaeology has a social order and an order of discourse, which involves a distinctive structuring of its "social space" into sets of situations where discourse occurs (the classroom, the field, the professional conference), a set of recognized "social roles" in which people participate in discourse (the professor, the student, the public), and a set of approved purposes for discourse (such as learning and teaching about the past) as well as a set of discourse types. The discourse types set up subject positions for the archaeologist and the student and it is only by occupying these positions that one becomes an archaeologist or a student, reproducing both the positions and white privilege in the process. We need to look at our position of white privilege and the social relations between archaeologists and American Indians and other interested communities as well as the subject positions that American Indians and archaeologists occupy.

As archaeologists, we can extend it further to recognize the white privilege in our social order and our order of discourse and develop initiatives that seek to increase the diversity in archaeology. The political and social consequences of the Kennewick case have led to new discussions around ethics, proprietary rights, and a redefined role of the archaeologist as participant and collaborator. Adding critical whiteness to the discussion allows us to challenge further the power *in* archeological discourse and to recognize different standpoints, power, and politics in the practice of archaeology.

ACKNOWLEDGMENTS
The initial inspiration for this chapter was offered from Sabihya Prince, who encouraged me to think about critical whiteness in the context of archaeology. For their thoughtful comments and suggestions, I would also like to thank Joan Gero and Kelly Ernst.

NOTE
1. The Confederated Tribes of the Colville Reservation, the Confederated Tribes of the Umatilla Reservation, the Confederated Tribes and Bands of the Yakama Indian Nation, the Nez Perce Tribe of Idaho, and the Wanapum Band filed claim to Kennewick Man.

REFERENCES
Aal, W. 2001. Moving from Guilt to Action: Antiracist Organizing and the Concept of "Whiteness" for Activism and the Academy. In *The Making and Unmaking of Whiteness*, edited by B. B. Rasmussen, E. Klinenberg, I. Nexica, and M. Wray, pp. 294–310. Durham, NC: Duke University Press.

Alexander, M. J., and C. T. Mohanty, eds. 1997. *Feminist Genealogies, Colonial Legacies, Democratic Futures*. London: Routledge.

Bérubé, A. 2001. How Gay Stays White and What Kind of White It Stays. In *The Making and Unmaking of Whiteness*, edited by B. B. Rasmussen, E. Klinenberg, R. Nexica, and M. Wray, pp. 234–265. Durham, NC: Duke University Press.

Blakey, M. L. 1994. American Nationality and Ethnicity in the Depicted Past. In *The Politics of the Past*, edited by P. Gathercole and D. Lowenthal, pp. 38–48. London: Routledge.

Blakey, M. L. 1996. Race, Nationalism, and the Afrocentric Past. In *Making Alternative Histories: The Practice of Archaeology and History in Non-Western Countries*, edited by P. Schmidt and T. Patterson, pp. 213–228. Santa Fe, NM: School of American Research.

Bonnichsen et al. v. United States. 2003. Opinion by Judge Gould. No. 02-35994, DC No. CV-96-01481-JE.

Brown, M. K., M. Carnoy, E. Currie, T. Duster, D. B. Oppenheimer, M. M. Shultz, and D. Wellman. 2003. Of Fish and Water: Perspectives on Racism and Privilege. In *Whitewashing Race: The Myth of a Colorblind Society*, edited by M. K. Brown, M. Carnoy, E. Currie, T. Duster, D. B. Oppenheimer, M. M. Shultz, and D. Wellman, pp. 34–65. Berkeley: University of California Press.

Derry, L., and M. Malloy, eds. 2003. *Archaeologist and Local Communities: Partners in Exploring the Past*. Washington, DC: Society for American Archaeology.

Dongoske, K., M. Aldenderfer, and K. Doehner, eds. 2000. *Working Together: Native Americans and Archaeologists*. Washington, DC: Society for American Archaeology.

Epperson, T. W. 2004. Critical Race Theory and the Archaeology of the African Diaspora. *Historical Archaeology* 38(1):101–108.

Fairclough, N. 1989. *Language and Power*. London: Longman's.

Frankenberg, R. 1994. Whiteness and Americanness: Examining Constructions of Race, Culture, and Nation in White Women's Life Narratives. In *Race*, edited by S. Gregory and R. Sanjek, pp. 62–77. New Brunswick, NJ: Rutgers University Press.

Frankenberg, R. 1997. Local Whitenesses, Localizing Whiteness. In *Displacing Whiteness: Essays in Social and Cultural Criticism*, edited by R. Frankenberg, pp. 62–77. Durham, NC: Duke University Press.

Hantman, J. L. 2004. Monacan Meditation: Regional and Individual Archaeologies in the Contemporary Politics of Indian Heritage. In *Places in Mind: Public Archaeology as Applied Anthropology*, edited by P. Shackel and E. Chambers, pp. 19–33. New York: Routledge.

hooks, b. 1992. Eating the Other. In *Black Looks: Race and Representation*, edited by b. hooks, pp. 21–39. Boston: South End Press.

Kerber, J. E., ed. 2006. *Cross-Cultural Collaboration: Native Peoples and Archaeology in the Northeastern United States*. Lincoln: University of Nebraska Press.

Kivel, P. 1996. *Uprooting Racism: How White People Can Work for Racial Justice*. Philadelphia: New Society Publishers.

Loring, S. 2001. Repatriation and Community Anthropology: The Smithsonian Institution's Arctic Studies Center. In *The Future of the Past: Archaeologists, Native Americans and Repatriation*, edited by T. Bray, pp. 185–200. London: Routledge.

Massey, D., and N. Denton 1994. *American Apartheid*. Cambridge. MA: Harvard University Press.

McDavid, C., and D. W. Babson, eds. 1997. *In the Realm of Politics: Prospects for Public Participation in African-American and Plantation Archaeology*, special issue. *Historical Archaeology* 31(3).

McGuire, R. 1989. The Sanctity of the Grave; White Concepts and American Indian Burials. In *Conflict in the Archaeology of Living Traditions*, edited by R. Layton, pp. 167–184. London: Unwin Hyman.

McGuire, R. 1997. Why Have Archaeologists Thought the Real Indians Were Dead and What Can We Do about It? In *Indians and Anthropologists: Vine Deloria, Jr., and the Critique of Anthropology*, edited by T. Biolsi and L. J. Zimmerman, pp. 63–91. Tucson: University of Arizona Press.

McIntosh, P. 1988. *White Privilege and Male Privilege: A Personal Account of Coming to See Correspondences through Work in Women's Studies*. Paper No. 219. Wellesley, MA Wellesley College Center for Research on Women.

Orser, C. E. 2004. *Race and Practice in Archaeological Interpretation*. Philadelphia: University of Pennsylvania Press.

Rasmussen, B. B., E. Klinenberg, I. J. Nexica, and M. Wray. 2002. Introduction. In *The Making and Unmaking of Whiteness*, edited by B. B. Rasmussen, E. Klinenberg, R. Nexica, and M. Wray, pp. 1–24. Durham, NC Duke University Press.

Roediger, D. R., ed. 1994. *Black on White: Black Writers on What it Means to Be White*. New York: Schocken Books.

Shackel, P. A., and E. Chambers, eds. 2004. *Places in Mind: Public Archaeology as Applied Anthropology*. New York: Routledge.

Society for American Archaeology Board of Directors. 2000. Position paper on The Secretary of the Interior's September 21, 2000 Determination of Cultural Affiliation for Kennewick Man. Available online at http://saa.org/repatriation/lobby/KennewickPosition.html (accessed September 14, 2004).

Swidler, N., K. Dongoske, R. Anyon, and A. Downer., eds. 1997. *Native Americans and Archaeologists: Stepping Stones to Common Ground*. Walnut Creek, CA: AltaMira Press.

Thomas, D. H. 2000. *Skull Wars: Kennewick Man, Archaeology, and the Battle for Native American Identity*. New York: Basic Books.

Trigger, B. 1980. Archaeology and the Image of the American Indian. *American Antiquity* 45(4):662–675.

Watkins, J. 2001. *Indigenous Archaeology: American Indian Values and Scientific Practice*. Walnut Creek, CA: AltaMira Press.

Watkins, J. 2003. Archaeological Ethics and American Indians. In *Ethical Issues in Archaeology*, edited by L. J. Zimmerman, K. D. Vitelli and J. Holowell-Zimmer, pp. 129–141. Walnut Creek, CA: AltaMira Press.

CHAPTER 27
OWNERSHIP OR STEWARDSHIP?
CULTURAL AFFILIATION AND
ARCHAEOLOGICAL ETHICS AS SOCIAL ETHICS
EDWARD A. JOLIE

The intersection of politics and identity are of central importance to contemporary archaeological practice, and these factors contribute to a number of prominent professional ethical issues that have emerged in the discipline over the past three decades (Barkan and Bush 2002; Kane 2003; Meskell 1998, 2002; Meskell and Pels 2005; Watkins 2005a). In the present context, and in its broadest sense, an ethic denotes a code of conduct. It is a set of values dictating what is right and wrong and is often closely tied to individual moral behavior.

My reading of the published literature on archaeological ethics suggests that the archaeological community acknowledges the impact that archaeology has on contemporary society, but that the ethical issues confronted by archaeologists are largely viewed as specific to the discipline. I submit that this view lacks an explicit recognition of ethical issues in archaeology as, simultaneously, equally relevant social ethics issues. Although this observation may appear to be a matter of semantics, I believe that the distinction has implications for how archaeologists have apprehended and approached the resolution of ethical issues in the past and may continue to do so in the future. Despite archaeological ethics being a form of professional ethics, and being principally concerned with moral issues that arise because of archaeologists' specialized knowledge, the field's engagement with many varied stakeholders on an increasingly global scale necessarily means that many of its ethical issues will have wider social significance. Archaeology's professional ethical codes are thus at a unique crossroads where they must continue to evolve to meet not just the disparate demands of a growing profession but also the many vocal communities who have stakes in the past.

Treating particular ethical issues solely as archaeological problems places conceptual and practical constraints on their broader social salience and divorces them from the context that can inform steps toward their resolution. My goal is to explore an approach to ethical issues in archaeology in which such issues are considered against the backdrop of a more general social ethic. I argue that ethical issues in archaeology are more productively thought of, and engaged in, as social ethics issues that have significance far beyond the discipline. Such an approach facilitates a response to growing trends in the literature that reflect a need for global perspectives on archaeology's context and practice (e.g., Fowler, Jolie, and Salter 2008; Meskell 2002) and, I believe, will open philosophical doorways that archaeologists can draw on to help guide our discipline through the 21st century and beyond.

I begin with a discussion of the relationship between social archaeology, identity, and ethics and then briefly outline some of the prevailing issues in current discussions of archaeological ethics. Next, I consider an approach to ethical issues in archaeology that draws on insights from social ethics and important work by Colwell-Chanthaphonh and Ferguson (2004, 2006) using virtue ethics. To demonstrate the utility of an approach grounded in social ethics for reframing and conceptualizing ethical issues in archaeology, I consider the North American controversy over the determination of cultural affiliation for the purposes of repatriating human remains, associated grave goods, and sacred objects under the Native American Graves Protection and Repatriation Act (NAGPRA) of 1990. The fundamental dichotomy between ownership and stewardship is shown to be a primary source of conflict, and I suggest that it can also be treated as a meaningful point of departure for developing a resolution to the problem of "culturally unidentifiable" human remains—of which the Ancient One, or Kennewick Man, is an exemplar.

SOCIAL ARCHAEOLOGY AND IDENTITIES

Though its intellectual roots run further back in time, a distinctive social archaeology emerged in the 1960s and 1970s in response to the charge that processual archaeology should reconstruct past social systems. The fundamentals of this approach to the social have persisted over the last two decades, but social archaeology itself has been greatly modified in response to postmodernism and the postprocessual critique (Hodder 2004). Today, social archaeology is very different from its predecessor but still emphasizes the centrality of the social. A current view of social archaeology offered by Preucel and Meskell (2004:16) acknowledges "the social construction of time, space, and material culture as constituent of social being … it engages with how different people inscribe meaning in time-space, spacetime, and embodied time and, through this process of inscription, construct themselves." Archaeologies of identity have thus become a focal topic in contemporary social archaeology and, increasingly, attention has been directed toward the relationship between contemporary politics and the archaeological study of identity.

Conceptually, identity subsumes social markers such as ethnicity, age, gender, and class but is often used more broadly in archaeology (glossed as "cultural identity") to refer to spatially and temporally discrete identity groups assumed to have shared a culture or language. The relationship between politics and identity as used in archaeology may seem opaque but it is long-lived and has been a source of social conflict for centuries. The "uses and abuses" of archaeology as a means to political ends have been widely discussed and its appropriation for nationalistic purposes well documented (Barkan and Bush 2002; Fowler 1987; Kohl 1998; Meskell 1998, 2002).

Archaeology and the knowledge derived from its practice are powerful tools that can be used to good or ill effect by and against states and their members. It is at this precise juncture that we find common ground between the politics of identity and archaeological ethics. Recent social and political assertions made by marginalized Indigenous communities since the 1960s, combined with recognition of the complexities of archaeological identifications of past cultural and ethnic groups, have forced archaeologists to take notice of their voices and claims to the past (Meskell 2002; Watkins 2000, 2003, 2005a). The response from archaeologists has been a growing awareness of ethical concerns and the political nature of archaeological practice. This is perhaps nowhere more visible than in a discussion of the identity politics coterminous with repatriation legislation.

Over the last three decades, it has become increasingly important for archaeologists to link Native American identity in the present to patterned variation observed in the archaeological record to assess cultural affiliation under NAGPRA. Historically within archaeology, ancient social groups were viewed as synonymous with archaeological culture areas and diagnostic material culture suites; this is the "pots equal people" fallacy. Contemporary anthropological formulations of "identity" underscore its fluid and dynamic nature (e.g., Díaz-Andreu et al. 2005; Jenkins 2004; Jones 1997), but this perspective contradicts identity's often-used definition as designating a sense (real or perceived) of sameness. This conceptual conflict ultimately undermines identity's usefulness as an analytical construct; identity either subsumes too much or too little (Brubaker and Cooper 2000). As a consequence, we need to examine critically the strength and validity of determinations of cultural affiliation and the contextual issues that surround the process of determination. This is particularly true as one moves further and further back in time because we reasonably assume that the identity groups of the present are the cumulative end products of centuries or millennia of social change. With these observations in mind, I now move to a consideration of archaeological ethics today.

ARCHAEOLOGICAL ETHICS TODAY

The literature on ethics in archaeology and, more generally, anthropology, has steadily increased over the past two decades (e.g., Fluehr-Lobban 2003; Fowler, Jolie, and Salter 2008; Meskell and Pels 2005; Scarre and Scarre 2006; Zimmerman, Vitelli, and Hollowell-Zimmer 2003). Recently, Fowler and colleagues (2008) provided a concise overview of the scope of current ethical issues in archaeology and found that archaeological ethics may be considered in four contexts that overlap in practice: (1) international, transnational, and national legal instruments; (2) knowledge-making and professionalism; (3) conservation, broadly considered; and (4) relationships with Indigenous peoples.

Diverse legal instruments (e.g., charters, covenants, conventions, declarations, and treaties) covering human rights, conservation, and preservation, although locally applied, are increasingly situated in the global realities of the 21st century. One benefit of this has been that the transnational and international contexts in which archaeological ethics are being developed facilitate mediation among many stakeholders (Appadurai 2001). Concerns over knowledge-making and professionalism have encompassed the practice of data collection, dissemination (including public archaeology), and professional accountability (e.g., codes of ethics or ethical standards).

A central assumption guiding epistemic and professional concerns has been the concept of stewardship, which refers to archaeologists' responsibility as both caretakers and advocates of the archaeological record. In this context, archaeology makes use of finite resources to produce useful knowledge about the human past to be held in public trust by archaeologist-stewards for the common good (Chippendale 1994; Fowler, Jolie, and Salter 2008; Lynott and Wylie 2000; Stapp and Burney 2002). This is related to trends in the ethic of conservation that recognize that archaeological sites and objects have value and are subject to a variety of threats.

At the scale of an individual site, the ethical response is necessarily situational in that it engages the appropriate measures to maximize the amount of information retrieved while inflicting the minimal amount of damage on the archaeological resource. On a broader scale, the collection of cultural property, looting, and the trafficking of antiquities are recognized as primary factors mitigating conservation efforts (Brodie and Renfrew 2005; Fowler, Jolie, and Salter 2008; Messenger 1999). The final trend in contemporary archaeological ethics denotes a set of ethical concerns arising from the emergence of Indigenous social movements. This is inclusive of archaeology's historical association with partisan politics, but also subsumes Indigenous claims to cultural and intellectual property that have gained more attention recently (Brown 2003; Greaves 2002; Nicholas and Bannister 2004).

Basic questions of who owns the past and who owns knowledge define many of these concerns, but the controversy over the ownership, identification, and repatriation of human skeletal remains, grave materials, and objects of cultural patrimony are, arguably, the most contentious manifestations. I will return to them later.

Identity politics, nationalism, postcolonialism, and globalism clearly figure prominently in discussions of archaeological ethics. Given this contextual background, I suggest that ethical issues in archaeology are, fundamentally, social ethics issues. They are concerned with the application of ethical principles to the whole of society, not simply individuals, and they provide the opportunity to complement more narrowly focused professional ethical codes. Following from this, I argue that the resolution of ethical issues requires greater consideration of social ethics models and an explicit treatment of archaeological ethics as social ethics, with attentiveness to the complex discourses with diverse publics that condition contemporary archaeological practice.

SOCIAL ETHICS AND ENGAGED ARCHAEOLOGY

In discussing strategies of moral reasoning, Wylie (2003) distinguishes between the terms "moral" and "ethical." An ethic denotes a set of specific standards applicable to individuals representative of a certain subgroup, like doctors, teachers, business people, or archaeologists. For archaeologists working in North America, the Society for American Archaeology's Principles of Archaeological Ethics (Society for American Archaeology 1996) form the most common ethical code. A moral code or standard, on the other hand, is more general and constitutes broadly acceptable social standards. It may contain a list of things like honesty, fidelity, beneficence, nonmaleficence, and respect (Wylie 2003:5). Archaeologists are subject to, not only the obligations of an archaeological ethic, but also the moral standards of their society.

This distinction between moral and ethical standards is an important one, but I think that part of the problem with current archaeological ethics is that they are based on codes or principles that are typically separated from more general discussions of moral standards and theory. Obviously, codes of archaeological ethics are of the utmost importance, but in practice they are not necessarily commensurable with the cultural values of the non-Western cultures that archaeologists may come into contact with and that may not recognize or appreciate a code's significance.

Given the impact of globalization on archaeology, I suggest that archaeology look beyond codes and principles to moral standards. Broadly construed, moral standards, informed by social ethics or moral theory, have the potential to offer more commonalities between Western and non-Western cultural values than codes or principles. I acknowledge that there is no single set of moral standards that apply cross-culturally, but I believe that there *are* suites of shared values or virtues that can be used as a starting point in conflicts between Western and non-Western values. Thinking about ethical issues in archaeology as social problems facilitates the use of moral standards (in conjunction with professional codes), and by recognizing that solutions to social ethics issues require a combination of structural change (e.g., legislation) and charity (e.g., good will and helpfulness), we can begin to work toward appropriate solutions.

The social ethics approach that I advocate here most closely resembles virtue ethics. Virtue ethics are generally defined by reference to the essential rationality of virtues in and of themselves (Rachels 1993; Slote 1992), where a virtue is "a trait of character, manifested in habitual action, that is good for a person to have" (Rachels 1993:163). Virtue ethics asks, in essence, what traits of character make a good person (Crisp and Slote 1997)? The fact that a virtue ethic considers the qualities of moral agents before identifying moral action makes it well suited to professional roles (Oakley and Cocking 2001).

In archaeology, Salmon (1999a) has noted similarities between virtue ethics and Watkins's (e.g., 1999, 2000, 2003) emphasis on trust and relationship building. Likewise, in his research on intellectual and cultural property, Brown (2003) has referred to "virtue pluralism" as fostering a relationship of trust and communication. Presently, only Colwell-Chanthaphohn and Ferguson (2004, 2006) have explicitly used virtue ethics in archaeology. They conclude from their experience that:

> An ethic of collaboration involves no simple rule or moral equation; it entails the cultivation of sincere relationships guided by virtuous ideals—civility, cooperativeness, tactfulness, patience, trust, honesty, thoughtfulness, tolerance and respect. In many ways, this ethical approach begins with questions of what constitutes a moral person before it addresses what makes a moral archaeologist. (Colwell-Chanthaphohn and Ferguson 2004:23)

Because virtue ethics place emphasis on an individual's moral qualities, many of which may overlap cross-culturally, virtues may be used together with archaeological ethical principles to help guide socially responsible action. In this sense, virtue ethics complements existing archaeological ethics to yield a set of mutually acceptable social standards. Obviously, virtue ethics is not a solution to ethical issues in and of itself but rather provides the best valuable tool for establishing common ground on which relationships may be built and through which solutions (compromises) may be achieved.

Barker (2003) distinguishes between "passive" ethics, which involve ethical behavior in response to ethical choices, and "active" ethics, which recognize that all actions have ethical consequences that should be considered as part of an individual's professional responsibility. A social ethics approach based on values and virtues is necessarily active in that it engages ethical issues in archaeology as current and imminent social problems requiring attentiveness to broader social context and a consideration of multiple contingencies. This view recognizes ethical issues as dynamic, fluid processes that are constantly changing in tandem with, and in response to, social factors.

Why has archaeology been slow to adopt a more active approach to resolving ethical issues? I suggest that archaeology's failure to treat its ethical problems as the broader social problems they are stems from the discipline's immaturity and uncertainty as to its ethical and scientific stature. A similar case has been made for anthropology as a whole (Gregor and Gross 2004), and I draw attention to recent debates over the place of archaeology within anthropology (Gillespie and Nichols 2003; Kelly 2002; Lees 2002; Wiseman 2002) and the discipline's public image problem (di Leonardo 1999; Kuhn 2002; Lamphere 2003). Other influencing factors may be anthropology's academic elitism, fear of "feminization" (Wilson 2003), and failure to acknowledge the contributions of female and minority anthropologists (Lamphere 2004).

Although many of these criticisms have been leveled against anthropology generally, I believe that they are equally applicable to archaeology and are allied with Lamphere's (2003) call for an "engaged anthropology." In her view, anthropology's moral commitment should outweigh the impersonal agenda of science. Of current anthropology in the United States, Lamphere writes:

> We have come to realise that we need to do three things as we become increasingly engaged with the world: first, transform our relations with the public in order to overcome entrenched stereotypes and foster current images that accurately depict anthropology today; second, continue to change our relations with the communities we work with, by attending to their concerns in formulating research questions and by viewing them as equal partners in carrying out research and educational activities; and third, work out effective ways of doing research on critical social issues that will expand the influence of anthropology in political arenas and policy debates. (Lamphere 2003:153)

Clearly, Lamphere's three points are similar to several prominent ethical concerns within archaeology. Following her lead, then, I support an "engaged archaeology" that places greater emphasis on the attendant social contexts of practice and treats archaeological ethics as social ethics. The flexibility and socially contingent nature of social ethics, generally, and virtue ethics, specifically, allows a confrontation of ethical issues on different scales without forcing either side to accept ethical relativism (Salmon 1999b). Although admittedly the intellectual product of Western philosophy, virtue ethics comes closest, I think, to satisfying the needs of an increasingly global archaeology in which we will continue to see the convergence of multiple voices and stakeholders.

REPATRIATION, IDENTITY, AND AFFILIATION

The so-called repatriation controversy in archaeology revolves around the disposition of human remains, grave goods, or items of cultural patrimony under the auspices of NAGPRA. The legislation itself constituted an important step to leveling the playing field between Native Americans and archaeologists and rapidly became controversial because, in many instances when materials are returned to claimant tribes, they are reburied and, in the eyes of some, lost forever as sources of valuable information about the past. Opinions vary widely on the impact of NAGPRA, but very few archaeologists see it as an entirely bad thing (e.g., Clark 2001; Meighan 1992) and many appreciate how it has improved relationships with Native Americans (e.g., Dongoske, Aldenderfer, and Doehner 2000; Ferguson 1996; Morenon 2003; Swidler et al. 1997; Watkins 2000, 2005a). Given the complexity of this legislation and the vastness of the resulting scholarly literature (e.g., Bray 2001; Bruning 2006; Dongoske, Aldenderfer, and Doehner 2000; Fforde and Turnbull 2002; Fine-Dare 2002; Jones and Harris 1998; Mihesuah 2000; Morenon 2003; Owsley and Jantz 2001; Swidler et al. 1997; Ubelaker and Grant 1989; Watkins 2003, 2004), I will focus primarily on the issues of cultural affiliation and identity as they relate to ethics and repatriation.

In practice, NAGPRA addresses "the rights of lineal descendants, Indian tribes, and Native Hawaiian organizations to certain Native American human remains, funerary objects, sacred objects, or objects of cultural patrimony with which they are affiliated." According to the law, such items are to be returned to those Native Americans who can prove a cultural affiliation with the object(s) in question, where cultural affiliation is defined as "a relationship of shared group identity which can reasonably be traced historically or prehistorically between a present day Indian tribe or Native Hawaiian organization and an identifiable earlier group."

Evidence based on anthropology, archaeology, biology, folklore, geography, history, kinship, linguistics, and oral tradition may all be brought to bear on the question of affiliation under NAGPRA. Unfortunately, NAGPRA provides *no* regulations for the disposition of remains for which cultural affiliation has not yet been (or possibly cannot be) determined. Although recent legislative developments at the time of this writing suggest that appropriate regulations may soon be developed, unaffiliated remains lie at the heart of much controversy over repatriation. Further complicating repatriation matters are cases of human remains of exceptional antiquity, such as

Kennewick Man and Spirit Cave Man, who underscore the extent to which the determination of cultural affiliation is clearly an issue of determining (and defining) cultural or ethnic identity, in particular how Native American identity is defined (Bruning 2006; Edgar et al. 2007; Watkins 2004, 2005b).

In a stimulating article on contemporary Indigenous identity, Weaver (2001:240) notes that "identities are always fragmented, multiply constructed, and intersected in a constantly changing, sometimes conflicting array ... in reality the various facets of identity are inextricably linked." Weaver's astute observations speak to the multiplicity of meanings that the term "identity" has. Her story about Lakota and Navajo basketball teams who argue over which group were "really Indians" is especially telling. Physical appearance, federal recognition, and native language ability were all put forth as hallmarks of a "real" Indigenous identity. Ultimately, they were unable to come to an agreement, as the ways in which they defined themselves were systematically contested by others. The "game" of exclusion these boys played bespeaks the extent to which identity, no matter what type, is inherently governed by power and exclusion (Weaver 2001:244).

Since the reservation period, Native American identity has largely been controlled by the federal government, forcing Native Americans to essentially prove they are Indigenous. Federal control of Native American identities has contributed to feelings of oppression and inferiority. Too often, Native Americans have been led to believe they are less than authentic, or no longer genuine. As Deloria (1973:33) famously observed, to many people, "the only real Indians were dead ones." Unintentionally, archaeology inherited these notions of power and exclusion when it integrated government standards into legislation like NAGPRA, which was developed for Native Americans' benefit. Native Americans and archaeologists have had to jockey for the power to exclude, with the ultimate question being: "Who owns knowledge of the past, Native Americans or archaeologists?" Most codes of ethics address this conflict by way of reference to professional accountability, but it is often left up to the archaeologist to go beyond lip-service and build the relationships necessary to effectively incorporate Indigenous viewpoints (Fowler, Jolie, and Salter 2008).

The construction of Native American identities has been a two-fold process and, in the context of repatriation, both Native Americans and archaeologists often create very different pictures. For many Indigenous groups, there is no question that they have occupied their traditional lands since the beginning of time, so determining who their ancestors are is a relatively straightforward task guided by oral tradition. With archaeological remains, the younger the age of the material, the more likely it is that ethnohistoric data or other lines of anthropological and historical evidence are available to establish cultural affiliation.

This issue is compounded the further back in time one moves. A prime example of this is the debate over Kennewick Man. Given his age, it is possible that he is related to a significant portion of living Native Americans or, alternatively, none at all if his lineage died out. Although this case is unique because of its age, we should remember that there are similar examples of "recent" archaeological cultures for which no historic ethnic analog has been established (e.g., the Fremont archaeological culture of Utah and eastern Nevada, ca. AD 400–1300).

The fact of the matter is that the cultures of the present and recent past are different from those that lived 500, 1,000, and certainly 5,000 or 10,000 years ago. Many of the culturally, linguistically, or politically defined groups of the present did not exist as discrete entities in the past, and we cannot assume that their historic territories reflect prehistoric territories. Stated another way, cultural affiliation is very difficult to prove if not impossible in some cases, according to NAGPRA's current standards. Furthermore, the repatriation debate marginalizes or altogether ignores the important fact that the social groups of today are not isomorphic with those of the past. My point here is that in the spirit of how NAGPRA was written to facilitate the determination of cultural affiliation, no guidance is offered for circumstances in which affiliation cannot be determined. The result is a repatriation stalemate that often appears to place Native Americans and archaeologists on opposite sides of the debate over the repatriation of unaffiliated remains. In many ways, discussion about the fate of the remains of Kennewick Man can be seen as the culmination of a debate on the nature of Native American identity that has been unfolding gradually over the past several hundred years.

OWNERSHIP OR STEWARDSHIP?

In the context of repatriation, proof of cultural affiliation is often equated with ownership. If a group can demonstrate affiliation, then they are, in essence, entitled by the government to a claim of ownership. The crucial questions have thus become: "Who owns the past?" or "Who owns these human remains?" In my view, these are the wrong questions because no one can own the past—only attempt to control it—and it is contradictory to many native worldviews to assert such ownership over human remains, objects, and the past or pasts they may reflect (but see Young 2006). A more appropriate question is: "Who are the most appropriate stewards of a particular set of unaffiliated human remains or objects?"

As part of an archaeological ethic, stewardship has historically been used to reference the responsibility of archaeologists as both caretakers and advocates of the archaeological record (Wylie 2005). However, by placing stewardship at the heart of the debate over the repatriation of unaffiliated remains we can promote a discourse of compromise between the competing stewardship interests of Native Americans and archaeologists. As the concept of stewardship does not presume ownership or control over archaeological materials (Lynott and Wylie 2000), it simultaneously provides the opportunity of accommodating multiple claims of affiliation by opening the door to the possibility of joint or collaborative stewardship (Groarke and Warrick 2006; Wylie 2005). In fact, joint stewardship is a far more logical course of action in light of the differing concerns many stakeholders have and the degree to which archaeological research suggests that many ancient societies were pluralistic.

Goldstein and Kintigh (1990) rightly observe that the repatriation issue at the heart of some NAGPRA-related disputes is not solely a problem of ethics. Rather, it is a conflict of cultural values that have become entrenched in the U.S. legal system. Current approaches to archaeological ethics have more to do with how archaeologists should conduct themselves with regard to their data in order to build a common knowledge base and less to do with telling archaeologists how they should act toward Native Americans (and other stakeholders) to resolve the dispute. The flaw is that, in practice, codes of archaeological ethics are not necessarily commensurable with the cultural values of the non-Western cultures archaeologists may come into contact with and they do not offer necessary guidance for how archaeologists should build productive relationships with Native Americans. By recasting the debate over the repatriation of unaffiliated remains within the context of stewardship and not ownership, I believe that we can begin to refigure archaeological ethics as part of a broader social ethic that engages such cultural value conflicts productively.

The question of who owns the past has been an important one guiding recent discussions of repatriation. Yet, it is important to note that these discussions have themselves been largely influenced by earlier legislation. Under the Antiquities Act of 1906, Native American skeletal remains and associated artifacts recovered from federal land were viewed as federal property (Moore 1989). In 1979 when the Antiquities Resource Protection Act was passed, human remains became archaeological "resources." By defining human remains in that way, the federal government chose to emphasize scientific and not cultural perspectives (Horn 1997). As a result, the management and protection of these cultural resources has largely fallen under property law (King 2004), effectively divorcing the significance of Native American skeletal remains and sacred objects from their social belief systems. These initial acts reflected "public sentiment that Native Americans represent relics of the past and are considered to be prime candidates of scientific research" (Horn 1997:504).

As property determines exclusive rights to things, ownership has become an important theoretical concept in both law and the social sciences (Earle 2000; Young 2006). With the passage of NAGPRA, Native Americans have been given a larger role in discussions over the disposition of human remains and artifacts that pertain to their cultural patrimony. However, many economically marginalized Native Americans lack the ability to effectively use the court system. The problem is compounded by the fact that cultural heritage preservation becomes a secondary concern for individuals struggling to survive (Watkins 2000, 2005). Clearly, effective repatriation legislation is an exceedingly complex topic that extends beyond property law and is influenced by many factors, not the least of which is the varied socioeconomic status of contemporary Native Americans.

Informed by a social approach that considers virtues, I suggest that it is more fruitful to proceed from the assumption that both Native Americans and archaeologists share in common their value of the virtue (or character trait) of respect toward others. Respect typically connotes the condition of being honored or highly regarded. As an extension, I argue that respect for the dead or for sacred objects is widely accepted cross-culturally (e.g., Carr 1995; Metcalf and Huntington 1991) and can serve as a starting point for discussions between conflicting stakeholders such as Native Americans and archaeologists.

If we consider that unaffiliated human remains and their associated funerary offerings can be thought of as the property of someone who is no longer living and, in some cases potentially unknowable, we move away from concerns over ownership to notions of stewardship and respectful relationship building among parties equally concerned with the care of human remains and associated objects. The question that logically arises from this realization is: "Who are the most appropriate stewards of a particular set of unaffiliated human remains or objects?" I think it is fairly straightforward that, at minimum, the best stewards are going to be a mix of archaeologists *and* contemporary Native Americans whose traditional lands encompass the site from which the remains and objects came.

Native Americans are undoubtedly better suited than any other group inhabiting North America today to care for the remains of other Native Americans respectfully, even in cases where cultural affiliation has not (yet) been determined. Archaeologists, on the other hand, are responsible for being both caretakers of, and advocates for, material and human remains on the behalf of all people. Archaeological ethics demand stewardship, that is, the preservation of the information potential represented by these remains, but also recognize simultaneously that potential descendent communities have an equally valid claim to stewardship (Groarke and Warrick 2006; Joyce 2002; Wylie 2005). With reference to the dispute over Kennewick Man, if an affiliation cannot presently be determined, then what matters is determining who is best suited to care for the remains respectfully and involving all concerned parties in the development of a solution based in compromise.

CONCLUSIONS

My aim in this chapter has been to highlight the benefits of a social ethics perspective on archaeological ethics and use it to suggest fruitful avenues for resolving ethical problems within archaeology. I have argued that archaeologists should adopt a view that openly acknowledges the social implications of archaeological practice and treats the field's problems as not just archaeological but broadly social. A virtue-based ethic provides the best approach to accomplish this because it actively engages the qualities of moral agents involved in conflict *before* identifying moral action and, in this, effectively complements existing archaeological ethics. In the case of repatriation and culturally unaffiliated remains, I suggest that the virtue of respect is integral to identifying a resolution for the conflict and one that must ultimately be based on compromise. Recognizing this, Native Americans and archaeologists involved in repatriation debates like that over Kennewick Man can move away from discussions of ownership to notions of joint stewardship and refocus their energies on respectful care of his remains. Perhaps, as Lynott and Wylie (2000) first suggested nearly a decade ago, it is time (again) to reaffirm stewardship as the centerpiece of archaeologists' ethical principles.

ACKNOWLEDGMENTS

I am grateful to Catherine S. Fowler, Don D. Fowler, and Joe E. Watkins for conversations that have greatly influenced my thinking on this subject over the past few years. The idea for this chapter first developed during a 2001 college ethics class with David Livingston, and I am indebted to him for stressing to me the importance of both structural change and charity in resolving social ethics issues. As a final note, I thank Chip Colwell-Chanthaphonh and T. J. Ferguson for their work applying a virtue ethics framework to ethical issues in anthropology. I believe strongly that it is an approach that holds great promise for cultivating a productive and socially responsible discipline.

REFERENCES

Appadurai, A. 2001. The Globalization of Archaeology and Heritage: A Discussion with Arjun Appadurai. *Journal of Social Archaeology* 1(1):35–49.

Barkan, E., and R. Bush, eds. 2002. *Claiming the Stones, Naming the Bones: Cultural Property and the Negotiation of National and Ethnic Identity.* Los Angeles: Getty Research Institute.

Barker, A. W. 2003. Archaeological Ethics: Museums and Collections. In *Ethical Issues in Archaeology*, edited by L. J. Zimmerman, K. D. Vitelli, and J. Hollowell-Zimmer, pp. 71–83. Walnut Creek, CA: AltaMira Press.

Bray, T. L. 2001. *The Future of the Past: Archaeologists, Native Americans and Repatriation.* New York: Garland.

Brodie, N., and C. Renfrew. 2005. Looting and the World's Archaeological Heritage: The Inadequate Response. *Annual Review of Anthropology* 34:343–361.

Brown, M. F. 2003. *Who Owns Native Culture?* Cambridge, MA: Harvard University Press.

Brubaker, R., and F. Cooper. 2000. Beyond "Identity." *Theory and Society* 29(1):1–47.

Bruning, S. B. 2006. Complex Legal Legacies: The Native American Graves Protection and Repatriation Act, Scientific Study, and Kennewick Man. *American Antiquity* 71(3):501–521.

Carr, C. 1995. Mortuary Practices: Their Social, Philosophical-Religious, Circumstantial, and Physical Determinants. *Journal of Archaeological Method and Theory* 2(2):105–200.

Chippendale, C. 1994. The Concept of the Commons. *Antiquity* 68(159):191–192.

Clark, G. A. 2001. Letter to the Editor. *The SAA Archaeological Record* 1(2):3.

Colwell-Chanthaphonh, C., and T. J. Ferguson. 2004. Virtue Ethics and the Practice of History: Native Americans and Archaeologists along the San Pedro Valley of Arizona. *Journal of Social Archaeology* 4(1):5–27.

Colwell-Chanthaphonh, C., and T. J. Ferguson. 2006. Trust and Archaeological Practice: Towards a Framework of Virtue Ethics. In *The Ethics of Archaeology: Philosophical Perspectives on Archaeological Practice*, edited by C. Scarre and G. Scarre, pp. 115–130. Cambridge: Cambridge University Press.

Crisp, R., and M. L. Slote, eds. 1997. *Virtue Ethics.* Oxford: Oxford University Press.

Deloria, V., Jr. 1973. *God Is Red: A Native View of Religion.* New York: Delta.

Department of the Interior. 1995. 43 CFR Part 10, Native American Graves Protection and Repatriation Act Regulations; Final Rule. *Federal Register* 60(232):62133–62169.

Díaz-Andreu, M., S. Lucy, S. Babic, and D. N. Edwards. 2005. Díaz-Andreu, M., S. Lucy, S. Babiæ and D. N. Edwards 2005. . London: Routledge.

di Leonardo, M. 1999. The Anthropologists' Public-Image Problem. *Chronicle of Higher Education* 45(28):B4.

Dongoske, K. E., M. Aldenderfer, and K. Doehner. 2000. *Working Together: Native Americans Archaeologists.* Washington, DC: Society for American Archaeology.

Earle, T. 2000. Archaeology, Property, and History. *Annual Review of Anthropology* 29:39–60.

Edgar, H. J. H., E. A. Jolie, J. F. Powell, and J. E. Watkins. 2007. Contextual Issues in Paleoindian Repatriation: Spirit Cave Man as a Case Study. *Journal of Social Archaeology* 7(1):101–122.

Ferguson, T. J. 1996. Native Americans and the Practice of Archaeology. *Annual Review of Anthropology* 25:63–79.

Fforde, C. J. H., and P. Turnbull, eds. 2002. *The Dead and Their Possessions: Repatriation in Principle, Policy, and Practice.* London: Routledge.

Fine-Dare, K. S. 2002. *Grave Injustice: The American Indian Repatriation Movement and*

NAGPRA. Lincoln: University of Nebraska Press.

Fluehr-Lobban, C., ed. 2003. *Ethics and the Profession of Anthropology: Dialogue for Ethically Conscious Practice*, 2nd ed. Lanham, MD: Rowman & Littlefield.

Fowler, D. D. 1987. Uses of the Past: Archaeology in the Service of the State. *American Antiquity* 52(2):229–248.

Fowler, D. D., E. A. Jolie, and M. W. Salter. 2008. Archaeological Ethics in Context and Practice. In *Handbook of Archaeological Theories*, edited by R. A. Bentley, H. D. G. Maschner, and C. Chippindale, pp. 409–422. Lanham, MD: AltaMira Press.

Gillespie, S. D., and D. L. Nichols, eds. 2003. *Archaeology Is Anthropology*. Archaeological Papers of the American Anthropological Association, Number 13. Arlington, VA: American Anthropological Association.

Goldstein, L., and K. Kintigh. 1990. Ethics and the Reburial Controversy. *American Antiquity* 55(3):585–591.

Greaves, T. 2002. Examining Indigenous Rights to Culture in North America. *Cultural Dynamics* 14(2):121–142.

Gregor, T. A., and D. R. Goss, 2004. Guilt by Association: The Culture of Accusation and the American Anthropological Association's Investigation of *Darkness in El Dorado*. *American Anthropologist* 106(4):687–698.

Groarke, L., and G. Warrick. 2006. Stewardship Gone Astray? Ethics and the SAA. In *The Ethics of Archaeology: Philosophical Perspectives on Archaeological Practice*, edited by C. Scarre and G. Scarre, pp. 163–177. Cambridge: Cambridge University Press.

Hodder, I. 2004. The "Social" in Archaeological Theory: An Historical and Contemporary Perspective. In *A Companion to Social Archaeology*, edited by L. Meskell and R. W. Preucel, pp. 23–42. Oxford: Blackwell Publishing.

Horn, A. L. 1997. The Kennewick Man Loses Sleep over NAGPRA: Native Americans and Scientists Wrestle over Cultural Remains. *Sovereignty Symposium* 10:501–524. Oklahoma City: Oklahoma Bar Association.

Jenkins, R. 2004. *Social Identity*, 2nd ed. London: Routledge.

Jones, D. G., and R. J. Harris. 1998. Archaeological Human Remains: Scientific, Cultural and Ethical Considerations. *Current Anthropology* 39(2):253–264.

Jones, S. 1997. *The Archaeology of Ethnicity: Constructing Identities in the Past and Present*. London: Routledge.

Joyce, R. A. 2002. Academic Freedom, Stewardship and Cultural Heritage: Weighing the Interests of Stakeholders in Crafting Repatriation Approaches. In *The Dead and Their Possessions: Repatriation in Principle, Policy and Practice*, edited by C. Fforde, J. Hubert, and P. Turnbull, pp. 99–107. London: Routledge.

Kane, S., ed. 2003. *The Politics of Archaeology and Identity in Global Context*. Boston: Archaeological Institute of America.

Kelly, R. L. 2002. Counterpoint: Archaeology *Is* Anthropology. *The SAA Archaeological Record* 2(3):13–14.

King, T. F. 2004. *Cultural Resource Laws and Practice: An Introductory Guide*, 2nd ed. Walnut Creek, CA: AltaMira Press.

Kohl, P. L. 1998. Nationalism and Archaeology: On the Constructions of Nations and the Reconstructions of the Remote Past. *Annual Review of Anthropology* 27:223–246.

Kuhn, R. D. 2002. Archaeology under a Microscope: CRM and the Press. *American Antiquity* 67(2):195–212.

Lamphere, L. 2003. The Perils and Prospects for an Engaged Anthropology: A View from the United States. *Social Anthropology* 11(2):153–168.

Lamphere, L. 2004. Unofficial Histories: A Vision of Anthropology from the Margins. *American Anthropologist* 106(1):126–139.

Lees, S. 2002. Counterpoint: Separation Versus a Larger Vision. *The SAA Archaeological Record* 2(3):11–12.

Lynott, M. J., and A. Wylie. 2000. Stewardship: The Central Principle of Archaeological Ethics. In *Ethics in American Archaeology*, 2nd ed., edited by M. J. Lynott and A. Wylie, pp. 35–39. Washington, DC: Society for American Archaeology.

Meighan, C. W. 1992. Some Scholars' Views on Reburial. *American Antiquity* 57(4):704–710.

Meskell, L., ed. 1998. *Archaeology under Fire: Nationalism, Politics and Heritage in the*

Eastern Mediterranean and Middle East. London: Routledge.

Meskell, L. 2002. The Intersection of Identity and Politics in Archaeology. *Annual Review of Anthropology* 31:279–301.

Meskell, L., and P. Pels, eds. 2005. *Embedding Ethics.* Oxford: Berg.

Messenger, P. M., ed. 1999. *The Ethics of Collecting Cultural Property: Whose Culture? Whose Property?*, 2nd ed. Albuquerque: University of New Mexico Press.

Metcalf, P., and R. Huntington. 1991. *Celebrations of Death: The Anthropology of Mortuary Ritual*, 2nd ed. Cambridge: Cambridge University Press.

Mihesuah, D. A., ed. 2000. *Repatriation Reader: Who Owns American Indian Remains?* Lincoln: University of Nebraska Press.

Moore, S. 1989. Federal Indian Burial Policy: Historical Anachronism or Contemporary Reality? In *Conflict in the Archaeology of Living Traditions*, edited by R. Layton, pp. 201–210. London: Unwin Hyman.

Morenon, E. P. 2003. Nagged by NAGPRA: Is There an Archaeological Ethic? In *Ethics and the Profession of Anthropology: Dialogue for Ethically Conscious Practice*, 2nd ed., edited by C. Fluehr-Lobban, pp. 107–140. Lanham, MD: Rowman & Littlefield.

Nicholas, G. P., and K. P. Bannister. 2004. Copyrighting the Past? Emerging Intellectual Property Rights Issues in Archaeology. *Current Anthropology* 45(3):327–350.

Oakley, J., and D. Cocking. 2001. *Virtue Ethics and Professional Roles.* Cambridge: Cambridge University Press.

Owsley, D. W., and R. L. Jantz. 2001. Archaeological Politics and Public Interest in Paleoamerican Studies: Lessons from Gordon Creek Woman and Kennewick Man. *American Antiquity* 66(4):565–575.

Preucel, R. W., and L. Meskell. 2004. Knowledges. In *A Companion to Social Archaeology*, edited by L. Meskell and R. W. Preucel, pp. 3–22. Oxford: Blackwell Publishing.

Rachels, J. 1993. *The Elements of Moral Philosophy.* New York: McGraw-Hill.

Salmon, M. H. 1999a. Ethics in Science: Special Problems in Anthropology and Archaeology. *Science and Engineering Ethics* 5(3):307–310.

Salmon, M. H. 1999b. Relativist Ethics, Scientific Objectivity, and Concern for Human Rights. *Science and Engineering Ethics* 5(3):311–318.

Scarre, C., and G. Scarre, eds. 2006. *The Ethics of Archaeology: Philosophical Perspectives on Archaeological Practice.* Cambridge: Cambridge University Press.

Slote, M. L. 1992. *From Morality to Virtue.* Oxford: Oxford University Press.

Society for American Archaeology (SAA). 1996. Principles of Archaeological Ethics. Available online at http://www.saa.org/aboutSAA/committees/ethics/principles.html (accessed January 16, 2008).

Stapp, D. C., and M. S. Burney. 2002. *Tribal Cultural Resource Management: The Full Circle to Stewardship.* Walnut Creek, CA: AltaMira Press.

Swidler, N., K. E. Dongoske, R. Anyon, and A. S. Downer, eds. 1997. *Native Americans and Archaeologists: Stepping Stones to Common Ground.* Walnut Creek, CA: AltaMira Press.

Ubelaker, D., and L. G. Grant. 1989. Human Skeletal Remains: Preservation or Reburial? *Yearbook of Physical Anthropology* 32:249–287.

Watkins, J. 1999. Conflicting Codes: Professional, Ethical, and Legal Obligations in Archaeology. *Science and Engineering Ethics* 5(3):337–345.

Watkins, J. 2000. *Indigenous Archaeology: American Indian Values and Scientific Practice.* Walnut Creek, CA: AltaMira Press.

Watkins, J. 2003. Beyond the Margin: American Indians, First Nations, and Archaeology in North America. *American Antiquity* 68(2):273–285.

Watkins, J. 2004. Becoming American or Becoming Indian?: NAGPRA, Kennewick and Cultural Affiliation. *Journal of Social Archaeology* 4(1):60–80.

Watkins, J. 2005a. Through Wary Eyes: Indigenous Perspectives on Archaeology. *Annual Review of Anthropology* 34:429–449.

Watkins, J. 2005b. The Politics of American Archaeology: Cultural Resources, Cultural Affiliation and Kennewick. In *Indigenous Archaeologies: Decolonizing Theory and Practice*, edited by C. Smith and H. M. Wobst, pp. 189–203. London: Routledge.

Weaver, H. N. 2001. Indigenous Identity: What Is It, and Who *Really* Has It? *American Indian Quarterly* 25(2):240–255.

Wilson, R. 2003. The "Feminization" of Anthropology. *Chronicle of Higher Education*

49(32):A13.

Wiseman, J. 2002. Point: Archaeology as an Academic Discipline. *The SAA Archaeological Record* 2(3):8–10.

Wylie, A. 2003. On Ethics. In *Ethical Issues in Archaeology*, edited by L. J. Zimmerman, K. D. Vitelli, and J. Hollowell-Zimmer, pp. 3–16. Walnut Creek, CA: AltaMira Press.

Wylie, A. 2005. The Promise and Perils of an Ethic of Stewardship. In *Embedding Ethics*, edited by L. Meskell and P. Pels, pp. 47–68. Oxford: Berg.

Young, J. O. 2006. Cultures and the Ownership of Archaeological Finds. In *The Ethics of Archaeology: Philosophical Perspectives on Archaeological Practice*, edited by C. Scarre and G. Scarre, pp. 15–31. Cambridge: Cambridge University Press.

Zimmerman, L. J., K. D. Vitelli, and J. Hollowell-Zimmer, eds. 2003. *Ethical Issues in Archaeology*. Walnut Creek, CA: AltaMira Press.

CHAPTER 28
ARCHAEOLOGY AS ACTIVISM
ADAM FISH

WALKING TO SCHOOL WITH THE ANCIENT ONE

In 1998, the Ancient One was two years unearthed and I was a junior archaeology student at the University of Idaho. A color transparency of a *USA Today* newspaper clipping depicting the Ancient One's facial reconstruction was slapped on the overhead in my Human Evolution class. Somebody shrieked, "Captain Picard!" and nervous laughter erupted from the class. *USA Today*, the most pop of American daily newspapers, sandwiched the cast of the Ancient One between advertisements, headlines, and celebrities, as if he was a prehistoric spokesman for a line of sneakers, a discount airline, or a science superhero: *K-Man!* He bumrushed the scene as the doppelganger of *Corpus Delicti*, a commodity and a cyborg, a corporate merger of sci-fi and bones.

Despite being an afternoon's drive in any direction to seven distinct tribal confederations, including each of the defendant tribes in *Bonnichsen et al. v. United States*, my primary educational interaction with Native Americans was through their representations in archaeological texts—typically twenty- to fifty-year-old salvage reservoir reports. By 1998, pedagogies of Indigenous archaeology were fomenting from the works of Vine Deloria, Jr. but were, and remain, outside mainstream teaching. As scientists and Native Americans coded Kennewick Ancient One with their particular brand of significance, students like me could relate to him as a *tabula rasa*, free floating between competing epistemologies, science and tradition, fossil dogma and cosmology.

The Ancient One taught me that archaeology is not science but politics, incapable of objective arbitration, needing a humanistic theory of the past. A fitting talking point for the Ancient One could be the pluralism and hermeneutic encouraged by "postprocessualism," but it is considered mischievous and dismissed as illegitimate in most anthropology departments in eastern Washington and northern Idaho. In many introductory classes, Indigenous and postprocessual archaeology have fifteen minutes of fame, straight by the textbook. Indigenous archaeologists have lectured at Central Washington University, and perhaps elsewhere, but in my tenure as a student, no Indigenous or postprocessual archaeology courses were offered in the two primary institutions of archaeological learning on the Columbia Plateau: Washington State University and the University of Idaho. The exclusion of Indigenous epistemologies in archaeological pedagogy is likely the same throughout most rural universities in the United States.

Outside the academy, along the Columbia River, archaeology is more a laborious description of the width of shovel test probes than significant interpretations of and for Native Americans. Throughout the late 1990s, many professionals and professors paired public sympathy with private disdain for the Ancient One. I remember that many of my co-students planning on entering the cultural resource management (CRM) profession openly scoffed at the Ancient One and supporters of his repatriation.

Orthodox archaeological education encourages the development of a subjective partition in the continua between the prehistoric past and its living expression.[1] Students are not encouraged to merge archaeology with political science (my graduate emphasis). For me, the Ancient One punctured that partition, remerging the spectrum between the past and the present, while exposing the conservative pedagogies of archaeology on the Columbia Plateau.

MODERN DAMS AND BURIAL EROSION IN THE NATIVE AMERICAN WEST
I entered archaeological training in 1997 as twenty-one-year-old budding applied archaeologist. I was immediately dissatisfied with archaeological hermeneutics, field methods, and the absence of civic responsibility. Through the Ancient One, archaeologists' complicity in modes of domination became transparent. Hegemonies of science and bureaucracy systematically control the landscape of the Native American past, reproducing a colonial historiography to facilitate natural resource exploitation. In my heart, I understood this history. My family settled along the Snake River of southern Idaho in the 1940s as pinto bean farmers. I grew up exploring the basalt plain creased by deep riverine canyons, waterfalls, and pictograph cracks, the integrity of which is threatened by the creeping tendrils of putrid reservoirs developed by the U.S. Bureau of Reclamation.

Since 1933, when the Bonneville Dam was constructed, archaeologists have dug up Native American burial grounds eroding from the riverbanks of the Columbia Plateau. The hydraulic-agrarian utopia for the post-Depression family promised to my great-grandparents by the U.S. Bureau of Reclamation and the U.S. Army Corps of Engineers (Corps) was propaganda. Today, in 2005, the military, agribusiness, federal agencies, farmers, archaeologists, and Native Americans are subsidized, and these working people remain serfs to the federal government and its subsidiary industries in impoverished rural towns. This is the context when the Ancient One was disturbed from his burial on the common ground of the Palus, Yakima, Umatilla, and Wanapum—land presently "owned" by the Corps.

NAGPRA IS A CIVIL LAW, NOT A TEST OF SCIENCE
Absolute knowledge of the past or present is impossible.[2] What is possible is archaeology for social justice. The Native American Graves Protection and Repatriation Act (NAGPRA) is a legal compact between Native Americans and the federal government. In this court case, scientists deconstructed indigeneity, as defined in NAGPRA, but NAGPRA should not be tested by a science that fails to find universal facts that enlighten society. Archaeology is better conceived less as a science and more as a tool for social justice and self-discovery. The Ancient One

doesn't present an opportunity to test the science of indigeneity, but a space in which the multicultural ideals of archaeology and democracy can emerge.

While working for the Sacred Land Film Project (www.sacredland.org) and the U.S. Forest Service and U.S. Bureau of Land Management in 2002, I was exposed to Native American topocentric rituals and learned how the National Park Service and other tourism industries commodify traditional cultural places. I returned to the Columbia Plateau in 2003 as an archaeologist employed by the Colville Confederated Tribes to write a cultural overview of the Snake River, an embattled river of dams, Folsom-Clovis burials, rockshelters, and endangered salmon species (Fish 2005). I integrated postcolonialism into western American history; melded traditional concepts of temporality into linear chronologies; performed sociologies on Columbia Plateau anthropological science; and in 2005 wrote the Determination of Eligibility for the National Register of Historic Properties for the Ancient One site. Unfortunately, I have the lonely feeling of being a maverick.

THE POST–KENNEWICK MAN FUTURE

In 2006, hundreds of archaeological reports were written confirming that the Native American past slowly evolved for over 8,000 years, but, according to Judge Gould, it is still not related to anyone Indigenous today (Gould 2004). Many archaeological reports inadvertently define Native American culture as ecologically and biologically determined. The scientific reports fueled the decision reached in *Bonnichsen et al. v. United States* that the Ancient One is not related to any living Native American (Gould 2004). The tribes submitted repatriation packets consisting of detailed ethnographic, archaeological, and traditional information to the Jelderks and Gould courts. Nevertheless, in the minds of the judges, the tribal packets did not surmount the immense library of archaeological science that marginalizes Indigenous knowledge while magnifying an empiricist's epistemology.

As highfalutin' as it seems, critical theory must inform the pedagogy of archaeology—even in rural U.S. universities. I envision a utopia in which tribal historic preservation officers embrace graduate students as human rights interns, where social work is as important as archaeological field schools. In this dream, more young archaeologists seek out experimental archaeological theorists, new mediasmiths, and Native American Elders for teachers. They return to integrate their newfound practice with their professional lives. Every site report is a small multimedia artwork of impeccable documentation, Elder interviews, and reflection, and is made available in the local vernacular to affected communities and on the Internet for online public contributions. When a future Ancient One is inadvertently discovered, the court is inundated—not only with indecipherable hieroglyphics of carbon 14 scatterplots—but by an engaged public and archaeologists more concerned with the living than the dead.

In the summer of 2004, I participated with tribal Elders, youths, and leaders in several day-long reburial ceremonies for over forty repatriated Colville ancestors disturbed from their rest because of dams and industrial undertakings. The Seven-Drum and Catholic prayers, rosewater, cedar boughs, Shaker bells, and brow sweat from hand digging the ancestors' graves are sensual evidence of NAGPRA's empowerment of contemporary tribal spirituality. The return of ancestors to the Earth is essential for Columbia Plateau traditional culture.

NOTES

1. Even the most fundamental archaeometry—not to mention historical and ethnoarchaeology—requires some reimagining of an "ethnographic present" or personal experience with which to contextualize empirical observations. This alone foils the objectivity-producing partition between the past and the present.

2. It is perhaps possible only to control the production of the future in experimental physics and microbiology.

REFERENCES

Fish, A. 2005. Social Archaeologies, Ethnographies, and Histories of the Lower Snake River: Cultural Overviews of the Lower Monumental Reservoir. Prepared by the History/Archaeology Program, Confederated Colville Tribes, in partial fulfillment of contract # DACW68-03-P-0154. Prepared for the Walla Walla Corps of Engineers, Walla Walla District. Copies available from the Walla Walla Corps of Engineers, Walla Walla District, Walla Walla, Washington.

Gould, J. 2004. Opinion and Order for *Robson Bonnichsen et al. v. United States of America et al.* Opinion and Order of the United States, Civil No. 96-1481-JE.

CHAPTER 29
MY OWN PERSONAL "KENNEWICK MAN"
IAN THOMPSON

I am honored to have been asked for my views about Kennewick Man. A graduate student in archaeology, my direct experience with Kennewick Man is far less than that of many of the other contributors to this volume; nevertheless he has played an important part in my life. I hope that the following personal account and comparison of the Kennewick Man controversy with a similar incident that happened in my grandfather's homeland will benefit this work.

My background is varied. I am Choctaw, Creek, and central and western European. I did not grow up in a predominantly Native community, but from an early age I was fortunate to be under the guidance of Choctaw traditional arts teachers, who taught me flint-knapping, hide-working, and many other wonderful things as I matured. I initially became interested in archaeology because I saw it as a way to continue to learn about certain aspects of the traditional arts in school and to end up eventually with a degree in the process.

I remember well the summer Kennewick Man came to light. It was two years after I started to consider archaeology as a potential career and about the time my freshman year of high school began. I learned about the recovery of the bones on the evening news. At the next monthly meeting of the local archaeological society, everyone was excited about the important find and concerned over the possibility that it might not get studied. In a way, Kennewick Man is what first made me acutely aware of the philosophical difference that often exists between traditional people and mainstream archaeologists. This came about the following week, when I discussed the situation with a mentor. Instead of being interested in the implications of the find as my archaeologist friends had been, he asked me how I would feel if some recently deceased relative of mine were exhumed for study, suggesting an equivalence between this and what was proposed for Kennewick Man. Ultimately, I was counseled that whatever information could be extracted from the remains of this human being would not bring about anything significant and that they should be left alone.

Initially in the Kennewick debate, I leaned a little more toward the primacy of science than what my mentor had recommended. My interest was captured by popular publications, such as the articles in the *New Yorker* (Preston 1997) and *Newsweek* (Begley and Murr 1999), which presented interviews with professional archaeologists who made some provocative statements. As an adolescent, although I did not wholeheartedly accept everything these archaeologists suggested, I did trust them as qualified scientists who could speak with some authority on the subject. Thankfully, the intervening years of my schooling in archaeology helped bring me back to my roots. Gaining a stronger understanding of the discipline shook my faith in the infallibility of its assertions, and I came increasingly to see the wisdom in what my mentor had taught me from the beginning about Kennewick Man, history, and respect for ancestors as well as the living. Now, eleven years after that first news story, I see Kennewick Man as a dual entity that has existed for me nearly as long as archaeology has: both as an individual who lived more than 400 generations ago and as an internationally publicized conflict. For me, this second facet of Kennewick Man has unfortunately and drastically overshadowed the first.

The conflict over Kennewick Man brings up a number of important issues in Native–Euro American relations, but I comment from my current vantage point on what I believe it indicates about the current state of Americanist archaeology. To me it seems that, despite the frequently made assertion that archaeology has moved on from its colonialist roots, the Kennewick Man controversy is unashamedly founded on a still-adamantly defended 500-year-old colonial assumption (see Garcia 1729), which holds that those trained according to the Western European tradition are, by default, the best qualified to interpret the history of the American peoples. The error of this assumption has been evidenced repeatedly by its fruits.

Poignantly, the Kennewick Man controversy shares a chilling number of similarities with something that happened in what is now the southeastern United States during the 19th century: the Moundbuilder controversy. Prominent features of the landscape in this region are earth mounds, created for millennia by many of the region's Indigenous peoples. These mounds are still revered, used, and constructed today (e.g., by the Choctaw Nation of Oklahoma Capitol Grounds), and there is no intervening point during which they were not. In spite of the contemporary 19th century evidence to the contrary, popular formulations of the Moundbuilder Hypothesis attributed the mounds to any number of Old World groups. Native Americans, on the other hand, were said to be descended from an underdeveloped mass of people who had invaded the Americas, annihilating the continent's original, advanced, and possibly "white," mound-building inhabitants. This was used as a justification for contemporary colonial practices, particularly removal.

A painful irony is that, at exactly the same time that one formulation of the Moundbuilder Hypothesis (Priest 1833) was becoming a best-selling book, Choctaw survivors of the Trail of Tears were constructing two new earth mounds at Nanih Waiya, Oklahoma (James Briscoe personal communication), resembling two other very sacred mounds in Mississippi that they had been forced to leave, partially as a result of the Moundbuilder Hypothesis. Even if the proponents of the Moundbuilder Hypothesis were aware of instances such as this, it is unlikely that much would have changed. To accept that Native people built the mounds would have contradicted the dominant paradigm, which held that Native inhabitants of the region were primitive and incapable of creating anything so complex. Such an acceptance would also have held up colonial "progress."

Similarly, in the Kennewick Man and related controversies, something has been found that most archaeologists did not expect according to the dominant racialist paradigm: skeletons possessing morphologies different from that of the constructed

Native American "type." Although the metrics of the bones fall outside the range of all other living populations, some of their traits have been said by some to look European. This has been combined with certain perceived similarities in the artifact forms of Pleistocene North America and Western Europe to suggest that the First Americans were of Western European origin (Bradley and Stanford 2004; Stanford and Bradley 2002).

Accordingly, the people who lived in the Americas 10,000 years ago are no longer to be called "Paleo-Indians," which implies a connection with the people living here when Columbus came; they are now "Paleo-Americans." It is asserted that certain types of stone projectile points, including the Cascade example lodged in Kennewick Man's hip, were produced by another group known as "Archaic Indians" (Preston 1997:80).

In case the implication is somehow missed, Chatters has said of the spearpoint: "It may be a sign of ethnic conflict" (Begley and Murr 1999:55). Stanford, a plaintiff in the Kennewick suit, is quoted as saying that America's original Caucasian inhabitants, such as Kennewick Man, were "obliterated," possibly intentionally, by the ancestors of the people living here when Columbus came (Begley and Murr 1999:55). Essentially the scenario for this is that an invading Mongolian horde— "Archaic Indians"—wiped out the original, advanced "high-tech forager," European inhabitants of this continent—the "Paleo-Americans"—through warfare and/or disease.

Although the hypothesis has profound evidential gaps and has been refuted within the professional community (see Straus 2000), it has been widely publicized to the general public through the previously mentioned *New Yorker* and *Newsweek* articles, where it has the appearance of being accepted by professional archaeology. Predictably, some have extrapolated a great deal from this interpretation, depicting the last 500 years of colonization as a just reclamation of land, and discounting the use for Native sovereignty in the 21st century (Ponte 1999). It is even suggested that the Native American reburial effort embodied in the Native American Graves Protection and Repatriation Act could be an attempt to hide the truth about these "Paleo-Americans" (Preston 1997:81).

In light of the above, the Kennewick Man and Moundbuilder controversies may be said minimally to share the following basic similarities: Archaeologists encounter something unexpected according to the dominant paradigm; it is interpreted as evidence of an early, advanced, and likely "white" civilization; despite available evidence to the contrary, the find is said to indicate that the late-arriving ancestors of today's Native Americans invaded the continent and exterminated these original inhabitants; the interpretation is immediately distributed to the popular press; it impacts the way the general public views living Native Americans; this affects national policy.

Recently, a very similar hypothesis and scenario has been formed around Pleistocene, "Polynesian-looking" bones from Serra Da Capivara, Brazil, which includes the violent annihilation of the original "American Aborigines" at the hands of American Indians who later arrived in that region. This hypothesis was disseminated to an international public (BBC News 1999). The evidence presented by all of these bones could have been interpreted in any number of ways. The repeated popular depiction of genocide at the hands of ancestral Native Americans makes it almost seem as if, when confronted with the unexpected, some researchers are predisposed to reach this particular conclusion and broadcast it as sensationally and as widely as possible.

What can be done to alter the cycle? Indigenous leaders have worked on aspects of this problem for centuries, and as evidenced by the outcome of the Kennewick court case, it is nearly as unlikely now that an immediate solution can be reached as it was in the past. This is because a final, mutually positive resolution would require broad, cross-cultural understanding and respect on a level that has rarely been achieved in colonial society. Speaking specifically in terms of Americanist archaeology, I think the beginning of the answer returns to a consideration of the human aspect of Kennewick Man.

The oral traditions of most Native communities and competent archaeology both suggest that the Indigenous past of this continent was incredibly dynamic. As is the case today, rapid change often occurred on a variety of levels and engaged with a great deal of linguistic, genetic, and political diversity to create a wonderful vibrancy and complexity, much more than is often acknowledged. The person who was Kennewick Man was part of this.

This does not make him something other than a Native American, or mean that he or his community originated anywhere other than the Columbia River Valley, or in any way imply that both are not directly ancestral to people living there when Columbus arrived. What it does imply is that the Native American past is not the static, unchanging, and dehumanized entity that is often found in history textbooks. For several reasons, textbook coverage sadly makes up a major part of the exposure most Americans have with the Native American past and present. Because of this, when some element of the real precolonial complexity is encountered, drastic explanations seem plausible to many because the evidence does not fit with the portrayal of Native Americans and the Native American past to which most have been exposed. Particularly when they are parallel with political goals, these explanations gain popularity. Sometimes this leads to unavoidable conflict, legal and otherwise.

The past sets the foundation for the present, not just literally, but also cognitively. Accordingly, I believe one important approach is for Indigenous people and other like-minded individuals to work toward the more regular incorporation of nonesoteric, Indigenous understandings of the past into "official," popular histories of Native American people, so that their depiction may become more emic and as detailed and human as current presentations of the U.S. past. On the broadest level, this will tend to discourage romanticism, stereotypes, and a general view of Native American people, past and present, as some type of mysterious "other."

In archaeological terms, if realistic views of this continent's precolonial human past become more prevalent, popularly accepted interpretations of that past, and actions based on them, may tend less often to reflect the recent history of the now-dominant society. Contributions to this volume and a great deal of other work done by Indigenous archaeologists, community leaders, and members are a strong start to this process. However, I believe much more remains to be done—perhaps most immediately for archaeologists this includes outreach, publication, and curriculum development—before a situation can be approached in which "Kennewick Man" and thousands of other exhumed individuals from across the continent can finally rest in peace, both in my mind and literally.

REFERENCES

BBC News. 1999. First Americans Were Australian. August 26. Available online at news.bbc.co.uk/hi/english/sci/tech/newsid_430000/430944.stm (accessed October 6, 2005).

Begley, S., and A. Murr. 1999. The First Americans. *Newsweek*, April 26, pp. 50–57.

Bradley, B., and D. Stanford. 2004. The North Atlantic Ice-Edge Corridor: A Possible Paleolithic Route to the New World. *World Archaeology* 36(4):459–478.

Garcia, G. 1729 [1607]. *Origins de los Indios de el Muevo Mundo, e Indias Occidentales*. Edited by A. Gonzalez de Barcia Carbadillo y Zuniga. Madrid: Francisco Martinez Abad.

Ponte, L. 1999. Politically Incorrect Genocide Part 2. October 5. Available online at http://www.frontpage.com/Articles/ReadArticle.asp?ID2658 (accessed September 14, 2005).

Preston, D. 1997. The Lost Man. *The New Yorker*, June 16, pp. 70–81.

Priest, J. 1833. *American Antiquities, and Discoveries in the West*. Albany, NY: Hoffman and White.

Stanford, D., and B. Bradley 2002. Ocean Trails and Prairie Paths? Thoughts about Clovis Origins. In *The First Americans: The Pleistocene Colonization of the New World*, edited by N. G. Jablonski, pp. 255–272. San Francisco: Memoirs of the California Academy of Sciences.

Straus, L. G. 2000. Solutrean Settlement of North America: A Review of Reality. *American Antiquity* 65(2):219–226.

CHAPTER 30
KENNEWICK MAN: WHAT DOES THE FUTURE HOLD?[1]

DEWARD E. WALKER, JR.

In 1990 and as part of a sometimes tense and conflicted process, Congress passed, and President George Bush signed into law, the Native American Graves Protection and Repatriation Act (NAGPRA), a result of more than thirty years of Native American political action. As with other legislation, such as the 1978 American Indian Religious Freedom Act, American Indians heralded the day as a victory, but a majority of anthropologists, and especially archaeologists, considered it a serious threat. Many in anthropology, archaeology, and sister disciplines believed that their basic right to conduct research as scientists was being compromised and they mounted their own campaign to defend their scientific right and authority to continue their historical practices of unfettered study of Native American peoples, cultures, and prehistory.

Beginning a historic set of events that are transforming U.S. anthropology, a skull and other bones were found eroding out of the banks of the Columbia River near Kennewick, Washington, in July 1996. Almost immediately, this discovery became the subject of a battle between anthropologists and American Indians, the latter insisting that the skeleton be repatriated for reburial. They were opposed by a vocal group of archaeologists who wanted to study the 9,000+ BP skeleton. A controversial legal case[2] (*Bonnichsen et al. v. United States*) was initiated by archaeologists following a press and media campaign more publicized than any other subject in U.S. anthropology or archaeology in several decades. Although tribes have lost the legal case for control of the Kennewick remains, many other issues remain unresolved and are taking both political and intellectual forms.

This complex mixture of science and politics includes such actions by archaeologists as denouncing tribal religious claims as mere politics, for example. A select group of archaeologists has also constructed a pre-Clovis framework within which to place the Kennewick and similar ancient remains, illustrated, for example, by Bonnichsen and Turnmire in *Ice Age Peoples of North America: Environments, Origins, and Adaptations of the First Americans* (1999). Bonnichsen and Turnmire (1999:back cover) attempt to "provide an up-to-date summary of important new discoveries earlier than 10,000 years old from Northeast Asia and North America that are changing our perceptions about the origin of the First Americans" and include articles by several of the archaeologists involved in the Kennewick litigation. A number of professional archaeologists and other related specialists have become involved in this and other forms of intellectual politics that have become all too familiar in the continuing Kennewick conflict. Some subscribe to a possible Ainu resemblance for Kennewick man, retreating from their initial claims for a

Caucasoid origin for the remains. These are undisguised attempts to limit the effects of NAGPRA on the Kennewick remains and other ancient skeletons and to seek support for expensive and complex scientific testing (see Chatters 2000).

Chronicling these developments and their probable impacts on the future of U.S. anthropology are two books that deserve careful assessment as windows on the future resulting from this controversy: *Riddle of the Bones: Politics, Science, Race, and the Story of Kennewick Man* (Downey 2000) and *Skull Wars: Kennewick Man, Archaeology, and the Battle for Native American Identity* (Thomas 2000).

Riddle of the Bones chronicles the discovery and the legal and ongoing political battle concerning Kennewick Man, with revealing details about the players and their personalities engaged in the intellectual politics surrounding this conflict. Beginning with the discovery of the Kennewick skeletal remains by a group of locals from Kennewick, Washington, in July 1996, Downey weaves a tale that includes fraud, folly, and the ineptitude of many. Throughout his narrative, Downey examines the validity of race, the development of U.S. archaeology, and how both academia and the federal government have historically dealt with American Indians. Although many are familiar with the story of Kennewick Man to some degree, most are unaware of all that took place in the four years following its discovery. By chronicling the step-by-step unfolding of the Kennewick controversy, Downey provides interesting and essential insights. For example, we learn that Jim Chatters was on the scene within a matter of hours, having received a phone call from the deputy in charge of the investigation. Not only was Chatters involved immediately, but he was permitted to take the bones home for further investigation. We also learn that Chatters conducted further excavations at the site prior to receiving a permit from the U.S. Army Corps of Engineers (Corps), a requirement under Archaeological Resource Protection Act guidelines. Downey describes a press conference in which journalists asked Colonel Curtis of the Corps if the bones were "Caucasoid" and resembled "pre-modern Europeans," and if so:

> why did the provisions of NAGPRA, intended to govern disposal *of only* Native American remains, apply at all? And apply or not, wasn't it necessary to submit the remains for further scientific study to determine exactly to whom they should be repatriated? Wasn't repatriation without examination merely an example of the progress of science being thwarted by religious superstitions? (Downey 2000:43, emphasis added)

In addition to describing details of the Kennewick case, a highlight of Downey's book is his critical review of the biological basis of race. Downey examines various biological and genetic theories employed in making racial distinctions, such as brachycephalization (increasing head breadth in relation to head length), mtDNA, and Y chromosome testing. This is beneficial not only for other scholars in the field who may not be familiar with these theories and methods, but it also allows the general public to better understand some of the foundations upon which the Kennewick case is being argued. Downey sums up the current state of population

genetics and its implications for Kennewick's alleged "Caucasoid" features as follows: "It's possible, of course, to claim that the reason for the drift is that an earlier
'Caucasoid' [group], was overwhelmed (absorbed) by later waves of brachycephal-
ic American Indians. Possible, but completely without evidential support" (Downey
2000:104).

Such speculation is also addressed in David Hurst Thomas's *Skull Wars:
Kennewick Man, Archaeology, and the Battle for Native American Identity*. Thomas
adopts a different approach in his projections concerning the future. Whereas
Downey deals with many of the events and personalities surrounding the
Kennewick case, Thomas takes a broader historical view following the example of
Stephen Jay Gould, who wisely and constantly reminded us that science is an assemblage of artifacts contingent on history, individual personality, and chance. Thomas
is curator of anthropology at the American Museum of Natural History in New York,
and his extensive background in anthropology and archaeology, as well as his famil-
iarity with Native American affairs, are clearly evident in his approach to the
Kennewick case. Introduced by Vine Deloria, Jr., the Thomas book provides a
recounting of the Kennewick remains, how they were discovered, and how their
alleged Caucasoid features all became highly controversial.

Thomas provides some historical context by describing how such figures as
Thomas Jefferson, Lewis Henry Morgan, Frank Cushing, Franz Boas, A. L.
Kroeber, and others contributed to the development of anthropology as a distinct
academic discipline in the United States. In *Skull Wars*, we also read about the
numerous injustices and outrageous acts committed toward American Indians in the
name of anthropology and archaeology. Thomas is to be credited for his forthright
description of abuses committed in the name of science, in which American Indians
have been routinely treated as objects of scientific study while having little voice or
authority over the process. Thomas also documents the actions of the federal government toward American Indians from the time of Thomas Jefferson (alleged by
some to have been the first U.S. archaeologist) up to the present and how they are
linked to anthropology and the Kennewick conflict. He provides the reader with
essential historical background concerning the frequent contradictions in federal
policy, ranging from policies based on the "Vanishing Americans" to "Noble
Redman"; from assimilation policies to "the Indian New Deal"; from "Red Power"
to the American Indian movement. Thomas is unusual in the extent to which he successfully presents the social, cultural, legal, political, and historical contexts and
background leading up to the Kennewick conflict. More archaeologists should pay
attention to his interpretation of the history of their discipline.

What, then, does the Kennewick conflict bode for the future of U.S. anthropology and archaeology? *Riddle of the Bones* and *Skull Wars* differ in their purpose, but
each deals with the Kennewick controversy and what it means for the future of
anthropology and archaeology. These are useful windows on the rapidly evolving
relationships between anthropologists and American Indians, especially as
American Indians take an increasing voice (scientific, administrative, and political)
in the conduct of research affecting them, their cultures, and their ancestors. Even

though both books cover the Kennewick conflict, they are different in content, style, and purpose.

Downey's book offers the reader an immediate, local view of the case. Here we see intellectual politics at play, including the postures of the many individuals involved, including Jim Chatters, Jeff Van Pelt, Robsen Bonnichsen, and others. "On close reading, it exposes a jagged fault line, largely generational, between investigators [archaeologists] still wedded to a traditional approach to investigating the human past, and others who embrace sophisticated techniques of investigation unknown to their teachers' generation" (Downey 2000:x). Thomas's book deals with the larger context of the conflict, including the history of anthropology, archaeology, and Native American affairs, and addresses the future of these fields.

One must read both books to grasp the situation and its implications for the future of anthropology and archaeology and their acceptance/reception by the tribes. For example, although archaeologists have sought protective legislation for their research, tribes are pursuing a more extensive political and legislative agenda that often conflicts with anthropological and archaeological goals and objectives. Failure by anthropologists to recognize and adjust to this transformation will only intensify current and future conflicts concerning Kennewick Man, Spirit Cave, and similar discoveries. We must accept the fact that Native people will play a leading role in deciding how the remains of their ancestors are to be treated, how places important to their cultural survival are to be protected, and, most importantly, how anthropologists and archaeologists will conduct their research in the future.

Apart from Downey and Thomas, numerous other researchers are calling for this change in our dealings and workings with American Indians (see, among others, High Plains Society for Applied Anthropology 2000; Stapp and Longenecker 2000). Ironically, in a publication by the Society for American Archaeology (SAA), distributed to all members of the SAA and entitled *Teaching Archaeology in the Twenty-First Century* (Bender and Smith 2000), there is only cursory mention of American Indians. This book attempts to chart the future direction of archaeology, in both teaching and practice. Unfortunately, in all of its 149 pages, American Indians are mentioned only four times as having any role in the future of American archaeology, a clearly misguided assessment of the future by some of the leaders of the principal professional archaeological society in the United States.

Part of the future will also include a growing number of disputes among the tribes requesting repatriation. Not only are there emerging conflicts between archaeologists and American Indians, but there are also intertribal conflicts among such groups as the Hopi and Navajo, the Great Basin NAGPRA Coalition, or the Yakama, Umatilla, Nez Perce, Wanapum, and Colville concerning how NAGPRA and similar legislation are to be interpreted and implemented. There is much work necessary before such tribal differences are resolved.

CONCLUSION

The time has now passed when anthropologists and archaeologists could conduct research on American Indian people, their culture, and their history in an unrestrained manner. Although *Teaching Archaeology in the Twenty-First Century* neglects to point it out, the best place to begin this process is in the universities and colleges where anthropologists and archaeologists are trained. *Riddle of the Bones* or *Skull Wars* should be required reading for all anthropology students. They should also be read by all who wish to understand the profound changes taking place in U.S. anthropology. As Vine Deloria, Jr. challenges us in the foreword to *Skull Wars* (Deloria 2000:xvi):

> David Hurst Thomas now marches into the swamp with the news, honestly stated but hardly welcome to his profession, that we should wash our dirty laundry now before things get completely out of hand, that we should carefully evaluate the present state of the discipline, and that we should build on the positive things now happening and work toward a more cooperative and productive future. Wise thoughts from a courageous thinker. Now, will we heed them?

Although our respected colleague Deloria has now joined his own ancestors, I earnestly hope that his advice and counsel will not be forgotten.

NOTES

1. This article derives from an original coauthored article completed with Peter N. Jones and published in *American Anthropologist*, December 2000. I take responsibility for all changes made to the original coauthored article.

2. A decision has been reached and described in the article in this volume by Darby Stapp and Peter Jones.

REFERENCES

Bender, S. J., and G. S. Smith, eds. 2000. *Teaching Archaeology in the Twenty-First Century*. Washington, DC: Society for American Archaeology.

Bonnichsen, R., and K. L. Turnmire, eds. 1999. *Ice Age Peoples of North America: Environments, Origins, and Adaptations of the First Americans*. Corvallis: Oregon State University Press.

Chatters, J. 2000. The Recovery and First Analysis of an Early Holocene Human Skeleton from Kennewick, Washington. *American Antiquity* 65(2):291–316.

Deloria, V., Jr. 2000. Foreword. In *Skull Wars: Kennewick Man, Archaeology, and the Battle for Native American Identity*, edited by V. Deloria, Jr. New York: Basic Books.

Downey, R. 2000. *Riddle of the Bones: Politics, Science, Race, and the Story of Kennewick Man*. New York: Copernicus.

High Plains Society for Applied Anthropology. 2000. *High Plains Applied Anthropologist* 20(1):67–71.

Stapp, D., and J. Longenecker. 2000. The Times, They Are A-Changin': Can Archaeologists and Native Americans Change with the Times? *Society for American Archaeology Bulletin* 18(2):18–20, 27.

Thomas, D. H. 2000. *Skull Wars: Kennewick Man, Archaeology, and the Battle for Native American Identity*. New York: Basic Books.

CHAPTER 31
ARCHAEOLOGY THE TRIBAL WAY: REESTABLISHING THE BOUNDARIES OF CULTURE

ORA MAREK-MARTINEZ

Kennewick Man was discovered in July 1996, below the surface of Lake Wallula, a section of the Columbia River behind McNary Dam in Kennewick, Washington (McManamon, Roberts, and Blades 2004). Several historic preservation regulations were set in motion because the human remains of the Ancient One were located on federal property, which seems to be the catalyst of the controversy among several tribes and teams of scientists. This situation testifies to the sad and often difficult state of affairs that many tribes face when working in the federal arena of cultural resource management (CRM). Events involving Kennewick Man exemplify the need for training Native American and/or Indigenous people in historic preservation, archaeology, and CRM so that tribes can create and maintain tribally specific archaeology programs.

The recent conflict concerning the Ancient One, or Kennewick Man, epitomizes the conflicted interactions between Native American tribes, anthropologists, and archaeologists that are inherent in areas such as managing cultural resources, artifact collection, and the implementation of historic preservation regulations. The lack of protection for sites and cultural resources significant to Native American tribes directly contributes to culture loss for many generations of Native peoples because ceremonial sites, sacred sites, other culturally significant sites, and cultural resources are important parts of the entire culture. The final decisions made concerning the final disposition of the Ancient One has many implications for future discoveries made on tribal lands, especially in the definition and later protection of cultural resources important to tribes.

The passage of laws such as the Native American Graves Protection and Repatriation Act (NAGPRA) and the National Museum of American Indian Act prompted many Native American tribes to raise legitimate grievances against the entire field of anthropology. These laws specifically protect cultural resources and human remains that are linked biologically, culturally, and historically to Native American tribes. Other regulations, such as the National Historic Preservation Act (NHPA) and the Archaeological Resources Protection Act (ARPA), which predate NAGPRA, protect the prehistory of America by categorizing these sites and cultural resources as archaeological resources. Although the intent of such laws is worthwhile, they undermine the relationship and importance of these sites and cultural resources to Native American tribes, as they are often created by nontribal members and are enforced by nontribal members who may not have an understanding of tribal worldviews.

Early historic preservation laws have strict guidelines and eligibility requirements for what constitutes a cultural resource or historic property, which are culturally constructed by the dominant white American culture and do not recognize the
significance of Native American concepts of cultural resources and sites. However,
recent amendments to national historic preservation legislation have provided for
the protection of sites that have special significance to Native American cultures.
Nevertheless, the problem remains that many tribal entities have attempted to secure
protection for cultural resources and sites having cultural significance because previously there were no means of protection under existing law. As these sites and cultural resources did not fit into Western definitions or categories of archaeological
sites and resources, many were destroyed or desecrated.

This is the situation with the Kennewick Man case. Initially, it was to be affiliated as "Native American" (Babbitt 2001), but later decisions by U.S. Magistrate J.
Jelderks repealed the decision made by Babbitt, and the remains of Kennewick Man
were turned over to a team of scientists for further study. The collected evidence
used to establish Kennewick Man as Native American as defined by NAGPRA was
based primarily on the oral histories of contemporaneous Native American tribes,
which is a legitimate source of evidence, but is strengthened when used in conjunction with other lines of evidence. However, in mainstream U.S. academic institutions, oral histories have not been considered a legitimate source of evidence and are
easily dismissed, which destabilizes tribal claims for cultural affiliation with the
Ancient One.

To ensure that their histories are seen as legitimate, tribes need actively to participate in the creation of their tribal histories—from the field research to the published report. This can be accomplished if tribes create archaeology programs that
will allow tribal management of cultural resources so they can create effective regulations to protect their cultural resources on and off the reservation. For Indigenous
cultures to survive and thrive in the future, the tribes will have to manage their cultural resources (Matero 2000; Salazar, Roberts, and Bohnert 2000; Swidler et al.
2000). Some methods to achieve this are integrating tribal perspectives in archaeological methodologies (Stapp 2000), including tribes throughout the entire process
of the project (Swidler et al. 2000), and utilizing tribal methods for conservation and
management of cultural resources (Matero 2000). The main intent behind this
movement is to maintain cultural traditions and provide training to the younger generations in appropriate management of cultural resources—a circular process that
will ensure the transmission of culture from one generation to the next.

The definition, categorization, and collection of cultural resources important to
Native Americans also need to be addressed if proper consultation and collaboration
are to occur. These acts epitomize the process of colonization (Hinsley 2000; Tsosie
1997) and, by performing these acts, archaeologists, anthropologists, and federal
bureaucrats are writing histories for tribal peoples and interpreting cultural values,
traditions, and perspectives through an ethnocentric lens that has damaging implications for the tribes and the public (Miri 2001; Shull 2001). In the case of the
Ancient One, the act of defining "cultural resources" is problematic for Native

American tribes, especially because white Americans have created the definitions for what is Native American and what is archaeological.

However, it is exactly through collaboration and consultation with tribes that problems associated with defining cultural resources can be laid to rest (Begay 1997; Dongoske and Anyon 1997; Shull 2001; White Deer 1997). Since initial consultation and collaboration began with tribal entities, the creation of inclusive definitions of cultural resources important to Native Americans has increased. For instance, the creation of *National Register Bulletin 38: Traditional Cultural Properties*, which provides guidance in nominating Native American cultural resources to the National Register of Historic Places, was the product of widespread consultation with tribes across the nation and the National Park Service. It is imperative that tribes, bureaucrats, and archaeologists work together in creating definitions that truly reveal the character and uniqueness of cultural resources that are important to Indigenous cultures (Begay 1997; Dongoske and Anyon 1997; White Deer 1997).

Through acts of legislation such as NHPA, ARPA, and NAGPRA, archaeologists must categorize cultural resources according to their scientific merit in order to provide some means of protection (Shull 2001; Tsosie 1997), a process that often degrades the cultural value of the resource. This approach is problematic to Native Americans, especially because resources become valued for their contribution to scientific knowledge, rather than to wider cultural, spiritual, or ethnohistorical information. The evidence used to disprove the initial decision of Secretary Babbitt was associated with a scientific perspective that in U.S. culture is seen as being superior.

The creation of tribally managed CRM programs allows tribes to enter into dialog with federal agencies and archaeologists beyond the simple stipulations for consultation with tribes that is mandated by various pieces of legislation. This action levels the playing field, so to speak, for tribal/Indigenous archaeologists and their CRM programs. In addition, many tribes feel that the creation of CRM programs tailored to their individual needs allows tribes to *perpetuate* their culture, rather than simply *preserve* it (Begay 1997; Welch, Mahaney, and Riley 2000).

By managing their own cultural resources, tribes are reclaiming their past, protecting the present, and preparing for the next generation who will be in charge of protecting cultural resources (Begay 1997; Martin 1997; Welch 2000). When tribes are managing their cultural resources in a manner consistent with their cultural beliefs, language, and worldviews about science and antiquity, they are practicing an Indigenous archaeology. Tribes are then effectively able to "play the game" of mainstream CRM legislation, defend their beliefs, history, and worldviews, and change their lives. If this were the status quo, the decisions regarding the Ancient One would be very different indeed!

The institutional practice of defining and interpreting objects plays a huge role in the protection and management of Indigenous cultural resources. In the past, this practice was an execution of power relations, because "to know something is to gain power over it" (Crawford 2000:229). Interpreting or defining then "becomes a battle over who is to control historical narratives and hence who is to have power over the categories of identity that dominate and control the present and the future" (Crawford 2000:230). Eventually, this becomes a battle over who is going to write Native American histories and who is the authority on Native American culture and history. The displacement of tribal narratives from mainstream American history and knowledge is proof of these power relations. Interpreting and defining cultural resources from the dominant white American perspective destroys the context and integrity of the resource, which enables curators and scholars to reorganize and recategorize tribal cultural resources in a manner that is familiar to their background, knowledge, and culture, thus ignoring and displacing tribal perspectives.

The issues confronted by the tribes in the Ancient One case highlight many of these issues, especially in violations of CRM legislation, the definition, categorization, and collection of remains and the unethical practice of archaeology, CRM, and anthropology. The five tribes that comprised the claimant's party were the Confederated Tribes of the Colville Reservation, the Confederated Tribes of the Umatilla Reservation, the Confederated Tribes and Bands of the Yakama Indian Nation of the Yakama Reservation, the Nez Perce Tribe of Idaho, and the Wanapum Band, each of which has remained strong in their claims. The trials and tribulations of the Nez Perce tribe of Idaho in their undertaking to repatriate the remains of the Ancient One, whom they see as an "ancestor" (Cannell 2005), will be used as a case study to illustrate the need for tribes to create and manage cultural resource and archaeology programs.

The Nez Perce tribe has a cultural resources program within the larger Natural Resources Department that serves to "protect, perpetuate, and preserve the cultural resources of the Nimiipuu" by monitoring federal, tribal, and state compliance with historic preservation legislation and regulations (Nez Perce Tribe website 2007). The Cultural Resources program has six components to it: archaeological, anthropological, cultural, language retention, knowledge of Elders, and arts. Like many other tribes, the Nez Perce tribe has a program that is understaffed and underfunded, demonstrating the need for a separate archaeology program with a separate staff and budget to the cultural resources program. A separate archaeology program will allow each program to develop and will begin to produce fully trained tribal archaeologists and tribal revenues.

However, since the Ancient One case, the Nez Perce tribal council voted to establish a code to support a Tribal Historic Preservation Office (THPO), the necessary preliminary step before being able to apply for one through the National Historic Preservation Act. However, the Nez Perce tribe has not established regulatory or procedural changes because the Kennewick Man case and the existing policies only address research designs from those who are applying to work within the reservation boundaries. With the establishment of a fully functioning THPO, the tribe will be able to manage cultural resources and sites on the reservation and have more say in state matters as well as create regulations that establish protocols for inadvertent discoveries of cultural resources, sites, and human remains.

The Kennewick Man case has important implications for tribes, and the precedents that will be set by this case will dictate the direction in which American tribal archaeology will proceed and will change the way archaeology is conducted on tribal lands. Tribes will have to take the responsibility to change or create new regulations and codes that will address research undertaken on and off reservations and on lands in which tribes have an interest in order to protect tribal interests and important cultural resources. Although there are national historic preservation regulations that tribes rely on, tribes must accept the responsibility to tailor these regulations to their specific cultures and worldviews if they want to avoid another Kennewick Man situation.

Another area that tribes need to acknowledge is the use of multiple lines of evidence when trying to prove affiliation or relationships, which includes using evidence from physical anthropology, anthropology, ethnography, history, and oral traditions. However, this will entail the education of tribal members in academic archaeology, so that they, in turn, can educate their people about archaeology and the archaeological process. In academia, it has been my experience that oral traditions are seen as inferior to physical anthropology and history; tribes need to use archaeological knowledge in conjunction with traditional knowledge to tie these lines of evidence together to form a cohesive and concrete package.

It is my opinion that, if tribes are to be successful in their CRM, anthropological, and archaeological endeavors, they need to have the proper infrastructure in place, such as separate archaeology and historic preservation programs, and be able to utilize different areas of expertise and knowledge to back their claims. Although oral traditions are an important part of my upbringing and education, I know that, as Indigenous people, we need to use other areas of knowledge to protect our cultural resources and sites. It is also important to create or overhaul tribal codes and regulations to protect cultural resources and sites adequately. These three areas are the main subjects that need to be addressed by all tribes that are interested in strengthening their cultural resource and associated programs.

As an Indigenous person pursuing my doctoral degree in archaeology, I feel that it is important for tribes to reclaim their sovereign right to protect and manage cultural resources and sites on and off reservations and on lands where tribes have an interest. It has been my goal throughout my academic and personal career to assist tribes in their historic preservation, anthropological, and archaeological pursuits, given that there is little information available to tribes about how to use archaeology on their lands. The goal of my dissertation research is to survey tribes about their archaeology and related programs to understand tribal needs and experiences with archaeology. The goals and reasons that many Indigenous archaeologists have for being archaeologists are varied and different, but it seems to me that we all believe in the sovereignty of our tribes and/or peoples to manage and protect cultural resources and sites important to our cultures. The decisions surrounding the Ancient One have stirred many of us to action, and it is these kinds of experiences that help shape Indigenous archaeology and the histories of Indigenous peoples.

REFERENCES

Babbitt, B. 2001. Letter from Secretary of the Interior Bruce Babbitt to Secretary of the Army Louis Caldera Regarding Disposition of the Kennewick Human Remains. National Park Service Cultural Affiliation Report. Available online at www.cr.nps.gov/aad/kennewick/ #cultaff (accessed December 8, 2007).

Begay, R. M. 1997. The Role of Archaeology on Indian Lands: The Navajo Nation. In *Native Americans and Archaeologists: Stepping Stones to Common Ground*, edited by N. Swidler, K. E. Dongoske, R. Anyon, and A. S. Downer, pp. 161–166. Walnut Creek, CA: AltaMira Press.

Cannell, K. 2005. Personal interview; notes in possession of author.

Crawford, S. J. 2000. (Re)Constructing Bodies: Semiotic Sovereignty and the Debate over Kennewick Man. In *Repatriation Reader: Who Owns American Indian Remains?*, edited by D. A. Mihesuah, pp. 211–236. Lincoln: University of Nebraska Press.

Dongoske, K. E., and R. Anyon. 1997. Federal Archaeology: Tribes, Diatribes, and Tribulations. In *Native Americans and Archaeologists: Stepping Stones to Common Ground*, edited by N. Swidler, K. E. Dongoske, R. Anyon, and A. S. Downer, pp. 188–196. Walnut Creek, CA: AltaMira Press.

Hinsley, C. M . 2000. Digging for Identity: Reflections on the Cultural Background of Collecting. *American Indian Quarterly* 20(2):180–197.

Martin, R. 1997. How Traditional Navajos View Historic Preservation: A Question of Interpretation. In *Native Americans and Archaeologists: Stepping Stones to Common Ground*, edited by N. Swidler, K. E. Dongoske, R. Anyon, and A. S. Downer, pp. 128–134. Walnut Creek, CA: AltaMira Press.

Matero, F. 2000. Beyond Compliance: Planning Heritage Preservation for Native American Ancestral Sites. *CRM* 23(9):4–8.

McManamon, F. P., J. C. Roberts, and B. S. Blades. 2004. Background and Scope for the Cultural Affiliation Reports—Chapter 1. National Park Service Cultural Affiliation Report. Available online at www.cr.nps.gov/aad/kennewick/#cultaff (accessed December 8, 2007).

Miri, A. A. 2001. Philosophy and Principles of Preservation in Practice. *CRM* 24(7):11–14.

Nez Perce Tribe website. 2007. Available online at http://www.nezperce.org/ content/Programs/cultural_resources_program.htm (accessed December 8, 2007).

Salazar, V., A. Roberts, and A. Bohnert. 2001. Cultural Sensitivity and Tribal Authority in Research Projects and Museum Collection Management. *CRM* 24(7):29–32.

Shull, C. D. 2001. Evaluating Cultural Resources: Challenging Issues for the 21st Century. *CRM* 24(7):44–47.

Stapp, D. C. 2000. Tribes Working with Agencies to Protect Resources. *CRM* 24(7):41–44.

Swidler, N., D. Eck, T. J. Ferguson, L. Kuwanwisiwma, R. Anyon, L. Panteah, K. Kelley, and H. Francis 2000. Multiple Views of the Past: Integrating Archaeology and Ethnography in the Jeddito Valley. *CRM* 23(9):49–53.

Tsosie, R. 1997. Indigenous Rights and Archaeology. In *Native Americans and Archaeologists: Stepping Stones to Common Ground*, edited by N. Swidler, K. E. Dongoske, R. Anyon, and A. S. Downer, pp. 64–87. Walnut Creek, CA: AltaMira Press.

Welch, J. R. 2000. The White Mountain Apache Tribe Heritage Program: Origins, Operations, and Challenges. In *Working Together: Native Americans and Archaeologists*, edited by K. E. Dongoske, M. Aldenderfer, and K. Doehner, pp. 67–83. Washington, DC: Society for American Archaeology.

Welch, J. R., N. Mahaney, and R. Riley 2000. The Reconquest of Fort Apache: The White Mountain Apache Tribe Reclaims Its History and Culture. *CRM* 23(9):15–19.

White Deer, G. 1997. Return of the Sacred: Spirituality and the Scientific Imperative. In *Native Americans and Archaeologists: Stepping Stones to Common Ground*, edited by N. Swidler, K. E. Dongoske, R. Anyon, and A. S. Downer, pp. 37–43. Walnut Creek, CA: AltaMira Press.

CHAPTER 32
AN INTERVIEW WITH CONNIE JOHNSTON[1]

I started to work on the Kennewick Man case for the Colville Confederated Tribes' (CCT) History/Archaeology Program in January 2000. I compiled and organized the administrative record for the tribes. I researched archival records located in the tribe's history/archaeology repository in order to gather information for the Kennewick Man Cultural Affiliation Claim submitted by the CCT. I gathered evidence supporting the fact that the area where Kennewick Man was found was within the traditional territories of the Palus people.

My involvement in the Kennewick Man case dated back to 1996. While employed as the legislative assistant/executive secretary to the Colville Business Council, I had traveled to Washington, DC, with council members to lobby Congress to support the Native American Graves Protection and Repatriation Act (NAGPRA) and the tribes' position in the Kennewick Man case. I was responsible for tracking NAGPRA-related legislation and updating the council on the Kennewick Man case.

My maternal grandfather was of Palus/Nez Perce descent. His father was Jim Billy and his mother was Eyomotwy (Umatwy). Their people lived along the Snake River. The Palus people lived along the Snake and Palus Rivers, and all were close-ly interrelated and intermarried with the lower Nez Perce. There was a Palus village located right in the vicinity of Kennewick, Washington, and, though it wasn't the exact location of my grandfather's family, it was still one of the places that all Palus people revered.

The sacredness of burials—of respecting the dignity of those who have gone before us—is a teaching and belief very basic and essential to who I am. My grand-father yearned for his home along the Snake River, and as a child I grew up know-ing that it was a place where my roots and identity were based. I traveled there with my grandfather and grandmother a few years before he died. The sadness and yearn-ing he felt for the place of his heart was so evident and real to me—I will never for-get it. The memory and feelings came flooding back when I traveled to the area again with my aunts and uncle last year. It was an overwhelming, emotional expe-rience for all of us. It was so sad, yet it made me feel so connected to my family and my people. I think this may be a universal feeling among Native peoples.

When I traveled to Canada with several councilmen a few years back, we went to reserves where there were descendants of Okanogan and Arrow Lakes people—people closely related to people enrolled on the Colville Reservation. The beauty of the land and the bonding with the people of those reserves was a wonderful experience. Even though I do not descend from either of those tribes, I felt that special connection to the people and the land, and they received us like we were all their long-lost brothers and sisters! It was another beautiful, unforgettable memory. To me, it is this feeling down deep in the depths of your heart and soul connecting you in a way that can't be described or articulated. The connection with the land and all the people who have gone before us in this land is something real and valid.

There is splendor in every culture; there is value in every culture. There is a place and a purpose for everyone and everything. Indians believe we were placed in specific areas for specific reasons. We have a cultural affiliation or relationship with Kennewick Man because he existed and died in the land where we were placed as caretakers by the Creator. In this case, the non-Indian court system has applied the standards, values, and beliefs of the dominant culture to our culturally unique Indian world. Tribes have been dismissed as superstitious backward people without a valid position, while the scientists are held up as "professionals" and "experts in their field," whose interests represent knowledge and progress. It sounds so familiar—just like back when they wanted the land and we were in the way of "progress."

To me, the balance on this Earth is so delicate and intricate that it was never meant for human control and manipulation. The Kennewick Man represents the basic dignity and respect due to a human being—to be allowed to rest in peace. He was laid to rest thousands of years ago in an area Native people are identified with and have cared for since time immemorial. All the tests that the scientists asked for in the beginning have already been done. They want to continue testing until there is nothing left of him to be buried. And, from what I have read, it is all just because they want to prove that we weren't here first or whatever. They seem to want to use him to prove a political point. Is that what science is about? Is that an honorable and valid reason to keep him above ground? They want to own him and be able to do what they want with him. I don't understand how you can own another human being, and to me, he is still a human being.

The formal position of the Colville Tribes back in 1996 was that we would agree to noninvasive testing. That was the position recommended to the Colville Business Council by the History/Archaeology Program. However, that does not mean that it was the personal opinion of individual tribal members. To a lot of really traditional tribal members, there is no testing that is noninvasive. Most people who belong to the Longhouse do not even allow autopsies or embalming, no matter what the circumstances.

The scientists, their lawyers, and some of the non-Indian people who have expressed their opinions publicly seem to be imposing or projecting their way of thinking onto us and assuming we look at things just like they do. Some people say we are doing this just because we want to continue to get special treatment and be able to have casinos. That is the furthest thing from the minds of most Indians. In general, Indians don't think that way. We tend to look at things from the heart and not the head—we don't analyze and strategize about what we're going to gain politically from something as sacred as this—that would be blasphemous. That's just crazy. Yes, the end result of all this could very well be an erosion of tribal sovereignty, but that's not our primary concern or what drives us to get him back in the ground. That is something the Colville Business Council might have to think about, but not your everyday tribal member.

I was taught not to present myself as speaking for all Indians, all tribal members, or even all Nez Perce/Palus people. So, this is my personal opinion based on how I was raised. Other tribal members will probably have different opinions, and some may even agree fully with the scientists. But the majority of Palus/Nez Perce people believe that the body should not be disturbed for any reason once it is laid to rest. That is taught in the 7-Drum Longhouse religion. Our right and ability to care for, protect, and preserve the dignity of our deceased is what is important to us.

NOTE

1. Interviewed by Adam Fish, January 14, 2005.

CHAPTER 33
AN INTERVIEW WITH
MARY A. MARCHAND[1]

The Ancient One affects me because I have handled so many reburials for the Colville tribes that have been dug up by public utility districts, state highway departments, and the telephone companies. From the oral teachings of my great-grandmothers, we were taught that all artifacts, be they skulls or bones, need to be left alone. We were taught that anything taken from the ground was put back in the ground. Not all Indians were taught the same, but we were all taught to respect one another's remains. We were taught that Mother Nature and the soil were our banks where we could put things to be saved and not disturbed. Those areas where these people were found were spiritual, but we were taught that all the grounds that tribes owned—which was all the land—should be protected. Anthropologists ask if this or that area is "spiritual," and I say all areas are spiritual.

According to our oral history brought down from our Elders, the sooner you go back in the ground, the sooner you decay back to Mother Nature. It was just a given fact that the faster you went back to the soil, then the faster you went back to your Creator. This was our teaching, and nowadays some believe that people should be back in the ground in three days. A lot of times, when hunters went out in the mountains to try to get food for their families, they got lost, frozen, were later found and finally laid to rest there or were brought home. Either way, they were put back in the ground as soon as possible. There were all different methods for burial in accord with the teachings of the different tribes. Our people traveled all over the land; wherever people died, they were either put in the ground right there, on the edge of a bluff, or in the rocks, wherever our people thought they would be the safest. A long time ago, they were rolled in a blanket or some type of cover and put in the ground. For some of the Indian people, if you died today you were back in the ground at sunrise, or before the sun went down the next day because the body started breaking down. Some people were put in the ground in a sitting position, or placed in a rocky area, in a place where there is a hole in a rock, with a big rock on top, which I have seen myself.

When I was on the Colville Business Council, we would go to archaeological excavations. It is not a good feeling. It is disturbing our history. For whatever reason, the Ancient One got buried and he should remain where he was found and stay there. We are disturbing ancestors that were supposed to be in the safekeeping of Mother Earth. I am a weird Indian because I have certain spiritual feelings that archaeologists do not have; other Elders are the same. The younger Indians visiting archaeology sites have not been taught these things and they get excited and say,

"What else did you find?" whereas people my age and older would say, "Don't disturb them." A long time ago, there were spiritual teachings that if our ancestors' remains are disturbed then their soul could come back and they could be angry to the point of sending destructive thoughts back at people that are holding them above ground.

Whatever affects one tribe can affect other Indian nations. For example, back East, this person dug a trench through a burial mound and installed a wall of plexiglass so people could view the Indian burial of a lady, baby, and a man. He charged entrance fees for the burial! That affected all of us. That is not history, it is just for greed. I think the Ancient One is similar.

Another recent example is the bridge at Hood Canal where they dug up that whole cemetery. They should not have gone beyond four burial boxes. You could tell just by looking that there was going to be a lot more. And they should have told the Washington State Department of Transportation that they could not go any further and needed to find another place to put the bridge.

The scientists want to prove that the non-Indians and explorers were here sooner than we want to admit. Our ancient connection to this land is strongly told in our language. We are *nxa?amxcin*, The People of the Land, not the people who came from somewhere else. We come from this land, this is our land, this is strongly stated, all the way down to our Indian names.

Ownership of land is through place names. We gave every nook, cranny, creek, lake, and river an Indian name that referenced what was important about that land or water, while the non-Indians come onto this continent and do not have place names. They name places after presidents—presidents who were not *ever* there! The Indians had a name for the area where the Ancient One was found. All of the lands of the people where Indians were are important. All the burial grounds, campsites, and pithouses, however deep they may be underwater, show that our people were here. There are living names associated with each place.

One time I was in Seattle and we went to dinner at a home and somebody said "Oh, I've got a beautifully framed collection of flints, stones, and arrowheads that I need to show you." He had this big wall of artifacts from Wells Dam on the Columbia River. I was born at Azwell, Washington, my great grandmother's orchard and allotment were drowned by Wells Dam. I do not think our people would be into studying ancient remains because we were told when we were younger that if we come up with remains we put them back in the ground. My great-grandma was emphatic: She taught us that when we found artifacts along the river that is Nature's banks and you leave them there. One day, my little brother and I brought an artifact to my great-grandmother's home and were told to take it back and protect it. To this collector I said, "I am sorry, I am not excited about your collection, I don't even want to look at it," because all I could see was Wells Dam. It is a collection that should never have been made, and it is a collection that should not be lining somebody's pockets with money.

People collect Indian artifacts because they value the *rare*. People in Europe will buy—if it is a proven fact—an Indian skull, lowest price $500 or $1,000, depending on that Indian chief's history, so they can put it in a display case in their home. We had an Elder who was a Chelan chief; they dug up his grave and the only thing that was stolen was his skull and it is still missing to this day, so he could be in England. And yet, he may be right close by with somebody thinking he may be as valuable as the Ancient One. I know some of the scientists in the case and I'd just as soon not speak to them; they are just trying to make big names for themselves. It all goes back to greed and fame.

This court case was decided against tribes because all that those in the court know about Indian people was learned in textbooks and in college. They handed down a decision on Indian people who they do not know and whose teachings they do not understand. They are in the wrong territories; they cannot learn about us through books. I do not care who writes the books; they can not really know Indians until they are on the reservation and can communicate with us, and there are very few Indians who will communicate because we were taught that we do not put our ancestry out there to be studied. And that is exactly what has happened. We try to protect something, but if something comes up like the Ancient One then all of a sudden they want it so badly that the courts are going to decide against you.

As far as I am concerned, until proven that there were other people here before us, the Ancient One belongs to us, courts or no courts. Indians always suffer when courts interfere. It is a given that everything stays in the ground. The non-Indians seem to think that research has to be done on everything; we think it is a violation of the people from our past. Remains do not need to be held, examined, or to go through tests.

The Ancient One was found because of a dam. Dams will always be a big hurt to our people. We still find a lot of remains; if you drive up Lake Roosevelt Reservoir behind Grand Coulee Dam you can see that we are losing land every day because those banks are sloughing off into the Columbia River. My great grandmother's allotment is now below Wells Dam. The tribes are losing land and burials to the dams; the settlement we get is a drop in the bucket in comparison to what we lost, including skulls that look like Europeans.

NOTE

1. Interviewed by Adam Fish, January 10, 2005.

CHAPTER 34
CULTURAL RETURN, RESTITUTION, AND THE LIMITS OF POSSIBILITY
LYNN MESKELL

In the United States, the Kennewick decision has underscored the serious need to depart from a narrowly construed and attenuated language of "affiliation" to the more ethically inflected language of cultural "restitution." In the first instance, one preferable shift would entail moving from the Native American Graves Protection and Repatriation Act's (NAGPRA) heavy reliance on "cultural affiliation" to one of "cultural patrimony," the latter focusing more intently on the imbued notions of inheritance, legacy, and heritage.

What the Kennewick case has brought into sharp relief is the duplicitous nature of the legal framing of NAGPRA. On one side, claimants are compelled to appeal to Western science to answer definitively the specificities of linear linkages to ancient identity. Spurred on by a positivist ethos in archaeology that advocated a literal match for artifacts and human remains with modern people, one would envisage that the discipline would learn from the lessons of past manipulation and misuse (Meskell and Preucel 2004:321). On the other side, archaeologists of a more theoretical persuasion have long problematized the connection between ethnicity and artifacts, thus arguing for a more fluid and ongoing constitution of identity. More worryingly, our attempts to decouple isomorphic relations between ethnicity and materiality have been hijacked by physical anthropologists who want unrestricted access to studying ancient human remains (Clark 2001:3). They impute that the ephemeral nature of ethnicity elides all connections over the long term and thus invalidates Indigenous knowledge claims. And what enables researchers to claim scientific primacy over human remains, and those communities that have rightful patrimony, is the flawed legacy of a positivist argument in today's political climate. Surely a more politically responsible and engaged archaeology can be forged without recourse to such reductionist science.

It is staggering that a discipline concerned with the very significance of ancient materiality—one that attempts to understand its culturally specific resonances—can have such difficulty honoring those culturally different and powerful spiritual meanings in the present. The material dimensions are key, as is a reorientation of our own taxonomic thinking. As Watkins (2004) has eloquently shown, the shifting language of Paleoindian to Paleoamerican in the case of the Ancient One, has had deleterious effects in the political arena.

NAGPRA's impossible guidelines of proof, the unknown techno-future of DNA, and the political ecologies of testing are just some of the reasons we must look beyond the mantle of science toward a more politicized, ethical, and just basis for our research and also its materialist underpinnings. There has to be an epistemic shift, entailing the legitimization of other discourses and taxonomies, rather than simply returning to something called "science," which, in turn, privileges the desire for certain knowledge at all costs, especially when those costs are borne by those who have already paid so dearly in the constitution of nationhood. Archaeology and anthropology have been complicit in the United States and elsewhere in the interventions of empires, governments, and capitalist forces to the combined detriment of native peoples. It is time that the discipline recognized its own inheritance and concomitant ethical responsibilities in the present. For many peoples around the world, "research" is an inherently dirty word (see Denetdale 2004; Smith 1999). What does it cost archaeologists to be major players in the call for cultural return? More importantly, how can we do our disciplinary part in the wider embrace of restitution?

Within the existing system, however, one could argue that emphasis should now be placed on the patrimonial relationship, which acknowledges that Native people can show traditional or historic continuity of connection instead of linear descent. Rather than trying to quantify past and present identities in the face of significant methodological hurdles, it may be more fitting to argue that specific groups constitute appropriate custodians because they have traditionally, or historically, legitimate cultural or spiritual responsibility for the cultural property at issue (Meskell 2002:321–322). This places more import on living groups and reconciliation in the wake of colonization, rather than attributing salience entirely to the archaeological record. Moreover, Ian Lilley (2000:109) has cogently demonstrated that Australian legislation, similar to that of other "settler societies," such as New Zealand, Canada, and South Africa, prioritizes Indigenous claims over those of all other interested parties. This situation stands in contradistinction to the United States, where many publics and multiple interests are acknowledged. As a result, Native Americans are simply one of several constituencies and are thus marginalized rather than prioritized.

NAGPRA only has jurisdiction over federal and tribal lands and cannot be enforced over private property, something that is inherently different than the postcolonial contexts of Australia and South Africa, where blanket protection is offered on all forms of land tenure. This is one major and negative disjuncture; another is premised on the impossibility of honoring and resolving multiple claims in the United States. I have often heard the argument that, as various Native American groups claim the Ancient One as ancestral, it is not possible to repatriate the remains. However, in the Australian case of human remains found in the Willandra World Heritage Area and named Mungo Lady, several Aboriginal groups (Barkandji, Muthi Muthi and Ngiyampaa) maintained joint and successful custodianship after appropriate resolutions. The return to Aboriginal custody, care, and control of Mungo Lady has been marked by cooperation and agreement between groups. In the United States, every argument is marshaled to polarize Native constituencies, to play each against the other to their communal disadvantage, and to retain and recapitulate an overarching "science as usual" approach. Axiomatic in this is the recognition that Native Americans must comply with the language of the law as set down by the very government that refuses them proper restitution and, more historically, the nation-state that perpetrated acts of repression and genocide. As eloquently argued by Taiaiake Alfred (1999:140):

> Aboriginal rights are in fact the benefits accrued by indigenous peoples who have agreed to abandon their autonomy in order to enter the legal and political framework of the state. After a while, indigenous freedoms become circumscribed and indigenous rights get defined not with respect to what exists in the minds and cultures of Native people, but in relation to the demands, interests, and opinions of the millions of other peoples who are also members of that single-sovereign community.

Moreover, the politics of recognition is, at the same time, a recognition of an Indigenous community *being*, alongside its *being* worthy of federal recognition. In that space, it similarly opens up the possibilities of being surveilled, examined, and scrutinized. Indigenous subjects ineluctably fail to match the liberal state's preconceived notion of what constitutes authentic "traditional culture," and, at the same time, justify the state legislating against them, thus setting them apart from dominant social values (Povinelli 1999, 2002).

Alternatively, I am suggesting here an ethical turn, described by some as political liberalism (Rawls 1993) or, more fittingly in the United States, postcolonial liberalism, the tenets of which aspire to a just society of equal citizens divided by reasonable religious, philosophical and moral doctrines. Postcolonial liberalism articulates "a space within liberal democracies and liberal thought in which these Aboriginal perspectives and philosophies can not only be heard, but given equal opportunity to shape (and reshape) the forms of power and government acting on them" (Ivison 2002:1). This stance recognizes a central tension, namely accepting the centrality of disagreement about political values such as justice, while still appealing to substantive values about democracy, equality, freedom, and well-being. Inbuilt in such a framing is the question: Why care so much for Indigenous claims as its host population is only a fraction of society at large?

Following Ivison, one answer is that the expropriation of Aboriginal lands and the forced assimilation or outright elimination of Aboriginal people represents the "original sin" of liberal democracies, such as Australia, Canada, New Zealand, and the United States. The historical injustices committed against first peoples in the process of nation-building seem to persist into contemporary lifeworlds in ways that affect internal as well as external perceptions of the moral character and national identity of these societies. Another counter is that most Indigenous peoples continue to live in intolerable conditions, presenting an acutely urgent challenge to any liberal democracy committed to social justice. Indigenous peoples are consistently among the most disadvantaged people on Earth, according to any number of different socioeconomic indicators, so that anyone concerned about justice must take heed of these facts (Ivison 2002:14–15).

If we take NAGPRA as one arm of governance, a state modality that works on Native Americans and to which they must comply, then postcolonial liberalism seeks to harness a broader social and political conversation about what is legitimate and illegitimate, specifically resting on the grounds of equality, compensation for historical injustice, and cultural difference. Even if one were to interrogate claims premised on compensatory logic based on the argument that repression has ceased and an equitable society prevails and therefore nothing is due, I would assert that cultural restitution for the past is still too powerful an ethos to elide. Though one could say more about the philosophical underpinnings of this position, archaeology works in the world and must recognize its colonial legacy and contemporary impacts, as the Kennewick case has made all too transparent. NAGPRA must be more progressive, keep in step with other cosmopolitan settler states, and make restitution to its Indigenous peoples.

ACKNOWLEDGMENTS
For their helpful comments, suggestions, and information, I thank Denis Byrne, Ian Hodder, Harvey Johnston, David Pearce, and Claire Smith.

REFERENCES
Alfred, T. 1999. *Peace, Power, Righteousness: An Indigenous Manifesto.* Oxford: Oxford University Press.

Clark, G. A. 2001. Letter to the Editor. Society for American Archaeology: *Archaeological Record* 1(2):3.

Denetdale, J. N. 2004. Planting Seeds of Ideas and Raising Doubts about What We Believe: An Interview with Vine Deloria, Jr. *Journal of Social Archaeology* 4(2):131–146.

Ivison, D. 2002. *Postcolonial Liberalism.* Cambridge: Cambridge University Press.

Lilley, I. 2000. Professional Attitudes to Indigenous Interests in the Native Title Era: Settler Societies Compared. In *Native Title and the Transformation of Archaeology in the Postcolonial World,* edited by I. Lilley, pp. 99–119. Sydney, Australia: Oceania Publications, Mongraph 50.

Meskell, L. M. 2002. The Intersection of Identity and Politics in Archaeology. *Annual Review of Anthropology* 31:279–301.

Meskell, L. M., and R. W Preucel, 2004. Politics. In *Companion to Social Archaeology*, edited by L. M. Meskell and R. W. Preucel, pp. 315–334. Oxford: Blackwell.

Povinelli, E. A. 1999. Settler Modernity and the Quest for an Indigenous Tradition. *Public Culture* 11(1):19–48.

Povinelli, E. A. 2002. *The Cunning of Recognition.* Durham, NC: Duke University Press.

Rawls, J. 1993. *Political Liberalism.* New York: Columbia University Press.

Smith, L. T. 1999. *Decolonizing Methodologies.* London: Zed Books.

Watkins, J. 2004. Becoming American or Becoming Indian?: Nagpra, Kennewick, and Cultural Affiliation. *Journal of Social Archaeology* 4(1):60–80.

CHAPTER 35
MOVING BEYOND KENNEWICK: OTHER NATIVE AMERICAN PERSPECTIVES ON BIOARCHAEOLOGICAL DATA AND INTELLECTUAL PROPERTY RIGHTS

GEORGE P. NICHOLAS, JOHN JULES, AND CARRIE DAN

The specter of Kennewick Man has loomed large over North American archaeology. In his wake, a wide array of issues relating to tribal sovereignty, reburial, and repatriation have dominated the relationship between archaeologists and Native Americans for much of the last decade and attracted the attention of the public more than virtually any other discovery. The Kennewick court case has not only challenged existing heritage legislation (Bruning 2006), it has also served as an important rallying point for many Indigenous peoples and as an opportunity for peripheral interest groups, such as the Asatru Folk Assembly, to lay claim to him. Regardless of their personal views, it is safe to say that every archaeologist has been affected in some way by this controversy. Even after the court case has finally been concluded, the relationship between archaeologists and Native Americans will remain tinged by unresolved issues.[1]

Largely lost in the continuing Kennewick controversy, however, are two important issues. The first is that the influence, and indeed knowledge, of the Kennewick case may be more limited in many Aboriginal communities in Canada (and likely elsewhere) than is commonly thought. Although many communities are very concerned about the welfare of found ancestral human remains, this is most often focused on local instances and issues.

The second issue is that other approaches to ancient human remains now being employed by some Aboriginal groups in Canada and the United States are significantly underreported, which skews perceptions about the relationship between Indigenous peoples and archaeology. We are personally familiar with more examples of positive working relationships between archaeologists and Indigenous peoples than negative ones regarding human remains. In Alaska and British Columbia, for example, First Nations have worked with archaeologists and other scientists, often setting the research agendas to obtain and study bioarchaeological and genetic data. This trend will likely increase as greater understanding of Aboriginal concerns is reached by archaeologists, facilitated by new approaches and protocols regarding the study of human remains developed by First Nations in Canada and the United States. Indeed, this is being nourished by the increasing frequency with which Aboriginal people are turning to archaeology to obtain information about their ancestors. As this occurs, new concerns regarding the cultural and intellectual property issues relating to archaeological and genetic information will emerge.

In this chapter, we examine Indigenous attitudes toward archaeology in south-central British Columbia and elsewhere that provide important points of comparison with the Kennewick case. We look specifically at two bands from the Secwepemc Nation, the Kamloops and Neskonlith, regarding their interest in archaeology and bioarchaeological data as well as other examples of innovative approaches. We also identify potential issues of concern regarding intellectual property rights and the dissemination of bioarchaeological data.

ALTERNATIVE MODELS FROM SECWEPEMC TERRITORY

In British Columbia, debate over human remains goes back for more than a century as Native peoples encountered explorers, scientists, and missionaries interested in their origins and history. The development of anthropology itself has deep ties to this region, because this was where Franz Boas conducted his early field studies, particularly on the coast. Boas and his contemporaries also worked throughout the interior part of the province, within the Plateau culture area, as part of the Jesup North Pacific Expedition (Lohse and Sprague 1998), conducting ethnographic studies with such groups as the Secwepemc, Nlaka'pamux, and Stl'atl'imx.[2] Today, the Secwepemc (or Shuswap) Nation consists of seventeen bands within the watersheds of the Fraser and Thompson Rivers. The range of attitudes regarding archaeology and human remains found today in Secwepemc traditional territory—from denying archaeologists permission to excavate and study human remains, to working together to do so—extends from the late 19th century. These early attitudes are known both through oral history and from letters written by ethnographer James Teit[3] to Franz Boas and others. For example, Teit wrote in 1897 that:

> Both [in Lytton] and at Kamloops the site of work is on Indian reserves—at both places I was welcome to take stone, shell etc. but refused human bones. At Kamloops they, after holding a big council where my side was presented by the Priest, telling them I came to get things to use to teach the people in N.Y., decided to let me have a few bones to teach with but I must cover up all I did not take so no bad white men would take them to make fun of the Indians. (Teit, cited in Carlson 2005:145)

What is significant in this account is that then, as today, the Kamloops Band is willing to support scientific research of human remains when it has been adequately justified and within certain parameters.

KAMLOOPS INDIAN BAND

The Kamloops Indian Band is one of the most politically savvy and organized groups in the region. Their development of a portion of their reserve as an industrial park and several housing developments has created a substantial tax base that supports a number of important activities, including the pursuit of major land claims. Many band members, including the former chief, are knowledgeable about archaeology, having worked on excavations or taken university courses.[4] The band has a cultural resources department, as well as a heritage policy that includes an archaeological permit system (Nicholas 2006).

The Kamloops Band has used archaeological information in past court cases to "prove our existence and our utilization of the land and its resources." Band members have also explored linkages between archaeology and traditional knowledge, "story and fable," and "cultural memory" regarding things that happened. For example, possible connections to glacial and postglacial events, such as ice-age conditions and knowledge of megafauna, may be reflected in stories about giants and larger-than-normal animals, or of Fox and Hare stealing the South Wind. Community members also see archaeology as a means to "prove conclusively" what the ancestors and the elders have been saying all along—"that we were here for as long as it matters to us politically and ideologically, no matter what those ancestors looked like."

ATTITUDES TOWARD REBURIAL AND THE SCIENTIFIC STUDY OF HUMAN REMAINS

The attitude of the Kamloops Indian band members toward human remains is based on the teaching of the ancestors and elders. In the cases of those who died on the war trail and/or deaths on the seasonal round where proper burial could not take place for whatever reason, relatives are expected to retrieve the remains from wherever they were within one year. If no immediate relative stepped forth to claim remains (including secondary burials), then the community took it on itself to honor, feed, bury, and fulfill ceremonial expectations for the dead. Postcontact-era burials were jealously guarded. Only in cases of formal requests for scientific study were remains allowed to leave the area and then only once certain provisions were agreed to. This attitude was formalized with the Kamloops Indian Band Heritage Policy and By-Law (1996), which allows the study of all remains for a finite term (generally one to five years).[5] The band has successfully repatriated human remains from Canadian and U.S. museums that had been removed decades ago and not returned, including those obtained by James Teit, which have been in the American Museum of Natural History in New York. A new ceremony, called the "Journey Home," was also created around the repatriation of remains returning from various institutions and excavations. The ceremony takes place in several Secwepemc communities when remains return to their homeland for reburial and is celebrated annually on the summer solstice.

There is widespread interest by community members in the information potentially available from human remains. Questions about their age (relating to "How long were we here?") and diet ("What did we eat?") are very common. Bioarchaeological studies on remains from Secwepemc territory, including isotope analysis on 8,250-year-old Gore Creek Man (Chisholm and Nelson 1983), have revealed much about changes in subsistence patterns that both support the longevity of the contact-period diet and identified a major dietary shift during the middle Holocene in the relative percentages of terrestrial mammals and anadromous fish, showing that the ancestors responded to changing environmental conditions in their diet. There is also interest in "What did we look like?" especially because most old timers always thought that "our ancestors were larger and more robust then present-day peoples." Finally, questions are always asked about relationship to the remains and genealogical tracing; indeed, most members interviewed (by Jules) are not averse to using DNA testing to find this out.

NESKONLITH INDIAN BAND

Like the Kamloops Band, the neighboring Neskonlith have had a variety of experiences with archaeology. In recent years, they have sought the assistance of archaeologists, such as Catherine Carlson, to recover burials exposed by erosion or construction. However, in Secwepemc territory, as elsewhere, feelings about human remains are complex. There have been instances of misunderstanding, as well as problems emanating from the historical power imbalance between Native people and archaeologists. Today, Indigenous communities are facing new challenges as they try to reconcile the potential of archaeological investigations with tribal politics and worldview, as illustrated by a recent controversy on the Neskonlith Reserve.

In 2004, the Canadian Pacific Railway (CPR) began a project to twin their tracks[6] through Secwepemc territory. Although an archaeological impact assessment (AIA) was not required, CPR nonetheless chose to conduct one and subsequently consulted with archaeologists and the four affected Indian bands: Adams Lake, Little Shuswap, Neskonlith, and Kamloops. Carrie Dan, a Secwepemc archaeologist, was hired by the Neskonlith Indian Band to participate in the AIA. After the investigations began, human remains were unearthed by heavy equipment during a monitoring task. CPR was asked to stop work immediately to allow the archaeology team to further assess the situation.

The band council, Elders, and community members were consulted and a unanimous decision was made to remove the remains, conduct a basic study, and then return them for reinterment at a different site. Before the remains were to be excavated, members of the Neskonlith and Adams Lake Indian Bands performed a pipe ceremony and prayers were said at the gravesite. However, immediately after the ceremony, a problem developed when another community member started to collect the exposed bones, which he took to his home for a four-day ceremony. The archaeology team went to his residence to inventory what he had taken. After the burial was excavated, further archaeological investigations exposed the floor of a housepit and a second set of human remains. Once again, the work stopped and a meeting was held to consult with the bands and Elders. They gave Dan their consent to exhume them and also to collect samples for radiocarbon dating[7] and DNA analysis. Meanwhile, Secwepemc Elders Mary Thomas and her son, Harold, made birch bark baskets in preparation for the reburials (Figure 35.1).

Although community protocols had been met, a small group of Native protesters from Neskonlith and other bands were outraged by the exhumation of human remains. The protesters set up camp at the site and all work ceased. The situation became heated to the point where the protesters even went to the band office to attempt to retrieve the excavated remains (being curated at a secret location with the

Figure 35.1. Carrie Dan places cedar boughs as she prepares recovered human remains for reburial in birch bark baskets (photo: G. Nicholas).

band council's permission). The protesters eventually vacated the site in December, at which time archaeological work ceased until the spring.

SIGNIFICANCE

What happened in the Neskonlith Reserve is an interesting and important case study to consider. Unlike Kennewick and similar examples, this is not a case of Indians confronting archaeologists about the sanctity of burials and the desire for scientific information, but rather Indians confronting Indians over the remains of individuals who could prove to be the ancestors of each, with an Indian archaeologist (Dan) in the middle. The problem is not about reburial, which was never in question, but the ability to study the remains to answer questions of interest to the Neskonlith band members. Who has claim to the remains? In this case, it is possible that the 5,000-year-old remains could be related not only to both those supporting the work (the band council and Elders) and those against it, but even to members of other Secwepemc Nation bands.

Of course, this issue could be resolved by agreeing to abide with the decision of the actual descendants of these ancient individuals, whoever they were, which could very likely be determined through the recovery and analysis of DNA. As with Kennewick, however, objections were raised about the possibility of *any* scientific analysis. In this case, the Neskonlith Band council has persevered and looks forward to receiving the results of the analyses when completed. Nevertheless, we caution against thinking about this in terms of "who won and who lost." Certainly, the community has supported archaeological research that can benefit it directly, but this was not unanimous and some individuals remain deeply offended by the disturbance of the remains. In addition, decisions made by a group now in power have, in other circumstances and communities, served as the impetus to replace chiefs or council members. The point here is that in Secwepemc Territory, and elsewhere, Indigenous peoples are increasingly becoming more involved in archaeology (Nicholas 2007). They may be collaborating with archaeologists, be hiring archaeologists, or be archaeologists themselves. As seen here, this can lead to new challenges for First Nations seeking to obtain archaeological data.

BIOARCHAEOLOGICAL INFORMATION AND INTELLECTUAL PROPERTY CONCERNS

Developments in bioarchaeology, especially those relating to human genetics, mark a revolution in archaeology of at least equal impact to that of radiocarbon dating half a century ago. The recovery and analysis of ancient DNA (aDNA) increases substantially what we can know about past population origins and movements, diet and nutrition, health, and even genealogy (e.g., Larsen 2000). Archaeologists are thus very interested in the recovery and analysis of aDNA from artifacts and archaeological sites.

Lost in the glare of the Kennewick case are bioarchaeological initiatives with and by First Nations. In both Canada and the United States, there are Aboriginal communities very interested in the information that such studies can potentially provide to them. Their research questions include corroboration of what is already known through oral histories and archaeology as well as the search for living relatives. Prominent examples of consultation and collaboration by and with Aboriginal communities that have a current or planned aDNA component and that provide important counterpoints to the Kennewick controversy include: the Champagne and Aishihik First Nations, with Kwaday Dan Ts'inchi, a 550-year-old glacier body in northern British Columbia (Beattie et al. 2000; Monsalve et al. 2002); the Tlinget Nation, with a 9,700-year-old individual from Prince of Wales, Alaska (Dixon 1999); the Canoe Creek Indian Band, with two 5,000-year old individuals from China Lake, British Columbia (Malhi et al. 2007); and Aleut communities, with middle Holocene through modern samples (Rubicz 2004; Rubicz et al. 2003). In the China Lake study, the Canoe Creek Indian Band fully participated in the discovery, and the majority of the community members voluntarily gave their DNA to help with the study, which they recognized as a means to distinguish their founding lineages (Malhi et al. 2007). Interest is not limited to human DNA: The Kamloops Band wants to know what the extinct Shuswap Hunting Dog looked like in the past and whether there are any extant strains.

CONCERNS

For their part, archaeologists, anthropologists, and others have to tread carefully, given both the legacy of scientific colonialism (Zimmerman 2001) and clear breaches of trust with Native peoples. An example of the latter occurred in British

Columbia following research on rheumatic diseases based on blood samples obtained from Nuu-chah-nulth communities, which were later used in mitochondrial DNA studies (Ward et al. 1991). As Cybulski (2001) points out, not only were the Nuu-chah-nulth unaware of the mtDNA research, they were never informed of the results of the original study.

DNA studies may be particularly problematic because they interface with both cultural property and intellectual property. They also eliminate some of the generalities of archaeological interpretation in that they are capable of connecting recovered remains, not only to modern populations but also to individuals. In England, for example, mtDNA from 9,000-year-old Cheddar Man was linked to a local schoolteacher, Adrian Targett (Barham, Priestley, and Targett 1999).

Another issue is *who* stands to potentially profit from vaccines and other discoveries made from information derived from ancient human remains—those who conducted the analysis or the descendants of the individuals from whom the DNA was extracted? How do groups contend with new information that challenges their traditional standing as original settlers, their cultural identity, or even their worldview (Figure 35.2)? Claims that Native Americans were not the first settlers of the continent are not limited to the purported Causacoid-like features of Kennewick Man, but also to genetic evidence from other sites. For example, aDNA has been recovered from the Windover site, an early Holocene burial ground in a Florida bog (Lawlor et al. 1991). An on-line discussion[8] of a film about the site, *Secrets of the Bog People* (Brighton Films 2003), included the following comments under the heading "European DNA Found in 7-8,000 Year Old Skeleton in Florida":

I just turned on *The Learning Channel* and caught about ten minutes of the ending. ... A doctor Gregory from Cornell said that preliminary DNA samples taken from the brains of some of the people indicate they are European. ... American prehistory is about to be re-written ...

All Right! Let's tell the Indians to go back where they came from. We got dibs! We got dibs!

Does that mean we can open up casinos in Florida?"

I demand reparations for my distant kin who were wiped out by invaders crossing the Bearing (*sic*) land bridge!

The Americas have long been known to have been the subject of many migrations/invasions. I recall that members of the Canadian "Objiway" tribe were also descended from a European migration.

In these cases, new genetic information from archaeological remains is not simply intellectual debate but a direct challenge to some of the very identity of the Aboriginal peoples of the Americas.

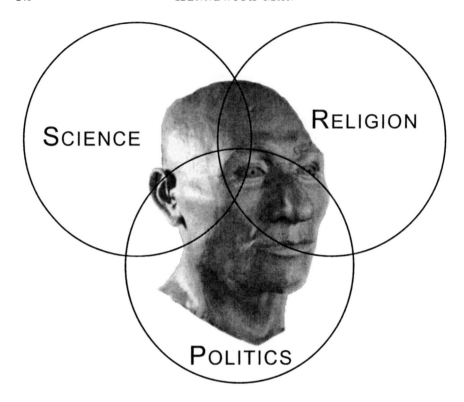

Figure 35.2. Points of intersection—why Kennewick Man is so problematic.

The debate now developing on intellectual property rights in archaeology (Nicholas and Bannister 2004; Nicholas and Hollowell 2004) also raises a host of contentious legal and ethical issues regarding who owns the products of archaeological research. Indigenous peoples increasingly find themselves involved in this debate as they move beyond seeking greater representation in the process of doing archaeology, to raising concerns of the products of archaeology that involves their heritage. The Kamloops Band, for example, is concerned about the potential of large-scale use or misuse of bioarchaeological information for personal and corporate gain. Issues have already arisen regarding the intellectual ownership of traditional ecological knowledge and the application of the knowledge usurped from Elders and cultural flame keepers. How might problems of intellectual property and scientific study be resolved?[9] Under the provisions of their heritage policy, joint copyright is required for research conducted under permit. More generally, the band requests sharing credit where it's due and giving some form of control to sources as to how information can be used and what is appropriate for public consumption as well as sharing any profits with the community.

To avoid the types of problems that have beset the Kennewick discovery, there is widespread need for new protocols that facilitate a more equitable relationship between stakeholders. Archaeology needs to be viewed as a negotiated practice among those participating in or affected by it (Nicholas and Hollowell 2004:8, 2007), and this requires a clear understanding of the control and dissemination of the products of research. Finally, Indigenous peoples will clearly benefit from being as knowledgeable as possible about current archaeological practices so that they would be in the best position to make informed decisions. They need also to be aware that "scientific data" may take on a life of their own—and thus can have potential uses that may be contrary to their interests.

CONCLUSIONS

In post-Kennewick times, we need to be careful in making assumptions about the way Indigenous peoples feel about archaeology. Although many Native Americans are against the disturbance and study of ancestral remains, others are not. Our understanding of the range and complexity of Indigenous perspectives on bioarchaeological research has been skewed by the Kennewick case, which has emphasized adversarial relationships and ignored varied responses and alternative models.

In the examples discussed here, it is evident that all parties benefit when archaeologists make the effort to spend time with the communities to identify and discuss their concerns (Colwell-Chanthaphonh and Ferguson 2007). A critical element of such dialog is the development of protocols that address community concerns and needs. Finally, Indigenous archaeologists may find themselves in the unenviable position of serving as a facilitator between different stakeholders. Speaking as someone in that position in the Neskonlith controversy, Carrie Dan notes:

> As a Secwepemc archaeologist I can understand the importance of proper analysis and the valuable information being collected. Whoever these ancient peoples were, whether they are Secwepemc ancestors or not, they have a story to tell and I will be the one telling it. Perhaps they wanted me to find them, so I could tell their story.

ACKNOWLEDGMENTS
We thank the Kamloops Indian Band, the Neskonlith Indian Band, and Golder Associates for their assistance in preparing this chapter and the editors of this volume for inviting us to participate. We have also benefited from discussions with Sheila Greer, Julie Hollowell, Jerry Cybulski, and Catherine Carlson.

NOTES

1. For informative overviews of some of these issues, see Bray 2001; Mihesuah 2000; Thomas 2000; Watkins 2000.

2. These Plateau peoples were semi-sedentary hunter-gatherer-fishers who spent the winters in villages comprised of semi-subterranean, earth-covered lodges and the remainder of the year following a well-organized seasonal round (see Walker 1998). Their economy was based on runs of anadromous salmon and on a wide variety of harvested foods. Following the influx of settlers in the early 1800s, their life-ways were transformed by the effects of the fur trade, missionaries, and a severe reduction in the land base.

3. Teit was a Scottish immigrant who was married to Nlaka'pamux Lucy Antko and spent much time with the community.

4. From 1991–2005, Nicholas directed a community-based archaeology program for Secwepemc and other Native peoples on the Kamloops Indian Reserve as part of a unique collaborative university degree program between Simon Fraser University and the Secwepemc Cultural Education Society (Nicholas 2006). Both Jules and Dan are graduates of this program. Jules is today head of the Cultural Resources Department of the Kamloops Indian Band.

5. This provision for study applies to instances of single or several (five or fewer) individuals; larger numbers indicate a burial site, which requires repatriation of all remains to another spot.

6. That is, to create a new line alongside the existing track.

7. These would produce dates ranging between 4,860 and 5,310 years BP.

8. www.freerepublic.com/focus/f-news/964408/posts

9. These and related questions are now being addressed through an international, multisectoral project, Intellectual Property Issues in Cultural Heritage: Theory, Practice, Policy, Ethics, directed by Nicholas, being funded by Canada's Social Sciences and the Humanities Research Council.

REFERENCES

Barham, L., P. Priestley, and A. Targett. 1999. *In Search of Cheddar Man*. Stroud, UK: Tempus Publishing.

Beattie, O., B. Apland, E. W. Blake, J. A. Cosgrove, S. Gaunt, S. Greer, A. P. Mackie, K. E. Mackie, D. Straathof, V. Thorp, and P. M. Troffe. 2000. The Kwäday Dän Ts'inchi Discovery from a Glacier in British Columbia. *Canadian Journal of Archaeology* 24(1):129–148.

Bray, T. L., ed. 2001. *The Future of the Past: Archaeologists, Native Americans and Repatriation*. New York: Garland.

Brighton Films. 2003. *Secrets of the Bog People*. Films for the Humanities & Sciences.

Bruning, S. B. 2006. Complex Legal Legacies: The Native American Graves Protection and Repatriation Act, Scientific Study, and Kennewick Man. *American Antiquity* 71(3):501–522.

Carlson, C. C. 2005. Letters from the Field: Reflections on 19th Century Archaeology of Harlan I. Smith in the Southern Interior of British Columbia, Canada. In *Decolonizing Archaeological Theory and Practice*, edited by C. Smith and H. M. Wobst, pp. 134–169. London: Routledge.

Chisholm, B. S., and D. E. Nelson. 1983. An Early Human Skeleton from South-Central British Columbia: Dietary Inference from Carbon Isotopic Evidence. *Canadian Journal of Archaeology* 7(1):85–86.

Colwell-Chanthaphonh, C., and T. J. Ferguson, eds. 2007. *The Collaborative Continuum: Archaeological Engagements with Descendant Communities*. Walnut Creek, CA: AltaMira Press.

Cybulski, J. 2001. Current Challenges to Traditional Anthropological Applications of Human Osteology in Canada. In *Out of the Past: The History of Human Osteology at the University of Toronto*, edited by L. Sawchuk and S. Pfeiffer. Available online at https://tspace.library.utoronto.ca/citd/Osteology/cybulski.html (accessed December 18, 2007).

Dixon, E. J. 1999. *Boats, Bones, and Bison: Archeology and the First Colonization of Western North America*. Albuquerque: University of New Mexico Press.

Larsen, C. S. 2000. *Skeletons in Our Closet: Revealing Our Past through Bioarchaeology*. Princeton, NJ: Princeton University Press.

Lawlor, D. A., C. D. Dickel, W. W. Hauswirth, and P. Parham. 1991. Ancient HLA Genes from 7,500-Year-Old Archaeological Remains. *Nature* 349(6312):785–788.

Lohse, E. S., and R. Sprague. 1998. History of Research. In *Handbook of North American*

Indians, Vol. 12: *Plateau*, edited by D. E. Walker, Jr., pp. 8–28. Washington, DC: Smithsonian Institution.

Malhi, R. S., B. M. Kemp, J. A. Eshleman, J. Cybulski, D. G. Smith, S. Cousins, and H. Harald. 2007. Mitochondrial Haplogroup M Discovered in Prehistoric North Americans. *Journal of Archaeological Science* 34(4):642–648.

Miheusuah, D. A., ed. 2000. *Repatriation Reader: Who Owns American Indian Remains?* Lincoln: University of Nebraska Press.

Monsalve, M. V., A. C. Stone, C. M. Lewis, A. Tempel, M. Richards, D. Straathof, and D. V. Devine. 2002. Brief Communication: Molecular Analysis of the Kwäday Dän Ts'ìnchi Ancient Remains Found in a Glacier in Canada. *American Journal of Physical Anthropology* 110(3):288–291.

Nicholas, G. P. 2006. Decolonizing the Archaeological Landscape: The Practice and Politics of Archaeology in British Columbia. Special issue on "Decolonizing Archaeology," edited by S. Atalay. *American Indian Quarterly* 30(1):350–380.

Nicholas, G. P. 2007. Native Peoples and Archaeology. In *Encyclopedia of Archaeology*, Vol. 3, edited by D. Pearsall, pp. 1660–1669. Oxford: Elsevier.

Nicholas, G. P., and K. P. Bannister. 2004. "Copyrighting the Past?": Emerging Intellectual Property Rights Issues in Archaeology. *Current Anthropology* 45(3):327–350.

Nicholas, G. P., and J. J. Hollowell. 2004. Intellectual Property Rights in Archaeology? *Anthropology News* 45(4):6, 8.

Nicholas, G. P., and J. J. Hollowell. 2007. Ethical Challenges to a Postcolonial Archaeology. In *Archaeology and Capitalism: From Ethics to Politics*, edited by Y. Hamilakas and P. Duke, pp. 59–82. Walnut Creek, CA: Left Coast Press.

Rubicz, R. 2004. Aleut Research Program. Available online at www2.ku.edu/~lba/Aleut_Results.htm (accessed December 18, 2007)

Rubicz, R., T. G. Schurr, P. L. Babb, and M. H. Crawford. 2003. Mitochondrial DNA Variation and the Origins of the Aleuts. *Human Biology* 75(6):809–835.

Thomas, D. H. 2000. *Skull Wars: Kennewick Man, Archaeology, and the Battle for Native American Identity*. New York: Basic Books.

Walker, D. E., Jr., ed. 1998. *Handbook of North American Indians*, Vol. 12: *Plateau*. Washington, DC: Smithsonian Institution.

Ward, R. H., B. Frazier, K. Dew-Jager, and S. Paabo. 1991. Extensive Mitochondrial Diversity within a Single Amerindian Tribe. *Proceedings of the National Academy of Sciences* 88(19):8720–8724.

Watkins, J. 2000. *Indigenous Archaeology*. Walnut Creek, CA: AltaMira Press.

Zimmerman, L. 2001. Usurping Native American Voice. In *The Future of the Past: Native Americans, Archaeologists, and Repatriation*, edited by T. Bray, pp. 169–183. New York: Garland.

CHAPTER 36
VOICES OF THE FUTURE: A VIEW FROM OUTSIDE THE UNITED STATES

MIGUEL AGUILAR

Scientists from outside the United States have long commented that respect for the rights of Indigenous people to believe in their spiritual and material cultural identity has been lacking in the Kennewick Man case. We find that the scientists involved seem to be against the rights of five Native American communities. Just as Indigenous people were forgotten and marginalized in the past, the rights that every nation and people enjoy in order to believe freely in their own religion, culture, costumes, or traditions are being marginalized today.[1]

The Indigenous people of the Columbia Plateau are staking a claim on the material and human remains of their ancestors. It is important for the scientific community to acknowledge that the respectful treatment of the remains of ancestors from every group is a basic human rights concern. Anthropologists who are not disconnected from the world and from humanity recognize this, but some scientists raise objections, particularly when they are opposed to the veneration, repatriation, and restitution of skeletal remains. These academics defend their positions apparently because they believe that repatriation would negatively affect the development of knowledge.

Kennewick Man, known as the Ancient One, has become one of the most controversial repatriation cases in the United States, pitting academics against a variety of Indigenous interest groups, in spite of a law that retains the right of contemporary tribes to have their ancestral human remains returned to them. The claim for restitution is complex, moreover, because the importance of the remains for science is being conceived and managed in opposition to the will of the tribes. According to the press release of the World Archaeological Congress (WAC),[2] physical anthropology has achieved much satisfactory work in the last fourteen years under the presence of the Native American Graves Protection and Repatriation Act (NAGPRA).[3] The negative reaction on the part of anthropologists to Kennewick's repatriation and the refusal to recognize all human remains in the United States prior to the so-called last wave of immigrants over the Bering Strait might be understood as a hostile reaction to native communities, causing distrust and damaging the discipline of anthropology.

A general assembly composed of academics and Indigenous groups is urgently needed, one in which all positions can be discussed openly, without reprieve or court orders. Many Indigenous groups, such as the Confederated Tribes of the Colville Reservation, are not against scientific investigation (Fish 2005). It is highly beneficial for the disciplines of anthropology and archaeology to use data from traditional knowledge and contact with living communities, as well as serving as a public voice for Indigenous concerns and needs. Certainly, international experience has shown that many anthropological investigations can obtain a substantial amount of resources and support with which to study human and cultural remains; these pursuits are much more fruitful when the descendants of past cultures work together and in cooperation with archaeologists.

For example, Hiram Bingham, who conducted expeditions to the Andes in 1911, was guided by local residents to Machu Picchu, the important ruins that now constitute one of the greatest legacies of Peruvian cultural identity. However, Bingham also exported many artifacts from his excavations there, a move that was approved at the time by the Peruvian State.[4] The Peabody Museum at Yale received some 5,000 of these artifacts from Bingham, although they were nominally on loan and supposed to be returned. Their continued presence in the United States has motivated the Andean community and the Peruvian government to call for the repatriation of these objects. The case of Machu Picchu is particularly interesting for its resemblance to Kennewick Man, because both involve living cultures that are historically alive and recognized by law and are known mostly through the works of social scientists who have worked extensively in these cultural areas.

The remains of Kennewick have been studied for seven years, whereas the Peabody Museum has held the material from Machu Picchu for more than ninety years. But those pieces haven't been the subject of any scientific publications that would allow for the verification of their analyses or clarify their state of preservation. This makes them inaccessible, not only to the direct descendants of Andean cultures, but also to local and other investigators in similar fields of study. In 2005, artifacts from Machu Picchu were exhibited in several North American museums[5] but not in Peru or Cusco, even though both have available facilities with sufficient storage and appropriate conservation environments.

Although there are significant spatial and chronological differences between Kennewick Man and Machu Picchu, the laws of NAGPRA and the court case of *Bonnichsen et al. v. United States* are an important precedent for the repatriation of the pieces from Machu Picchu. In both cases, the native groups are the ones most affected by the lack of access to their material culture and by being unable to venerate their ancestors. Andean archaeologists believe those remains have always belonged to the native peoples of Machu Picchu; living Indigenous groups are the biological and/or cultural heirs of their ancestors. It is important to recognize that the cultural remains also belong in some sense to all of humanity, but it is clear that keeping the artifacts in their place of origin is key to promoting cultural identity and continuity between the past and the present. NAGPRA, in this sense, has recognized the legal bond between Kennewick Man and the tribes of Colville, Nez Perce, Umatilla, and the Wanapum Band from the Columbia Plateau; therefore, restitution should proceed as supported by law.

In the case of Peru, the law establishes that cultural patrimony is the property of the nation, independent of its private or public disposition which is protected by state law.[6] Although none of these laws are applicable outside their own country, the UNESCO Convention of 1970 (UNESCO 1983:63–80) has defined cultural patrimony as including religious and lay objects, regardless of whether they were acquired in legal or illicit archaeological excavations. Countries that signed this convention (Peru ratified it in 1974 and the United States did so in 1983) agreed to prevent their national museums from acquiring cultural goods illegally and to return any illegally acquired cultural property at the request of the nation of origin.

In North America, Native Americans have achieved recognition of their rights through laws that respect most religious and cultural beliefs. U.S. legislation has implemented laws that recognize the importance of cultural elements with religious significance, respecting both their origin and their existence as cultural property. In the same way that Native Americans, as contemporary people, are entitled to preserve their patrimony and be respected at death, the conservation and veneration of their ancestors should also be respected as a universal principle of human rights. The fact that Kennewick Man has been recognized by the Department of the Interior as an ancestor to the tribes of the Columbia Plateau is a reflection of the substance of these claims.

Although institutions such as UNESCO, the International Council on Monuments and Sites, WAC, and the Society for American Archaeology all recognize the special and respectful treatment of mortal remains as a fundamental matter of human rights, and cultural patrimony as integral to the survival of diminishing Indigenous groups (UNESCO 1983:67 [11.14.1970]), the laws that create equality of treatment and respect without discrimination are not universal. The inhabitants of discriminated and oppressed nations and groups are entitled to life and health; we are all entitled to respect for those issues which men and women believe in, for our own human body and for our belongings, which should no longer be exhibited as "rarities" because they originate from cultures different to ours (Pease 2000:17). Globalization means that human rights are internationalized in diverse circumstances; the preservation of these liberties should not create one homogeneous culture.

NOTES

1. WAC, "Kennewick Man," press release, June 27, 2003.

2. "World Archaeological Congress Supports NAGPRA Amendment," press release, October 20, 2004.

3. They were given these in 1911, 1912, and 1916. Only the human remains have been returned, not the material objects (Mould de Pease 2004).

4. Machu Picchu: Unveiling the Mystery of the Incas. Exhibition organized by the Peabody Museum of Yale University, presented at Yale University, New Haven, CT (January 26–May 4, 2003, and on permanent exhibit after February 2005); Natural History Museum of Los Angeles County (June 22–September 7, 2003); Carnegie Museum of Natural History in Pittsburgh (October 18, 2003–January 4, 2004); Denver Museum of Nature and Science (February 13–May 9, 2004); the Houston Museum of Natural Science (June 12–August 29, 2004); Field Museum in Chicago (October 8, 2004–February 1, 2005).

5. There have been many pronouncements on this topic in the city of Cusco, supported by numerous researchers from Cusco and Peru.

6. 21st article of the Peruvian Political Constitution.

REFERENCES

Fish, A. 2005. A Critique of Archaeological Science on the Columbia Plateau. Available online at http://www.landarte.org/Kennewick_Plateau_Science.htm (accessed February 22, 2005).

Mould de Pease, M. 2004. *Machu Picchu y el Código de Ética de la Sociedad de Arqueología Americana*. Lima: CONCYTEC, PUCP Fondo Editorial.

Pease, G. Y. 2000. Prólogo. *Machu Picchu: Patrimonio Cultural en Peligro*. Lima: Alberto Martorel, Editorial Malze.

UNESCO. 1983. *Convenciones y Recomendaciones de la UNESCO Sobre la Protección del Patrimonio Cultural*. Lima: PNUD/UNESCO.

CHAPTER 37
LEARNING FROM OUR[1] OLD PEOPLE AND THE POLITICS OF BEING INDIGENOUS: A NGARRINDJERI RESPONSE TO THE ANCIENT ONE CASE

CHRISTOPHER WILSON

> For many Indigenous communities the control of ancestral human remains is not only about defending their beliefs systems, but is embedded in wider struggles to control identity. (Smith 2004:408)

The "discovery" of the Ancient One[2] has raised many significant issues related to the dichotomy between the objectives of science and the belief systems of Native Americans.[3] In a global context, this case is representative and symbolic for many Indigenous peoples within colonized societies who continue to struggle for acknowledgment of their cultural heritage rights and recognition of their continued existence.

Within the repatriation and reburial debate there are several aspects of identity politics at play. These include the relationships that Indigenous peoples share with their ancestors and with themselves; the relationships that Indigenous peoples share with archaeologists who support repatriation and reburial; and the collective identity of archaeologists seeking to retain "scientific" values for archaeology. Finally, it also includes Indigenous peoples trained in archaeology who are in a unique position to reshape and redefine the discipline through sharing their experiences.

This chapter is a response to the Ancient One case from the perspective of a Ngarrindjeri archaeologist.[4] In this chapter, I discuss the concept of identity as it relates to repatriation, reburial, and archaeology as well as emphasize the politics of being Indigenous and working within the archaeological discipline. In particular, I draw on my own experiences working with Ngarrindjeri Elders[5] during the repatriation of some of my Old People[6] from Museum Victoria in 2004. Through sharing my experiences, parallel to the views of my Elders, I highlight how, through processes of negotiation, successful repatriation outcomes can be achieved that do not necessarily engage with legislation.

In writing from this position about the Ancient One, I acknowledge my social, political, and cultural contexts and must admit that, although I have been asked to write into this space, I feel somewhat cautious about engaging with this subject. This is partly because I am a recent graduate and therefore only a beginner in this field, but more importantly because I do not wish to speak on behalf of another group's ancestors. So, I do not intend to provide an extensive analysis of the Ancient One case. Instead, I will relate my own experiences of identity in Australia, as one of the key issues emerging from the Ancient One case.

REPATRIATION, REBURIAL, AND IDENTITY

Following decades of debate and controversy between Western science and the belief systems of Indigenous peoples, the reburial issue continues to be widely discussed within archaeology (Bowdler 1992; Fforde 2004; Fforde, Hubert, and Turnbull 2002; Zimmerman 1989, 1992). Regardless of who undertook it or how it occurred, the theft of human remains from their resting places and their subsequent "study," "display," and "storage" continues to have an impact on Indigenous peoples today; it is an element of our shared history that should not be dismissed lightly. Despite the specifics of the ongoing debate, what becomes a focal point is the relationship between archaeology and Indigenous peoples, encompassing collaboration, negotiation, and conflict (see Fforde, Hubert, and Turnbull 2002; Hubert 1989; Layton 1989; Mulvaney 1991; Simpson 2001; Swidler et al. 1997; Watkins 2000; Webb 1987).

Many Indigenous peoples rightfully request the return of their ancestors to rebury or care for them in accordance with their cultural beliefs. This may include the decision to engage in scientific research or negotiate an alternative outcome, but usually on the condition that the community—rather than the researcher—is in the position of power and control. However, more typically Indigenous peoples' beliefs are at odds with scientific interests, the latter of which claim to retain human remains for the benefit of all humanity. While in the possession of researchers, the treatment of human remains continues to be one of several issues of concern for Indigenous communities. In many instances, human remains were (and continue to be) devalued from "human" to "specimens" of science (e.g., Hemming 2003; Lippert 2006; Russell 1997). This treatment ultimately causes distrust, pain, and anxiety for Indigenous peoples who hold strong spiritual and cultural connections with their ancestors. And, although some archaeologists (e.g., Pardoe 1990; Zimmerman 1989, 1992) have adopted proactive approaches to the repatriation and reburial process, some institutions continue to facilitate investigations and analysis of Indigenous human remains in the interest of generating public knowledge without appropriate community involvement.

At the heart of this contentious and political area is the right to determine the fate of Indigenous human remains and other cultural heritage—issues of power, control, and authority as well as affirmation of cultural identity. In her analysis of the reburial issue, Fforde (2002:38) has argued that repatriation and reburial are "loci for processes which both construct and reaffirm Aboriginality, empowering its participants by enabling them to assert, define (and thus take control over) their own identity." Although much of the debate is centered on the reclamation and control over Indigenous identities, Meskell (2002) has also argued that individual and collective identity is crucial for the existence of archaeologists within the discipline. Further, Smith (2004:406) suggests that previous debates between cultural beliefs and science fail to conceptualise the overall issue: "The issues are political ones that revolve around the politics of identity and recognition—in which the disciplinary and individual identity of archaeologists and other scientists are as much at stake as those of Indigenous peoples."

Ultimately, the question of "whose past?" becomes pivotal to the overall debate—one that draws on "identity" as a determinant to "authenticity" of Indigenous peoples (claimants) and the right to have control over certain aspects of the past (Jemison 1997; Langford 1983; Layton 1989; McBryde 1985).

THE ANCIENT ONE AND NAGPRA

In light of the opposing perspectives, conflicts relating to Indigenous human remains in the United States have highlighted some fundamental issues that all parties can learn from. The passing of the National Museum of the American Indian Act (1989) and the Native American Graves Protection and Repatriation Act (NAGPRA) in 1990 has provided opportunities for Native American communities to obtain ownership and control over human remains, provided that their "cultural affiliation" can be established (Parker Pearson 2003; Swindler et al. 1997; Thomas 2000; Watkins 2000). Although NAGPRA in some respects enabled Native Americans and archaeologists to engage in more effective dialog, the outcomes of NAGPRA proved to be more complex than first expected (Downer 1997).

One of the main criticisms of NAGPRA is its failure to extend to the repatriation of human remains and objects from locations other than federal and tribal lands (Tsosie 1997:71; Watkins 2000). The most controversial claim put forward under NAGPRA to date—the return of the Ancient One—has drawn vast media attention since its "discovery'" in July 1996. It is a prime example of the contested values between Indigenous peoples and science and, nearly a decade later, continues to be a hotly debated topic globally within archaeology, cultural heritage, human rights law, and Indigenous studies (see Parker Pearson 2003; Swidler et al. 1997; Thomas 2000; Watkins 2000).

Like many repatriation cases, the case of the Ancient One is linked to the politics and debates surrounding Native American identity (Meskell 2002:9). Although situated within human rights law, NAGPRA challenges Native American identity such that proving the relationship between present-day communities and those of the past (ancestors) becomes a critical requirement for successful repatriation through demonstration of "connection," "cultural affiliation," and "descent." Western notions of connection and affiliation typically differ from Indigenous peoples' beliefs. For example, some Indigenous people continue to maintain their country and thus accept responsibility to care for their cultural heritage regardless of Western concepts of genetics or antiquity. This includes caring for human remains in accordance with present-day cultural beliefs in a similar way to caring for one's closest relatives.

REPATRIATION AND AUSTRALIAN
CULTURAL HERITAGE DEBATES: AN OVERVIEW

The reburial issue in the Australian context is similar to that in North America in that there is conflict between scientists in pursuit of the past and Indigenous peoples' claims for rights over their cultural heritage (Layton 1989:12). Although a range of resistance movements emerged in Australia in the 1960s (see Hollinsworth

1998; Lippmann 1994), so, too, did major developments in cultural heritage management (i.e., the Aboriginal sites legislation of the 1960s and 1970s that aimed to protect Aboriginal "relics" and the establishment of the Australian Heritage Commission in 1975). Developments in legislation, however, did not situate control of Indigenous cultural heritage and archaeological sites with Indigenous people; it was the "white" establishment that continued to act as "protectors." Australian museums, archaeologists, and physical anthropologists also began to consider Indigenous peoples' concerns regarding the duration and scientific use of culturally sensitive material (Fforde 2002:34). In the 1970s and early 1980s, museums began to change some of their policies to deaccession and repatriated Indigenous human remains of "named individuals" (i.e., the Crowther Collection; see Hubert 1989:150).

Professional archaeological organizations were also active in this process. In the 1980s, Webb (1987) carried out a research project for the Australian Archaeological Association (AAA) that was designed to open up communication between archaeologists and Indigenous peoples in relation to the reburial issue. After consultation with Indigenous communities associated with the Murray Black Collection, Webb (1987) concluded that concerns could only be overcome through considerable discussion and negotiation. The AAA continues to support and respect Indigenous peoples' rights to cultural heritage by encouraging its members to abide by its code of ethics (AAA 2004).

Although there is no legislation equivalent to NAGPRA in Australia, there are heritage acts within each state and territory that have provisions to protect Aboriginal sites, objects, and remains (e.g., the Aboriginal Heritage Act 1988 [South Australia]). In addition, the Native Title Act of 1993 provides a process by which Indigenous peoples can reclaim lands and waters through the demonstration of "connection" to country, similar to demonstrating "cultural affiliation" under NAGPRA. Indigenous groups (claimants) must demonstrate continuous maintenance and access to country (even though many communities were forcibly removed from it), knowledge and connection to country (which corresponds to historical evidence), and maintenance of a similar way of life compared to documented sources (see McDonald 2000). The consequence for many Indigenous communities is that only those "authentic" or "traditional" groups that can prove continued physical use and connection to country will be awarded native title (see chapters in Lilley 2000).

One of the main flaws of this act is that the definition of "traditional laws and customs" is open to interpretation, such that popular perceptions of "authentic" and "traditional" situate Indigenous peoples in the past, or as existing only within remote regions of Australia (Harrison 2000). This is definitely the case in southeast Australia, where invasion of traditional lands occurred earlier than the northern, central, and desert regions. Although no current legislation exists within Australia, repatriation of human remains is funded through federal government programs: the Repatriation Program, administered by the Office of Indigenous Policy Coordination, which funds international repatriation cases; and the Return of Indigenous Cultural Property Program (RICP), administered by the Department of

Communication, Information Technology and the Arts, which funds domestic repatriation from Australian museum collections. Under the RICP initiative, eight Australian museums are eligible to access this funding; however, they are not required by law to repatriate, making it dependant on the good will of the "gatekeepers" within each museum.[7] Overall, both programs have achieved some success, but they fail adequately to support Indigenous communities throughout the whole repatriation and reburial process, which extends beyond the "handover" of the Old People (Wilson 2005). Ongoing financial support is critical throughout all stages of repatriation and reburial on a case-by-case basis to ensure that Indigenous human remains are cared for appropriately.

Indigenous peoples' concerns over cultural heritage, including requests for repatriation, have been influential in the way in which archaeology has operated (Murray 2000). As a result of ongoing consideration of concerns lobbied by Indigenous peoples, archaeologists in Australia became increasingly involved in constructive consultation and involvement with Indigenous peoples (Colley 2002; Flood 1989).

Removal and Repatriation of Ngarrindjeri Old People: Museum Victoria

The Ngarrindjeri Nation, like many Indigenous communities, has been subject to research since the early period of European colonization in the 19th century (see Berndt 1940; Hale and Tindale 1930; Jenkin 1979; Meyer 1843, 1846; Stirling 1911; Taplin 1864). During the late 1800s and early 1900s, thousands of Old People were removed from Ngarrindjeri *ruwe*,[8] exploited for a range of purposes, and dispersed to numerous institutions locally, nationally, and internationally (Fforde, Hubert, and Turnbull 2002). Not only have individuals, through their careers and science, benefited from research on the Old People, the countries that acquired them, such as Australia and the United Kingdom, also obtained substantial economic and other benefits (Smith 2004:408). The ongoing battle for ownership over cultural heritage and repatriation of human remains from museum collections has become an aspect of maintaining cultural responsibility for the Ngarrindjeri people. This also includes caring for *ruwe* and burial sites (Hemming 2000). This practice reflects moral and cultural respect for all human remains within the Ngarrindjeri landscape, regardless of age, and is a belief system that continues to be central for Ngarrindjeri people today.

In the latter half of the 20th century, a paradigm shift within the discipline saw anthropologists and archaeologists begin to work more closely with Ngarrindjeri people and thus engage in more collaborative research (e.g., Bell 1998; Hemming 1994; Hemming, Jones, and Clarke 1989; Hemming, Wood, and Hunter 2000; Roberts 2003, Roberts et al. 2005; Trevorrow, Hemming, and Wallis 2005). This shift allowed the Ngarrindjeri people to reclaim limited control over archaeological practices conducted within the region and therefore better positioned them to request repatriation.

In 2003, after more than 100 years of removal, over 300 Old People were repatriated to the Ngarrindjeri from the University of Edinburgh—one of the largest repatriation events to occur in Australia to date (see Fforde 2002; Haxton 2003a,

2003b). The following year, another seventy-four Old People were returned from Museum Victoria (Barnes 2004; Hemming and Wilson 2005; Wilson 2005). As a member of the delegation that traveled to Museum Victoria, I obtained a deep insight into the repatriation process and thus learned about some of the issues being dealt with by Ngarrindjeri Elders. In particular, Uncle Tom Trevorrow offered valuable insights into the cultural and spiritual implications of repatriation during the formal handover ceremony at Museum Victoria:

> Once again it's like a day for us, the Ngarrindjeri people, of a mixed feeling, mixed emotion. We feel goodness in us that we're able to come and do this, we know it is the right thing to do, it has to be done, but we feel sadness knowing what has happened and that these Old People have been removed from their traditional burial grounds upon our land and taken by people who had no authority to do that. They've been used in ways, which is culturally wrong, in our culture. So we have to look at it as a very sad part of Australia's history. We're coming together now, we're attempting to make amends for what has happened but there's a long way to go, a lot more to be done. (Trevorrow, cited in Wilson 2005:65)

Although Uncle Tom viewed the repatriation as positive, he also argued that the process was not complete, with the formal handover marking only the beginning of a long process that should receive recognition and support from all museums and institutions in possession of human remains. A stepping-stone toward such support began in this case with an apology from the CEO of Museum Victoria and its acceptance by the community. This apology not only bridged a gap between the museum and the Ngarrindjeri people, it also formed the basis for building a positive relationship in the future.

In addition to this apology, Museum Victoria and Ngarrindjeri Elders signed a Kungun Ngarrindjeri Yunnan Agreement[9] (see Hemming and Trevorrow 2005; Wilson 2005) recognizing Ngarrindjeri people and Ngarrindjeri culture. This process also returned ownership and control over the fate of Ngarrindjeri Old People in the Museum Victoria collection back to the Ngarrindjeri Nation. This marked one of the first agreements, if not *the* first, to be negotiated and signed between a museum and an Indigenous community during a repatriation event in Australia.

As a young Ngarrindjeri archaeologist working with the community, a more interesting component of this process was returning home to Ngarrindjeri *ruwe*. At this point, Ngarrindjeri Elders began to discuss some of their major concerns, such as overcrowding of Old People at Camp Coorong; whether the documentation was accurate; how land would be obtained and negotiated for reburials; which ceremonies each individual should be given during reburial; and the lack of time and resources to follow this process through. The priority for the Ngarrindjeri was to get the Old People back to Ngarrindjeri *ruwe*; other concerns could be dealt with later.

Many people gathered at Camp Coorong the following day to welcome the Old

People home to *ruwe*. The ceremony was open to the wider public, with invitations issued by the Ngarrindjeri Lands and Progress Association to a wide range of community organizations and individuals—both Indigenous and non-Indigenous. This was an opportunity for Ngarrindjeri people to educate the wider public about past injustices, the repatriation of Old People, and Ngarrindjeri culture. It was also a learning experience for me. I was not only learning from Ngarrindjeri Elders with whom I traveled to Melbourne and back, I was also learning from my Old People:

At approximately 1:15 pm the ceremony began. It was an experience that blew me away. The expressions of the dancers, the sound of clap sticks, the smell of tea tree burning and the smoke from the campfires set a strange mood in my body. Looking through the camera made this experience even more daunting as at times the Ngarrindjeri danced in and out the screen and often disappeared in the smoke from the camp fires. Ngarrindjeri men carried the Old People through the smoke and into the storage facility. They, too, would disappear through the smoke. Inside the already crowded storage room the Old People were laid with over 300 other individuals who were brought back home the year before. Inside people paid their respects. Quietly and cautiously people walked around the boxes, some would brush their hands across the top of the boxes others tried to avoid even looking at them. There was only silence then, maybe a cough or two and the sound of the tape rolling through the camera. (Wilson 2005:70)

The repatriation of Old People from Museum Victoria was an important step toward bridging relationships between Indigenous peoples and museums in Australia. As a result, relationships between museums and Indigenous peoples are slowly becoming processes of negotiation and collaboration, and museums that are engaging in repatriation are returning more than human remains—they are also returning ownership, power, authority, and a sense of identity to Indigenous peoples.

MY RELATIONSHIP TO INDIGENOUS ARCHAEOLOGY(IES) AND THE ANCIENT ONE

Indigenous archaeology(ies) and the contribution to archaeology by Indigenous peoples in the broader movement are shaping a future for the discipline, a promising framework for younger people globally to build on (see Deloria 1992; Grossman 2003; Langford 1983; Langton 1993; Million 2005; Richardson 1989; Smith 1999; Watkins 2000). These valuable insights, unique perspectives, and different ways of doing and theorizing help generate new knowledge and interpretation within archaeology and become dynamic spaces that bring together a range of critical and constructive viewpoints. Prior to studying archaeology, my learning experiences were always centered on my identity. Understanding my position as an Indigenous person within the discipline and within the broader Australian society was a major step toward raising self-awareness of the meanings attached to labels (given to me by others), such as Indigenous, Aboriginal, black, and Native. It was not until I began my honors research on the repatriation of my Old People that I felt a sense of control over my identity. The ability to construct and direct my own research enabled me to apply my knowledge and skills to the benefit of my community (see Wilson 2005).

The process of working with my community on the repatriation of Old People has enabled me to "rediscover" my Ngarrindjeri heritage, while obtaining additional skills and training outside of the university under the guidance of Ngarrindjeri Elders. This process is reciprocal: Not only did I witness the repatriation of Old People back to Ngarrindjeri country, I also underwent a transformation and repatriation to my community. From here on, my understanding of identity and the importance of knowing my position was clear.

Identity continues to be an issue I battle with on a daily basis. I have entered the discipline of archaeology with the complexities and politics attached to meanings and perceptions of who is Indigenous and what an Indigenous person is. As an Indigenous researcher, one of the largest responsibilities I carry is to ensure that my research (whether involving human remains or not) is conducted in negotiation and collaboration with my Elders—a responsibility that many non-Indigenous archaeologists are increasingly adopting. As I continue to mold the spaces in which I work to suit my understandings and interests, I can only hope that the work carried out before my existence by Indigenous and non-Indigenous archaeologists has paved a strong foundation for a future that I can build on collectively with both my community and others who seek to walk the same path.

From repatriation to identity politics, my position as an Indigenous person and archaeologist practicing what is loosely termed "Indigenous archaeology(ies)" has been mostly my choice. To some extent, however, I have felt "boxed into" these categories without any control. Either way, I continue to learn from my Old People, Elders, teachers, peers, as well as through my own experiences, and I awake each day with more knowledge and experience than before. The Ancient One case has influenced my work as a Ngarrindjeri archaeologist in Australia, as it has provided the opportunity for other Indigenous peoples, both young and old, to continue learning about culture, history, politics, and cultural identity.

CONCLUSION

The Ancient One case provides an example of contesting values between Indigenous peoples and archaeologists and allows interesting comparisons to be drawn with the Australian context (see also Hemming, Rigney, and Wilson in this volume). Some of the major issues emerging from the Ancient One case relate to cultural heritage, Indigenous cultural affirmation, authenticity, objectivity, and cultural identity. What is apparent in many respects is that science is too often privileged over the cultural beliefs of Indigenous peoples to the extent that cultural identity and proving affiliation to our ancestors, our country, and our culture are open to the public for their criticism, contestation, and interrogation.

Within the Australian context, the Ngarrindjeri have engaged in agreement-making processes as a positive method to engage with museum professionals.

Likewise, relationship building between archaeologists and Indigenous peoples is pivotal in developing collaborative research, which has dual outcomes and benefits for all parties involved. These strategies are critical in processes involving cultural heritage, repatriation, and human remains, as each community and repatriation case is distinct. Repatriation cases, such as the Ngarrindjeri experience, are a model for proactive repatriation and demonstrate that legislation is not necessarily the only viable option to providing equality for Indigenous peoples and Indigenous cultural heritage.

An intriguing aspect of the repatriation process is that we continue to learn from the Old People through debate, research, and practical experience. It is therefore important that both archaeologists and Indigenous peoples continue to engage in dialog and continue to work toward developing practices with Indigenous peoples to further enhance the prospects for an archaeology that engages in processes for the benefit of Indigenous communities—a philosophy and practice that grounds my purpose and vision as a Ngarrindjeri archaeologist.

ACKNOWLEDGMENTS

I would like to thank Naomi Anderson Sibosado, Steve Hemming, and Lynley Wallis for comments and feedback on earlier drafts of this chapter. Thanks to Uncle Tom Trevorrow, Uncle Matt Rigney, and the Ngarrindjeri Lands and Progress Association for providing the direction, leadership, and inspiration to continue learning about Ngarrindjeri culture. Thank you to Lori Richardson for information related to the RICP Program. And, lastly, I thank Simone Ulalka Tur for the tireless but thoughtful discussions about the politics of being Indigenous.

NOTES

1. I do not claim ownership over another group's ancestors by using the term "our"; rather, I acknowledge "our" collective struggle as Indigenous peoples.

2. For the purposes of this chapter, the term "Ancient One" will be used to describe the human remains referred to elsewhere as "Kennewick Man."

3. The term "Native American" refers to Indigenous people within the United States.

4. The Ngarrindjeri are a nation of Indigenous peoples of the Lower Murray Lakes and Coorong in South Australia.

5. The term "Elders" also refers to Senior Ngarrindjeri leaders.

6. The term "Old People" refers to Ngarrindjeri "human remains."

7. The eight museums eligible to participate in the program include: the Australian Museum, Museum and Art Gallery of the Northern Territory, Museum Victoria, National Museum of Australia, Queensland Museum, South Australian Museum, Tasmanian Museum and Art Gallery and the Western Australian Museum.

8. *Ruwe* is a Ngarrindjeri word meaning country or lands and waters.

9. Kungun Ngarrindjeri Yunnan means "Listen to Ngarrindjeri talking." Similar agreements have been signed with other local councils in South Australia.

REFERENCES

Australian Archaeological Association (AAA). 2004. *Code of Ethics of the Australian Archaeological Association*. Available online at http://www.australianarchaeologicalasso-ciation.com.au/codeofethics.php#3 (accessed May 29, 2006).

Barnes, R. 2004. We're Sorry, Says Museum. *The Advertiser*, August 26, p. 13.

Bell, D. 1998. *Ngarrindjeri Wurruwarrin: A World that Is, Was and Will Be*. Melbourne, Australia: Spinifex Press.

Berndt, R. M. 1940. Some Aspects of Jaralde Culture, South Australia. *Oceania* 11(2):164–201.

Bowdler, S. 1992. Unquiet Slumbers: The Return of the Kow Swamp Burials. *Antiquity* 66(250):103–106.

Colley, S. 2002. *Uncovering Australia: Archaeology, Indigenous Peoples and the Public*. Sydney, Australia: Allen and Unwin.

Deloria, V., Jr. 1992. Indians, Archaeologists and the Future. *American Antiquity* 57(4):595–598.

Downer, A. S. 1997. Archaeologists-Native American Relations. In *Native Americans and Archaeologists: Stepping Stones to Common Ground*, edited by N. Swidler, K. Dongoske, R. Anyon, and A. Downer, pp. 22–34. Walnut Creek, CA: AltaMira Press.

Fforde, C. 2002. Collection, Repatriation and Identity. In *The Dead and Their Possessions: Repatriation in Principle, Policy and Practice*, edited by C. Fforde, J. Hubert, and P. Turnbull, pp. 25–46. London: Routledge.

Fforde, C. 2004. *Collecting the Dead: Archaeology and the Reburial Issue*. London: Gerald Duckworth.

Fforde, C., J. Hubert, and P. Turnbull, eds. 2002. *The Dead and Their Possessions: Repatriation in Principle, Policy and Practice*. London: Routledge.

Flood, J. 1989. *Archaeology of the Dreamtime: The Story of Prehistoric Australia and its People*. Sydney: Collins Australia.

Grossman, M., ed. 2003. *Blacklines: Contemporary Critical Writing by Indigenous Australians*. Melbourne, Australia: Melbourne University Press.

Hale, H., and N. Tindale. 1930. Notes on Some Human Remains in the Lower Murray Valley, South Australia. *Records of the South Australian Museum* 3(2):145–218.

Harrison, R. 2000. Challenging the "Authenticity" of Antiquity: Contact Archaeology and Native Title in Australia. In *Native Title and the Transformation of Archaeology in the Postcolonial World*, edited by I. Lilley, pp. 35–53. Sydney, Australia: University of Sydney.

Haxton, N. 2003a. *Ngarrindjeri Remains Returned to Ancestral Lands*. Available online at http://www.abc.net.au/am/content/2003/s851655.htm (accessed March 22, 2004).

Haxton, N. 2003b. *Aboriginal Community Wants Ancestor Remains Returned*. Available online at http://www.abc.net.au/am/content/2003/s857217.htm (accessed March 22, 2004).

Hemming, S., ed. 1994. *Troddin Thru Raukkan Our Home: Raukkan Re-union 1994*. Adelaide: Raukkan Community and South Australian Museum.

Hemming, S. 2000. Ngarrindjeri Burials as Cultural Sites: Indigenous Heritage Issues in Australia. *World Archaeology Bulletin* 11. Available online at http://wac.uct.ac.za/bul-letin/wab11/hemming.html (accessed May 12, 2003).

Hemming, S. 2003. Objects and Specimens: Conservative Politics and the SA Museum's Aboriginal Cultures Gallery. *Overland* 171:64–69.

Hemming, S., and T. Trevorrow. 2005. Kungun Ngarrindjeri Yunnan: Archaeology, Colonialism and Re-claiming the Future. In *Indigenous Archaeologies: Decolonising Theory and Practice*, edited by C. Smith, and M. H. Wobst, pp. 243–261. London: Routledge.

Hemming, S., and C. Wilson. 2005. Returning Old People: The First Stolen Generations. Unpublished conference paper delivered at the Museums Australia National Conference. Available online at: http://www.museumsaustralia.org.au/dbdoc/Hemming%20and%20 Wilson%20-%202005.pdf (accessed June 1, 2005).

Hemming, S., P. Jones, P. Clarke. 1989. *Ngurunderi: An Aboriginal Dreaming*. South Australian Museum, Adelaide.

Hemming, S., V. Wood, and R. Hunter. 2000. Researching the Past: Oral History and Archaeology at Swan Reach. In *The Archaeology of Difference: Negotiating Cross-*

Cultural Engagements in Oceania, edited by R. Torrence and A. Clarke, pp. 331–359. London: Routledge.

Hollinsworth, D. 1998. *Race and Racism in Australia*, 2nd ed. South Melbourne, Australia: Social Science Press.

Hubert, J. 1989. A Proper Place for the Dead: A Critical Review of the Reburial Issue. In *Conflict in the Archaeology of Living Traditions*, edited by R. Layton, pp. 131–166. London: Unwin Hyman.

Jemison, G. P. 1997. Who Owns the Past? In *Native Americans and Archaeologists: Stepping Stones to Common Ground*, edited by N. Swidler, K. E. Dongoske, R. Anyon, and A. S. Downer, pp. 57–63. Walnut Creek, CA: AltaMira Press.

Jenkin, G. 1979. *Conquest of the Ngarrindjeri*. Adelaide, Australia: Rigby.

Langford, R. 1983. Our Heritage: Your Playground. *Australian Archaeology* 16:1–6.

Langton, M. 1993. *Well I Heard It on the Radio and I Saw It on the Television*. Sydney: Australian Film Commission.

Layton, R. 1989. Introduction: Conflict in the Archaeology of Living Traditions. In *Conflict in the Archaeology of Living Traditions*, edited by R. Layton, pp. 1–19. London: Unwin Hyman.

Lilley, I., ed. 2000. *Native Title and the Transformation of Archaeology in the Post-Colonial World*. Sydney, Australia: University of Sydney.

Lippert, D. 2006. Comment on "Dwelling at the Margins, Action at the Intersection? Feminist and Indigenous Archaeologies, 2005." *Archaeologies: Journal of the World Archaeological Congress* 1(1):63–66.

Lippmann, L. 1994. *Generations of Resistance: Mabo and Justice*, 3rd ed. Melbourne, Australia: Longman.

McBryde, I. 1985. *Who Owns the Past?* Melbourne, Australia: Oxford University Press.

McDonald, J. 2000. Archaeology, Rock Art, Ethnicity and Native Title. In *Native Title and the Transformation of Archaeology in the Postcolonial World*, edited by I. Lilley, pp. 54–64. Sydney, Australia: University of Sydney.

Meskell, L. 2002. The Intersections of Identity and Politics in Archaeology. *Annual Review of Anthropology* 31:279–301.

Meyer, H. A. E. 1843. *Vocabulary of the Language Spoken by the Aborigines of South Australia*. Adelaide, Australia: Government Printer.

Meyer, H. A. E. 1846. *Manners and Customs of the Aborigines of the Encounter Bay Tribe, South Australia*. Adelaide, Australia: Government Printer.

Million, T. 2005. Developing an Aboriginal Archaeology: Receiving Gifts from White Buffalo Calf Woman. In *Indigenous Archaeologies: Decolonizing Theory and Practice*, edited by C. Smith and H. Wobst, pp. 44–55. New York: Routledge.

Mulvaney, D. J. 1991. Past Regained, Future Lost: The Kow Swamp Pleistocene Burial. *Antiquity* 65(246):12–21.

Murray, T. 2000. Conjectural Histories: Some Archaeological and Historical Consequences of Indigenous Dispossession in Australia. In *Native Title and the Transformation of Archaeology in the Postcolonial World*, edited by I. Lilley, pp. 65–77. *Oceania Monograph* 50, University of Sydney, Sydney.

Pardoe, C. 1990. Sharing the Past: Aboriginal Influence on Archaeological Practice, a Case Study from New South Wales. *Aboriginal History* 14(2):208–223.

Parker Pearson, M. 2003. *The Archaeology of Death and Burial*. Gloucestershire, UK: Sutton Publishing, Phoenix Mill.

Richardson, L. 1989. The Acquisition, Storage and Handling of Aboriginal Skeletal Remains in Museums: An Indigenous Perspective. In *Conflict in the Archaeology of Living Traditions*, edited by R. Layton, pp. 185–188. London: Unwin Hyman.

Roberts, A. L. 2003. Knowledge, Power and Voice: An Investigation of Indigenous South Australian Perspectives of Archaeology. Unpublished PhD thesis, Department of Archaeology, Flinders University of South Australia, Adelaide.

Roberts, A. L., S. Hemming, T. Trevorrow, G. Trevorrow, M. Rigney, L. Agius, and R. Agius. 2005. Nukun and Kungun Ngarrindjeri Ruwe (Look and Listen to Ngarrindjeri Country): An Investigation of Ngarrindjeri Perspectives of Archaeology in Relation to Native Title and Heritage Matters. *Australian Aboriginal Studies* 2005(2):45–53.

Russell, L. 1997. Focusing on the Past: Visual and Textual Images of Aboriginal Australia in

Museums. In *The Cultural Life of Images: Visual Representation in Archaeology*, edited by B. Molyneaux, pp. 230–248. London: Routledge.

Simpson, M. G. 2001. *Making Representations: Museums in the Post-Colonial Era*. London: Routledge.

Smith, L. J. 1999. *Decolonizing Methodologies: Research and Indigenous Peoples*. London: Zed Books.

Smith L. J. 2004. The Repatriation of Human Remains—Problem or Opportunity? *Antiquity* 78:404–413.

Stirling, E. C. 1911. Preliminary Report on the Discovery of Native Remains at Swan Port, River Murray with an Enquiry into the Alleged Occurrence of a Pandemic among the Australian Aborigines. *Transactions of the Royal Society of South Australia* 35:4–46.

Swidler, N., K. Dongoske, R. Anyon, and A. Downer. 1997. *Native Americans and Archaeologists: Stepping Stones to Common Ground*. Walnut Creek, CA: AltaMira Press.

Taplin, G. 1864. *Lessons, Hymns and Prayers for the Native School at Port Macleay in the Language of the Lake Tribes of Aborigines, Called Narrinyeri*. Adelaide, Australia: Aborigines' Friends' Association.

Thomas, D. H. 2000. *Skull Wars: Kennewick Man, Archeology, and the Battle for Native American Identity*. New York: Basic Books.

Tsosie, R. 1997. Indigenous Rights and Archaeology. In *Native Americans and Archaeologists: Stepping Stones to Common Ground*, edited by N. Swidler, K.E. Dongoske, R. Anyon, and A. S. Downer, pp. 64–76. Walnut Creek, CA: AltaMira Press.

Trevorrow, T., S. Hemming, and L. Wallis. 2005. Parnka: Reflections on the History of Archaeological Research in South Australia. Unpublished conference paper delivered at The Uses and Abuses of Archaeology for Indigenous Populations, World Archaeology Congress (WAC) Inter-Congress, November 8–12, Auckland, New Zealand.

Watkins, J. 2000. *Indigenous Archaeology: American Indian Values and Scientific Practice*. Walnut Creek, CA: AltaMira Press.

Webb, S. 1987. Reburying Australian Skeletons. *Antiquity* 61(232):292–296.

Wilson, C. 2005. Return of the Ngarrindjeri: Repatriating Old People Back to Country. Unpublished BArch (Hons) Thesis, Department of Archaeology, Flinders University, Adelaide.

Zimmerman, L. J. 1989. Made Radical by My Own: An Archaeologist Learns to Accept Reburial. In *Conflict in the Archaeology of Living Traditions*, edited by R. Layton, pp. 60–66. London: Unwin Hyman.

Zimmerman, L. J. 1992. Archaeology, Reburial, and the Tactics of a Discipline's Self-Delusion. *American Indigenous Culture and Research Journal* 16:37–56.

CHAPTER 38

LISTENING AND RESPONDING ACROSS
GENERATIONS AND BEYOND BORDERS:
THE ANCIENT ONE AND KUMARANGK
(HINDMARSH ISLAND)

STEVE HEMMING, DARYLE RIGNEY, AND CHRISTOPHER WILSON

The Hindmarsh Island (Kumarangk) issue has more twists and turns than a
pit full of snakes and a bite just as deadly. Ten years have passed since the
Ngarrindjeri people sought protection of Aboriginal heritage sites on and
around Hindmarsh Island. It has been a sustained attack on people's spiritual and cultural beliefs, and has caused deep emotional and physical
stress. (Sandra Saunders, Ngarrindjeri Elder and former director of the
Aboriginal Legal Rights Movement [South Australia], 2003:60)

The links between the Ancient One (Kennewick) case and the Kumarangk
(Hindmarsh Island) case make for some sobering reflections on the politics of identity and the relationship between archaeological practice and related laws in the
making of contemporary national identity in settler societies. The Ngarrindjeri
Nation of South Australia and the Confederated Tribes of the Umatilla Indian
Reservation (CTUIR) of the Columbia Plateau have recently worked together over
international First Nation treaty development. It is tragic and ironic that major "heritage" controversies have arisen on the lands of these First Nations as a consequence
of archaeological practice and have led through legal battles to the redefinition of
Indigenous peoples in relation to the United States and Australian nation-states (see
Hemming 2006; Watkins 2001, 2003). Both cases raise questions that seriously
challenge the authenticity of settler colonial states. Importantly and sadly,
Indigenous people have learned that legislation aimed at protecting heritage, such as
the Native American Graves Protection and Repatriation Act (NAGPRA) and the
Aboriginal and Torres Strait Islander Heritage Protection Act, 1984, also contain
and restrict Indigenous sovereign rights. In an attempt to work beyond colonialist
political and legal boundaries, the Ngarrindjeri, the CTUIR, and the National
Congress of American Indians (NCAI) are working toward strategic alliances
between First Nations on the Pacific Rim.
    Perhaps at first glance the Ancient One case of North America bears no rela-
tionship to the Kumarangk case of South Australia, but shared traditions and shared
histories provide valuable insights. Kumarangk became part of the Australian media
landscape in 1994, only two years before the Ancient One's resting place was disturbed in Washington State (e.g., Bell 1998; Thomas 2000; Smith and Wobst 2005;
Watkins 2005). These issues are contemporary; they emerge out of a shared tradition of settler colonialism and a shared tradition of archaeology as the scientific dis-

course that patrols the white nation's past. Importantly, as Geonpul scholar Aileen Moreton-Robinson has recently pointed out, the power of this discourse is dependent on the "possessive logic of white sovereignty":

The possessive logic of white sovereignty is deployed to promote the idea of race neutrality through concepts attached to the ideals of democracy, such as egalitarianism, equity and equal opportunity. This allows patriarchal white sovereignty to remain transparent and invisible—two key attributes of its power. Yet as the premise of white national identity it defines "the human condition … it alone defines normality and fully inhabits it." (Moreton-Robinson 2004:2)

In the Kumarangk case Ngarrindjeri fought to protect sacred land and waters (*ruwe*) from desecration by the building of a bridge between Kumarangk and the township of Goolwa, near the Murray River mouth in South Australia (e.g., Hemming, Trevorrow, and Rigney 2002; Trevorrow 2003). The area holds particular significance for Ngarrindjeri women's traditions, and the case became characterized as "secret women's business." A royal commission was staged by the South Australian government to determine whether the women's business was a fabrication—to interrogate the religious and spiritual beliefs of Indigenous people (Stevens 1995). The Hindmarsh Island Bridge Royal Commission dominated the media with headlines such as "lies, lies, lies," "fabrication," and "hoax." In cases such as Kumarangk and the Ancient One, the dominant forces in the media, the scientific community, the legal system, the business community, and conservative politicians form a powerful alliance. In a devastating blow to the Ngarrindjeri, Commissioner Iris Stevens found that all the Ngarrindjeri women's traditions were fabricated.

In a 2001 landmark decision in the federal court, Justice von Doussa's findings contradicted the royal commission and supported the credibility of the Ngarrindjeri traditions (von Doussa 2001). This win for the Ngarrindjeri people has received little attention in the Australian media (Simons 2003). Along with the building of the "genocide bridge," the phrase "secret women's business" has entered the Australian vernacular as a derogatory devaluation of Indigenous and women's knowledge.[1]

Part of Ngarrindjeri concern for the Kumarangk area revolved around threats to burial sites of Old People (the preferred Ngarrindjeri term for those who have gone before) (Hemming 2000). In 2002, the local council disturbed the remains of some Old People during excavations for the redevelopment of the wharf area directly adjacent to the new bridge (Hemming and Trevorrow 2005). On this occasion, the Ngarrindjeri leadership decided not to evoke the Aboriginal Heritage Act, 1988 (South Australia), having already experienced the futility of its power in the face of development and non-Indigenous interests. The Ngarrindjeri fight to protect the sacred waters around Kumarangk and the burial places of the Old People had gone all the way to the High Court and led to a retrograde reinterpretation of the Australian Constitution and powers to make laws relating to "Aboriginal people" (Bell 1998:600–603). Instead, Ngarrindjeri leaders negotiated a Kungun

Ngarrindjeri Yunnan agreement (Listen to what Ngarrindjeri people are saying) and an apology from the local council. Ngarrindjeri people gained recognition as traditional owners and received a broad apology from the Alexandrina Council.

As experienced by the CTUIR in the case of the Ancient One, heritage protection legislation leads to a legal process dominated by the "possessive logic of white sovereignty." The conservative governments in Australia and the United States have also made strategic appointments to their highest courts—the Australian High Court and the U.S. Supreme Court. In the present conservative environment, it has become increasingly necessary to avoid the courts and the evocation of supposedly "protective legislation," which most often leads to negative legal findings and reactionary legal precedents. In 2004, the CTUIR made the following public statement:

> Today the Confederated Tribes of the Umatilla Indian Reservation's Board of Trustees decided not to appeal the Ancient One/Kennewick Man case to the US Supreme Court. The decision was based on the availability of financial resources, the uncertainty of whether the Supreme Court would even hear the case, and the risk that an unfavorable Court decision could become law. (CTUIR 2004)

PARTNERSHIPS, RESISTANCES, AND NEW DIRECTIONS

In June 2004, NCAI adopted a resolution, as proposed by the CTUIR,[2] "to establish a special committee of Tribal delegates to meet with Indigenous Nations of the Pacific Rim."[3] At the October 2004 annual convention of the NCAI, a Special Committee on Indigenous Nations Relationships recommended a series of working meetings on key questions of Indigenous nation relationships to consider the development of a "United League of Indigenous Nations."

Ngarrindjeri attended both meetings and made formal presentations proclaiming their support for the establishment of a Ngarrindjeri Ngia-ngiampe (treaty/trade partnership) with other Indigenous nations to address issues of common concern and in furtherance of common goals.[4] Ngarrindjeri agreed at these meetings that there is strength in developing international unity among Indigenous First Nations through a structure for international cooperation that:

- recognizes that the laws of each Indigenous nation regarding its own cultural property take precedence;
- formulates joint strategies and initiatives on common issues and concerns; and
- through consultation and negotiation, develops rules and procedures for Indigenous nation diplomacy based on protocols that are grounded in the culture and traditions of Indigenous peoples.

In their participation with the CTUIR and the NCAI, Ngarrindjeri are asserting their inherent rights to governance as a nation at a time when the need to come together to create political, cultural, and economic benefit to the community has never been greater. In August 2007, on the lands of the Lummi Nation, Washington State, eleven Indigenous nations from around the Pacific Rim signed the inaugural United League of Indigenous Nations Treaty. In so doing, Ngarrindjeri have recognized that engagement with other Indigenous nations through an effective program of nation-to-nation diplomacy and strategic alliance would positively add to the local process of agreement making, bringing value to both the Ngarrindjeri nation and Australian governments around matters such as: protection of cultural properties, natural resource management, native title, education, research, scholarly exchange, and a framework for mutually beneficial trade and commerce.

Governance in this context is not unproblematic and moves beyond being merely a matter of state authority and becomes a matter of authority and legitimacy in other social arrangements at local, national, and international levels. Indigenous peoples organizing across geopolitical boundaries challenge colonial and postcolonial processes of state formation, which are typically framed through discourses of "discovered territory" and "unoccupied land." Ngarrindjeri, as a minority in the political space created by the colonial nation state's pursuit of its interests, recognize their marginalization in the economic and political economies as being based on the denial and/or subjugation of their rights, cultures, and interests by the Australian nation-state. In December 2003, Ngarrindjeri asserted to the South Australian government through the "Ngarrindjeri Proclamation of Dominium 2003" that sovereignty was never ceded to the Crown and that what is needed is a process of recognition and agreement making in relation to future well-being.

The Ngarrindjeri struggle for just recognition of the damage done to their cultural economy through assertion of principles of social justice and their sovereignty, and the questioning of what constitutes a nation-state has led Ngarrindjeri to look to points of intersection with other Indigenous nations. These points offer the opportunity to make it more difficult for dominant nation-state-based political interests to simplify and obscure the details of local political struggle. Broadening the audience beyond the isolation of the Australian domestic arena at a time when there is "great uncertainty for Indigenous peoples, with significant changes underway in the federal government's approach to Indigenous affairs and how it engages with Indigenous peoples" is important when there are "very few mechanisms remaining that are able to independently monitor the activities of governments from a national perspective" (Aboriginal & Torres Strait Islander Social Justice Commissioner 2005:1).

All too often, Ngarrindjeri have experienced threats to their survival and well-being as Ngarrindjeri, as Australian governments have designed the facilitation of their political possibilities through the silencing or exclusion of the political possibilities of Ngarrindjeri. Add to this selective and/or coercive "consultation" and a lack of funded representative structures and there is a strong case to be made for Indigenous nations to coordinate strategies and processes to develop common positions, political concepts, and linkages to communicate their case at an international level. Failure to do so locks the struggle into a biased Australian political and legal system where Ngarrindjeri voice remains captured by Australian political policy.

Tensions between colonial nation-states and Indigenous peoples, during which Indigenous people and their communities have sought to determine and exercise their political status through the pursuit of economic, social, and cultural development, take many forms. In settler colonial societies, the protection of cultural heritage has become a central site in the struggle for Indigenous survival. Archaeology as a discipline must better understand its historical and contemporary role in securing the authenticity of settler democracies such as Australia and the United States. As Joe Watkins has recently pointed out:

> It is contingent on archaeologists to appreciate the importance of the wider contexts within which archaeology is practiced and the political realms within which those contexts are situated. It is imperative that anthropology, as a discipline, realizes that American Indians and other Indigenous populations worldwide have more at stake in the study of their heritage than merely the information "contained" therein. (Watkins 2005:202)

ANCIENT ONE, KUMARANGK, AND ARCHAEOLOGY: SOME REFLECTIONS

The continuing common experience of Indigenous First Nations in settler societies around issues such as the Ancient One and Kumarangk illustrates the value of close relationships between First Nations across the Pacific Rim. Archaeology continues to play an exaggerated role in determining the status of First Nations in settler societies in this region. Tim Murray, a senior archaeologist, said the following about Ngarrindjeri traditions:

> It should be self-evident that the temptation to create a seamless link between past and present where none is there, or to produce convenient pasts to support Native Title claims, will serve to do little more than to bring both history and archaeology into disrepute. The consequences of the Hindmarsh Island Royal Commission for the heritage of South Australia are a pretty dramatic case in point. (Murray 2000:76)

Murray provides no evidence that he is familiar with the Kumarangk case, and his sweeping statement about the continuity of Ngarrindjeri traditions can only be described as a privileged, colonizing intervention. It clearly highlights the critical role that archaeology plays in the Indigenous struggle for land rights and self-determination in south-eastern Australia, through its occupation of the scientific "high ground" and in the last few decades through its dominance of Aboriginal heritage "management" (e.g., Byrne 2003; Hemming and Trevorrow 2005; Smith 2004). The following remarks by senior Ngarrindjeri woman Sandra Saunders highlight the continuing damage of the Hindmarsh Island Bridge Royal Commission:

> Ten years on Ngarrindjeri culture is still being destroyed; burial grounds are still being dug up. Ngarrindjeri have no access to Kumarangk except by

a bridge that destroyed their heritage. Nationally the Howard Government continues to attack and dismantle Aboriginal heritage. The fabrication tag still remains with the Government refusing to take up the issues raised in the von Doussa judgement and no apology has been made to the Ngarrindjeri. (Saunders 2003:61)

In October 2004, the World Archaeological Congress (WAC) "offered its unreserved support for the Senate Indian Affairs Committee's" proposed amendment to NAGPRA, "which would recognize as Native American all human remains found in the United States that date prior to the documented arrival of European explorers" (WAC 2004:1). We, the authors of this chapter, unreservedly support this amendment. The chairs of the Ngarrindjeri Tendi, Ngarrindjeri Heritage Committee, and the Ngarrindjeri Native Title Management Committee, George Trevorrow, Tom Trevorrow, and Matt Rigney directed that their support for this amendment be recorded in this publication.

So far, the Ngarrindjeri have had nearly 400 individuals repatriated back to Ruwe (country).[5] The priority and culturally appropriate protocol for the Ngarrindjeri people today is to lay the Old People at rest in their country. As Ngarrindjeri Elder Tom Trevorrow made clear:

The wrongs of the past are the inheritance of the present. The unbelievable acts of stealing, desecration, abuse and genocide upon our people will never be forgotten. The return of our old people to their true resting places is a significant step but only one step in the continuing journey for justice that the Ngarrindjeri must travel. (National Museum of Australia 2003:1)

Conclusion

The complex political, legal, and media landscape is the context of Indigenous heritage debates in Australia and the United States. This is the space in which crucial cases such as Kumarangk and the Ancient One are contested. Courts in Australia and the United States are becoming increasingly more conservative—particularly in the highest courts (the U.S. Supreme Court and the Australian High Court). Battles over land and legitimacy are being resolved in courts dominated by a patriarchal, white, ruling-class culture. The scientific archaeologist is a recognizable and understandable expert witness in these spaces. The language of "fact," underpinning Western legal systems and scientific disciplines, joins forces with conservative, colonial interests to restrict Indigenous rights and interests in country, culture, and a just stake in the future. There should be no underestimation of the power of this continuing and strengthening alliance. Australia under John Howard and the United States under George W. Bush have been political landscapes in which 1980s justice, empowerment, and self-determination agendas are out-of-place and increasingly friendless.

Certainly in Australia there is an urgent need for archaeology students to engage more directly with general studies of society and a broad range of cultural and critical theory. Indigenous theorists must be essential parts of any archaeology degree in a settler, colonial democracy (e.g., Deloria 1995; Langton 1981; Moreton-Robinson 2004; Smith 1999).

NOTES

1. In early 2003, Daryle Rigney met Alan Parker, a Cree man from Rocky Boy Reservation and professor of Native law and policy at Evergreen College, Washington State, in Aeoteroa, New Zealand. The meeting led to further discussion with other scholars and Indigenous leaders about the establishment of an international forum on Indigenous strategies of self-determination. The Ngarrindjeri Nation leadership acknowledge Professor Parker, the CTUIR, and the NCAI in this most important initiative.

2. National Congress of American Indian, Resolution MOH 04-005. Available online at http://www.ncai.org (accessed April 12, 2005).

3. NCAI Mid-Year session, Uncasville, Connecticut, June 20–23, 2004. In attendance: Tom Trevorrow, Elder and chair, Ngarrindjeri Heritage Committee, Ngarrindjeri Nation and Steve Hemming, advisor to Ngarrindjeri Heritage Committee and Ngarrindjeri Native Title Management Committee.

4. NCAI 61st Annual Convention, Fort Lauderdale, Florida, October 10–15, 2004. In attendance were: Daryle Rigney, Ngarrindjeri and director, Yunggorendi, First Nations Centre for Higher Education and Research, Flinders University, Adelaide, Australia.

5. On May 8, 2003, the largest return of Indigenous remains in Australia's history took place at Camp Coorong, Race Relations and Cultural Education Centre in South Australia. Three hundred Old People were returned to the Ngarrindjeri people. Their remains were stolen by Dr. William Ramsay Smith from graves between 1898 and 1906 (see Fforde, Huburt, and Turnbull 2003). Thousands of Ngarrindjeri Old People still remain in public and private collections in Australia and overseas.

REFERENCES

Aboriginal & Torres Strait Islander Social Justice Commissioner. 2005. *Social Justice Report 2004*. Sydney, Australia: Human Rights and Equal Opportunity Commission.

Bell, D. 1998. *Ngarrindjeri Wurruwarrin: A World that Is, Was, and Will Be*. North Melbourne, Australia: Spinifex.

Byrne, D. 2003. The Ethos of Return: Erasure and Reinstatement of Aboriginal Visibility in the Australian Historical Landscape. *Historical Archaeology* 37(1):73–86.

Confederated Tribes of the Umatilla Indian Reservation (CTUIR). 2004. Ancient One/Kennewick Man. Press statement: CTUIR will not pursue case in the US Supreme Court, July 19, 2004. Available online at www.umatilla.nsn.us/kman14.html (accessed April 11, 2005).

Deloria, V., Jr. 1995. *Red Earth, White Lies: Native Americans and the Myth of Scientific Fact*. New York: Scribner and Sons.

Fforde, C., J. Hubert, and P. Turnbull, eds. 2002. *The Dead and Their Possessions: Repatriation in Principle, Policy and Practice*. London: Routledge.

Hemming, S. 2000. Ngarrindjeri Burials as Cultural Sites: Indigenous Heritage Issues in Australia. *World Archaeological Bulletin* 11:58–66.

Hemming, S. 2006. The Problem with Aboriginal Heritage. In *Sharing Spaces: Indigenous and non-Indigenous Responses to Story, Country and Rights*, edited by G. Worby and L-I. Rigney, pp. 305–328. Perth: API Network.

Hemming, S., and T. Trevorrow. 2005. Kungun Ngarrindjeri Yunnan: Archaeology, Colonialism and Re-Claiming the Future. In *Indigenous Archaeologies: Decolonizing Theory and Practice*, edited by C. Smith and H. M. Wobst, pp. 243–261. London: Routledge.

Hemming, S., T. Trevorrow, and M. Rigney. 2002. Ngarrindjeri Culture. In *The Murray Mouth: Exploring the Implications of Closure or Restricted Flow*, edited by M. Goodwin and S. Bennett, pp. 13–19. Adelaide, Australia: Department of Water, Land and Biodiversity Conservation.

Langton, M. 1981. Urbanising Aborigines: The Social Scientists' Great Deception. *Social Alternatives* 2(2):16–22.

Moreton-Robinson, A. 2004. The Possessive Logic of Patriarchal White Sovereignty: The High Court and the Yorta Yorta Decision. *Borderlands e-journal* 3(2):1–8. Available online at http://www.borderlandsejournal.adelaide.edu.au/vol3no2_2004/moreton_possessive.htm (accessed April 21, 2005).

Murray, T. 2000. Conjectural Histories: Some Archaeological and Historical Consequences of Indigenous Dispossession in Australia. In *Native Title and the Transformation of Archaeology in the Postcolonial World*, edited by I. Lilley, pp. 65–77. Oceania Monograph 50, University of Sydney, Sydney.

National Museum of Australia. 2003. Largest Return of Aboriginal Remains. Media release. Available online at: http://www.nma.gov.au/media/media_releases_index_/28_april_2003_largest_return_of_aboriginal_remains/ (accessed April 28, 2003).

Saunders, S. 2003. Are They Going to Pull It Down? *Overland* 171(Winter):60–61.

Simons, M. 2003. *The Meeting of the Waters*. Sydney, Australia: Hodder Headline.

Smith, C., and H. M. Wobst, eds. 2005. *Indigenous Archaeologies: Decolonizing Theory and Practice*. London: Routlege.

Smith, L. 2004. *Archaeology Theory and the Politics of Cultural Heritage*. London: Routledge.

Smith, L. T. 1999. *Decolonising Methodologies: Research and Indigenous Peoples*. London: Zed Books.

Stevens, I. 1995. *Report of the Hindmarsh Island Bridge Royal Commission*. Adelaide: Government Printer.

Thomas, D. H. 2000. *Skull Wars: Kennewick Man, Archaeology and the Battle for Native American Identity*. New York: Basic Books.

Trevorrow, T. 2003. A Shocking Insult. *Overland* 171:62–63.

von Doussa, Justice J. 2001. *Chapmans vs Luminis & Ors, Federal Court of Australia* (Summary of Judgment August 21, 2001).

Watkins, J. 2001. *Indigenous Archaeology: American Indian Values and Scientific Practice*. Walnut Creek, CA: AltaMira Press.

Watkins, J. 2003. Beyond the Margin: American Indians, First Nations, and Archaeology in North America. *American Antiquity* 68(2):273–285.

Watkins, J. 2005. The Politics of American Archaeology: Cultural Resources, Cultural Affiliation and Kennewick. In *Indigenous Archaeologies: Decolonizing Theory and Practice*, edited by C. Smith and H. M. Wobst, pp. 189–206. London: Routledge.

World Archaeological Congress (WAC). 2004. *World Archaeological Congress Supports NAGPRA Amendment*. Media release, November 20.

CHAPTER 39
LAW OR LORE?
SPEAKING SOVEREIGNTY IN THE
KENNEWICK CASE
SVEN OUZMAN

Anyone who thinks artifacts are silent is not listening or hasn't heard of "Kennewick" (e.g., Thomas 2004). This Ancient One has sparked judgments about research ethics, Indigenous rights, peopling of the Americas, and the ability to speak for oneself.

I speak as a South African in the hope that a non-American voice may help reformulate the polarized continuum of Kennewick debate. Kennewick's convoluted history has caused us to hush basic questions such as why, when two sovereign nations dispute, does the legal system of one nation routinely adjudicate that dispute? Using only Western law suggests that Native Americans are either incapable of full participation in this system or that their opinions are not valued. This incapacity stems from the Native American Graves Protection and Repatriation Act provision that claimants prove direct links to deep pasts.

The ruling that Kennewick cannot be claimed by modern Native Americans because he does not physically resemble them is a willful distortion of ancestry. Of course people today don't resemble their 8,500-year-old forebears. Today's British citizens are well above the 1.6 m height, 50 kg body mass, and thirty-five-year longevity of the Medieval English (Kunitz 1987), yet individual links are nonetheless made to, for example, 9,000-year-old "Cheddar Man" (Sykes 2001:169–183).

Kennewick exposes the deficiency in how we think we connect to the past. This is especially so when "firsts" or very old artifacts are classified as part of "world heritage" at the expense of specific and even sensitive or painful histories. Similarly, "the" law is a set of historically specific protocols that should not be presented as "natural" or "normal." Cultural "heritage"—a legal term deriving from "inheritance"—is better served by a custodial rather than proprietal ethos. I find U.S. property law fundamentally unfair to "true owners" and their descendants. Any artifact on private land is deemed the property of the land's current owner, disinheriting other claims. Yet artifacts on federal land (which comprises 2.1 million km² of the U.S.'s 9.1 million km²) are state property held in trust for the "nation," often serving to dissipate specific claims. With Kennewick, the U.S. Army complied with U.S. law that recognizes Native American lore as law but was overruled—making a very old Indigenous person common property in name—but the de facto property of a very few non-Native physical anthropologists in practice.

But to caricature Western law as unyielding would be as misplaced as romanticizing Indigenous legal systems, which include repressive gerontocracies.

Kennewick is a high-profile case that masks Euro American and Native American cooperation. Here, the most significant collaboration centers on Indigenous notions that certain places and artifacts are sentient and people are obligated to them. In parallel, Western law has *in rem* (against the thing) and *lex loci* (law of the place) actions. In the former, artifacts can stand trial as defendants and even claimants (Cunningham 1999:49–51). In the latter, an assembly of legal systems is permitted such that no single system dominates (Dworkin 2000). Thus, Gerald Vizenor wrote twenty years ago of "bone courts," in which:

> The rights of bones are neither absolute nor abolished at death: bone rights are abstract, secular and understood here in narrative and constitutional legal theories. The rights of bones to be represented in federal court are substantive; these rights are based on the premise that human rights continue at death. (Vizenor 1986:319)

The key to radical scholarship like Vizenor's is a rather conservative attention to detail that exposes critical occlusions in seemingly hegemonic structures like "the" law. Kennewick is, in Suzanne Crawford's phrase, a "productive body" (2000), because he shows us the wear and tear in the fabrics of U.S. and Native American jurisprudence. Vizenor's "bone rights" changes the question from "What do we want of these bones?" to "What do these bones want of us and what are our obligations to them?" Archaeology, with its twin focus on artifacts and sites, is ideally suited to mediate these two legal principles (of the "thing" and the "place") using a more adaptable notion of time.

Not everyone views time as inevitable succession. Otherwise we could argue that Kennewick is common property as, according to evolution, we are all ultimately "Africans" and the African Union is thus the appropriate "court" to rule on Kennewick's future. Such are the absurdities of hard-line adherence to legal protocols, and they resurrect the specter of European colonial excess. Indeed, how is using Kennewick to support notions of non–Native American colonization of the Americas different from colonial theories about non-Africans building Great Zimbabwe and painting the "White Lady" in Namibia?

Similarly, parading images of Kennewick both in the media and physically to select Burke Museum visitors is not substantively different than displaying the live and dead body of Sara Baartman (Holmes 2006) to 19th-century European anatomists and voyeurs. As a nation-to-nation negotiation, Sara Baartman's repatriation from France to South Africa in 2002 was initially considered legally impossible for fear of establishing precedent. Then KhoeSan poet Diana Ferrus wrote a poem that so moved French Senator Nicolas About that he had a special repatriation provision enacted within the same seemingly "impossible" law. Sara's return added a vital compassionate element to relations between Indigenous people, governments, and anthropologists. Similarly, Kennewick's return to an earthly, rather than cardboard, resting place would be more socially productive to a divided society than would his scientific study. Kennewick is not as rare as some non-Native scientists claim—there are over a dozen human remains from 7,000–10,000 years ago that are or have been available for study (Fiedel 2004:Table 1). This more interactive spirit suggests we should be consistent in how we treat people today and in the past. Measurements can be both precise and untrue. Using blood quanta to establish minimum levels of Native American-ness (Jaimes 1992) creates the impression that "indigeneity" is finite and constantly dissolving through miscegenation with non-indigenes, weakening links to ancestral pasts. Yet, inter-marriage, group hybridity, and evolution are on-going and essential to species survival. How do ninety-nine drops of "pure" blood make you any more Indigenous than a single drop (see Watkins 2004)? You can't, after all, be a little bit pregnant. Indeed, why does the United States not insist on blood quanta for all citizens, or is their identity self-evident? Such measurements and subjection of people to measurement is not helpful. Instead, social scientists can use their analytical precision to responsibly but compassionately ease the congress of lore and law, recognizing both as sovereign systems. Although Kennewick may be an artifact, he was and remains a person, and we, as fellow people, should listen to his wishes.

ACKNOWLEDGMENTS
I thank Henry Bredekamp, Richard Cunningham, Jon Daehnke and Adam Fish for their comments.

REFERENCES
Crawford, S. A. 2000. (Re)constructing Bodies: Semiotic Sovereignty and the Debate over Kennewick Man. In *Repatriation Reader: Who Owns American Indian Remains?*, edited by D. A. Mihesuah, pp. 210–236. Lincoln: University of Nebraska Press.

Cunningham, R. B. 1999. *Archaeology, Relics and the Law*. Durham, NC: Carolina Academic Press.

Dworkin, R. 2000. *Sovereign Virtue: The Theory and Practice of Equality*. Cambridge, MA: Harvard University Press.

Fiedel, S. J. 2004. The Kennewick Follies: "New" Theories about the Peopling of the Americas. *Journal of Anthropological Research* 60(1):75–110.

Holmes, R. 2006. *The Hottentot Venus*. London: Random House.

Jaimes, M. A. 1992. Federal Indian Identification Policy: A Usurpation of Indigenous Sovereignty in North America. In *The State of Native America: Genocide, Colonization, and Resistance*, edited by A. M Jaimes, pp. 123–138. Boston: South End Press.

Kunitz, S. J. 1987. Making a Long Story Short: A Note on Men's Height and Mortality in England from the First through the Nineteenth Centuries. *Medical History* 31(3):269–280.

Sykes, B. 2001. *The Seven Daughters of Eve: The Science that Reveals Our Genetic Ancestry*. London: W. W. Norton.

Thomas, D. H. 2004. The Kennewick Man Dispute: Courts of Last Resort? *Before Farming: The Archaeology and Anthropology of Hunter-Gatherers* 2004/2 article 8:1-3.

Vizenor, G. 1986. Bone Courts: The Rights and Narrative Representation of Tribal Bones. *American Indian Quarterly* 10(4):319–331.

Watkins, J. 2004. Becoming American or Becoming Indian? NAGPRA, Kennewick and Cultural Affiliation. *Journal of Social Archaeology* 4(1):60–80.

CHAPTER 40

BODY AND SOUL: CROSSING A GREAT DISTANCE

ALEJANDRO F. HABER

We used to believe that the treatment of human remains, besides evoking an ethical dilemma, is also enclosed in one. I am suspicious about such an ethical prison. Knowledge is a universal value for advocates of the scientific right to know. Given that, at the end of the road, knowledge will save humanity, any obstacle to science is inconvenient. On the other hand, for those advocating the cultural regulation of access to human remains, these have potency that should not be violated. Violation of the norms in which the world is inscribed is, at the same time, a violation of that world and of everyone who is sustained by it. Thus, our dilemma.

Taking advantage of this commentary, I'll go back to the intimate origin of my interest in this issue. Being an archaeologist, I had my own death. I have written about the skeleton of the newborn premature baby that I found beneath a big boulder at the entrance of a house in Tebenquiche Chico, Argentina, and the important place this had in the house (as part of the domestic stage) and in the understanding of the life-cycle (Haber 2007). The baby was buried, quite literally, at the entrance of the house, before the ritual entrance to social life. Every person, as a live person, had their place in the interior of the house, and, after death, was deposited inside underground chambers, some of which had been studied before me by Vladimir Weiser (Weiser 1923) and Pedro Krapovickas (Krapovickas 1955).

In my interpretation (Haber 2007), the house was the stage for social life; those who had already lived dwelled in the tombs, and those who had not yet lived— would not have lived—remained in the fragile *ad limine* space of the door. Space and time were thus conjoined to give place to my story of that baby. But that is not all. Given that the burial of the newborn was below the house, and that the timing of the building of the house could not necessarily be thought of as being in concordance with the sad circumstance of the baby's death, the possibility of a sacrifice remained open. The sacrifice, even if it could not be demonstrated, was concordant with other sacrifices that were part of the building of the house. A decorated small jar and two big vessels—probably filled up with food—were deposited inside other walls and excluded from human consumption, while the corpse of the baby-who-would-not-be-raised was deposited below the entrance.

In mentioning this, I want to underline the fact of having talked about that other, knowing that she or he would not talk about me. You'll tell me if I am right or wrong, that I should do this or that in support of my ideas, or you could silence my words, retain them at the doorway of your person, or silently suggest condescension or indifference. Like me, you can, if you want to, talk to me or to the reader beside you about those who cannot talk about us; our talking is structured in that asymmetry. We can see now that what seemed to be enclosed in an ethical dilemma is, instead, allocated in the particular way in which science, and archaeology as part of it, creates the world. It is an interrogated-, analyzed-, de-scripted-, talked-about world. We act on the world following how we talk about it.

We take a picture of some bones, we collect them, we take them to a specialist, and then we talk. The fact is that our action in the world cannot be supported in what we say about the world; we assume that the world is disposed to action in the same way that we assume it is disposed to knowledge. We assume that it is as it appears in our description of it; that is, we not only talk about other beings, we act on other beings in the way we talk. I can now make the same point in a different way.

Everything we say from our scientific province is about knowing. Our own limitations in the possibility of knowledge articulate what we say about other beings. We can talk about other beings, about the possibility of knowing about them, but not about the being of those other beings. Nonetheless, we act on other beings as a result of the fiction that our knowledge of them mirrors their being. For others—those for whom the world is not lived like this through the knowledge of it—knowing and its possibilities do not limit life in the same way. Other beings, including those bones we wanted to photograph, collect, or analyze, cannot be understood as objects of knowledge, because they were already in life. They were never pure bodies without soul prepared to be known by the pure mind, soul without body. In the fabric of actions and interactions in which we are, those beings were—openly or hidden—acting and talking with other beings, even with us.

To be able to take myself to life from the place from which I interpret the world, I should disclose here that, before talking, writing, analyzing, collecting, and taking pictures, before having developed my whole machinery for domination, those bones had already caused a first cry, a nonexplicated, long-lasting pain that takes me far apart from my role and my place and throws me once and forever into the life that suffers death. Life was always there. I was there in life, living in-life relationships, sometimes relating myself to the same beings that here, in the place of science, are objects of knowledge as much as I am a knower of them. But life is also here; life is both before and after science.

There is no essential distance between body and soul, not in the plane of being. There is nothing that authorizes us to act on other beings as if they were not able to act themselves. Our action in the world, and particularly that relative to human beings, is already inside the flux of life and not outside it, as if we could see it at a distance. It is not that these sentences will make us know more or better. Maybe I am just trying to reconcile myself with my small life and small death and with the plurality of beings, some of them human, others nonhuman, with which we, as beings, interact. Our relationships in life—as beings with other beings—are not essentially asymmetrical, as our relationship as knower or the world is intended to be.

Any discussion about human remains should not remain enclosed in an ethical dilemma, even less in an epistemological one. It is a discussion that should risk the foundations of our understanding of the world, and of our place in it. It is thus a philosophical discussion. It is also part of the same discussion about our actions in the world. It is thus a political discussion. But it is inadequate to arrive at these discussions as if we were in a pristine situation. At the end, we will acknowledge that the question was not reduced to discussion, to talk about the world. We arrive at these discussions from our life, and it is in that same mud that we sit down and talk to each other. In that conversation, as in this one, I would allow myself, barefoot, to see and say, with Jaime Sáenz:

I am divided from myself by the distance I find myself in,
the one who is dead is divided from death by a great distance.
I plan to cross this distance, resting on the way.
Face up, in the dwelling of desire,
stock still, in my place—opposite the locked door,
with a winter's light at my side.

In the corners of my room, in the chairs arena.
With wavering memory splitting off from the void—on the ceiling of the vault,
the one who is dead must communicate with death.

Contemplating the bones on the plank, numbering the darknesses with my fingers starting from you.

Seeing that things are, I fill with desire.
And I find myself crossing a great distance. (Sáenz 2002)

ACKNOWLEDGMENTS
I read a previous version of this chapter at the end of the session Of Body and Soul: Transgressions between Biology and Society at the Meeting of the Argentine Association of Biological Anthropology, San Fernando del Valle de Catamarca, October 9, 2003. What I read (and the session as a whole) was not that tasty for several people in the room (mostly biological anthropologists). When the session was over, a Bolivian student came to the desk with tears in her eyes and said something about my signature. I saw myself in the happy eyes of Santiago and Ignacio (Ini was a baby when I excavated the baby tomb at Tebenquiche Chico in 1995). Gonzalo Aráoz introduced me to the world of Jaime Sáenz during my visit to his house in St. Andrews, Scotland. The text is dedicated to them all.

REFERENCES
Haber, A. F. 2007. *An Archaeology of the Oasis: Domesticity, Interaction, and Identity in Antofalla, Puna de Atacama, Argentina.* Oxford: Archaeopress.
Krapovickas, P. 1955. *El Yacimiento Arqueológico de Tebenquiche (Puna de Atacama).* Buenos Aires: Publicaciones del Museo Etnográfico.
Sáenz, J. 2002. *Immanent Visitor: Selected Poems of Jaime Saenz.* Berkeley: University of California Press.
Weiser, V. 1923. Diario de la II Expedición Muniz Barreto. Unpublished. Museo de La Plata. La Plata, Argentina: Universidad Nacional de La Plata.

EPILOG

CHAPTER 41
THOSE FUNFUNFUNNYBONES
Roger Echo-Hawk

The idea of race manifests itself in our world as a cult of belief that enshrines a lie. Racialism promotes the dehumanizing notion that humankind can be reliably divided into races, but this falsehood warps our humanity and the stories we tell about ourselves. This cult is popular. Its tenets are enshrined throughout American society, serving as one of our foremost unifying cultural ideas. And the ideology of the cult of race has powerfully shaped the communal storytelling that surrounds the identity and fate of Kennewick Man. For most of my life, everyone did race unquestioningly and I did it that way, too. I believed in the cult of race. But one day I gave it up. I became a race-atheist.

There are an increasing number of race-atheists and agnostics out there. I know who some of them are, because they occasionally write serious books on the subject. One such person is Alexander Alland, Jr., a distinguished anthropologist and author of *Race in Mind* (2002). He's "distinguished" because I like what he says. Alland's book features a chapter entitled "Race: A Flawed Category," in which he explains why the ideology of race leads to "a funny-mirror distortion of reality." I suspect that some readers won't get his meaning, because if you live long enough in a funhouse full of curved mirrors, the oddly distorted images will eventually look normal and very real.

Many distinguished scholars have written serious books and papers about race and why belief in the precepts of race is merely a faith-based cultural enterprise. I sometimes get the impression that I'm the only person in America who looks for stuff like this at the bookstore. I'm just guessing about this, of course. There aren't any surveys on the topic of race faith versus race atheism and agnosticism. What would be the point? In terms of public awareness about the truths of race, it's as though the scholars who challenge race have been talking about beings on some far-off imaginary planet, dissecting their strange cultures and reporting weird things to readers who then go about their lives undisturbed by what they've read. It isn't real to anyone, somehow.

It seems dismayingly irrelevant to American racialists that race is invalid as a way to sort people and that race is not a biological reality but a purely cultural social artifact. Inheriting the funhouse truths of race for generation after generation, it seems quite convincing to peer into the distorted mirrors and think we see arbitrarily defined racial groups when we look at one another.

But my Pawnee and English ancestors long ago were not "Indian" or "white." One day, not so long ago, they all went into the funhouse and looked at themselves in the warped mirrors and they laughed as they embraced the idea of becoming Pawnee Indians and white Anglo-Saxons. They embraced the distortion of race. And it's so easy to just go along with the funhouse mirror joke. I laugh to think of the power that race wields in our lives. It's an unnatural laughter. Everyone writhes together in its humorous grip. It's been so much fun for everyone, terribly fun.

And the fun thing about Kennewickman is that you get to vote on his race. The sadly ironic fun-thing about this vote is that the whole idea of race is like a sitcom laff-track—everyone chuckles along with the unnatural laughter as though it were real. And the crazy ironic-fun-thing is that the people who laugh the loudest are the least likely to ever get the joke.

Because in the sad-crazy-ironic-fun-thing comedic plot that surrounds Kennewickman, people believe totally in race and all the hilarity that ensues is totally side-splitting! They view race as a scientifically proven biological reality. BUT IT'S NOT!

Ha-ha-ha!

When Kennewick Man first appeared on the scene long ago, the invention of race lay far off in the distant future. Few people seem to understand how race happened, historically. Only two or three centuries ago, researchers turned the primitive lanterns of enlightenment science on humankind. And they did their best to think through what they knew, to explain the nature of the human world as it unfolded before them. Judging from the results, these researchers wisely determined that we needed a sense of humor. We needed race! In the sitcom world to come, they decided that a lifelike laff-track would be terrific fun!

Some people may be content to blame this outcome on "white" Europeans and their "white" American cousins. But *everyone* liked the weird science of race, and one day, *everyone* daubed it on like make-up, and then *everyone* stood around for the next several centuries laughing at one another.

This was indeed quite a silly stroke of comic genius!

But because race has very little to do with any inherent quality of human biology and because race is a recent cultural invention, it's doubly inaccurate to think of Kennewick Man as being racially "white" or "Indian."

See, he lived a race-free life. He didn't just laugh at everything like we do today.

When Kennewickman came back onto the scene more than 9,000 years later, he was in for an amusing surprise. Everyone had recently made big changes. Things were twisted in a funny sort of way, and people now very much enjoyed the novelty of being "white" people, "black" people, "Indian" people, and other such things.

When Kennewickman returned to the scene, people were having lots of fun, enacting the laws of race and displaying racialism in all its lighthearted latter-day forms at the end of the century before the next millennium.

All the laughter was unsettling. At first, Kennewickman didn't know what to make of the underlying laff-track of race.

Race had evolved through many plotlines since it had first appeared in the world during the 18ᵗʰ century, catching everyone up and blowing them relentlessly through story after story. The theme of the main madcap racial sitcom in America was now "multiculturalism." People could be divided into "people of color" and "white people."

Race is such a complicated gag!

Ha-ha-ha!

It's particularly delightful because there are so many practical jokes that one can make with racialism. Like voting on Kennewickman's race! You're surely a white guy, said the first two people to look him over and cast votes on the topic. Surely!

But ... but ....

But there's a serious side to this topic. Even though people can decide for themselves whether to treat race as a lifelong laughing matter, the question of Kennewick Man's identity deserves serious attention. Because the idea of race as a biological reality is not real, and racial identity has a shallow history, inquiry into the connection between Kennewick Man and his ancestors and his descendants must look somewhere beyond race and racial identity.

The anthropologists who made Kennewick Man an issue of academic freedom versus religious belief have chosen to publicly defer to the inclination of the news media to treat the whole matter as an issue of race. This is because the sitcom of racial identity is our most popular comedy of errors—it's so outrageous, you just have to laugh along!

Ha-ha-ha!

Anyway, race puts everything in a certain light, and it's funny how the warping alchemy of race has the amazing ability to transform whatever it touches in our lives. Having given it strange superpowers that it doesn't deserve, race drives assumptions in our lives that we take for granted without even pausing to chuckle a bit.

As a tenet of race, for example, racial Indian people feel that Indians should have the final word over the fate of Kennewick Man if he's Indian or racial white people will understand something interesting about themselves if he's white. The general idea is that races are real and thus have histories that rise like great monoliths from the ancient past into the present.

But because race is a recent distortion of humankind, it is forced to write itself retroactively into deep time. And it doesn't deserve this sense of history, so when we agree to give it an ancient past in the stories we tell, we have abandoned history—we have instead intoned a faith-based liturgical spell that transmutes everything it touches.

A conservative viewpoint suggests that Kennewick Man has no knowable descendants and thus lacks any living next of kin. It is also possible, however, to speculate that he could have millions of people worldwide on his family tree, regardless of their present-day racial identities, phenotypes, or national citizenships. Whether his descendants dribbled out of existence or are legion, it's difficult to see how giving him race retroactively would be helpful in tracing branches of his family tree.

With our public discourse about Kennewick Man completely driven by racial imperatives, I sometimes feel a little lost when I think of him. To help with this sense of disorientation, about the time the last millennium turned into this one, I published a technical article in a technical archaeology journal. My article touched on oral traditions and cultural affiliation and archaeology, and in the course of writing it, I found myself constructing a model of the ancient past in which I'm descended from Kennewick Man and his peers. I didn't mention him by name, but I argued that my Pawnee ancestors have traceable roots reaching back to his time and his region of the world.

This historical model implies that it would be highly unlikely for Kennewick Man's descendants to just neatly descend into four or five present-day communities of the Pacific Northwest. A lot of very diverse people would appear by now on the many branches of his family tree, not an exclusive few.

But capitalizing on the great success throughout American life of the triumph of race, a movement got going in 2004 to amend the Native American Graves Protection and Repatriation Act (NAGPRA) with an "or was" designed to ensure classification of Kennewick Man and his peers as racial "Native Americans." Some see this as a social justice remedy—a means of empowering a dispossessed race and their racially identified governments. Others see a defeat for the practice of science—the fettering of science by governments driven by politics and religion.

Whatever one makes of the important issues of social justice and academic freedom, legislating retroactive race doesn't make sense, given what we know about race and its short history in the world. For the moment, it is unremarkable for us to make laws that perpetuate race and endow it with a legally falsified ancient past.

It seems I've traversed a complex future into your present with its fascinating past.

—That's right, Kennewickman! And in my technical paper I tried to think of how your world flowed into mine. A lot of flowing went on for a long time in the world that followed your world—over 9,000 years worth of flowing. Things got pretty muddled along the way. My Pawnee ancestors took part in that muddling. But don't tell anyone. It'll be our secret.

Okay. I won't say a word about your technical paper. But what about that other paper you read before the Society for American Archaeology a couple years later? You talked of how the government and its consultants used your work and yet everyone still ignored what your research really implied about me. I sat in the audience and listened.

—You were there? I spoke about how the Department of the Interior cited my research when they made their findings of NAGPRA cultural affiliation for you, and

the disinterest of tribes in my work, and the attack on scholarship by the Kennewick plaintiff-scientists. I stated that there were seven plaintiffs, leaving one out—I'm not much of a mathematician. In any case, all of them kept quiet about the implications of my work.

Ha-ha-ha! I remember how I sat there laughing to myself at your version of scholarly accountability. Given their huge silence about your work, it's funny to hear them lauded as defenders of good scholarship! But tell me again what you said about how your distant past and my distant future occupy the same moments in time.

....

—Okay. In the second year at the beginning of the tenth millennium after you lived and died, I stood up somewhere in Denver, Colorado and I said...

The evidence for the past exists in remnants. Inevitably, an impressionistic coalescence of occurrences and circumstances serves as the source of our communal and personal identities, and we deliberately fabricate a history that mimics a seamless remembrance. Because a sense of history is essential to the ongoing production of our self-aware humanity, historians have an obligation to tell complex stories that encourage the building of complex identities. Academic scholarship must assess fragmentary evidence to explain ongoing patterns of identity in time.

In constructing what happened in the past, scholars have an obvious duty to submit information to appropriate critical tests and then to make use of all the relevant evidence. Toward this end, if oral traditions can contribute to the study of ancient history, then professional organizations like the Society for American Archaeology (SAA) have a responsibility to encourage such research.

These issues of scholarship lie at the heart of the debate that surrounds efforts to understand the identity of the person known as Kennewick Man. As the Department of the Interior (DOI), the plaintiff-scholars in the Kennewick court case, SAA, and others have wrestled with each other and with Indian tribes over Kennewick Man, we learn from the very best that American scholarship has to offer that the study of the past is an inherently political process. In recent years, SAA has made inquiry into oral traditions a matter of professional discourse among archaeologists, but examination of the Kennewick case shows that SAA must make a greater effort to match words to actions if it is to provide the best possible service to the production of good scholarship on oral traditions.

SAA published my article, "Ancient History in the New World" in the April 2000 issue of *American Antiquity*. Drawing on both oral traditions and archaeology, I suggested that the Arikaras, Pawnees, and Wichitas are descended from Paleo Indian ancestors who resided west of the Rocky Mountains. The archaeological record and Caddoan oral traditions suggest that the first Americans entered the New World from a region of lingering darkness. As recorded in Arikara origin stories, these people entered a world that featured a great forest, a body of ice-bound water, and an impassable canyon. They then journeyed into the Rocky Mountains and from there they looked out into their future homeland.

This sequence of events finds support in the archaeological record, where some research suggests that Paleo Indians of the Pluvial Lakes tradition gave rise to the Mountain tradition here in Colorado. One Mountain tradition component, known as the Hogback phase, served as the source for the later Apishapa phase, which is generally viewed as the westernmost element of Plains Caddoan populations.

In this model of the past, Kennewick Man is my likely ancestor. The Paleo Indian human remains from Spirit Cave and Wizard's Beach are my likely ancestors. Whether one views such assertions with skeptical sympathy or skeptical antagonism, I am greatly intrigued by the response to my work by the DOI and SAA.

Investigating the cultural affiliations of Kennewick Man as required under section 3 of NAGPRA, the DOI drew on detailed reports commissioned from various experts, as well as information collected during consultations with five tribes. DOI concluded that Kennewick Man is culturally affiliated with five present-day tribes that reside in Washington along the Columbia River. DOI summarized the basis for this finding in a report entitled "Human Culture in the Southeastern Columbia Plateau, 9500–9000 BP and Cultural Affiliation with Present-Day Tribes," otherwise known as "Enclosure 3."

By my count, DOI cited my *American Antiquity* article four times in "Enclosure 3." These citations accurately draw on my work to support observations on the general state of academic inquiry into oral traditions, on the need to identify historical information by viewing oral traditions in the context of other data, on the malleable nature of oral documents, and on the possibility that more detailed study of the oral traditions used by DOI might ultimately support different scholarly conclusions.

As explained in "Enclosure 3," DOI did the best it could to assess the readily available oral traditions of the five Washington tribes in conjunction with other evidence. Following this process, DOI determined that those five tribes have a cultural affiliation to Kennewick Man. It is puzzling, however, that DOI drew on my work, but included no discussion of my theory of Caddoan ancient history. In conducting a credible investigation of Kennewick Man's cultural affiliations, DOI arguably had an obligation under NAGPRA, as well as a scholarly duty, to consider the readily available Caddoan oral traditions and archaeological information in my paper. "Enclosure 3" sheds no light on why DOI neglected to conduct such inquiry.

Under NAGPRA, findings of cultural affiliation are driven by evidence and are formulated after consultation with affected tribes. In the course of investigating affiliation under section 3 of NAGPRA, when a federal agency is aware of a demonstrated or likely affiliation, consultation must be initiated. In my opinion, when DOI learned of my research sometime after April 2000, it should have initiated consultations with the Three Affiliated Tribes of the Fort Berthold Reservation, the Pawnee Nation of Oklahoma, and the Wichita and Affiliated Tribes.

Under NAGPRA, consultation must be arranged with tribes for whom evidence shows a likely affiliation, even if the tribes in question do not assert any affiliation. In accordance with standards of scholarship, available evidence must be investigated and weighed, not ignored. Under NAGPRA, findings of cultural affiliation must be based upon the review of readily available, relevant evidence. In accordance with standards of scholarship, one must go where the evidence goes, without regard for the popularity of the outcome. DOI is accountable for the manner in which it has implemented these various standards.

I shared my research with the three Caddoan tribal governments listed above, and I spoke with the Arikara NAGPRA representative, the Pawnee NAGPRA representative, and the Wichita tribal archaeologist. To date, none of the Caddoan tribal governments has expressed interest in claiming the remains of people who lived and died long ago in the west beyond the Rocky Mountains, and tribal governments have no obligation under NAGPRA to endorse affiliations suggested by any researcher. But in failing so definitively to explore and assert the affiliation of these three Caddoan tribes in Kennewick Man, DOI has left intact an imposing barrier to any effective future action on the part of these tribes.

Ostensibly defending the precepts of academic scholarship, the plaintiff scholars and their lawyers in the Kennewick court case have condemned the use of all oral records that have religious content. This extreme view is completely out of touch with the growing professional interest of archaeologists in oral traditions. In scrutinizing religious information, researchers need encouragement to adhere to scholarly analytical standards while cultivating a sensitive appreciation for the impact of scholarship on religious belief and practice. The advancement of good scholarship thus requires an informed, multifaceted discourse—not automatic dismissal. It is disappointingly clear that these seven nationally respected scholars have chosen to elevate the goals of scholarly litigation at the expense of scholarship on oral traditions.

SAA disagrees with the seven plaintiffs regarding the use of oral traditions. In seeking to reflect a cross-section of the views of American archaeologists, SAA has properly argued for critical assessment of oral traditions rather than simple rejection. We might wonder, however, whether SAA actually hinders the useful development of scholarship on oral traditions by setting standards that would have destroyed archaeology as a discipline, had these standards been applied in the infancy of the profession. SAA must support responsible professional standards, but should not expect scholarship on oral traditions to spring fully formed from our communal minds.

SAA cites my published article in setting forth its opposition to DOI's findings on Kennewick. And like DOI, SAA neglects to mention the implications of my model of Caddoan ancient history for the cultural affiliation of Kennewick Man. The membership of SAA may well feel that by opposing the applicability of NAGPRA to Kennewick Man, SAA and the seven Kennewick plaintiffs have properly defended the legitimate interests of scholarship. In seeking to divorce Kennewick Man from NAGPRA, however, SAA and the seven Kennewick plaintiffs have trampled on the very ideals of good scholarship they purport to protect. In representing American archaeology as a discipline, SAA has an arguable obligation to point out a meaningful technical flaw in the DOI cultural affiliation process, and, to encourage the best possible scholarship, SAA should do more than defend oral traditions from unwarranted dismissal from the classroom. It should openly advocate consideration of all readily available oral traditions—including Caddoan oral traditions.

In the end, I do not know whether scholarship can clearly and convincingly tell me whether I am descended from Kennewick Man and his contemporaries in the West. But when we openly decline to investigate questions of this kind, we can hardly claim to be upholding the standards of scholarship.

As scholars, when we look back in time, the world of our ancestors typically resembles a place of indefinite journeying. Ephemeral travelers come and go, weaving their shared group identities for thousands of years from oral literatures, from their ceremonial enactments, and from their interactions over time. And through archaeology, physical anthropology, and many other forms of study, we can discover the same past that lingers in oral records.

Peering into the immense remnants of the past, we see the mysterious places where we gradually became who we are. When we deliberately close our eyes, and when we deliberately edit the immensity, we dehumanize ourselves and pass on a distorted humanity to our heirs. It is therefore important for us to explore the past in partnership with one another. Archaeology and oral traditions must find each other in this world. For the sake of our very humanity, we must know the past that gave rise to our world. As we struggle over the meanings of remnants of the past, it is crucial for us all to find ways to connect the surfaces of archaeological America to the surfaces of spoken America.

Listening intently to what the spoken surfaces of the world might be saying, Kennewickman said nothing at first. He had a lot to think about. How was his historical world connected to this one? For now, race guided what people had to say about the meaning of the past, the realities of the present, and the fate of the future.

He sat there on the table observing how everyone went 'round & 'round, caught up in the unnatural grip of the joke of race.

It looked like great hilarious fun! And soon Kennewickman decided he didn't want to be left out; he had to have a race, too! So he called a press conference and got together a bunch of reporters and editorialists and they put their heads together and merrily invited everyone across the land to vote on a race for Kennewickman!

They chorused together, shouting in glee: Those old bones don't have to just be old bones; we'll toss in some race and they'll be funfunfunnybones! We'll scurry to our phones & our email & our websites & our editorial pages and we'll cast our votes! Then we'll lafflafflaff like mad!

Vote white! Vote red! Vote for the right choice! And if it doesn't add up quite right, we can always sneak in a droll "or was" after the "is!"

Race is such a scream!

Come on everyone, scream!scream!scream! It's a whole jumpin' buncha lotta gasgasgas, this race thing!

But we'd better laugh it up while we can, Kennewickman! Ha-ha-ha as you votevotevote!!! & then let's hurry on down to the punch-line of the joke! I can hardly wait, you see, because when you finally get it; well, I just can't wait for the look on your face!

Kennewickman looked around at their faces.

Some people around the table heard him saying how he wanted them to know many interesting things. He wanted them to discover all the little details and figure out how those little details fit into the big picture. Others circling the table heard something different. They heard him murmuring about religion and ancestry and sovereign rights. And everyone who heard him felt inspired anew to enact and fulfill their most profound certainties. And in the midst of their certainties lay a deeper passion.

Race.

Kennewickman saw that having race was not like putting on make-up or having a TV show or casting a vote. All these things—as important as they might be in their own right—seemed pale and trivial compared to race.

Race seemed an unshakable edifice towering into the world. And people were fierce about upholding it. Through it they sought self-esteem, jobs, careers, hobbies, friendships, loves, hatreds, and power.

Race seemed so convincingly authentic and authoritative because it assigned everyone compulsory social roles. Things could change over time, but you had little choice about your fundamental service to the cause; you could only choose the degree of your zeal about it. Unfortunately, the passions of race also clouded the innermost truths that really account for humankind. Racialism held forth an impassioned falsehood to embrace.

Kennewickman lay back to think.

Race is a distortion of humankind. An intensely meaningful, hopelessly towering distortion. What an amazingly alien world the earth had become! And humanity had become something wonderfully odd and terrifying and filled with unyielding passions. He smiled to think of this. Then he thought about how the rules of race didn't give him much choice and he might as well go along with it and anyway having race is such a whole lot of sad crazy fun!

Kennewickman smiled to himself as all the faces anxiously circled his table. They had already bestowed race upon him. It just needed a moment or two to take effect.

He thought of floating relentlessly through story after story.

Then he began to laugh. ...

REFERENCES
Alland, A., Jr. 2002. *Race in Mind*. New York: Palgrave Macmillan.

INDEX

ABOUT THE AUTHORS

MIGUEL AGUILAR DIAZ is director of the Cultural Association Supay in Lima, Peru, and editor of the archaeological magazines *Supay, the Journal of Humanities and Sciences of Man,* and *Unay Runa,* dedicated to Amazonic archaeology. He is dedicated to promoting and protecting the archaeology of Peru.

BARBARA FRIEDLANDER ARIPA works for the Environmental Health–TOSHA-Emergency Medical Services Department as staff assistant and as the tribes' culture resources recording secretary to the Culture Committee of the Colville Business Council. Barbara is an enrolled member of the Confederated Tribes of the Colville Reservation descended from former leaders of several tribes. She is a respected Elder knowledgeable in the traditions, history, and ways of the Colville Confederated Tribes.

JODI BARNES is a doctoral candidate in the Department of Anthropology at American University, Washington, DC.

WALTER BIGBEE is a member of the Comanche Nation, and a renowned professional photographer and editor. He studied photography at the Rochester Institute of Technology, Rochester, New York, and has taught college courses and workshops. BigBee has documented many museum collections, including at the Smithsonian Institution, the Library of Congress, and the Institute of American Indian Arts. He has lectured on Indigenous topics and has participated on numerous panels. He has served as an advisor to the Northern Pueblos Institute, the Crow Canyon Archaeological Center, and the Southwestern Association on Indian Arts. BigBee feels that Native photography continues the tradition of storytelling once expressed through petroglyphs, pictographs, and ledger art.

HEATHER BURKE is senior lecturer and head of the Department of Archaeology at Flinders University, Adelaide, Australia.

LYNN COPES is a graduate student in paleoanthropology at Arizona State University, Tempe. She is interested in questions of functional morphology, especially of the cranial vault. Her research currently focuses on Homo erectus vault morphology, but she is broadly interested in the evolution of mammalian cranial shape as well as the emergence of the genus *Homo* in the fossil record. Her favorite fossil is Bodo, the cannibalized *Homo heidelbergensis.*

CARRIE DAN is a working Secwepemc archaeologist who is currently enrolled in the Graduate Program at the University of British Columbia–Okanagan. Her interests of study are ancient and modern mitochondrial DNA of the Secwepemc people in the Canadian Plateau Culture area. Carrie is a member of the Kamloops Indian Band, Kamloops, British Columbia, and a current member of the Society for American Archaeology.

ROGER ECHO-HAWK is a composer of aural, verse, narrative, and photo dream meditations.

ADAM FISH is presently a Ph.D. student in anthropology at UCLA and a television producer for the cable network Current TV. He studies cultures of media production at the emergent

KENNEWICK MAN

confluence of new media and television industries. His documentaries—usually about nationality, religion, sexuality, and technology—advance the method of an activistic and reflexive journalism.

ADELINE (SAM) FREDIN was born on April 11, 1934. She is a 4/4 enrolled member of the Colville Confederated Tribes (CCT). Her father was Harry Sam, his father was Pink-Steet-Sah, of the Methow Tribe, his mother was Ke-kie-met-sak, her given white name was Madeline Moses of the Moses/Palouse Tribes. Her mother was Christine (James) Sam, her mother was Yahx-Kew-Malks, her given white name was Lucy (Machel) James of the Okanogan Tribe. Her mother's father was Joe James, Chief of the SanPoil Tribe. Adeline's grandmother married Wil-wah-net-sah, his given white name was Jim James, who was also a Chief of the SanPoil Tribe and other tribes of the Colville Reservation. Adeline lives a traditional life hunting, fishing, gathering, and collecting natural foods, materials, and resources. She has a good understanding of tribal customs and traditional territories and was the program manager for the CCT History/Archaeology Program from 1974 to 2002. In 1996, she became one of the first twelve tribal historic preservation officers in the United States.

JOEL GILMAN was born and raised an hour's drive north of Kennewick, Washington, and has always felt a deep affection for the landscape and the history of the region. Admitted to the practice of law in 1983, he has resided in Australia since 1999 where he has done postgraduate study in heritage and archaeology and earned a Master's degree in Law in 2005. He currently is the legal officer for the Heritage Council of Western Australia.

KRISTI A. GRINDE graduated from the University of Sheffield (UK) with an MSc in Human Osteology and Funerary Archaeology. She has worked in Papua New Guinea, Spain, the United States, and Malta and has embarrassing cultural immersion stories from her various travels. She currently resides in Minnesota.

ALEJANDRO F. HABER is a well-known Argentinian archaeologist and ethnographer who has published widely on issues of theory in South American archaeology. One of his current archaeological concerns is the issue of reburial and the debate over ownership of Indigenous remains in Argentina.

MICHELLE D. HAMILTON is an assistant professor of forensic anthropology at Texas State University, San Marcos. She was formerly the Section 106 officer for the Tribal Historic Preservation Office of the Eastern Band of Cherokee Indians in Cherokee, North Carolina.

STEVE HEMMING lectures in Australian Studies and Indigenous Studies at Flinders University, Adelaide, Australia. He was formerly an anthropology curator at the South Australian Museum. He has worked with Ngarrindjeri leadership for several decades as an interdisciplinary researcher. This work has included Native title research, cultural heritage protection, and the repatriation and reburial of Ngarrindjeri Old People.

CONSUELO "CONNIE" JOHNSTON was born in Nespelem, Washington, in 1949. She is a member of the Confederated Tribes of the Colville Reservation of Palus and Nez Perce descent. She held numerous positions with the Colville Tribes for twenty-five years and lives on the Colville Reservation. She received an AA degree from Green River Community College and a BA degree from Eastern Washington University. Connie worked in the legal field for most of her career, but also spent several years in the CCT History/Archaeology Program specifically working on the Ancient One case. She has four children and six grandchildren; all are enrolled tribal members.

EDWARD A. JOLIE is a French and Oglala Lakota/Hodulgee Muscogee Indian Ph.D. candidate in archaeology at the University of New Mexico, Albuquerque. He is interested in anthropological ethics, Native American–anthropologist relations, the prehistory of the Americas, and perishable technologies. For his dissertation research, he is using basketry to explore social diversity in the Chaco regional system (AD 850–1140) in the Four Corners region of the U.S. Southwest.

PETER N. JONES is director of the Bauu Institute and Press, where he works on issues of cultural affiliation and natural resource management. He has worked on several cases involving NAGPRA in the American West, including the Kennewick Man and Spirit Cave cases, as well as natural resource damage assessments and environmental impact assessments. He is also editor of *Indigenous Issues Today*.

JOHN JULES is head of the Cultural Resources Department, Kamloops Indian Band. He is a Kamloops Band member.

ANN M. KAKALIOURAS is an assistant professor of anthropology at Whittier College, near Los Angeles, California. She is a bioarchaeologist whose research interests also include the history of Native American–anthropologist relations and the ways in which repatriation can transform the practice of physical anthropology.

THOMAS F. (TOM) KING is a consultant, educator, and writer in cultural resource management, based in Silver Spring, Maryland. He has worked since the early 1960s in historic preservation and environmental impact assessment in the United States and the Pacific Islands and is the author of a number of textbooks, journal articles, and government regulations and guidelines on cultural resource management topics. He specializes in the review of project and policy impacts under Section 106 of the U.S. National Historic Preservation Act, which emphasizes broad-based consultation to resolve conflicts, and in the identification and management of "traditional cultural properties," including spiritual places.

CHARLES LORING BRACE is professor of anthropology and curator of biological anthropology at the Museum of Anthropology at the University of Michigan, Ann Arbor.

MARY L. BRACE is at Kilauea Caldera, Hilo, Hawaii. She has assisted with data collection in Europe, Japan, China, and Southeast Asia, as well as working as a technical illustrator.

MARY A. MARCHAND was born in 1927 and raised on the Iswald Allotment on the Columbia River north of Wenatchee, Washington, in the town of Azwell. Mary's people were from the Wenatchee, Entiat, Chelan, Methow, and San Poil Tribes. Mary was taught traditional ways by her great grandmother and has a deep spiritual relationship to the land, her people, and the Creator. When Mary's father, Jerome Miller, was in his final days he told Mary that she was to serve her people, no matter if they were white, red, yellow, brown, or polka-dotted. That is what she has been doing ever since, even though she hasn't found any polka-dotted people yet. Mary worked for five years recording the Wenatchi language with Dr. Dale Kinkade and her father. Her first tribal job was driving the seniors' bus. She worked her way up to running all five community centers for the Colville Reservation. Mary successfully ran for tribal council and served with distinction. For many decades now, Mary has been called on to represent the Confederated Tribes of the Colville Reservation at meetings and on committees. Her people look to her for spiritual guidance and she actively participates in church and religious functions. Her prayers blessed many high-level conferences and consultations between the Colville Confederated Tribes and other people. Mary interviews and records tribal Elders about their lives along the Columbia River system. She documents the joys and heartaches of a lifetime. She captures the true history of the Indian people, the way things were, and how the encroachment of the modern world forever changed our lives. It is often sad work.

ORA V. MAREK-MARTINEZ is an enrolled member of the Dine' Nation, and of Nimiipuu descent. While growing up on the Nez Perce reservation, Lapwai, Idaho, she discovered the need for the protection of cultural resources important to her people. She graduated from Northern Arizona University, Flagstaff, with a B.A. in anthropology and history, and with a M.A. in cultural anthropology. She is currently conducting dissertation research at the University of California, Berkeley, concerning the needs and experiences of tribes in archaeology.

LYNN MESKELL is a professor in the Faculty of Cultural and Social Anthropology at Stanford University, Stanford, California. Her most recent publications include *Embedding Ethics,* with Professor Peter Pels, and the forthcoming, *Cosmopolitan Archaeologies.* Her research interests cover a broad range of fields, including Egyptian archaeology, identity, sociopolitics, gender, and ethics.

ARMAND MINTHORN is a Board of Trustees member and religious leader with the Confederated Tribes of the Umatilla Indian Reservation.

HARVEY MOSES, JR., is a full-blooded member of the Confederated Tribes of the Colville Reservation, a member of the Chief Joseph Nez Perce, Moses-Columbia, and Okanogan Tribes. He has lived on the Colville Indian Reservation all his life and is a veteran of the Vietnam conflict, honorably discharged. He was on the Colville Business Council for six years, from 1995 to 1997 and for two consecutive terms between 2001 and 2005.

GUY F. MOURA is employed by the Confederated Tribes of the Colville Reservation as the traditional cultural property coordinator with the History/Archaeology Program and has been involved with the Ancient One case since 1996. Mr. Moura received a Bachelor's degree in anthropology from the University of Maine at Orono, where Dr. Robson Bonnichsen was one of his major professors. Guy also holds a degree in education and a 5th-Year Teaching Certificate.

JAMES D. NASON is Professor Emeritus in the Department of Anthropology at the University of Washington, Seattle, and an enrolled member of the Comanche Nation.

GEORGE NICHOLAS is associate professor in archaeology and anthropology at Simon Fraser University, Burnaby, BC, Canada, in collaboration with the Secwepemc Education Institute in Kamloops, BC. He received his doctorate in archaeology from the University of Massachusetts in 1990, and has coedited (with Thomas Andrews) *At a Crossroads: Archaeology and First Peoples in Canada* (Archaeology Press 1997).

SVEN OUZMAN is an archaeologist whose work charts the use of archaeology artefacts, sites, symbols in the present, especially with regard to contemporary identity formation. Previously head of the Rock Art Department at the National Museum, Bloemfontein, South Africa, Sven is now senior lecturer at the University of Pretoria.

JOSEPH A. PAKOOTAS is a past member of the Colville Confederated Tribes ruling body, the Colville Business Council Colville. Elected to council several times, Joe was chairman when this request for perspectives on the Ancient One controversy was forwarded to the Colville Confederated Tribes. Joe holds an MBA from the University of Washington, Seattle.

DARYLE RIGNEY is an associate professor in education and Indigenous studies in the Yunggorendi, First Nations Centre for Higher Education and Research, Flinders University, Adelaide, Australia. As an Indigenous academic and advisor to the Ngarrindjeri Nation, South Australia, he has been principally responsible for developing relationships internationally with Indigenous nations, including a resolution to establish social, cultural, economic, and scholarly exchange with the Confederated Tribes of the Umatilla Indian Reservation, Oregon.

STEVE RUSSELL is a Cherokee Indian, born and raised in Oklahoma. He dropped out of high school in the 9th grade and joined the Air Force. After acquiring a GI Bill education, he had his first career as an elected judge in Texas. He is currently associate professor of criminal justice at Indiana University, Bloomington. In 2001, he was voted into the Native Writers Circle of the Americas and would really like to have enough time to write books.

DONALD SAMPSON is a member of and currently the executive director for the Confederated Tribes of the Umatilla Indian Reservation.

NORIKO SEGUCHI earned her Ph.D. at the University of Michigan, Ann Arbor, in 2000 and is now an assistant professor of anthropology at the University of Montana, Missoula.

JOHN ELI SIROIS (SAY' AY') is a father, son, grandson, brother, and committed community member of the Colville Confederated Tribes (CCT). He is an enrolled member of the Okanogan and Wenatchi Bands of the Colville Indian Reservation who was born and raised on the Colville Reservation in Omak, Washington. He completed degrees at Dartmouth College, Hanover, New Hampshire (AB in history, minor in Native American studies) and a Masters of Public Administration at the University of Washington, Seattle. For several years, John was the cultural preservation administrator for the CCT. He continues to advocate, learn, teach, empower, and revitalize the original languages/cultures/histories of the Colville Indian Reservation.

CLAIRE SMITH is at the Institute of the Advanced Study for Humanity, Newcastle, Australia, and president of the World Archaeological Congress. Although she has conducted field research with Aboriginal communities in Australia, Asia and North America, she mostly works with Aboriginal people from the Barunga region of the Northern Territory, and with Ngadjuri people from South Australia.

LAURAJANE SMITH is reader in cultural heritage studies and archaeology at the University of York, UK. Her research interests include heritage and the construction and negotiation of cultural and social identities, public policy and heritage management, archaeological theory, tourism, and ethics.

RODERICK SPRAGUE is Emeritus Professor of Anthropology and Emeritus Director of the Laboratory of Anthropology at the University of Idaho, Moscow. He is well known for his study of beads types from the early Historic Period in North America, as well as the study and description of Native American burial practices.

DARBY STAPP works for Pacific Northwest National Laboratory in Richland, Washington, where he is project manager for the Hanford Cultural and Historic Resources Program. Along with Michael Burney, he is the author of *Tribal Cultural Resource Management: The Full Circle to Stewardship* published in 2002 by AltaMira Press.

IAN THOMPSON is Choctaw, Creek, and European. A doctoral student at the University of New Mexico, Albuquerque, his research employs Indigenous experimental archaeology to document the traditional knowledge incorporated into precolonial Choctaw arts and tools. Ian has been active in a variety of Native American student organizations and in teaching the Choctaw traditional arts at the community level.

DEWARD E. WALKER, JR., is professor of anthropology and ethnic studies at the University of Colorado, Boulder. He is the author and coauthor of numerous books, among them *Nez Perce Oral Narratives* (1989), *Indians of Idaho* (1982), *Conflict and Schism in Nez Perce Acculturation* (1985), *Myths of Idaho Indians* (1980), *Nez Perce Culture and History* (1973), and *Nez Perce Legends* (1973).

CHRIS WILSON is academic advisor/associate lecturer within Yuggorendi First Nations Centre and Ph.D. candidate in the Department of Archaeology at Flinders University, Adelaide, Australia. As a young Ngarrindjeri man from the Lower Murray Lakes and Coorong in South Australia, he has also been involved in various community-related projects with Ngarrindjeri Elders, including repatriation of Old People from museums.

PEI-LIN YU is currently an assistant professor of anthropology at Sacramento State University. In addition to teaching and research, she serves as the university's NAGPRA specialist and archaeological collections manager.

LARRY ZIMMERMAN began his academic career at the University of South Dakota, Vermillion, leaving in 1996 as Distinguished Regents Professor. He has served as chair of American Indian and Native Studies at the University of Iowa, Ames, and as head of the Archaeology Department at the Minnesota Historical Society; he is currently professor of anthropology and museum studies and Public Scholar of Native American Representation at Indiana University–Purdue University, Indianapolis. His one consistent research interest has been Native Americans, from precontact times to the present.